Peter Townsend

The Social Minority

Allen Lane

Allen Lane
A Division of Penguin Books Ltd
21 John Street, London WC1N 2BT

ISBN 0 7139 0425 9

Printed in Great Britain by
Lowe & Brydone (Printers) Ltd., Thetford, Norfolk

For Adam

Contents

Acknowledgements

These papers owe much to my friends and colleagues, first at the London School of Economics and then, from 1963, at the University of Essex: in particular to Brian Abel-Smith, Max Atkinson, Sheila Benson, Geoffrey Hawthorn, Hilary Land, Tony Lynes, Dennis Marsden, Robert Pinker, Charles Posner, Sally Sainsbury, Lucianne Sawyer, Adrian Sinfield, Richard Titmuss, Sylvia and Jeremy Tunstall, and Caroline Woodroffe. Among others to whom I was and am indebted for help at different times are George Brown, F. Le Gros Clark, Amelia Harris, Norman Mackenzie, Peter Marris, Sybil and George McRobie, John Rex, Ethel Shanas, Ann Shearer, Geoffrey Smith, John Vaizey, Dorothy Wedderburn, Peter Willmott, Barbara Wootton, and Michael Young. I owe much also to the secretarial help given first by Sue Best and then by Marion Haberhauer. Finally, I must acknowledge a different kind of debt to people who have contributed so much to choice of subject and manner of its handling. They divide into three: my wife and family, individuals and families who have lived or live in the same locality, and families I have interviewed in different parts of the United Kingdom. In different ways each has provided the emotional resources and incontrovertible first-hand evidence needed to sustain social inquiry.

These papers were first published in the following books and publications: Chapters 2 and 3 in the *British Journal of Sociology*: Chapters 13 and 21 in *New Society*; Chapter 19 in the *New Statesman*; Chapter 8 in the *Observer*; part of Chapter 9 in the *Listener*; the postscript to Chapter 12 in the *Sunday Times*; Chapter 10 in the *International Social Science Journal*; Chapter 17 in *Case Conference*; Chapter 18 in *The Sociological Review Monograph*; Chapter 5 in *Political and Economic Planning*; Chapter 6 in the Fabian Research series; Chapter 11 in *Nursing Homes in England and Wales* (the National Corporation for the Care of Old People); Chapter 20 in *Proceedings of Seminars, 1961-5* (Duke University Council on Gerontology); Chapter 1 in N. Mackenzie (ed.), *Conviction* (©MacGibbon & Kee); and parts of Chapter 16 in E. Shanas *et al.*, *Old People in Three Industrial Societies* (Routledge).

The author and publishers would like to thank the editors and publications concerned for permission to include these papers in this collection.

Introduction

This book makes a plea for more systematic study by sociologists of social minorities and of their relationships to social structure. Individuals or families who have some characteristic in common which marks them off from 'ordinary' people and which prevents them from having access to, or being accorded, certain rights which are available to others, and who therefore are less likely to receive certain kinds and amounts of resources, can be defined as belonging to a social minority. This definition is broader than sometimes understood and links at least two social categories. There are ethnic and racial minority groups whose members have a common history and culture and carefully induct offspring into conformity with the beliefs and values of the group. They have close relationships among themselves, whether they are tightly or only loosely integrated with the rest of society. They can usually be shown to be in a relatively disadvantaged position in society and may feel it keenly. This type of social minority is well-recognized and studied by social scientists.

But secondly there are those who through appearance, physical condition, manner or speech and employment, family or residential status, find themselves frequently or regularly treated as second-class citizens. Their identity as members of groups is uncertain or ambiguous. Their social position is often very exposed. Some have a well-developed sense of group-consciousness, and may have a network of relations with similar households or families though this is never, nor can it be, as extensive as in an ethnic community. Others may be unaware of families or persons with identical problems and may turn in upon themselves and lead an extraordinarily self-contained or individuated existence. Some minorities are even best regarded as an aggregation of individuals. Their social roles are in various ways supplementary: dependent, subservient or acquiescent. They may be objects of pity or derision. Their attitudes and behaviour adjust to an inability to observe social norms in particular respects. They develop defensive or self-protective behaviour. Some elderly and disabled people, homeless families, one-parent families and even large families, as well as people living in different types of hospitals and other institutions, display these traits. Yet fundamentally they are individual victims of an arrogant and self-perpetuating social order.

xii The social minority

This second category can only with certain qualifications be regarded as consisting of social groups. If they have an identity in groups it is in a number of special senses. Society defines and accords deviant status to some types of individuals through its legislation, bureaucratic procedures and provisions in welfare, social security and employment. Less formally, local communities or the mass media, for example, may by their treatment of people invest them with collective attributes which they may or may not possess and may or may not accept. Again, uniformities in behaviour or need on the part of some individuals may cause them to be set apart and treated as a different species. The sociologist must investigate and demonstrate how these different processes work. Unless he does so he cannot show how social inequalities arise and are maintained and therefore cannot fully analyse and explain social structure.

Social minorities in this second sense of the term are endowed by society with virtues which are the opposite of those which it upholds. They have to be negative symbols of thrift, willing toil, self-reliance and abstemiousness, for example. We have to recognize this ruthless process for what it is — a gigantic piece of social self-deception — and one which is characteristic of all countries. We create scapegoats and deviants to ensure conformity with the values to which we subscribe and are sometimes extravagant both in their production and punishment. People who fall out of work, who are deserted by their husbands, beget a handicapped child or a child out of marriage, are crippled after an accident at work, or fleeced by an unscrupulous landlord or employer are transformed from being regarded not as victims but, in conventional opinion, as profligate work-dodgers, scroungers who live on the Welfare State and unfortunates who cannot survive the highly-principled competitiveness of the market. People come to believe this. How else could they feel comfortable with the unemployed, the poor and the dispossessed in their midst? Although poverty, deprivation and homelessness are the prices we pay for the social system we have, we pretend instead that people experiencing them do not deserve to enjoy its fruits.

Some minorities are extremely vulnerable. While ethnic or racial status may apply equally to all members of a household, and even many residents in a single locality, other kinds of minority status, like disability or unemployment, may apply specifically to one member. There is the risk of friction and dissension within the household, and though other members of the household often compensate the individual for his stigmatized existence they tend also to be contaminated by it. The household as a whole acts and feels differently from other households and is also regarded differently by the outside community. These are just some of the problems which arise.

Some minorities are still barely recognized. It is only in the last few years that the deprivation of the fatherless family, the long-term hospitalized, the disabled and the single woman with an adult dependant, for example, have come to be discussed more than cursorily in Britain. Tenants deprived of reasonable living conditions by the operation of a private market in housing, and communities of consumers in poor districts who are exploited by supermarkets and tallymen alike, for example, still require adequate description and analysis. What is important is the classification of groups and the definition and measurement of their relative numbers and conditions. Such classification of the subtleties and nuances of social structure has to be undertaken not just to achieve better sociological generalization but to oblige Government and public to recognize the needs and rights of certain groups in the population and discuss more rationally how they might be met.

The essays and papers in this book have been selected to illustrate this principal theme. Needless to say, like all collections of essays they fall short of presenting a sustained and neat argument. They are no more than attempts made over recent years to contribute to the understanding of different minority problems, and how these problems have to be set in the context of the changing structure and distribution of resources in society as a whole. Some papers have not previously been published and some were first published in rather inaccessible journals. They are reproduced almost entirely as originally written. A few passages which had been omitted upon first publication have been restored. I have also added references to some papers which had lacked them and a few notes at points where I felt it was important to call attention to subsequent developments. I have also corrected a few errors and some of the worst lapses of style.

The book falls into three parts. The papers on poverty (Chapters 2, 3, and 4) overlap to some extent. I have included them partly because they all contain some new data or arguments but also because they illustrate a certain evolution of thought. My first serious piece of research was into poverty and the subject has remained my central preoccupation. No one has yet produced a wholly satisfactory formulation of the concept. Several times since 1951 I have experienced the excitement of believing that I have contributed something fresh towards its definition and measurement, rather like taking a run at a particularly precipitous slope and getting a little higher each time without ever surmounting the summit. Readers who are interested in tracing one man's fitful attempts to analyse one of the most fundamental problems of society should read these chapters in conjunction with two other works (*The Poor and the Poorest*, with Brian Abel-Smith, London, Bell, 1965; and *The Concept of Poverty*, London, Heinemann, 1970).

The papers in the middle part of the book (Chapters 5 to 14) take as their subject-matter specific social minorities: the unemployed, coloured immigrants, the disabled, long-stay psychiatric patients, the mentally handicapped, the elderly, the Catholic minority in Northern Ireland, and the institutionalized. If there is a theme it is that the conditions in which these minorities live can be understood only in relation to the styles of life and resources enjoyed by the rest of society, and how society jealously guards and justifies such privileges as well as negatively denies them to minorities.

The final group of papers (Chapters 15-21) illustrates how diversities in the social structure, and hence the dimensions and characteristics of social minorities, arise and have to be explained sociologically. A paper which discusses what empirical substantiation there is for different theories about the place of the elderly in industrial societies is followed by a paper which takes up the concepts of isolation, desolation and loneliness, and attempts to measure and begin to explain these phenomena. These two are placed with five papers on the immediate and extended family, which are intended to illustrate how individual minority situations are so often related to the structure and disposition of the family network.

1 A society for people*

During the war I lived in London. For a youngster there was much excitement. As soon as the barrage balloons began to perch on their wires I started building an air-raid shelter in the garden, and it was not long before I took my turn as a fire-watcher and learned how to handle a stirrup-pump. When the London docks were first bombed I cycled for miles through the East End to see what had happened. I remember many days spent in improvised classrooms in the school crypt and nights curled up on a mattress under an iron bedstead, or huddled at the foot of the basement stairs with my mother and grandmother and the other tenants in our large, gloomy Victorian house. There was less reserve between neighbours and everyone seemed to be in and out of one another's houses, papering over pin-pricks of light in blackened windows, claiming access to stairways and roofs, keeping meaningless records of alerts and all-clears, drinking cups of tea at all hours and, increasingly as time went on, arguing about the kind of society he or she wanted after the war.

I was not old enough to take much of an interest in proposals for social change but I was aware of the lowering of social barriers and of the popular support for social reform. This had a profound influence on me and, so it seems now, on many others of my generation. At the start of the war my mother was on tour in Blackpool and some evacuees from Liverpool were lodged temporarily in our boarding-house. A poorly-dressed woman with leaden eyes climbed off the bus with a tearful baby and, without a thought for the landlady and two sharp-nosed women guests, undid her blouse and pulled out one of her breasts to comfort the child. I remember how shocked the three women were by her unselfconscious behaviour and, more important, how shocked they and many others were too by the poverty of the evacuees. In the early part of the war the upheavals of evacuation caused many people to understand for the first time how the other half lived, and what the years of unemployment had wrought. Here were two nations confronted.

The rich were chastened by this sudden revelation of social misery,

* First published in Mackenzie, N. (ed.), *Conviction*, MacGibbon & Kee, 1958.

and the young wanted to put an end to it. Involvement in the problems of others, and a respect for them, as well as mere patriotism, made people prepared to accept sacrifices. National assistance was liberalized, welfare foods and all kinds of benefits for mothers were introduced, stiff taxation was accepted and the most envied rationing system of the war raised the living standards of the poor. Experts who had been arguing seriously whether the number of 'unemployables' in the population was half a million or one million were shamed into silence. Other experts who had predicted widespread war neurosis and panic to get out of the cities were humbled by the calm and steadiness of the people. Infant and child mortality fell sharply, morbidity was amazingly low and, despite the apparent rigours of rationing, the submarine blockade, the bombing and everything else, a near-miracle occurred — there was in 1942 a greater sense of national well-being than in any year of the thirties.

Although social objectives which had been sought from one Royal Commission to another were now secured within weeks and months, few people were satisfied. The guilt of the thirties had to be erased. The Beveridge Report successfully competed with the battles in Russia and North Africa for the front pages of the daily press. A Coalition Government produced the first White Paper on a National Health Service, more remarkable, in some respects, than the plan finally agreed; *The Times* even complained in the middle of the war that the Government was dragging its feet in putting forward proposals for social reform; and a Tory who had been one of the Foreign Office spokesmen in Parliament at the time of Munich actually piloted through the Education Act of 1944. These were measures of the agreement that existed. A new post-war society seemed ready to emerge.

The details of the plan seemed not to matter. The will was there and that was enough. The public was determined that there must be no return to pre-war conditions and sought a government which could maintain the momentum of social change. Those people who believed Winston Churchill's charges in his ill-phrased 'Gestapo' speeches, like the two old women in our street who bolted their doors for four whole days after the 1945 election, belonged to another world.

Looking back now at the popular feeling generated by the events of the war years it is difficult to understand how anyone could have been surprised by the Labour Party's victory. A transformation had taken place. In the Britain of 1945 it seems possible to detect the two human impulses which, as I understand it, are necessary to any Socialist society. Tracing what has happened to these two provides, in a sense, the theme of this essay. There was an attitude of trust, tolerance, generosity, goodwill — call it what you like — towards others; a pervasive faith in human nature. Then there was a prevailing mood of self-denial, a readiness to share the good things in life and to see that others got the same privileges as oneself; an urge to give everyone, including the poor, the sick, the old and the handicapped, the chance of having certain elementary rights or freedoms so that they could achieve individual self-respect. Am I wrong in supposing that these were the really important attitudes struck by society then, despite the effects of a long war? After all, millions of people were thankful to be safely home once more, and their memories were still fresh with the suffering of the victims of the war.

Perhaps I exaggerate. Perhaps I am being sentimental about the carry-over of a popular mood from the period of the blitz. Or maybe I am simply recollecting some of the ideals of adolescence, fed on such unforgettable books as Richard Hillary's *The Last Enemy*. Whatever the truth, many others of that generation felt much the same. From wartime experiences of evacuation, sleeping in shelters, civil defence, farming and forestry camps during school holidays and finally service in the armed forces, many of us gained a sense of fair shares, of common effort, of mixing with people of different class and of planning for the future which came at the most impressionable age and which could at times be intoxicating.

At first all seemed to go well. In the early years after the war a daunting programme of legislation was undertaken which seemed to match popular feeling. By the middle of 1948 national insurance, industrial injuries and assistance benefits, as well as family allowances, were being paid and the Health Service had started. There were new charters for the care of children, the sick and the old. For a nation struggling with the economic consequences of the war the programme was little short of breathtaking. But instead of gaining a sense of purpose and of confidence as the wartime plans began to take recognizable shape the Labour Government hesitated more and more; doubts crept into the discussion of social policy and the first flush of post-war enthusiasm began to wane. Concessions were made to interest-groups by men uncertain of their direction. There was no steadying voice to remind the Government of its objectives, to say that more was required than the institutional framework for a new society (even supposing it was the right framework), or to say that it takes more than acts of Parliament, however well-intentioned, to establish trust and equality. The staff who had worked the poor law, to take one example, could not be changed overnight. A long process of education, and education by example, was required.

By 1950 the momentum following the war was spent and the Labour Party's victory at the polls was a hollow one, the succeeding year before the defeat of 1951 being one of the most painful and degrading in recent political history. It is true that the Government was severely handicapped by the Korean war and the decision to buy weapons at any price. These were enough to make anyone neurotic, and the slim parliamentary majority was scarcely helpful. But, quite apart from these extenuating circumstances, there was a succession of minor decisions, like the imposition of Health Service charges, the abandonment of a large part of the Exchequer share of social insurance and the faint-hearted singling out of the cement and sugar industries for nationalization, which showed how quickly the Labour Party had reached a dead end. It was not simply that the two most formidable leaders, Cripps and Bevin, had been lost, nor that the Bevanite split had occurred without offering adequate alternative leadership, nor even that the party needed to recover its breath before resuming the assault. No one knew what to assault. Instead of realizing that their work was only beginning the Labour Party leaders thought it was at an end. They seemed to be drained of initiative by the effort of legislating. They no longer believed in any tangible social aim and had increasingly lost touch with ordinary people. These were the two frightening facts at the start of the 1950s.

From 1948 to 1951 I was at Cambridge. In 1949 Orwell's *1984* was published. In the next year or two few undergraduates failed to read it. The impact of this book, coinciding as it did with the tragic death of Orwell himself, was very great. It is a masterpiece of cynicism. Orwell had shown how the highest political ideals could be, and had been, perverted. He had revealed the mechanisms by which the unsophisticated could be, and had been, misled. More than anyone else, and despite the many occasions on which he laid himself open to mockery, he had taught that Socialism was a code of conduct to live by and not an uneasy compromise with vice. His last book gave the final twist in the wounds of 1950 and 1951. Those who had discussed the plans for a new society so ardently during and immediately after the war found their hopes sadly deflated. They were completely disillusioned.

During the last seven or eight years this disillusion with Socialism has persisted. I think it can largely be explained by the meaning given to the simple, but crushingly cold and complacent phrase, 'the Welfare State'. I want to attack this phrase, and all it is supposed to represent, because it suggests, or rather is taken to mean, first that a country which is a Welfare State is soft and makes people soft, and secondly, that in a country which is called a Welfare State there can be, in some strange way, no just causes left.

The strict values of the unbending spinster have always had a cherished place in British society — the peculiar and varying disciplines of the public school, the Church of England and the outside lavatory have seen to that — and it is not surprising to find them being expressed with peculiar vehemence as soon as the new health and social security services began to operate in July 1948. The general satisfaction created by the legislative achievements was quickly undermined. Britain, so the argument went, was going soft and everyone was being supervised from the cradle to the grave. Wage-earners had been granted improved insurance and assistance benefits in sickness and unemployment: no doubt they would be feckless and stay off work. Mothers were actually being paid a small allowance when they had two or more dependent children: no doubt they would spend it on perms or the pictures. The middle-aged and old were making extraordinary demands for wigs, spectacles and dentures: no doubt they would acquire them irresponsibly to entertain their grandchildren. Services were wasted on people who could not be trusted, who toddled off to the nearest doctor or national assistance officer to get what they could when they needed nothing.

All this may read like exaggerated parody. I only wish it were. The line of criticism could be documented at tedious and uniformly depressing length. When, in February 1958, the director of the Conservative Political Centre wrote in *The Future of the Welfare State* that we were 'squandering public money on providing indiscriminate benefits for citizens, many of whom do not need them and some of whom do not want them', he was simply repeating, in a characteristically vague way (which benefits? which people?), the complaint that has been made down the years in the correspondence and editorial columns of the *Telegraph*, *The Times*, *Economist* and, perhaps most revealing of all, the *British Medical Journal*.

It is quite remarkable what happens when we submit the various charges to the cool test of evidence. What about 'malingering' and 'abuse', for example? Everyone knows, or thinks he knows, of the individual instance, but is it significant nationally? Early in 1958 *The Lancet* published data showing that in one area a small minority of people made claims for sickness benefit said to be unjustified by the doctor, but the money they received was only three per cent of the total paid. A year or two previously the National Assistance Board took a special look at those who had drawn assistance for long periods during unemployment. Its officers found that about 2,000 of the total of 32,000 were 'work-shy' (less than one per cent of the unemployed, or 0.001 per cent of the total working population at that time). What is more, nearly *two thirds* of this tiny group were physically or mentally handicapped. As for the run on spectacles, dentures and the rest that took place after July 1948, no proof has ever been offered of the widespread belief that many people were queueing up for these for no other reason than that they were free.

It is important to ask for the evidence. It is also important to remember historical precedent. The same severe views have been pressed with considerable force for generations by one section of society. The Poor Law reforms of the nineteenth century and the Old Age Pensions Act of 1908 were attacked as bitterly as any recent measure by those who saw them as 'undermining the sense of family responsibility' and who fought to preserve the distinction between the 'deserving' and the 'undeserving' poor. They believed firmly in charity and in the division of the population into first- and second-class citizens. In his film masterpiece *Intolerance*, made in 1916, D. W. Griffith mercilessly satirized the 'uplifters' of his day, who perpetrated so much cruelty under the guise of charity. I shall never forget those women, acting like agents of the Lord's Day Observance Society — sternly moral, if not openly pious, inflexible and frequently outraged.

The journals of the Establishment, such as the *Economist, The Times* and the bank reviews, have taken the criticism a stage further. They have given a good deal of support to the idea that the social services are an indulgence or an extravagance which should be withdrawn as soon as possible. With increasing national prosperity, it is said, more and more people should look after their own health, education and social security; the dwindling numbers of the destitute should be covered by selective services which assuage guilt by employing more palatable means tests. This is the 'self-liquidating' theory of the social services. So far as I am aware it has never been expressed in practicable details suggesting how the chronic sick, the disabled and the poor can pay for their own services and how State schools and hospitals can be handed over to private individuals. It is little more than a semi-articulate protest drawing on self-interest and class mistrust.

This has not stopped the theory from being used freely in recent years to support the sustained attack on the social services and on taxation. Nowhere from the political Right or Left has much resistance been shown. Ironically enough, it has been left to Enoch Powell to stress that the social services are as necessary to modern society as sewage systems to Victorian society. (1)*

I have discussed one assumption about the Welfare State. The other, that there are no just causes left, is more pernicious. It implies that everything has been achieved. But were the achievements of 1945-8 as remarkable as so many people suppose? Future historians will, I think, pick out the uncritical acceptance of the Beveridge recommendations as one of the most significant phenomena of domestic politics from 1942 to 1946. Here was a set of proposals for social security which caught the imagination of the public. Central to them was the idea that

---

* Figures in brackets refer to notes and references at the end of each chapter.

benefits should be enough without other resources for subsistence, yet this idea was never scrutinized. Beveridge took over the kind of measure used by those who had carried out surveys of poverty before the war. It looked bogus, was bogus and has been shown to be bogus, yet right up to 1954 successive governments stuck to it bravely and pretended that they were trying to live up to it. The subsistence standard, even as Beveridge worked it out, has never, by a good many calories and proteins, been attained. How many people know that the unemployment and sickness benefits for a man in 1958 form a much smaller percentage of the average wage than they did in 1938, or indeed in 1912? Full employment and not social insurance has been responsible for the reduction in poverty since the war. The Beveridge scheme tidied up numerous anomalies and extended social insurance to the whole population (largely, it must be said, to the benefit of the self-employed and the middle classes, some of whom now qualify for the full retirement pension of £2 10s. for a single person or £4 for a married couple after only ten years of tax-free contributions), but it belonged to the past, to the 1930s and not the 1950s. It is difficult now to understand the enthusiasm of only ten or twelve years ago.

All governments pretend to the public that their achievements are greater than they are. In a democracy one hopes the pretences will be probed ruthlessly by an alert Opposition. But where are the informed critics of today? Labour politicians have been happy to exaggerate the achievements of the Welfare State because they feel they can gain most of the credit. Tory politicians have been loath to disavow them because they can follow less guiltily a policy of cutting 'marginal' social service expenditure and reducing 'redistributive' taxation. 'Nothing', as they say, 'is sacrosanct'. This policy has indeed been followed since 1951: up to that year the proportion of the nation's resources devoted to the social services had been growing steadily, and then stood at about 11 or 12 per cent (compared with about 9½ per cent in 1938). Even now, in its Health Service, Britain is strikingly ahead of most other countries, but in many other services it has fallen strikingly behind. Germany, for example, is now spending half as much again as Britain on social security from a smaller national income.

The achievements in what is unreflectively called 'income redistribution' have also been exaggerated. Were the post-war trends so much in favour of the working class as both Socialists and Tories supposed? During the war, differences in living standards had narrowed sharply and only grudgingly did the Labour Government begin to let them widen again. That seems to be as near to the truth as we are likely to get. A 'redistribution' of income occurred in the war rather than afterwards. Not for some time did the middle-class counter-revolution come into full swing. Not until 1947 was the first important step taken to increase regressive, and lighten progressive, taxes. Bank chairmen have now talked unceasingly about the plight of the impoverished middle classes and the *Manchester Guardian* and *Observer* have joined the other journals in printing lengthy discussions. Gradually an elaborate protective system has been built into the tax system and industry. Successive Chancellors of the Exchequer have loosened the rules by which tax is collected. Allowances have been granted for more kinds of dependants, for some dependants for longer, for superannuation and life insurance. Income-tax consultants have become prosperous and more individuals have become aware of the expenses which, quite legitimately, count for tax relief. Just before I began to write, the 1958 Budget introduced allowances for subscriptions to professional societies. Many of these changes may appear to be reasonable in themselves, but the cumulative effect should not be forgotten.

The changes outside the tax system have been even more important. Indirect income benefits today have reached such a pitch that mere comparisons between two persons' incomes tell us little about the real differences in their standards of living. There are luxurious cars bought and maintained at the expense of the firm, meal vouchers, season tickets, subsidized and free housing, salaries paid in full during sickness, large superannuation contributions, holiday expenses and free travel abroad. The recent Royal Commission on Taxation recognized all this, but failed to appreciate its significance. Examples are not hard to come by. Claims for as much as £28 for one lunch for four people are not infrequently made by the executives of one big company. I know of one extreme instance where the expenses for forty people for a lavish four days' conference in a seaside resort amounted to over £8,000. At a time when the number of people with incomes over £5,000 a year is supposed to be small the increase in the number of very expensive cars on the roads is impressive. The production of Rolls-Royces has more than trebled within the last ten years. In April 1958 *The Times* was advertising a new Rolls-Royce for £9,015 and a Bentley for £8,388. Admittedly these appeared to be the prices for rather exceptional models. Those who were prepared to rough it a bit could get by with the standard Rolls-Royce for £5,500 or the Bentley at £3,700.

Subsidies to income explain part of the middle-class counter-attack. Capital gains explain another. Throughout the last ten years inflation has meant a large series of non-taxable capital gains. The seven- and eightfold increase in undistributed profits since 1938 has given a powerful boost to the value of shares (partly concealed by free and cheap issues of new shares to shareholders) and so a much bigger proportion than previously of the shareholder's income has come from capital gains than from dividends. Moreover, heavy death duties have caused the rich to look for ways of avoiding them. They can pass on their wealth late on in life, more than five years before they expect to die; or they can buy agricultural land and expand the family business, on which they pay less tax. The recent history of the reaction to the high tax rates of the war and early post-war years teaches that no economic measures intended to narrow income inequalities can last unless the Chancellor of the Exchequer remains both Socialist and vigilant.

All this could be documented better and in greater detail. But would the argument be conclusive? Would it answer those like A. J. P. Taylor, who recently wrote an article for the *Manchester Guardian* entitled 'Nothing left to Reform — Political Consequences of 1945-50'? I have been destructive rather than constructive. What *is* there to reform? To answer this question we have to know more about people's needs and how they live.

I work as a sociologist. I should like this to mean that I explore, and write about, present-day society so that others may understand it better. I should like it to mean that I spend a good deal of time observing and interviewing small cross-sections of the population before writing detailed reports which aim to keep human beings to the forefront. Above all, I should like it to mean studying very carefully the life of the poorest and most handicapped members of society.

Why do I emphasize this last point? In the British population of 50,000,000 there are nearly 5,000,000 retirement pensioners, 500,000 widows receiving special benefits, nearly 2,000,000 war pensioners, not far short of 250,000 people receiving industrial injuries and disablement allowances; 450,000 unemployed (at present) and therefore around 1,250,000 men, women and children dependent on unemployment benefit; and, on any average day, nearly 1,000,000 wage-earners and their families dependent on sickness benefit. Altogether about 2,250,000 people are dependent at any one time on national assistance allowances, most of them for extremely long periods. There are many more people, particularly the old (as a number of studies make clear), who would qualify for national assistance, but do not apply. There are 300,000 mental defectives and persons of unsound mind, most of whom are in mental hospitals and other institutions; over 750,000 disabled persons, including spastics and the blind; there are hundreds of thousands of persons in chronic sick hospitals, institutions for the aged, children's homes, and even more chronic sick living at home. There may be nearly 1,000,000 old people who cannot leave their homes unassisted. Finally there are many adults and children in large families, among whom recent surveys have confirmed nutritional deficiencies; many young and middle-aged widows with children to support and many working men still earning less than £7 or £8 a week. The figures I have given may overlap in some instances but if we are trying to estimate the proportion of the population with special difficulties over a long period, who cannot and could not be expected to overcome their problems on their own resources, we should think in terms of the submerged fifth and not the submerged tenth. The total numbers are nearer 10,000,000 than 5,000,000. Did Mr A. J. P. Taylor have them in mind when he said there was nothing left to reform?

Mine is a personal view of what should be emphasized in sociology. In fact the term covers an enormous range of different subjects. A university lecturer addressed one of the few meetings of the British Sociological Association during the present year on the subject of 'Protestantism and Capitalism in Sixteenth-Century Germany'. Articles in the sociological journals with titles like 'The Dimensions of Syntality in Small Groups I: The Neonate Group', 'Suffragium: From Vote to Patronage' and 'Palaeolithic Religion and the Principles of Social Evolution' are by no means rare. Many sociologists are in fact interested exclusively in social philosophy, in history or social evolution or in rather mechanical experiments in closed laboratories. These interests have their place, of course, but one wonders whether the balance is right and why so few research workers study the submerged fifth (2). Among the last hundred main articles in the *British Journal of Sociology* only twenty report research into present-day society, six of these twenty dealing with overseas affairs (three with the social background of African students), six with social status and ranking of occupations, and two with the employment of sociology graduates. Clearly the graduates are not much employed on surveys of everyday life.

Those who are doing social research seem to be preoccupied with the specialized techniques of questionnaire design, coding and computing and administrative tasks like the supervision of junior interviewers. The subjects of investigation seem to be depersonalized behind screens of subordinates and paper tape. This is one way of acquiring professional status, as market research agencies have been quick to appreciate, and of building up recognition for an academic discipline which until recently did not exist in Cambridge and Oxford. (3) However, the preoccupation with method and with status is symptomatic of a disease which goes much wider than sociology. This is the general problem of professionalism in Britain, whereby groups of specialists with a technical training, their own language and their own ethics multiply and form their own protective associations. It is one of the long-term problems we have hardly begun to identify. A professional association seeks privileges at the expense of the common good. It attaches more importance to respect for seniority, conformity to professional rules of conduct and the growth of tradition than it does to individual freedom and inventiveness. Its members are conditioned to interpret their duties more in terms of professional skills than in terms of the needs of clients. Professional people must not get involved in their clients' affairs; they must be wholly detached, formal and objective; they must be neutral and never, never get mixed up in politics. Perhaps this is why the strongest associations tend in practice to be so reactionary.

The same pressures are now exerting themselves on the sociologist, yet the more he tries to study and interpret contemporary society the more difficult it is for him to isolate his work from daily politics. If he visits a cross-section of people in their homes and tries to understand their lives and problems he is made aware of their needs and how government affects them. It should be terribly hard for him to write his report without revealing, or at least implying, what their needs are, even if he shirks the separate duty of going on to suggest how these needs may be met. This difficulty is much more acute for him than for an anthropologist concerned only with a remote non-industrialized society, or for an economist, still less for a biologist, a historian or a physician. It may cost him his bread and butter. Is it surprising to find wealthy foundations shy of giving money for social research, or university specialists tending to concentrate on subjects which they hope are politically neutral?

It may be best for the sociologist to admit this dilemma rather than pretend it does not exist. He may then be less inhibited about studying social needs; readier to concede that government officials and politicians always will, and perhaps should, look to sociology for evidence on which to base reform; and readier too to face up to his own worst failings and prejudices, rather than conceal them by depending too much on the reports of others.

I have never realized the importance of these things more clearly than during the first more-or-less formal interview of my life. I was supposed to be trying to find out what had been the effects of prolonged unemployment in 1952 on many thousands of people living in the Lancashire cotton towns. Already I had talked to officials of the National Assistance Board and of the Ministries of Labour and National Insurance and done my best to penetrate the fog of their statistics; I had done the rounds of borough councillors, trade union secretaries, personnel officers and welfare workers without finding much enlightenment. I could avoid the hardest job no longer. The first address I had chosen at random proved to be a dark, terraced house and I remember the whitened doorstep and the tall chimneys rising above the roofs in the distance. Twice my courage failed me and I walked past without knocking. My hands were thrust in my raincoat pockets and I can still remember fumbling with some scraps of paper and tearing them into minute pieces while I stood at the corner of the street and pretended to be looking for a bus.

I knocked hesitantly and when the door opened explained myself rather abjectly to a woman in her early twenties. She was friendly and showed me into a rather bare sitting room where her two-year-old son was romping around. She had another boy of five who was at school. My questions were bad, my manner worse, and I felt a complete charlatan — a bungling amateur with no right to scientific pretensions. Yet somehow she patiently coached me through my interview, tactfully answering the really important questions which it had not occurred to me to ask. She and her husband had both been weavers earning a combined income of £12 a week (the grandmother used to look after the children). Both had been unemployed for twenty weeks and while their social security benefits totalled £3 14s. their unavoidable outlay on rent, rates, life insurance and fuel totalled £2 12s. (including 10s. to keep alive a hire-purchase agreement on a suite of furniture). No more than £1 2s. was left for food, clothing and the rest. Early on in unemployment they had spent their few pounds of savings on tinned foods and for four months the family lived largely on these and on bread and jam. No meat was bought, no butter, eggs or fresh milk (the children relied mainly on tinned dried milk, though one had started getting fresh milk at school and the other had lived for several weeks with a better-off relative), only part of the bacon and margarine ration, no sweets, little fruit, few vegetables and practically no clothing (indeed, some clothing was sold). Although the 2s. a week on the football pools was abandoned, husband and wife bought a few cigarettes and still went occasionally to the cinema. 'Life wouldn't be worth living without *something*.' The family had developed its own idiosyncrasies during this time of crisis. They went to bed early to save fuel and electricity and they had entered vainly for newspaper crossword competitions. When he had no chance of trying for another job the husband stayed in bed until lunchtime so that he would need no breakfast. Relatives had given them food from time to time but were mostly in no position to help. The family had not sought national assistance although they qualified. 'That's for the people who are really poor.'

As I called at other homes I began to understand something of the problems of the submerged fifth, even though I had not learned to be at ease during an interview. (I tried to identify myself with the people I met, yet half realized I never could.) One person I met was a widow with three young children and no close relatives. Another was a mother with two illegitimate children. A third was a widower living in a hostel who suffered from double incontinence. Then there was a couple with two boys at grammar school — 'when our children were born we made up our minds that they would never go into cotton'; a bachelor living with his parents — 'the dole is nowt at all for a single man'; two middle-aged spinsters, one with chronic bronchitis; a family with a long history of tuberculosis, and many others.

Again and again I found I was wrong in assuming that doctors, social workers, local government officers, trade union secretaries and others who spent most of their lives working in the area would have first-hand knowledge of the peculiar circumstances and problems of the people living there. For one thing they were often acquainted with no more than one odd corner of local society. On matters of detail falling within their specialized field of work they were helpful; on general matters involving the life of whole sections of the population, whether children, young families, the unemployed or the chronic sick they were unbelievably wide of the mark. Many seemed to have little comprehension of the needs and circumstances of people living right under their noses. A trade union secretary said he knew of no one in his union who would qualify for national assistance, yet he was wrong in at least five of the ten instances where members of his union were interviewed. It is easy to be misled by people believed to be so much more eminent and knowledgeable, especially if they are charming and share some of the same sentiments. I found this very hard to understand. Go easy. Ask for the evidence. If you want to believe it, don't. What people like to happen, what people say happens, and what in fact does happen, are very different things.

The journey through Lancashire had left me in a confused but excited frame of mind. It had come in the middle of a two-year period of research among White Papers and Blue Books and I determined to seek the earliest opportunity to do more continuous research among people living in their own homes. I had set off with some questions I had been unable to answer. I returned with different questions, with a deeper respect for people like Charles Booth and Mayhew and also for D. H. Lawrence and George Orwell, and with a greater mistrust of the Welfare Establishment subscribed to by Socialists and Tories alike. At that time criticism was, however, so rare that it was easy to doubt one's judgement, and Richard Titmuss was the only university person of repute to give confidence and inspiration to a number of people like myself who were beginning to feel their way towards a critical evaluation of the progress that had been made since the war. In fact he was the only person who seemed to understand what had been happening. The public debate about social policy had a strange air of unreality alongside the facts of people's lives. Some of the strengths of working-class life and many of the needs of the submerged fifth had been overlooked.

In 1954 Michael Young started the Institute of Community Studies to do a job the universities were not doing, and I had the opportunity to interview old people in Bethnal Green. What struck me hardest was the extraordinary diversity between people of similar age living in the same locality. It was deeply puzzling. All the stereotypes in one's mind had to be taken to bits. By the time I had finished counting exceptions to the politician's traditional picture of Darby and Joan living on the old-age pension there was nobody left. It was hard to fill in a truthful picture. At one extreme I met a man who was one of twenty-two children, married to a woman who was one of eighteen, and between them they had seventeen children, of whom twelve were alive. They had about sixty relatives living within a mile and on every occasion I called the house was alive with grandchildren. The family kept a stall in the local market and had many friends. At the other extreme was an elderly spinster who was the only child of an only child. Her father died when she was a baby and her mother some fifteen or twenty years ago. Since then she had had literally no relatives whatsoever. She lived in a single room at the top of a tenement block and consistently refused to apply for national assistance. She had virtually no friend in the world and no close contacts with any of the neighbours. Her holiday consisted of visiting Southend once or twice a year just for the day; she sat on the front by herself and watched the crowds. I found it almost impossible to believe she was so isolated and I was not convinced until I visited her on Christmas Eve and found no sign of Christmas but a sheet of wrapping paper from Woolworths pinned up above the mantelpiece.

Between these two were ranged people of every imaginable kind. Dimly I tried to make sense of them and to group people so that generalization might be possible. All the time I wrestled with and never properly resolved the apparent contradiction between the comforting conclusion that the majority of old people lived reasonably secure lives within an affectionate family and the disturbing conclusion that a frightening number of physical, financial, occupational and social needs went unmet and, what is more, undetected, particularly among the minority of isolated or semi-isolated people with few or no relatives. I wondered vaguely if the surprising range of people was due to my catching people towards the end of life, yet when I did another spell of interviewing with people of all ages in a single tenement block in Stepney the diversities seemed even wider. I have yet to read a theoretical work which properly captures and reflects this diversity.

One day's experience may show what I mean. First of all I climbed a stone stairway and knocked on a brown-painted door at the end of a gloomy passage. It opened almost before I had lowered my hand. Standing there, with her head cocked on one side, was a small stocky woman with a mop of yellow-grey hair splaying out from her head. A bedraggled blouse was held together with at least four safety pins and below it a misshapen velvet skirt had dropped three or four inches to reveal a vest partly concealed by a red sash. Her face was fleshy and pallid and she kept placing stubby fingers against a cheek in thought. She rambled disconnectedly in reply to my explanation of my call, talking in one breath about washing her hair and the problem of an H-bomb world, but she motioned me inside.

The room was small and an inside door led to an even smaller room, not much bigger than a large cupboard..There was very little furniture and, except for one strip of old lino, the floor boards were bare. There was a terrible armchair, dilapidated and broken with a rope mat thrown over it, a small table in the centre, a wooden chair, a small iron bedstead, and little else. The bedstead possessed no mattress. A carpet lay on the springs and there was a grey pillow and coverlet rolled up at the foot. Slung under the mantelpiece and above an old open firegrate was a large cardboard box in which there were all kinds of knick-knacks – pins, cotton-reels, bits of wool and cloth, and scraps of paper. By the fireplace stood a single gas ring on top of a cylindrical tin which in turn rested on another tin. On one wall was a magazine-illustration of an eighteenth-century lover wooing his lady by a lake; it was clipped to a board with three clothes-pegs. In the middle of the small table I noticed a child's toy lorry in which had been placed a few tiny flowers, their stalks nipped off.

The woman put a bowl of cold water on the table to wash her hair, went behind me to fetch a bar of soap and later transferred some hot soapy water from a zinc tub – in which she had been washing some clothes – into the bowl on the table. These actions were spread over the half-hour I was there. At first we were in semi-darkness and she shuffled around the room, eventually finding a small step-ladder, which she placed against the door in order to reach the gas meter and put a shilling in the slot. She left the step-ladder against the door and, with momentary alarm, I saw her place a heavy gas fire and a flat-iron against the door. 'You're in a strange world. It isn't England at all. They say they want to put a stop to wars . . . but with all the bombing everyone got unsettled and we had to leave the shelters. It all started with that . . . It's very hard to live and perhaps you'll call tomorrow. But it's always nice to welcome friends.' Her brother and her only daughter lived in the next street and saw her every day. One provided her with a small cleaning job and the other often gave her meals. But for their support and perhaps the considerateness of her neighbours it is reasonably certain she would have been in a mental hospital. She answered some questions lucidly, but then trailed off into confused meanderings. She kept speaking of her separation from her husband. 'You keep wondering, wondering where he is, right now. Wondering if he's with someone. You're used to married life and you want a partner. You can't go down the road and have a drink unless you've got a husband. They say absence makes the heart grow fonder. It's true. Your heart aches. But you've got to dismiss it.' And she began busying herself with soap and water.

I then called on a middle-aged married man who had several relatives in the same block and many more in the neighbouring streets, and he and his wife seemed to be meeting dozens of them every day. There was another couple with nine brothers and sisters and twenty-six uncles and aunts, many of them in the immediate neighbourhood, who also led a tight family life. Then there was a young couple waiting to move out to Crawley New Town and away from their family; a young single woman who had taken a room in the next street from her parents to be sure of a home after her marriage a few months hence, and an enormously fat widow who had that utter casualness of many working-class Mums and who cross-examined me shrewdly, if not mercilessly, about my own life. Finally there was a neurotic man living alone who was separated from his wife. He was one of the real desolates of society who seem to turn up in poor housing in fairly large numbers. He had left his wife and family in Liverpool years before and had had no contact with them since. His room smelt stale. He complained of 'breakdowns' at work and kept rubbing his head. Nevertheless he was intelligent and talked knowledgeably of the people in the locality who had many relatives. 'You have to be careful what you say. You'll go to a pub and you'll be talking about someone and he'll suddenly say, "He's my cousin." There's so many people related to each other in some way — it's like a little village.'

Besides those who were very poor perhaps as many as a fifth or more of the inhabitants were isolated and handicapped. They were elderly bachelors and spinsters whose parents and contemporaries had died, or merchant seamen who had drifted in from the docks, or divorced, separated or deserted people whose family life had been disturbed. Then there were the few who seemed to have led a hermit-like existence because of some deformity or disability or whose past was something of a closed book. Many of them were pathetic individuals who had found cheap shelter in a place where their anonymity could be preserved, where there was a general air of sociableness but of respect for privacy, where they could be accepted with indulgence but not interfered with. 'He's a poor old soul.' 'He means well. He can't help it.' 'She acts a bit queer, but she's very quiet. I think it was the war.'

Around them was preserved the main texture of working-class society, the people whose parents lived there, whose brothers and sisters worked around the corner and whose children either lived there or near by. Some two thirds of the inhabitants were closely related to several people in the same block, parents, brothers, and sisters, children,

and grandchildren. Relationships ramify, and many people were aware
of distant connexions to other extended families in the same block and
nearby. Thus part of the sense of community, of solidarity and of
neighbourly restraint arose and was in fact created by the ties of
kinship.

What lessons are there here for social policy? I believe that it is possible
to get a better understanding of what are the needs of the submerged
fifth and how they can be met by learning what are the strong features
of working-class life. That is why the analysis of social diversity seems
to me to be so important. The happiest and most secure relationships
between adults in a family, for example, seem to be those in which all
kinds of services are exchanged, as when the old grandmother cooks the
meals and cares for the grandchildren, and her daughter does the
shopping and cleaning and works part-time outside the home. One-sided
dependence is disliked and the ability to give, to be of use to others, to
do one's share and to be independent, is venerated. This simple fact
explains a lot of things. It explains why working people (supported,
incidentally, by the trade unions) have always preferred to pay for
social security by specific 'contributions', because they earn thereby
their right to benefit in a way that they feel would not be possible
through ordinary taxation. It explains why social services administered
by systems of charity, patronage or means tests have never succeeded
and will always be disliked if not hated. A man does not want to get
anything according to his degree of misery or destitution: that is
humiliating. It affronts his dignity.

Yet it is difficult to reject the hand of the unbending spinster and
her world of the privileged and the unprivileged, the strong and the
weak, the deserving and the undeserving. She turns up in unexpected
places and in unexpected guises. She never admits failure. More
important, she never wants to succeed. Hers is an ambivalent attitude,
wanting to do good works providing the reason for doing them is never
removed. So long as she does not expect to gain, so long will there be
inequality. It has taken us more than a decade to realize that beneath
the New Look of social security the same old lady lurks. For, shrewdly
adapting herself to the slogans of progressives, she has adopted
wholeheartedly the policy of the national minimum.

The central choice in social policy lies in fact between a national
minimum and equality. Support for the establishment of a national
minimum in some or all social services has a long history, and especially
from the work of the Webbs at the turn of the century to the present
day. All one has to worry about, so the belief runs, is the need to raise
health and living standards to a bare minimum, a subsistence level from
which individuals can themselves build by their own efforts. It is in the

State's interest to ensure that this minimum is attained: to go further would be to interfere with individual freedom and to waste national resources. In theory the idea seems wonderful. In practice it evaporates. It is extraordinarily difficult to define what can be meant by a 'minimum' (bread? tea? cake? newspapers? books? cortisone? 'invisible' hearing aids? plastic surgery?). It is all the more difficult to readjust one's ideas continuously during a period of inflation. Even when a pound is worth half its value the fact takes time to get used to. Has anyone tried running up a downcoming escalator? Supporters of the national minimum are all too likely to find themselves defending a policy which widens rather than narrows the gap between living standards and depresses the opportunities for recovery of the poor, the sick and the dispossessed.

The source of confusion is that the national minimum has been held to be the badge of equality. How noble for all citizens to be treated alike. What could be more equal than flat-rate benefits for all, financed by flat-rate contributions? Unfortunately this is a perfect example of doublethink. When the rate of benefit is kept below a 'national minimum', when the national insurance stamp takes a far larger share of the wage of the lowest paid than of the salaried earner, and when part of the population is allowed to exploit the tax system through a plethora of private insurance and 'top hat' pension schemes to gain very generous extras, the result is the opposite of equality. According to a recent *Manchester Guardian* supplement half the pension contributions of those earning a few thousand pounds a year would otherwise go in tax. 'The greatest gainers are those with the highest rate of surtax. Thus the man with an income of £15,000 a year would lose only £7 10s. of net income per £100 premium, the remainder of the premium being offset by tax saving.'

Two separate standards of social value exist at one and the same time. In old age the living standards of the poor now fall more sharply than do those of the rich. I have interviewed middle-class people whose incomes were about the same or higher after retirement than before. They had paid off the mortgages on their houses, some had received large tax-free gratuities; and some were getting the advantage of the generous tax concessions now allowed on any further earnings. Their difficulties are as nothing compared with those of people now living on £3 or £4 a week who were recently earning a wage of £10, say, or more. There are millions of people living on £3 or £4 a week — and some on even less.

The problem for the future is to refuse to tolerate two standards of social value and apply one: to see that the privileges of the few can be transferred to the many. One obvious course is a complete recasting of social security, to reduce poverty and gross inequalities in living standards. The Labour Party has tentatively approved the principles of a national superannuation scheme with graduated contributions and benefits which favours the lowest paid. The plan could be the biggest contribution to social equality since the end of the war. I say 'could be' because the interpretation of a few of the crucial principles of the scheme remains in doubt. It will be interesting to see how far the traditional opponents of social equality can undermine the scheme. But the changes in social security cannot stop there. The same principles will have to be applied to sickness, unemployment, widows' and industrial injuries benefits. They may be applied partly by obliging the employer to pay full wages (as well as full salaries) for the first months of sickness and also by obliging him to make adequate redundancy payments (one day's notice and one week's pay are still all too frequent). Children's allowances (both direct family allowances and tax allowances) need to be reviewed and family allowances increased. This general reform would logically entail the drastic revision of the tax concession laws and the eventual withering away of the National Assistance Board, with people whose needs cannot be met by social insurance being transferred to the care of casework agencies.

Too many social services, and not only those concerned with payments of money, are still governed by the belief in a 'minimum'. These clothes will do for the boys and girls in this children's home; they are cheap but hard wearing. The meals in this institution only cost 15s. a week per person but they give adequate nutrition; the inmates are used to simple meals. The children in this school are far from reaching eleven-plus standards (what do you expect in such a district?); that is why they are housed in an ancient building in classes of fifty. The people queueing up outside this surgery (housing office, labour exchange, welfare office) have been waiting a long time; but they are used to waiting.

We have hardly begun to understand how to abandon the double standard of values in the social services and to treat people as we ourselves would like to be treated. What can be done? To a large extent the deficiencies can be remedied by good legislation and government. Take housing, for example. As many as 2,500,000 households in this country (17 per cent of the total) have no piped water, well over 3,000,000 no water closet (23 per cent) and 6,500,000 no fixed bath (45 per cent). When we know that millions of people must live for decades in old housing, why there is no adequate plan, supervised by the Ministry of Housing, for its modernization and maintenance? Why do we allow slum clearance schemes to remove many solidly built terraced houses (sometimes, as in Bethnal Green, to make it easier to view the hideous old tenement blocks of Victorian England which are the worst slums and about which nothing much is being done) and to be carried out with gross insensitivity to community and family life? Housing management seems to be almost as much of a national scandal as the procedure by which patients lodge complaints against doctors and others in the Health Service. Local authorities should perhaps be answerable to regional housing associations (with consumer representation) set up by the Ministry of Housing.

Or take the services provided in the home. Part of the business of treating people as we ourselves would like to be treated is respecting the desire to be independent and to live a normal home life. Throughout recent years there has been growing professional emphasis, in the medical and psychiatric as well as the social-work world, on the value of care at home rather than in an institution. Most children taken into care by local authorities and by voluntary societies, old people in need of care and attention, and young and old in mental and general hospitals may be better cared for in ordinary private homes within the environment of a normal or substitute family rather than in institutions. For one thing the selfless devotion of institution staff makes more acute the separation of patients or residents from society. The idea that others are giving up their lives for your benefit and that you can do nothing much about it makes you give up trying, or it makes you aggressive because you want your independence. The trend towards smaller hospital wards and smaller old people's Homes (including many single and double rooms); the establishment of more contacts between institution and community (shown in the more generous visiting hours and more frequent 'holidays' outside institutions); the development of boarding-out schemes for both children and the aged taken into care — all these are indications of a complete change in outlook. Experiments in Worthing, Nottingham, Oxford and elsewhere give a hint of the enormous role which the domiciliary services will play in the future. The growing number and proportion of old people in the population strengthen the argument for a new policy.

In the first place, therefore, priority should be given to the home and community health services, including district nursing. By comparison with hospital services (except for mental hospitals) far too little money is being spent on domiciliary health and preventive services. The development of health centres and group practice has been much too slow; and the education of general practitioners barely touches on psychological and social medicine and thus offers no training for over two thirds of their future work.

In the second place, a family help service should be created. The purpose of this would be to enable the old, the sick and the handicapped to lead a normal life at home within an ordinary community, by supplying those who have no relatives or who are separated from them with the services normally provided by the family

— like shopping, cleaning, cooking meals, washing laundry and so on — and by giving support to those relatives bearing a heavy burden of care (through personal attendance allowances, for example, or relief at night and during holidays). In the population there are many with few or no relatives. About a quarter of the old are unmarried or childless. There is the nucleus of a home help service and no doubt this would form the basis of the new service. It would have many additional functions, like the systematic visiting of the isolated aged by skilled workers to assess need, the supervision of special housing schemes and welfare homes and the provision of occupations for the homebound. The emergence of a major new service to take its place alongside Social Security, Health, Education and Housing may be justified.

If there is any lesson in the experience of the last ten years it is that no social aim can be achieved merely by planning, and passing, the necessary legislation. The various services do not exist as self-perpetuating systems untouched by worldly sin. They need money and they need good staff. They therefore depend on political decisions about priorities and on all the subtle twists and turns of social, and human, change. Almost imperceptibly since 1945 the needs of the submerged fifth have grown and the differences between the rich and the poor in their living standards have widened. Powerful arguments can be advanced, as I have tried to show, for a new and ambitious policy, geared to the principle that the best possible standards of service should be available to all on the basis of equal sacrifice. This could be followed with imagination, hope and enthusiasm. There is just one condition. It is useless paying lip-service to equality. Better nothing than that.

You cannot live like a lord and preach as a Socialist. Equality of sacrifice is not an ideal which applies to others but not to yourself. It is essentially personal and is not just a matter of avoiding ostentatious displays of wealth. To be scornful about cigars, extravagant receptions, hunt balls, or a Rolls or Bentley with its superior number plate (like the elegant Bentley — UUU 100 — which I recently saw parked outside the House of Commons) would be easy. The real test comes in all the trivial details of life — in choosing whether to dodge some taxes, use the firm's stamps for personal letters, add a pound or two to the bill for expenses, or jump the queue at the hospital; in asking repeatedly whether certain of our privileges look as reasonable to others as they so often do to ourselves. How many business lunches cost more than the National Assistance Board is paying a man to keep himself for a whole week? How many professional people, and how many workers, have four, six, or eight weeks' holiday, a working week of less than thirty hours, and a centrally-heated and carpeted workroom? The more privileges you have the fewer there are for others.

Everything turns on the way people behave towards each other. The handicapped, for example, are still treated too often as second-class citizens who have no rights and no feelings. I once went round an old people's Home with a matron who swept into rooms and lavatories without making any apology to the people who were sometimes there. I saw one of her staff changing an old man's trousers in full view of thirty other people in the room. In another Home the warden, an ex-army officer, took me into a room where there were a dozen aged women. He stood and pointed at each one in turn, saying in a loud voice, 'That's eighty-five, that's eighty-eight, that's ninety-two . . .'

It is more than a personal ethic of self-respect, of fighting hard to avoid conforming to a double standard, and failing often. It is also a faith in people, in the fundamental goodness of man. People live very differently and it is sometimes hard to understand what drives them to act as they do. To give them the benefit of the doubt, to assume they have good rather than bad motives when we know little or nothing about them, and to concern ourselves with their needs rather than their failings — these are generally regarded as being Christian virtues, and yet they are the essence of Socialism. They come naturally to some people. I have never known my grandmother bear a grudge against anyone. As the eldest in a large family in Middlesbrough she worked hard to help her own parents. She lost her husband when she had three small children, took in washing and tried to live on £1 a week. Yet whenever I meet anyone who knew her then, I hear stories of her helping neighbours in illness, injury and death. Throughout her life everyone has imposed on her, yet I never remember her making a single complaint. Even now, at the age of eighty-three, she is looking after her widowed son of sixty who lost his legs in the First World War. Perhaps, because of my love of her, I exaggerate her qualities. Yet there are many as unselfish.

It is more difficult for those who have to make a conscious effort of will to achieve as much. The sort of Socialism advocated by William Morris, or any simple expression of faith in the goodness of man, frightens and embarrasses the intellectual. He does not want to be taken for a sucker in public and you rarely find him saying anything so straightforward and naïve. He is much too cynical and self-conscious. Yet if he is not prepared to live his Socialism it stands little chance of attainment. He wants to stand apart from the crowd, to be original, to wear an outrageous shirt, condemn the mass media and talk of commitment, positivism and free cinema. He wants to reject many of the values of society. He may be right but continually he runs the risk, in his thoughts and actions, of alienating himself from ordinary people. There are few harder conflicts to resolve. Somehow he must preserve his independence and his right to criticize and yet keep in touch with people of every age and class, and laugh and cry with them in his private life as well as in his public utterances. This is his one hope of becoming a constructive and not simply a destructive critic of society. For to believe in people is to subscribe to their strengths, their pride, their capacity to recognize humbug or to shrug off propaganda, their fair dealing, their unselfishness and their willingness to bear pain without fuss, but above all the strengths given them by their lives within their families.

Influenced by Marx and Engels, who in their theories on the family were far less perceptive than in their other theories (4), many Socialists have either ignored the family, because they believed it to be irrelevant to the future quality of society, or have openly tried to weaken it — alleging nepotism and the restrictions placed upon individual fulfilment by family ties. Extreme attempts to create societies on a basis other than the family have not had much success, perhaps because they failed to assess all the complex functions of the family. But there is a much closer link between aspects of family relations and social relations than many people suppose. It is significant that a Socialist usually addresses a colleague as 'brother' and a Communist uses the term 'comrade'. Some aspects of the family can be used to support Socialist values and organization. For most people the chief means of fulfilment in life is to be a member of, and reproduce, a family. There is nothing to be gained by concealing this truth. Most of the supreme moments of life come not only in falling in love but in marrying, in having children and in maintaining one's love for one's parents. A man's public activities, especially as a politician, can be explained to a large extent by his possession or lack of a family.

Terms such as 'equality', 'privilege', 'the Establishment' and 'class' are imprecise and call up different images for different people. One is conscious of the risks in using them. But if that overdone phrase 'a classless society' means anything it is a society where differences in reward are much narrower than in Britain today and where people of different background and accomplishment can mix easily and without guilt; but also a society where a respect for people is valued most of all, for that brings a real equality.

At a Bank Holiday Fair on Hampstead Heath I once watched a stolid, heavily-built man in his late forties heave at a rather ancient collection of horses, motor-bikes and cars which comprised a child's roundabout. After he had got it going he continued his labours on an iron wheel at the centre of the roundabout. It was then about 4 p.m. and he had been at it for hours. His forehead shone with sweat, yet despite this and the waiting throngs he was giving the children a fairly long ride for their sixpences. The small daughter of a young woman in slacks and a cashmere cardigan — probably the wife of a writer or a university lecturer — started wailing. The man stumbled between the circulating toys of iron, caught the child gently and handed her to her mother, placing his body in the way of missiles so that he could do so. Humbly, matter-of-fact, he took a terrible blow in the middle of his back. His expression did not change and he moved clumsily back to the wheel to continue his job. The woman and her husband had not thanked him, had not even looked at him. 'We shouldn't have brought her,' the mother said to her husband, 'she's so sensitive.'

Notes and References

1 *The Future of the Welfare State*, Conservative Political Centre, 1958.

2 [Partial improvements took place in the late 1950s and early 1960s, after this was written. The swift expansion of university departments of sociology has been accompanied by heavier investment by Foundations, Government and other bodies in research. The Department of Education and Science, the Department of Health and the Home Office, for example, are now important sponsors of research. However, the volume of sociological research into, for example, handicap, poverty, unemployment, retirement, household relations, fringe benefits and the use of the social services, to list a few examples, is still relatively small.]

3 [In the late 1950s two papers in sociology were introduced as an optional part of the Economics Tripos at Cambridge. A two-year B.Phil. in sociology was introduced in Oxford in 1965. In 1969 Cambridge University approved a degree course allowing specialization in sociology.]

4 See, for example, Engels, F., *The Origin of the Family, Private Property, and the State*, New York, International Publishers, 1942.

2 Measuring poverty*

One of the basic aims of social policy in the years immediately following the war was the elimination of poverty. In order to find how far this aim has been realized there must be adequate inquiries from time to time in the form of social surveys which adopt certain definite standards of measurement. In the ten years preceding the war at least ten surveys of the extent and causes of poverty in particular areas were carried out. In the nine years since the war only one study of this type has been published. This in itself may be an indication that the problem of poverty is less pressing than it was, but, on the evidence of a single study, we cannot claim much detailed knowledge about the living conditions of poorer people, or about the effects of the new social security services. My object is to consider on what basis this knowledge may be acquired in the future. I will discuss briefly the standards used in measuring poverty in the past, and in the course of this will argue for an entirely different approach.

The standard selected is important not only to the research worker intent on measuring the extent of poverty or general living conditions in any locality. A standard of a similar kind has been used in framing social policy. Social security benefit payments are intended to be related to a rough standard of subsistence, and this relation will have to be considered when the quinquennial review of the social security scheme is presented to Parliament in the near future. It is therefore appropriate to examine what is meant by a subsistence or poverty standard.

Early Attempts at Measurement
The sociological study and measurement of poverty in this country dates from the pioneering work of Charles Booth and B. Seebohm Rowntree at the end of the last century (1). In introducing his study Rowntree said that families living in poverty may be divided into two sections:

1. Families whose total earnings are insufficient to obtain the minimum necessaries for the maintenance of merely physical

* Presented at a conference of the British Sociological Association and first published in the *British Journal of Sociology*, vol. V, no. 2, June 1954.

efficiency. Poverty falling under this head may be described as 'primary' poverty.

2. Families whose total earnings would be sufficient for the maintenance of merely physical efficiency were it not that some portion of it is absorbed by other expenditure, either useful or wasteful. Poverty falling under this head may be described as 'secondary' poverty.

The 'minimum necessaries for the maintenance of merely physical efficiency' were calculated by estimating the nutritional needs of adults and children and by translating such needs into quantities of different foods and hence into money terms, and by adding on to these figures certain minimum sums for clothing, fuel and household sundries, according to the size of family. The poverty line for a family of five was: food 12s. 9d., clothing 2s. 3d., fuel 1s. 10d., household sundries 10d., totalling 17s. 8d. per week. Rent was treated as unavoidable outlay and was added to this sum. A family was considered to be in poverty if its total income fell short of the poverty line plus rent. The studies that followed in the next forty years adopted the same approach, and although there were some minor alterations the standards used for measuring poverty were broadly the same, adjusted according to change in prices, as that used by Rowntree in 1899 (2). In the 1930s a standard applicable in 1904 was taken to be the best method of measuring poverty (3). By and large the changes in the conditions of life brought about in the intervening years were ignored.

In 1936 Rowntree made a second survey of York, in the course of which he used a more generous standard of poverty. This differed in degree, but not in kind, from the standard used at the end of the last century. The list of necessaries was lengthened to include compulsory insurance contributions, trade union subscriptions, travelling to and from work, and personal sundries such as a daily newspaper, a little stationery, and a few other odds and ends. A similar list was adopted in his and G. R. Lavers's third survey of York in 1951 (4). A discussion of these standards and of those used in earlier surveys will be found in a P.E.P. review (5).

In considering all these poverty standards in detail, one cannot help feeling that they are too arbitrary. If clothing, money for travel to work and newspapers are considered to be 'necessaries' in the conventional sense, why not tea, handkerchiefs, laundry, contraceptives, cosmetics, hairdressing and shaving, and life insurance payments? Are we indeed so sure that a list of necessaries must exclude cigarettes, beer, toys for children, Christmas gifts and cinema entertainment? The question of what were regarded or what ought to have been regarded as necessaries was very rarely raised in any of the surveys.

In attempts to reduce the arbitrariness of the standards some investigators had tried to find out the actual spending of families on certain items. In 1899 and 1936 Rowntree based his allowances for clothing and fuel and light on information and opinions passed on to him by 'a large number of working people', though in 1936 he admitted that in arriving at an allowance for personal sundries 'I was forced to rely largely on my own judgement', and in both years his findings on the food consumption and expenditure of 18 and 28 families respectively did not affect his formulation of the poverty line. In the third survey of York in 1950 Rowntree found out the spending of 29 women on clothing and household sundries, and of 32 men on clothing and fuel and light. In the last case, for example, the amounts to be included in the poverty standard for women's and children's clothing and for household sundries were based on the average expenditure of three women whose expenditure on these items was the smallest of those from whom information was obtained. Finding out the expenditure of the poorest families on clothing, fuel and light and household sundries is perhaps a less arbitrary method of compiling a standard, but why should these items be selected from budgets for consideration and not others as well? And secondly, does the average expenditure of those who spend least on clothing or fuel provide a standard of what people *need to spend* on such items to be out of poverty?

The most defensible constituent of the poverty line has always been the amount allocated to food. Experts on nutrition have worked out the average nutritive needs of broad classes of the population, in terms of calories, protein, vitamins, iron, calcium and so on. These needs, as stated earlier, can be translated into quantities of different foods and from foods into money terms. The diet, as derived, gives adequate nutrition at the lowest possible cost, and demands considerable knowledge of the most nutritious and cheapest foods on the market. It may well be argued that few families have the knowledge or opportunity to attain such a standard. In a study of the diets of 28 families in different income groups in his 1936 survey of York Rowntree said:

> It is true that, at 1936 prices, a family of five could be adequately fed for this sum [20s. 6d.], but . . . the housewife must possess an unusual amount of knowledge of the nutritive value of different foodstuffs. Among the 28 families, some of which were very poor, not one succeeded in selecting a dietary anything like as economical as that used in our minimum standard of living (6).

The same point applies to the half-yearly papers on the cost of a 'human needs' diet, which stem from the standard used by Rowntree in 1936, written by Miss T. Schulz of the Oxford University Institute of

Statistics (7). If indeed, few working-class families attain this standard, then it may not be a practicable one to use in measuring poverty.

The main fault in the standards used has been their lack of relation to the budgets and customs of life of working people. Many who are considered to be above the poverty line because their income exceeds the total cost of meeting basic needs do, in fact, spend less on the individual items included in the standard — food, clothing, fuel and light and household sundries — simply because they spend money on other things. This can be illustrated by comparing the poverty standards used immediately before the war (and the subsistence standard outlined in the Beveridge Report) with the budgets of poorer families in 1938, details of which were collected by the Ministry of Labour (8). Lord Beveridge, for example, arguing for a subsistence standard similar in kind to the poverty lines used in the surveys before the war, allowed a man, wife and three small children 53s. 3d. a week at 1938 prices, including 31s. for food (58 per cent of the total). But in 1938 families of the same size with roughly the same total income were spending less than 22s. on food (41 per cent of the total income) (9). How those on the borderline of poverty ought to spend their money is a very different thing from how they do spend their money. It would be unrealistic to expect them, as in effect many social investigators have expected them, to be skilled dieticians with marked tendencies towards puritanism.

In all the definitions of poverty in the social surveys there is the implication that many poor people ought to limit their spending to a short list of 'necessaries' laid down by those in charge of the surveys and that if they do not do this they are in poverty only through their own fault. 'Our definition is such that a family is deemed to be in poverty if the joint income of the members, *supposing it were all available and wisely spent,* would not suffice to purchase for them the necessaries of life . . .' (my italics) (10). Many critics have fastened on to the large numbers in what Rowntree called 'secondary' poverty as evidence of the need for moral regeneration, and have said that these people lack merely the strength of will to pull themselves out of poverty. It is not appreciated that many in this class would need virtues of self-denial, skill and knowledge not possessed by any other class of society if they were to spend their money as it is thought they should spend it.

Judgements of one social class on another are notoriously untrustworthy, and things which are treated as necessaries by one group may not be so regarded by another. A few drinks in a pub on a Saturday night after watching the local football match may be as necessary, in the conventional sense, to membership of the poorest stratum of society as a Savile Row suit and business lunches at the Savoy to membership of a wealthier stratum of society. Recent experience of the effects of unemployment in the cotton towns in Lancashire showed that when incomes were reduced from a full wage to an unemployment insurance allowance many families were apt to cut down on things such as meat and fruit in order not to forgo an occasional visit to a cinema or football match (11). In considering the spending habits of poor people, it seems that due regard must be paid to the conventions sanctioning membership of their community, to the influence of economic and social measures currently adopted by society as a whole, such as rationing, welfare foods services, food subsidies and indirect taxes, and to the standards encouraged by advertisers (12), the press, the B.B.C. and the Church.

A New Standard

The pattern of spending among poor people is largely determined by the accepted modes of behaviour in the communities in which they live, and these in turn are determined to some extent by the practices adopted by the society as a whole through central and local government. A yardstick for measuring poverty can only be devised in the light of knowledge about family budgets. How can this be done with the least arbitrariness?

One improvement was suggested in a study of a Birmingham community, carried out in 1939 and published in 1942 (13). In this study poverty was measured in two ways: (i) by comparing *net income* (i.e. total income less rent, compulsory insurances, and fares to and from work) with an assumed minimum standard of expenditure on food, fuel, light, clothing and cleaning materials; and (ii) by comparing with a minimum standard of expenditure on food the *balance out of housekeeping money theoretically available for food,* after paying the assumed minimum on non-food items in (i) plus voluntary insurances and regular hire-purchase instalments. The first, the usual type of measurement adopted in social surveys, was said to take 'less account of actualities' and the second was 'a more realistic measure of the standard of sufficiency of the family'. But it was acknowledged that both these methods could be criticized, though the second to a lesser extent, for 'ignoring certain types of necessary expenditure, such as that on household utensils, medical treatment, and holidays, as well as expenditure on tobacco, beer, newspapers, and recreation, which are, to say the least of it, customary' (14).

The second method, although open to many of the criticisms expressed above, gives prominence to expenditure on food as a criterion of poverty. In future, it would seem reasonable to accept such a criterion, with certain qualifications, simply because nutritional needs are more susceptible of measurement than clothing, fuel and other needs.

The following procedure might be justifiable in future surveys: (i) the collection of data relating to the food consumption and expenditure as well as the income of working-class households; (ii) the comparison of these data, assembled according to constitution of household and income group, with a scale of nutritive needs, such as that in the Report of the Committee on Nutrition of the British Medical Association, 1950; (iii) the isolation, from all those securing minimum nutrition, of, say, the 25 per cent in the various household groups who achieve it on the smallest incomes, or rather, the smallest incomes less one or two fixed involuntary overheads, such as rent and compulsory insurances. The average total expenditure of these households, less the overheads, according to their different sizes, can be taken as the poverty line.

Such a standard may be justified on the ground that it is, in fact, attained by a fair proportion of working-class people, and is therefore realistic. It would obviate the need for subjective decisions about the sums of money required for clothing, fuel and light and so on. Inevitably, a subjective element remains, and this is involved in the choice of the proportion of working-class households whose members have an adequate diet and whose spending is to be considered in fixing the standard. But this element need not be obtrusive, particularly if the choice is made with full knowledge of the dispersion, and the reasons for the dispersion, around the budgetary mean of each income and household group.

Part of the information essential to the application of this method is already obtained in the course of the National Food Survey. The Report for 1951 (15) analyses the adequacy of diet by social class, but the classes are rather broadly defined (16) and the diet and expenditure of those in the lowest income group is not set out in any detail. A great deal of information about family budgets will issue from the new survey of household expenditure being made at present by the Ministry of Labour. It is to be hoped that this will be tabulated by household size and constitution, for each income group.

It is true that the method suggested is basically a method of measuring the extent of malnutrition not attributable to wasteful spending, but I think it would give the fairest index of poverty, particularly if the results gained by its use were correlated with other findings based on standards of overcrowding, household amenities, education and so on.

The Level of Benefit
The different approach which has been urged has an important bearing on the standards adopted in social policy for levels of benefit. Lord Beveridge, in his *Report on Social Insurance and Allied Services,*

formulated a subsistence standard very similar to the poverty lines used in the social surveys before the war, as a reasonable way of fixing benefit rates. This was generally regarded as the central idea of the Beveridge Plan (17). Lord Beveridge has himself reaffirmed this point in recent months. The national assistance scales are determined by means of a similar standard, and although the national insurance scales fall short of the Beveridge standard, they are still in principle related to it. Neither the Labour nor the Conservative Party has explicitly abandoned this principle.

Whether, in fact, the subsistence basis for benefit payments should be accepted by the nation in the future is one of the fundamental questions that will have to be faced by Parliament next year when the quinquennial review of social security is considered. The adoption of a true subsistence minimum would add greatly to the costs of the scheme. It is true that in recent years an increasing number of people have received wages during sickness and have entered superannuation schemes, and income from the social security services in times of adversity may therefore be less important now than it was. For short periods of unemployment or sickness, families, at least if they have only one child or two children, seem to manage quite well because, apart from insurance payments, they frequently get deferred wages, trade union allowances and P.A.Y.E. refunds, and need to purchase few items of clothing or household materials. There would appear to be a case for two scales, one for a short and one for a long period of need. In any event, the acceptance of a standard such as the pre-war poverty line or the Beveridge subsistence minimum implies that poor working-class people should and could live as social scientists and administrators think fit. There has been little attempt to discuss the distinction between luxuries and necessities in terms either of economic and social sanctions for spending behaviour, or of individual and class differences. And there has been no attempt to distinguish between the humanly attainable and the desirable in the pattern of family budgets.

I have tried to set out the difficulties of arriving at a satisfactory standard for measuring poverty, which can be used in social surveys, and the difficulties of eliminating class judgements from that standard. The conclusion seems to be that the problem of whether or not a family is in poverty is best decided by finding whether its expenditure, save for one or two involuntary overheads, such as rent and compulsory insurances, is less than that which actually secures minimum nutrition for a large number of working-class families.

Notes and References

1 Booth, C., *Life and Labour of the People in London*, Macmillan, 1889-1904. Rowntree, B. S., *Poverty: A Study of Town Life* (York), Macmillan, 1901.

2 A Survey of Five Towns: Bowley, A. L. and Burnett-Hurst, A. R., *Livelihood and Poverty*, 1915, and Bowléy, A. L. and Hogg, M. H., *Has Poverty Diminished?*, 1925.

Kingstanding (Birmingham): Soutar, M. S., Wilkins, E. H. and Sargant, Florence P., *Nutrition and Size of Family*, 1942.

3 For example, the standard used in London: *New Survey of London Life and Labour*, 1930-35; see also, George, R. F., 'A New Calculation of the Poverty Line', *Journal of the Royal Statistical Society*, 1937.

4 Rowntree, B. S. and Lavers, G. R., *Poverty and the Welfare State*, Longmans, 1951.

5 Political and Economic Planning, *Poverty: Ten Years After Beveridge*, Planning, no. 344, 4 August 1952.

6 Rowntree, B. S., *Poverty and Progress: A Second Social Survey of York*, Longmans, 1941, p. 173. In the *New Survey of London Life and Labour*, vol. VI, p. 320, discussing working-class culinary and dietic standards, Miss F. A. Livingstone argued that full weight must be given 'to all the handicaps and difficulties, such as cramped space, absence of storage, defective water supply or cooking apparatus, and the severe limitations of time arising from other pressing duties', besides working-class 'habits and prejudices'.

7 In a summary of her studies Miss Schulz said: 'It needed, indeed, exceptional knowledge of food values as well as considerable skill in cooking for the adequate nutrition of a family to be attained at the figures of cost computed by us since 1941.' *Human Needs Diets from 1936 to 1949*, Bulletin of the Oxford University Institute of Statistics, October 1949.

8 Ministry of Labour, *Weekly Expenditure of Working-Class Households in the United Kingdom in 1937-8*, Detailed Tables, July 1949.

9 Based on data in Henderson, A. M., 'The Cost of a Family', *The Review of Economic Studies*, vol. XVII (2), 1949-50.

10 Caradog Jones, D. *et al.*, *Social Survey of Merseyside*, Liverpool University Press, 1934, p. 148.

11 Political and Economic Planning, *Social Security and Unemployment in Lancashire*, Planning, no. 349, 1 December 1952.

12 'To [the advertiser] a bride is not a young woman on the edge of a great adventure; she is a conditioned consumer who, by buying the right cosmetics and right brassière has captured her man, and who, when she returns from her honeymoon, will go into the grocer's and automatically recite those branded names which have been the most loudly dinned into her ears from the last twenty-one years.' Turner, E. S., *The Shocking History of Advertising*, Penguin, 1952, p. 12.

13 Soutar, M. S. *et al.*, op. cit.

14 ibid., p. 47.

15 *Domestic Food Consumption and Expenditure, 1951, Annual Report of the National Food Survey Committee*, H.M.S.O., 1953.

16 The sample was divided into the following income groups: £20 and over per week (1 per cent of the population), £13-20 (2 per cent), £8-13 (13 per cent), £4 10s.-8 (64 per cent), and under £4 10s. per week (20 per cent).

17 De Schweinitz, K., *England's Road to Social Security*, University of Pennsylvania Press, 1943. Political and Economic Planning, *After the Beveridge Report*, Planning, no. 205, 20 April 1943.

3 The meaning of poverty*

The belief that poverty has been virtually eliminated in Britain is commonly held. It has been reiterated in Parliament and the press and has gained authority from a stream of books and papers published by economists, sociologists and others in the post-war years (1).

The proposition rests chiefly on three generalizations which are accepted as facts. The first is that full employment, combined with larger real wages and the enormous increase in the numbers of married women in paid employment, has brought prosperity to the mass of the population. The second is that there has been a marked redistribution of income from rich to poor and, indeed, a continuing equalization of income and wealth. And the third is that the introduction of a Welfare State has created a net — though some prefer to use the metaphor a feather bed — which prevents nearly all those who are sick, disabled, old or unemployed from falling below a civilized standard of subsistence. Each of these generalizations needs to be examined carefully. We might, for example, ask whether a population of the present size, with 400,000 registered unemployed, constitutes a society with 'full employment'; or whether we should add to the official numbers of the unemployed many thousands of married women, handicapped persons and persons of pensionable age who do not register with employment exchanges, but who would take certain forms of paid work, particularly light or sheltered work, if it were available. Again, we might ask whether post-war Britain justifies the epithet of a 'Welfare' State in relation either to contemporary needs and resources or to the social services which existed during and before the war.

The crucial concepts embedded in these three generalizations are those of 'prosperity', 'equality' and 'subsistence'. I shall say something about the last of these, which appears to govern much contemporary thought about the subject of poverty. My main thesis is that both 'poverty' and 'subsistence' are relative concepts and that they can only be defined in relation to the resources available at a particular time to the members either of a particular society or different societies.

* Presented at the 1962 conference of the British Sociological Association and first published in *The British Journal of Sociology*, vol. XIII, no. 3, September 1962.

The state of almost dazed euphoria which seems to have overtaken social scientists in the latter 1940s has gradually given way to a more lively, if cautious, examination of the peripheries of the Welfare State and even of a few of its nerve centres. Dr J. H. Sheldon's revelations about the state of chronic sick hospitals in the Birmingham region (2), Mr Peter Marris's study of widows in East London (3), Mr Merfyn Turner's account of life in lodging-houses (4), Dr John Wing's and Mr George Brown's detailed analyses of conditions in some mental hospitals (5), Miss L. A. Shaw's and Mrs M. Bowerbank's description of the hardship experienced by families whose breadwinners die or are ill (6) and Mrs Harriet Wilson's description of the economic stress experienced by families with problems (7) comprise just a few of the revealing studies which have been published in recent years. As a result of such work and of public interest in the problems of some groups in the population — for example, homeless families and gipsies — there has been greater readiness in the last few years to concede the existence at least of 'residual' poverty.

The Numbers in Poverty

But what are the dimensions of poverty? Everything turns on the precise meaning given to the term. Charles Booth and Seebohm Rowntree each developed a rough definition towards the end of the nineteenth century and the latter's was broadly followed, with various modifications, in a series of surveys during this century. In 1941 Lord Beveridge was guided by these in working out benefit rates to be paid under the new scheme of social security to be introduced after the war. Even today the amounts paid in national insurance benefits and national assistance allowances derive what logic they have from his approach. Beveridge leaned heavily on Rowntree's work.

In 1950, with G. R. Lavers, Rowntree undertook his third and final survey of the City of York (8). Whatever criticisms we might make of its methods it listed the levels of income said to be needed by different types of households to keep clear of poverty. For example, an income of £5 0s. 2d. per week, excluding rent, was said to be needed by a family consisting of man and wife and three children, and £1 13s. 2d. by an unemployed or retired woman living alone. The chief conclusion was that 1½ per cent of the total population of York was in poverty in 1950, compared with 18 per cent in the similar, but not identical, survey of 1936. Most of this small group were retirement pensioners.

Even accepting the methods used, would the conclusion have been as true of the whole country as many people supposed at the time? The Ministry of Labour carried out a detailed survey of the expenditure (and income) of a random sample of nearly 13,000 households in the United Kingdom during 1953 and the early weeks of 1954. These households comprised some 41,000 persons. A report was published in 1957 (9) but this did not allow more than intelligent guesses to be made about the number and type of households falling below certain levels of expenditure. Lately, with the help of the Ministry, my colleagues and I have had an opportunity of studying the results in more detail and particularly the distributions of expenditure. We adjusted Rowntree's income standards according to the rise in prices between 1950 and 1953, and then applied them to the budget data collected by the Ministry (10). We found that 5.4 per cent of the households, comprising 4.1 per cent of the persons in the sample, were in poverty, according to Rowntree's criteria. Another 10.6 per cent of persons were living at a standard lower than 40 per cent above the poverty line; 14.7 per cent of the persons in the sample were in poverty or near-poverty. Applied to the whole population these figures would suggest that there were 2.1 million people in poverty, and another 5.4 million only marginally better off, giving a total of 7½ million.

The rather lower subsistence standard of the National Assistance Board was also applied to these data. In 1953 the ordinary amounts payable to the Board were 35s. for a single householder, 59s. for husband and wife, and amounts ranging for children and other dependants in the household from 11s. to 31s., according to their age. Usually the actual rent paid by the household could be added to these amounts. For each type of household in the Ministry of Labour sample of 1953-4, we worked out the minimum sum which it would normally receive in adversity from the National Assistance Board. The total expenditure of each household was then compared with the national assistance rate.

We found that 2.1 per cent of households, comprising 1.2 per cent of the people in the sample, had an average weekly expenditure below the basic national assistance rates plus rent, and that another 6.6 per cent had less than 40 per cent above these rates. Altogether 10.1 per cent of households and 7.8 per cent of persons were living at a standard less than 40 per cent above the basic national assistance rates. Some details are shown in Table 1.

These figures may under-represent the proportions in poverty in the United Kingdom at that time. In its report the Ministry points out that people aged sixty-one or more were under-represented in the sample by about a quarter (11) and our scrutiny of the data also suggested that there was some under-representation of the sick. It is after all understandable that the poor, particularly those who are aged or sick, may find it more difficult than other people to keep detailed expenditure records for a period of three weeks. With this important reservation, the figures imply that almost 4 million people in the United Kingdom were in 1953-4 living below, or less than 40 per cent above,

36 The social minority

Table 1 Percentage of households and people with low expenditure (national sample surveyed by the Ministry of Labour, 1953-4)

Total household expenditure as percentage of national assistance scale rate plus rent	Households	People
Under 90	1.09	0.48
90-99	1.02	0.72
100-119	3.56	2.85
120-39	4.43	3.77
140-59	5.02	5.13
160 and over	84.88	87.04
Total	100	100
Number in sample	12,911	41,090

the national assistance level. Twenty-nine per cent of these were children under the age of sixteen (about a third of whom were children under five). As would be expected, a large proportion of the total, in fact nearly half, consisted of elderly persons or couples living alone. Another substantial proportion consisted of households in which the head was sick or unemployed. But what may be surprising to some is that over a third were living in households where the head was working full-time, as shown in Table 2. Most of these were people living in households containing three, four or more children. The data showed that the poorest people in the United Kingdom are mainly the old and members of large families.

The reasons for drawing a line at a level of 40 per cent above the basic national assistance rates are important and should be explained.

Table 2 Percentage of poor persons living in households, according to employment status of head

Employment status of head of household	Percentage of poor people (a)
Working full-time	34.5
Working part-time	3.6
Unemployed	5.3
Sick	7.2
Retired	49.4
Total	100
Number in sample	3,224

(a) Living in households with total expenditure of less than 40 per cent above national assistance rates plus rent

First, in deciding entitlement to assistance the Board disregards certain kinds and amounts of income, and of savings. For example, in 1953 earnings up to 20s. a week and superannuation up to 10s. 6d. or a disability pension up to 20s. could be wholly disregarded, as also could war savings up to £375 or other capital up to £50. A substantial proportion of national assistance beneficiaries receives some income which is disregarded by the Board. There is also a reasonable presumption that its officers ignore gifts of money and small allowances, as for example from adult children to retirement pensioners, which are nonetheless reflected in the expenditure of the latter. They also probably ignore small windfalls such as occasional gifts from charitable organizations and winnings on the football pools.

Secondly, the Board often adds certain small amounts to its basic benefits, at the discretion of its officers, for special needs, to take account of expenditure on special diets in old age and sickness, laundry, fuel and domestic help. Thus, in 1954 some 621,000 of the allowances, or over a third of the total number, were increased by an average amount of 5s. 3d. per week. The Board also makes single grants for exceptional needs and repays prescription charges. Of course, to calculate an average figure to allow for all these grants or disregards and add it to the basic rate would be difficult as well as unrealistic.

These points may be put in a more practical way. From the 1953-4 sample we found that the expenditure of people living alone who were dependent wholly or partly on national assistance averaged 26 per cent, and of married couples 44 per cent, above the basic assistance rate. If therefore we aim to find out how many people are living below, at, or just above the standard of living actually attained by national assistance recipients, it would appear to be justifiable to take the criterion of 40 per cent above the basic rates. It should be remembered, of course, that the expenditure of a substantial number of households in the sample was several hundred per cent larger than the national assistance rates and that the expenditure of the average household was around 260 per cent of these rates.

It must be emphasized that by no means all of those living around the national assistance level in 1953-4 were receiving assistance. A large number were in households primarily dependent on the earnings of the head. Another large number were in households primarily dependent on the insurance benefits. The Ministry of Labour data suggested that a group of households depending on social insurance benefits, not wages, and representing about 900,000 people in the population, were living at a standard which, *prima facie,* might have allowed a very large number of them to qualify for supplementary allowances from the National Assistance Board. Moreover, substantial numbers of people in households with an expenditure of more than 40 per cent higher than the level were nonetheless receiving some assistance. Some of these were pensioners living alone. A large number were pensioners living, usually with children, in households primarily dependent on a wage. Some were people receiving the higher rates payable to those suffering from tuberculosis and blindness.

To summarize, it would appear that in 1953-4 there were in the United Kingdom (i) approximately 1,350,000 retirement pensioners and their dependants; (ii) approximately 900,000 widows, disabled, sick, handicapped and other persons, including members of their families, primarily dependent on other forms of social security; and (iii) 1,750,000 other persons primarily dependent on wages, all 4 million of whom were living in households with a total expenditure less than 40 per cent above national assistance scale rates plus rent. There were also (iv) approximately 600,000 retirement pensioners (and their dependants) and (v) approximately 700,000 others who were actually receiving or dependent on a national assistance allowance of some kind, although the total expenditure of the households in which they lived was 40 per cent or more above the basic assistance rates. This gives a total of approximately 5,300,000.

A secondary analysis has also been undertaken of the data collected by the Ministry of Labour in its Family Expenditure Survey of 1960. Although at the time of writing the analysis has not been completed (12) our counts show that 4 per cent of the population were living below the basic national assistance rates plus rent, 5 per cent less than 20 per cent above those rates and a further 5 per cent less than 40 per cent above, giving a total of 14 per cent, equivalent to about 7½ million people in the population. It is, however, difficult to compare in detail the 1953-4 and 1960 results, because the former are based on total expenditure, while the latter are based on total income, less tax and national insurance contributions. The 1953-4 income data were not reliable enough for detailed analysis. We used definitions of income and expenditure which were broadly comparable but it is well known that budget surveys tend to produce under-estimates of household income and, to a lesser extent, over-estimates as well as under-estimates of certain kinds of household expenditure. In comparing the results for 1953-4 with those for 1960 differences in size of sample and methods of inquiry must also be remembered (13).

The Problem of Defining 'Subsistence' and 'Adequate' Nutrition

But is this approach to the question of defining the nature and extent of poverty good enough? The income standards applied above to the Ministry budget data are determined by the rather special meaning that has been given to the term 'subsistence'. In 1901 Seebohm Rowntree stated that families living in poverty were those 'whose total earnings are insufficient to obtain the minimum necessaries for the maintenance of merely physical efficiency' (14). He drew up a list of necessities under the headings of food, clothing, fuel and household sundries, and estimated how much it would cost to buy them. Other students of the subject afterwards adopted a similar approach.

Many people have been uneasily aware of the problems of defining necessities like housing, clothing, or fuel and light. A family might maintain its physical efficiency just as well in a caravan, a nissen hut or even a railway waiting room as in a three-bedroom council house. It could go to bed early and spend nothing on electricity. It could salvage wood from the neighbourhood rather than buy coal, and scrounge clothing from the W.V.S. or the Salvation Army. The breadwinner might be more physically efficient if he walked to work and saved train fares. We could go on interminably debating such issues and it is evident that any standard we might adopt would be an arbitrary or conventional one.

Uncertainty about such matters has been excused because the definition of a family's food requirements has always been supposed to be more scientifically certain, and food, from the beginning of this century onwards, has remained the largest component of the measure of subsistence or poverty.

Shrewdly, and originally, Rowntree saw at the end of the nineteenth century that the work of nutritionists could be used in social surveys of populations to illuminate, more objectively than in the past, the living standards of poor families. Excluding rent, the amount allocated for food in his poverty standard for a family of man and wife and three children accounted for 72 per cent of the total (15). He leaned heavily on the work of an American nutritionist, Atwater, in fixing on the nutrients required by adults and children. Broadly speaking, what he did was to select, from conflicting data, figures of the number of calories and amount of protein thought to be required by an average man, translate these nutritional components into a standard diet and thence into the cost of purchasing such a diet.

Yet the determination of the income needed to purchase minimum nutrition has always been a hazardous exercise. The special report in 1950 of the authoritative committee on nutrition set up by the British Medical Association demonstrates this (16). We learn from the committee that 'Nutrition is a young and rapidly growing science. Much of the field is still unexplored or is only half explored . . .' There are 'many gaps in the existing knowledge of the quantitative aspects of a man's needs' (17). A man who spends the day in bed requires about 1,750 calories, if he is up and about he requires another 370 and if he walks for two miles at 3 m.p.h. a further 130. He needs another 30 for each hour of work if it is sedentary, 70 if light effort is involved, and 200 if heavy, and 450 if exceptionally heavy effort is involved. These are the committee's estimates, which have been followed faithfully in annual food surveys. Women tend to have lesser requirements. The difficulties of applying such estimates (even if they were less rough and ready than they are) to a diverse population are pretty obvious. Little work has been done on the effort actually expended at the present time in different occupations. With the data available, the committee in fact concluded that the problem of classification was 'insoluble' (18).

When we turn to the amounts of fat and protein said to be required in an adequate diet we find even less scientific precision. There is no convincing evidence that any individual fatty acids are indispensable for the nutrition of man, although nutritionists generally agree that they have psychological significance and therefore should provide at least 25 per cent of the calorific value of the diet in order to maintain the general character of the food habits of the British population. Estimates of protein requirements are little more than 'intelligent guess-work' and no convincing evidence exists of the need for animal as distinct from vegetable protein (19). Doubt also exists about the desirable intakes of calcium, iron and various kinds of vitamins, particularly vitamin C (20).

It is therefore important to remember that calculations of nutritional requirements are rough estimates subject to a wide margin of error. When putting them to practical use and converting them into fixed quantities of foodstuffs, other hazards must be recognized. The nutritional content of certain foodstuffs varies from place to place in the country and according to season. For example, the vitamin C content of old potatoes is much less than that of new potatoes.

The first step in the traditional approach to the question of defining and measuring poverty is difficult enough. The next steps become more difficult still. Having obtained estimates of nutritional requirements the investigator seeks to translate these into the cheapest possible diet. From his knowledge of nutritional values and market prices he might tend to produce a diet giving prominence to potatoes, cabbage, bread, margarine and cooking fat, cheese, and fish such as herrings. Purely on nutritional and financial grounds he would be led perhaps to exclude from the diet meat, citrus fruit, tinned vegetables, frozen foods, sweets, chocolates, and fish and chips. But already we can begin to see how unrealistic this procedure might be. Should an allowance for sweets be made in the diet? The same energy value could be provided by sugar or jam and at cheaper cost. But can we ignore that fact that nearly all households are accustomed to eating sweets as a regular, if perhaps marginal, part of their diet? Surely it is important to take account of eating habits which have endured for generations and which have their physiological as well as their psychological consequences. And it is also important to remember that housewives living on low incomes are influenced in making their purchases of foodstuffs not only by the tastes of their families and friends but also by commercial advertising. They are educated to take account of the virtues of particular brands and particular forms of packaging. We cannot assume that they are well informed about the nutritional content of certain foods and where to obtain them most cheaply, nor, if they are, can we assume that they are activated only by the need to maintain the physical efficiency of those in their households.

Tea is an even better example for it has little or no nutritional value. Should any allowance be made for this in the minimum diet? Drinking tea is a widespread custom in Britain. But to say that it is 'customary' may also mean that it is 'necessary', in two senses. It may be psychologically necessary, in the same sense that a habit-forming drug is necessary. Individuals have grown up to accept and expect it. Secondly, it serves an important social function. When a neighbour or a relative calls, a housewife will often make a cup of tea. True, in another society she might prepare coffee or open a bottle of wine, but this is what she will generally do in Britain. The reciprocation of small gifts and services, and sharing the enjoyment of them, is one of the most important ways in which an individual recognizes and maintains his social relationships.

This line of analysis suggests that we cannot depend solely on a narrow interpretation of 'physical efficiency' or nutritional value in choosing a list of necessary foodstuffs. But this is not the only difficulty. Are the foodstuffs on the list everywhere available? The list also has to be priced. How far should some allowance be made for variation in prices between different districts of a country or even of a town? Indeed, could some items on the list be obtained not by buying them in markets or shops, but by growing them more cheaply in gardens or allotments?

Rowntree and others who carried out surveys of poverty were aware of some of these difficulties but tended to skate over them, eschewing anxious discussion and depending on crude methods which, even for their time, could have been bettered. Rowntree, for example, referred in his first and possibly his finest book to the different calorific value of the diet required by men and women and by children of different ages, and yet made no allowance for such differences in the standard which he used in measuring poverty. Like other students of poverty, he sought to produce a simple and uniform standard which would be relatively easy to compare with household income. But this was done at the price of neglecting wide variations in nutritional and other needs. Social and economic truths can often be blurred or concealed in inquiries which depend on an over-assiduous application of the law of averages.

The advantages of hindsight can always mislead us into being unduly severe in our judgements of men of distinction who pioneer difficult paths. Rowntree, Booth, Bowley and others did much to awaken Britain's social conscience and reveal the deprivations of the poor. But we have allowed our respect for their vision and methods to dull the critical sensibilities which we need to investigate modern society.

The Need for a New Approach

Although other evidence would be required to provide a conclusive argument, perhaps enough has been said to suggest that the study of poverty has not developed theoretically during the course of this century. One mistake has been to narrow attention largely to the preservation of physical efficiency, whatever that may mean, and by implication to assume that the physical efficiency of individuals can be divorced from their psychological well-being and the organization and structure of society. Another has been to draw up a list of basic necessities, translate them into a certain income, and call this 'subsistence'. All students of poverty have in fact made some concessions to psychological and social needs and conventions, but they have tended to write as if their subsistence standards consisted of a list of absolute necessities which could be applied irrespective of time and place, rather as if a fixed yardstick could be devised and measured against a given population, whether in 1900, 1930 or 1950, and whether in York, London, Sicily or Calcutta.

Poverty is a dynamic, not a static, concept. Man is not a Robinson Crusoe living on a desert island. He is a social animal entangled in a web of relationships — at work, in the family, in the community — which exert complex and changing pressures to which he must respond, as much in his consumption of goods and services as in any other aspect of his behaviour. And there is no list of the absolute necessities of life to maintain even physical efficiency or health which applies at any time and in any society, without reference to the structure, organization, physical environment and available resources of that society. As Alfred Marshall pointed out in 1890:

> ... differences in climate and differences in custom make things necessary in some places, which are superfluous in others . . . But . . . a more careful analysis has made it evident that there is for each rank of industry, at any time and place, a more or less clearly defined income which is necessary for merely sustaining its members; while there is another and larger income which is necessary for keeping it in full efficiency . . . Every estimate of necessaries must be relative to place and time.

He even took the enlightened (for this time) view that 'some consumption of alcohol and tobacco and some indulgence in fashionable dress' was 'conventionally' necessary (21). Over a century previously Adam Smith had adopted much the same approach.

In our own day there is everything to be said for returning unashamedly to the broad theoretical outlook of these early economists. Economics and sociology sometimes seem to be imprisoned within narrow specialisms which discount the flesh and blood and the problems of ordinary life. Partly as a consequence, serious misconceptions about the nature and direction of our society are commonly held.

The Level of Income in Relation to Levels of Nutrition

A new approach might be developed. First, despite all criticisms, more imaginative use could be made of nutritional studies. But instead of seeking the minimum cost of 'adequate' nutrition and finding how many families do not have an income sufficient to meet this cost, we could study random samples of the population to find which and how many families, and at what levels of total income, only just achieve, or fall short of, certain levels of nutrition. To establish a minimum income standard is meaningless unless we also show that there are some families with that income who do in fact secure a defined level of nutrition. This fundamental criticism could be made of nearly all studies of poverty.

There is little to prevent this information from being obtained. Each year the Ministry of Agriculture publishes the results of a national food survey. Some of the tables published in the reports compare the energy value and nutrient content of the diets of different types of households with the allowances recommended by the British Medical Association, expressed as an average percentage. We see, for example, in the report for 1959, that the average household containing a man and woman and four or more children had a diet with an energy value falling below 100 per cent of the requirement, in all social classes. Again, the average diets of households containing a man and woman and two or three children vary, according to social class, from 100 to 103 per cent of the requirements (22). But it is strange, in view of the importance of these data, that the Food Survey Committee do not see fit to publish tables showing the distribution of households around the averages. Surely it is more important to know how many households of a particular type fail to achieve a certain food standard than to know what they achieve on average. And there is no reason why information about the total income and source of income of such households should not be obtained and published.

We cannot define 'adequate' nutrition except in relation to the conventions and resources of any particular society which we happen to be studying. The problem is rather like that of trying to define 'adequate' individual height. We know that a man must have some height but cannot say whether it should be 4 feet or 7 feet. But we can show how many men are less than 4 feet tall, from 4 feet to 4 feet 6 inches, and so on, and relate the figures to income and other characteristics. This, by analogy, seems to be the only fruitful procedure.

Fluctuations in Living Standards over Life

Secondly, the living standards of individuals might be studied in relation to the standards those individuals had previously experienced. In common speech we often say that a man is poor or in poverty because he has 'come down in the world'. Our reference point is some previous standard of living. A man who experiences a drastic fall in income when he retires, becomes sick or disabled, or is forced to take a much less well-paid job, is often described in this way, whether he falls from £3,000 to £1,000 a year, or £10 to £5 a week. He cannot go on living in his accustomed manner, and has to move to a smaller house, give up a car, reduce his expenditure on food or forgo new clothes and house furnishings. It would be illuminating to study how people manage in certain adversities and whether sharp fluctuations in living standards are common experiences.

This kind of study would amount to a revival of interest in the 'life-cycle of poverty', referred to in the past by some social scientists but never properly explored (23). It would offer a means of finding out what individuals actually treat as expendable budget items and what as necessities. A few pilot studies have shown that when household income falls, say, from £10 to £5 a week, the members of the household take a very different view from that of moralists and economists of what goods and services they must continue to buy (24).

Relative Insufficiencies of Income and Wealth

Thirdly, living standards can be studied on the basis of the number of households or families of certain types having a total income of less than, say, half or two thirds of the average. As Professor Galbraith has said, 'People are poverty-stricken when their income, even if adequate for survival, falls markedly behind that of the community' (25).

The studies of income distribution that have been carried out since the war are inadequate for this purpose, because they rest chiefly on statistics produced by the Board of Inland Revenue. Many economists treat these statistics with awe and believe they offer conclusive evidence not only of greater redistribution of income in post-war, as compared with pre-war, years, but also of a continuing equalization of income and wealth (26). In fact they have been of diminishing value as a general guide to relative standards of living in Britain. The Board's figures refer to a haphazard mixture of individuals and tax units, and are not reworked in terms of households or families. They relate to a narrow definition of income. Comparisons over time do not take account of sharp changes in the demographic structure of the population. As Richard Titmuss emphasizes in an important new work, the statistics are increasingly presenting a 'delusive picture of the economic and social structure of society' (27).

In what ways is the picture delusive? I can do no more than pick up a few threads in answer to this question. Many employees receive benefits in kind in addition to their salaries or wages, which are largely excluded from official statistics. Most big companies help some of their employees with the purchase of housing and own property which is let at a nominal rent. Meals, entertainment, cars and travel which enhance the living standards of some groups are partly allowed as business expenses. Employers often contribute to private educational establishments. The real scale of such fringe benefits in this country is unknown, though in America they are estimated to be a quarter of payroll costs (28).

Sometimes such benefits are accepted in substitution for equivalent monetary additions to taxable income. But figures of taxable income are unrepresentative of real income in other ways. Taxable income is sometimes deliberately reduced to spread income into retirement, to spread it to other members of the family or friends — via irrevocable settlements, discretionary trusts, family and educational trusts and gifts *inter vivos* in favour of children, and to secure bonus shares or other tax-free capital gains. The object is to avoid taxation and enjoy at least part of the income that would otherwise be forgone, though perhaps at a different time or in a different way. These activities are now sufficiently common and on a large enough scale to make hay of recent statistics of income distribution.

The statistics are misleading as a guide to variations in standards of living perhaps most of all because of the vague distinction made between capital and income. The Royal Commission on Taxation did little to remedy this, although a few of its members argued in a memorandum of dissent that 'in fact no concept of income can be really equitable that stops short of the comprehensive definition which embraces all receipts which increase an individual's command over the use of society's scarce resources — in other words his "net accretion of economic power between two points of time" ' (29). Untaxed realized capital gains and capital receipts do not fall within the present definition of taxable income (30). In 1951 the Board of Inland Revenue estimated annual capital appreciation at £150 million and in 1954 at between £200 million and £250 million. The minority of the Royal Commission on Taxation said that these estimates were much too low and that the real figure was between £600 million and £1,000 million. Since the mid-1950s there has been a boom in capital appreciation. According to the *Economist*, an investment of £100 in a group of fifty leading ordinary shares at the end of 1957 was worth £220 by the end of 1959 (31).

For various reasons some taxpayers and their employers have taken advantage of opportunities to translate taxable income into forms of capital appreciation. A long account could be given of the avoidance of taxation through dividend stripping, bond washing, one-man companies, shares for executives, overseas investment, hobby farming, payment of large lump sums masquerading as compensation for loss of office and so on.

All this suggests why we need to devise more sensitive indicators of the living standards enjoyed by different sections of the population. Perhaps more use might be made of the concepts of 'average disposable income per head' (32), or 'average household income' for different types of household. Those households having a total income of less than, say, 50 per cent or 66 per cent of the average would be carefully studied. To give an illustration from the Ministry of Labour budget data for 1953-4, 14 per cent of the households in the sample consisting of man, wife and three children were spending less than 66 per cent of the average for households of that type.

Inequitable Distribution of Housing, Medical, Educational and Other Resources

Fourthly, more study must be given to the distribution of non-monetary resources. Some families with relatively large incomes might be obliged to live in slum houses or send their children to grossly over-crowded schools. They might therefore be 'poor' only in certain limited respects. We must remember that to some extent the concept of 'poverty' is independent of that of income. The housing standards enjoyed by different classes and types of household might be carefully described. Account would be taken of facts such as that, in 1951, there were 2½ million homes without piped water, 3 million without a W.C. and 6½ million without a bath; and that in 1958 about 150,000 people in England and Wales, other than gipsies, were living in caravans, often because they could not get a house (33).

Again, the differential enjoyment of educational resources might be examined more fully. Account would be taken of facts such as that over a fifth of secondary school classes in England consist of thirty-six or more pupils (34), while a large number of classes in grammar and independent schools consist of less than half this number; and that the proportion of able working-class children leaving school at fifteen is much larger than that of middle-class children. Half the National Service recruits to the army in 1956-7 who were rated in the two highest ability groups had left school at fifteen (35).

These kinds of studies are also important in medicine and welfare.

Staffing ratios, amenities and standards of comfort in the better types of general hospitals, nursing homes and old people's Homes might be compared with those in chronic sick and mental hospitals and former workhouse accommodation retained as residential Homes by local authorities.

Many other examples could be given. To achieve point and precision such internal comparisons would have to be placed in context and related to the allocation of resources as between different regions of the country and as between public and private services. There is considerable evidence of the co-existence of poverty and plenty and of stark contrasts between public squalor and private opulence.

Inequitable Distribution of International Resources

Finally, the development of theories of poverty and deprivation cannot be based solely on studies in Britain. It has always been evident that what most people would call poverty in one society would be comparative affluence in another. To give one vivid example, the standard of living chosen by Rowntree in 1899 to define poverty in York was certainly at least three or four times higher than the average standard enjoyed today by the populations of such countries as India, Pakistan, Indonesia and Bolivia. The United Nations has done much to prompt comparative studies of economic and social conditions. Included among the measures adopted are income *per capita*, energy consumption *per capita*, starchy staples as percentage of total calories consumed, expectation of life, infant mortality rate and number of inhabitants per physician. In one recent study, for example, national income *per capita* in one group of countries (including the United States, Australia and Sweden) was estimated to average 1,366 U.S. dollars per annum, while in another group (including India, Pakistan and Bolivia) it was estimated to average 72 U.S. dollars. The average number of inhabitants per physician was 885 and 13,450 respectively (36).

No one pretends that the measures so far used for comparative purposes are anything but extremely crude. Available statistics vary in quality and are not often based on similar definitions. 'No satisfactory and practicable indicators of actual nutritional status of people have yet been developed . . .' (37) and 'no single comprehensive measure of levels of living (has been) found acceptable' (38). Estimates made by United Nations experts of 'subsistence' needs in different under-developed countries vary widely and no proper basis for comparison exists (39). What is clear is that until more reliable indicators are devised for any single country, and I have argued that these must all be relative indicators, no reliable basis exists for international comparisons.

Relative Deprivation

The vague concept of 'subsistence' is an inadequate and misleading criterion of poverty, partly because it does not have the scientific objectivity sometimes claimed for it, but also because it is essentially a static concept. It tends, with the passing of time, to become outgrown. By using it we have convinced ourselves that there is almost no poverty in Britain. In fact there seems to be a substantial amount, and more, by any reasonable criterion, than we care to admit.

Of course we are more prosperous than were our grandparents fifty years ago. That is a claim which can be made by each generation and one, no doubt, which our grandchildren will be making fifty years hence. But this is a different matter from eliminating poverty. One can no more proclaim the abolition of want than the abolition of disease. Poverty is not an absolute state. It is relative deprivation. Society itself is continuously changing and thrusting new obligations on its members. They, in turn, develop new needs. They are rich or poor according to their share of the resources that are available to all. This is true as much of nutritional as monetary or even educational resources.

Our standpoint, then, should be that those individuals and families are in poverty whose resources, over time, fall seriously short of the resources commanded by the average individual or family in the community in which they live, whether that community is a local, national or international one.

Notes and References

1 See, for example, the reference to 'the virtual elimination of primary poverty', by Kirk, J. M., the Chairman of the National Food Survey Committee, in his preface to the Annual Report of the Committee. *Domestic Food Consumption and Expenditure: 1958,* H.M.S.O., 1960.

2 Sheldon, J. H., *Report to the Birmingham Regional Hospital Board on Geriatric Services,* Birmingham Regional Hospital Board, 1961.

3 Marris, P., *Widows and their Families,* Routledge & Kegan Paul, 1958.

4 Turner, M., *Forgotten Men,* National Council of Social Service, 1960.

5 See, for example, Brown, G. W. and Wing, J. K., 'A Comparative Clinical and Social Survey of Three Mental Hospitals, Sociology and Medicine, Studies within the framework of the British National Health Service', *The Sociological Review Monograph,* no. 5, 1962.

6 Shaw, L. A., 'Living on a State-Maintained Income — I', *Case Conference,* March 1958; and Bowerbank, M., 'Living on a State-Maintained Income — II', *Case Conference,* April 1958.

7 Wilson, H. C., 'Problem Families and the Concept of Immaturity', *Case Conference,* October 1959.

8 Rowntree, B. S. and Lavers, G. R., *Poverty and the Welfare State: A Third Social Survey of York dealing only with Economic Questions,* Longmans, 1951.

9 Ministry of Labour and National Service, *Report of an Enquiry into Household Expenditure in 1953-4*, H.M.S.O., 1957.

10 The study was carried out in collaboration with Brian Abel-Smith and with the full-time assistance of Mrs Caroline Woodroffe. In preparing this paper I have also benefited from help and advice given by Mrs Vivien Sober, Royston Lambert and Tony Lynes. Because of complexities in the way the data were arranged we found that our resources did not allow us to scrutinize the figures of expenditure extracted from information relating to every household in the sample. We confined ourselves to all those in the low- and middle-income groups, and selected a one-in-four sample of these. This procedure introduces a further element of possible sampling error to the error already recognized and discussed by the Ministry in its report of the results of the survey. But in view of the size of the national sample studied in 1953-4 this is not likely to have invalidated the broad results.

11 *Report of an Enquiry into Household Expenditure*, p. 12.

12 See the subsequent publication, Abel-Smith, B. and Townsend, P., *The Poor and the Poorest*, Bell, 1965.

13 A report on the 1960 survey is also given in a paper by Wedderburn, D., 'Poverty in Britain', *The Sociological Review*, 1962.

14 Rowntree, B. S., *Poverty: A Study of Town Life*, Macmillan, 1901, p. 86.

15 In the war, when Beveridge looked to Rowntree and others for guidance in deciding what rates should be paid in the new system of social security, the minimum income thought to be sufficient for subsistence for a family of five included an amount for food which represented 72 per cent of the total (rent excluded).

16 The standards recommended by this committee have been used up to the present day by the National Food Survey Committee, which reports on annual food surveys carried out throughout Britain.

17 *Report of the Committee on Nutrition*, B.M.A., 1950, pp. 7 and 11.

18 ibid., p. 13.

19 ibid., pp. 13-14.

20 The National Research Council of the U.S.A. recommends intakes over three times larger than the British Medical Association. See Ministry of Agriculture, Annual Report of the National Food Survey, *Domestic Food Consumption and Expenditure: 1956*, H.M.S.O., p. 20.

21 Marshall, A., *Principles of Economics*, eighth edition, Macmillan, 1946, pp. 68-70.

22 Ministry of Agriculture, *Domestic Food Consumption and Expenditure: 1959*, H.M.S.O., 1961, p. 65.

23 See, for example, Tout, H., *The Standard of Living in Bristol*, 1938.

24 For example, Political and Economic Planning, *Social Security and Unemployment in Lancashire*, no. 349, 1 December 1952.

25 Galbraith, J. K., *The Affluent Society*, Hamish Hamilton, 1958, p. 252.

26 See, for example, Lydall, H. F., 'The Long-Term Trend in the Size Distribution of Income', *Journal of the Royal Statistical Society*, vol. 122, part I, 1959; Paish, F. W., 'The Real Incidence of Personal Taxation', *Lloyds Bank Review*, January 1957; and Seers, D., *The Levelling of Incomes Since 1938*, Blackwell, 1951.

27 Titmuss, R. M., *Income Distribution and Social Change: A Study in Criticism*, Allen & Unwin, 1962. I have drawn heavily on this study in the following paragraphs.

28 Macaulay, H. H., *Fringe Benefits and their Federal Tax Treatment*, 1959.

29 *Report of the Royal Commission on Taxation*, Cmd. 9474, H.M.S.O., 1955, p. 8.

30 'The immunity from taxation which in Great Britain, unlike the United States, such speculative plunder continues to enjoy, has as much justification as a close season for sharks.' Tawney, R. H., *Equality*, fourth edition, Allen & Unwin, 1952, p. 243.

31 16 January 1960.

32 As adopted in Lynes, T., *National Assistance and National Prosperity*, Occasional Papers on Social Administration, no. 5, Welwyn, The Coldicote Press, 1962.

33 Ministry of Housing and Local Government, *Caravans and Homes*, Cmnd. 872, H.M.S.O., 1959.

34 See, for example, Ministry of Education, *15-18, Report of the Central Advisory Council for Education* (the Crowther Report), vol. I, H.M.S.O., 1959, p. 434.

35 ibid., p. 453.

36 Department of Economics and Social Affairs, *Report on the World Social Situation*, New York, United Nations, 1961, Chapter III.

37 *International Definition and Measurement of Levels of Living*, New York, United Nations, 1961, p. 7.

38 ibid., p. 1.

39 For Chile in the early 1950s, for example, it was estimated that an income equivalent to over 137 U.S. dollars per month was required by a family of man and wife and three children, while for Ecuador and Libya the estimated requirement was 20 U.S. dollars per month. Wages tended to be less than half these estimates. Department of Economic and Social Affairs, *Assistance to the Needy in Less-Developed Areas*, New York, United Nations, 1956, pp. 19-21.

4 Poverty in western countries*

That poverty is still an immense contemporary problem in Britain, the United States and elsewhere in the West, as well as in other parts of the world, has only just begun to seep through to public consciousness. Indeed, there is evidence lately that it has been increasing. I want to trace the history of the information which has become available in recent years. My thesis is that there is no such thing as absolute poverty, that poverty can only be defined in terms of relative needs and that this has profound implications not only for our understanding of society but also for social policy.

Britain ended the war on a note of high enthusiasm for social reform. A new Education Act had already been passed and a mandate was given for a series of important measures which represented, at the time, the public's detestation of the social order of the 1930s — with unemployment, slums, inadequate medical services — everything that tended to be symbolized by the poor law and the means test. Though some are inclined to forget it now, there was in fact considerable agreement between people of different political opinion on much of the so-called Welfare State legislation of the mid- and late 1940s. In the latter stages of the Labour Government's six-year term of office, poverty was widely assumed to have been virtually abolished. We had full, or almost full employment; a rising number of married women taking paid employment; the maintenance of high taxation and of systems of rationing and other public restraints or controls; and a web of welfare services which seemed to be preventing everyone from falling below a civilized minimum standard of living. And after carrying out a third socio-economic survey of the city of York, Seebohm Rowntree emerged in 1951 with the conclusion that less than three per cent of the working-class population in that city were in poverty (1). He was supported indirectly at the time and afterwards by economists such as Dudley Seers, F. W. Paish and Harold Lydall, who told us that the differences in income between rich and poor were smaller than they

* A paper given to a colloquium on handicapped families, organized by the Bureau de Recherches Sociales and held under the auspices of UNESCO, Paris, 10-12 February 1964.

had been before the war; moreover, that this egalitarian trend was continuing well into the 1950s (2).

Thus were the seeds of complacency and indifference sown. Government departments did not possess research or intelligence units adequate to the task of telling the public what exactly was happening. The social sciences had not yet sufficiently developed to provide good independent evaluation. Several years passed before it was realized that although the post-war achievements were considerable, they were by no means as complete — nor, what is just as important, as lasting — as was commonly supposed. In a sense the system of public social services in particular was marking time while the rest of society moved on. Social historians may judge the 1950s as a period of stagnation in British social policy, compared with what went before and even with what has been happening in the early 1960s.

Articles and books began to appear offering exceptions to what was supposed to be the general rule. The families of those who were unemployed in a cotton recession in Lancashire (3) and those who were sick for more than a brief period (4) were shown to be really poor. The problems of the homeless were vividly portrayed (5). A gipsy population of some 50,000 and a distinct caravan population of perhaps 150,000 was found to be living mostly in insanitary as well as penurious circumstances (6). The special problems of immigrants living in overcrowded conditions gradually attracted more notice (7). A trickle of important studies turned into a stream. More people began to admit the existence of 'residual' poverty. But a number of the studies seemed to be limited. Most were confined to small localities or were based on interviews with a very small number of people.

Perhaps the first realization that the problem was large-scale came with the various studies of old people. Since J. H. Sheldon's pioneering survey in Wolverhampton just after the end of the war we have had in Britain over fifty regional and local studies of the living conditions of old people (in places as far removed as the Orkneys, Aberdeen, Bristol, Liverpool, Sheffield, Oxfordshire and East London), several of them, interestingly enough, carried out by general practitioners. Not all of these gave economic data. When they did they showed, as did Dorothy Cole Wedderburn's survey of old people in six areas (8), that more than half the elderly population, which in the whole population could amount to over three million, lived at or around the national assistance level. It seemed that there were at least half a million old people who would qualify for supplementary national assistance but who were not getting it.

The Scale of Poverty

More recently new evidence has begun to show the true scope of the problem. A study by Brian Abel-Smith and myself of data collected in surveys by the Government of income and expenditure shows that there were 7½ million, or 14 per cent of the population, in poverty or on the margins of poverty in 1960. Although our secondary analysis had to be hedged with various qualifications, it seemed that the number in poverty had increased since 1953. An independent set of data was to be found in the reports of the annual National Food Survey. My colleague Royston Lambert is shortly to publish a report on nutrition in Britain in which he shows that during the decade 1950-60 the proportion of persons in the sample whose diet was below the nutritive standard of the British Medical Association for two, three or four items increased significantly and that, rather surprisingly, the Food Survey Committee seems to have failed to publicize and investigate the poor standards of large families (9). There are other data which point to a relative fall in living standards of certain sections of the population. For example, there has been a slowing down since 1954 in the annual increase found in the height of schoolchildren in London of a given age, and data on heights and weights from other parts of the country suggest that this may be a general phenomenon.

More disturbing evidence is emerging from the United States. Estimates of the fraction of the American population living in poverty range from around 20 per cent to 33 per cent. S. M. Miller has spoken of the 'rediscovery' of poverty in the United States (10). Studies undertaken by James Morgan, Leon Keyserling, Michael Harrington, Lenore Epstein and others have shown that negroes, the aged, the sick, the unemployed, the poorly educated and the unskilled comprise this large minority (11). The official monthly publication of the U.S. Social Security Administration contained a recent article by Mollie Orshansky, a staff member of the Division of Research and Statistics, saying that 'some 17-23 million youngsters, or from a fourth to a third of all our children, are growing up in the gray shadow of poverty'. Some studies, such as those by Gabriel Kolko and Robert J. Lampman, have also shown that the wealthiest one per cent have grown relatively wealthier (12), while there is other evidence to show that, after a real improvement in the income position of low-income groups during the war, there has been no marked improvement since. Dr Kolko actually found a deterioration in the relative income position of the 20 per cent with the lowest income. The level of negroes' incomes is no longer advancing relatively to that of whites. Public and private insurance schemes to make good wage losses during sickness have made little or no headway in recent years (13). These are just a few of the signs of what may prove to be a retreat from greater equality.

Why the Problem is Growing
In Britain, as well as in the United States, the problem has increased and may increase further. Why has there been an increase in the

numbers living at or below the official standard of subsistence (corresponding, it might be noted, with an increase in the 1950s from just over 2 million to around 3 million people partly or wholly dependent on national assistance)? There has been a relative as well as an absolute increase in the population aged sixty-five or over, particularly people aged seventy-five and over. And pensions and national assistance benefits, as Tony Lynes has demonstrated (14), have not kept pace with average disposable income.

Secondly, there has been a relative as well as an absolute increase in the number of families with four, five or more children, as shown by the annual reports of the Ministry of Pensions. There has been an increase, in fact, in dependency at either end of the life span, but the crucial group is large families. Direct family (or child) allowances have been raised only twice since 1948, although other insurance and assistance benefits have been raised seven or eight times; male weekly earnings in many unskilled or semi-skilled occupations are still around £10 or below. The sudden rise in unemployment just over a year ago drew attention to the pernicious effect on large families of the so-called 'wage-stop'. A man with several children who qualified for supplementary assistance larger than his previous wage often found that his entitlement was reduced by up to two or three pounds. I calculate from a recent report of the Board that nearly half of the unemployed with three or more children who are receiving assistance must be receiving a reduced grant. The fault lies not so much with the Board as with the Government for not improving children's allowances and ensuring a good minimum wage in different industries.

Large families in the Common Market countries are better off. For example, Professor Goetz-Girey has shown that the allowances paid to a family with six children in the Netherlands, Italy, Germany, Luxemburg, Belgium and France range from 42 to 108 American dollars a month, compared with $29 in Britain. The allowances range from $6 to $27 for a family with two children, compared with less than $5 in Britain (15). The real differences in living standards may be rather smaller than these figures indicate, however. Allowances in kind, by which I mean subsidies for cheap milk and school meals, are important in Britain. Many large families also benefit from subsidized public housing, as well as the national health, national insurance and education services. If account were taken of the total effect of redistribution through the social services the large family in Britain might be found to be in a favourable position compared with that in other countries. A comparative study would be valuable.

In the Common Market countries cash allowances play a much bigger part than in Britain; they do not exist in the United States. Yet in relation to other social security allowances and in relation to gains in total income, these allowances have been dwindling in value (16). Though there may be exceptions, it would appear that in Western Europe generally, as well as in the United States, the large family has suffered a fall in recent years, relative to other families, in its standard of living. In France, for example, M. Paul Paillat has shown the fall since 1951 and particularly since 1956 jn the standards enjoyed by families with only one child and by married couples without children (17). In general, then, even if other Western countries have not been experiencing a general *increase* like the United States and, to a lesser extent, Britain, in the numbers of the population living at subsistence standard, they have shown signs of transferring less income to large families than a decade earlier.

There are other reasons for believing that there has been an increase in poverty. The *proportion* of men in their fifties and early sixties who are chronic sick or disabled has grown. The proportion of persons in fatherless families may also have grown. Widowed and divorced women and wives separated from their husbands who are bringing up small children are a vulnerable group. Unlike certain Scandinavian countries, Britain does not underwrite maintenance payments and many unsupported women bringing up children have to turn to the National Assistance Board. Miss Orshansky shows for the United States that between 1950 and 1962 such families increased as a percentage of total families from 6 to 8½ (18). The latter percentage is the same as the current estimate for Britain (19) but appears to be lower than the figure for Germany (20).

The Ministry of Labour budget data for 1960 showed that of all the persons living in those households at or around the basic standard of subsistence laid down by the National Assistance Board, about 35 per cent were wholly or primarily dependent on retirement pensions, 23 per cent on other state benefits, 4 per cent on miscellaneous sick pay, superannuation, etc., but 38 per cent on earnings. The great majority of these households comprised families with several children.

The Difficulties of Using an Absolute or Static Concept of 'Poverty'

In 1960, Professor Galbraith's *The Affluent Society* was published. He did much to reawaken interest in poverty and the role of the public services, but he referred to poverty in terms which suggested that it involved pockets or islands of the population rather than a major sub-stream. He was one of the first to point out that economic growth was not the answer to poverty, that the conditions of certain minorities would not necessarily improve if the nation gave priority to the task of increasing productivity. He argued that the 'myopic preoccupation with production and material investment has diverted our attention from the more urgent questions of how we are employing our resources and, in particular, from the greater need and opportunity for investing in persons' (21). What has to be asked is whether the problem may become endemic in present Western society and whether more drastic changes than traditional 'welfare state' improvements in housing and social security benefits are required to prevent inequality increasing.

Other American writers have since shown that the islands of population are in fact much larger than Galbraith implied. Their measures, however, are based on the traditional approach to human needs pioneered by Charles Booth and Seebohm Rowntree at the turn of the last century, and I would like to emphasize this because I believe it is crucial to a new appraisal. In America there is an economy food plan priced by the Department of Agriculture (and there is also a slightly more generous low-cost food plan) (22) which has been used to find which and how many families do not have enough income to buy an adequate diet (23). Essentially, as in Britain, this assumes that *absolute* dietary needs can be objectively measured and translated into quantities of meat, vegetables, milk, fruit and so on and hence into a fixed market cost. This is the theoretical basis for many of the attempts to define 'minimum' standards for social security in this century. But when we look at the dietary standards worked out by nutritionists and by the American and British Medical Associations the word 'objectivity' dies on our lips.

According to the special report in 1950 of a committee set up by the British Medical Association, estimates of the need for calories vary according to activity. A man who spends the day in bed requires about 1,750 calories. Mobility other than at work adds another 500 calories. Sedentary work adds a further 30, and, at the other extreme, exceptionally heavy manual work adds a further 450 calories. But no attempt is made to base such estimates on empirical findings. No account is taken of whether sedentary workers play rugby or go ballroom dancing in their leisure hours or devote a large proportion of their time travelling to and from work, for example. The recommended estimates for different categories are in fact crude averages. The committee is appropriately reticent about its claims, although I have not noticed the B.M.A. reminding the National Food Survey committee of the limitations of this procedure.

The problem could be discussed in a lot more detail. My point is that nutritional needs, like the needs for housing, warmth and clothing, are relative, not absolute. I am told that it is possible to live in Calcutta, if barely, on just over 1,000 calories a day. Yet in measuring adequacy in the West, estimates tend to vary around 3,000. When Rowntree first defined in 1899 what was required if a family was not to live in poverty, the income he chose was three or four times larger, in comparative purchasing terms, than the income of the average family today in India. This example provides a sharp reminder of the variability of the 'basic' standards which have been used in the past.

A man's needs depend not only on his physiology and his metabolism but on the climate, the house he lives in, the family and the community of which he is a member, and the way he spends his leisure as well as the kind of work he does in the day. This seems obvious, perhaps, but the implication is that we can only measure poverty, or meet it, in relation to the resources and style of life currently available in the society under study — which presumably forms an organic or administrative whole. And every society creates psychological and social as well as material needs. Let me give one simple example. Suppose a socio-economic study was carried out of families whose incomes were about to be halved, say, such as families whose heads were about to retire or otherwise to lose their jobs. I am sure that the changes in the consumption patterns would not reflect conventional economic distinctions between 'luxuries' and 'necessities'. An illustrative study along these lines which was undertaken in Lancashire during the recession in the cotton industry in 1952 showed that many families stopped or drastically reduced their expenditure on meat, fruit, milk and so on without abandoning expenditure on children's toys, cigarettes, cinema and sports outings (24). There are acquired psychological as well as socially controlled compulsions which are reflected in family consumption patterns. In relation to physical or bodily needs, they should not be underestimated.

To describe poverty, then, is to describe the conditions of families or households receiving much less than the average income of all families or households of the same size and type. They may also experience much less than the average standard of housing and schooling and doctoring and hospitalization, or they may be unlucky in only one of these respects. Some families have only brief or partial experience of poverty. Others may be totally immersed. They may live in a slum house, with a poor wage or social security income, served by an overcrowded slum school, a badly staffed and out of date hospital and an employer who is always dodging the factory inspectorate.

A Provisional Definition

A dynamic definition of poverty is therefore required. *Individuals and families whose financial resources and/or whose other resources including their educational and occupational skills, the condition of their environment at home and at work and their material possessions, fall seriously below those commanded by the average person or family in society may be said to be in poverty.* 'Society' can mean local, national or international society, according to the frame of reference.

Poverty may be total in the sense that a family may, in respect of a wide range of resources, fall seriously short of what is usual or average in that society for a family of similar composition. This form of poverty may be experienced by many of those living in the slum areas or shanty towns of a city, such as the French bidonvilles. Or poverty may be partial in the sense that a family which commands an average income may live in poor housing; the young children may attend a slum school, or the adolescent children may have fewer opportunities than are generally available in society to enjoy secondary and university education, apprenticeship training or other educational, cultural and sports facilities. No doubt it would be possible to develop varied, if related, terminology, for example, 'financial', 'environmental' and 'educational' poverty, in the analysis of total and partial poverty.

Poverty may be temporary or long-term, and scientific measures of it will, of course, depend on the different kinds of resources that are available. Persons who, for example, are poor for a few weeks because of sickness may rely on continued payments of wages by the employer, income tax rebates or temporary loans from relatives. Some of the temporary unemployed may rely principally on lump sum redundancy payments. Those who are seriously injured while at work and enter a long period of poverty may rely predominantly on social insurance or assistance and occasional gifts in kind (such as bedding and clothing) from religious and voluntary associations. They may also require regular medical aid and physiotherapy.

It follows that poverty may be a condition which most individuals experience in at least one respect for at least some part of the life cycle. Definitions which tend to imply that there are 'two nations' may be useful only at one point of time in rousing public sympathy for social reforms but it would be wrong to believe that there are two permanently exclusive categories of the population — the rich or prosperous and the poor.

The term 'fall seriously short' is deliberately general. Much will depend on the measure of poverty being used. I have in mind measures of income distribution which show for different countries how many families of a given type have less than, say, 50 or 75 per cent of the median income for that type of family. Quality of housing might be measured objectively by using a scale. The choice of the point on any scale at which 'poverty' begins may be subjective, in that it represents individual or collective opinion, or objective, in that behaviour can be shown to be restricted or the prevalence of illness increase sharply. It would be possible to establish the extent of agreement among (a) a selected group of professional persons, e.g. economists, sociologists or dieticians, or (b) a sample of the general population on the question of the point at which they subjectively feel they *would* descend or *have* in the past descended into poverty, and the point at which *others* would descend or have descended into poverty. Ratings of social status or prestige have been carried out along these lines.

Quantitative measures of the *distribution* of resources would be necessary. For example, a scale might be devised to establish how many of ten facilities each household enjoys: for example, piped water, indoor W.C., electricity, running hot water, refrigerator, more than 100 square feet house-space per person. Educational resources might be measured in terms of the number of children in a class, the educational qualifications of the teacher and so on. It would be possible to show for all families of a particular type whether their children attend classes of average size, according to national standards, or whether the classes are grossly overcrowded. Considerable ingenuity will be required of sociologists and psychologists to further develop objective measures of such a kind to show the relative command of different groups of society over certain resources.

One logical consequence of the above definition is that families who are in total or partial poverty may or may not be socially 'maladjusted', in whatever sense society applies that term. But there may be a considerable overlap and research is urgently needed to establish whether this is so.

Practical Consequences

If this is how we define the problem it cannot be solved by making grudging offertories to the sick, the retired, the disabled and, now, the workless adolescent and middle-aged persons who are made redundant, while holding out the bait of greater material incentives to a growing class of professionals, technocrats and young skilled manual class. We will only make the situation worse by setting in sharper juxtaposition the haves and have-nots. A society can create more poverty in various ways, some of them perhaps unwitting. It can do so by sharpening professional and trade union restrictive practices. Workers who are made redundant or who are otherwise seeking new jobs are excluded from the opportunity of taking them by the necessity to go through prolonged and cumbersome rituals or by ill-concealed social inclusiveness. A society can also create more poverty by conferring more educational opportunities on a minority of the population, as in higher education or special training schemes in a few industries, or even streaming in primary schools, instead of distributing such opportunities widely. It can do so by restricting the scope of a man's job, as in many automative processes which inevitably restrict the man's adaptability for future employment. It can do so by restricting education and re-training to the young, instead of also to the middle-aged. It can do so, again, by promoting policies which widen existing income differentials. These could take the form of failing to maintain pension rates as wages and prices rise or offering increased rewards to certain professional men and workers whose contribution to production is believed to be crucial. Are professionals and technocrats paid too much? Are they really as interested in having their incomes increased, say, from £4,500 to £5,500 as they are in the conditions and nature of their work?

By acting from a psychological sense of insecurity and a desire for the recognition of our self-importance, do we attach too much importance, as a society, to professional and social status, to material perquisites, and unwittingly cancel out the effectiveness of the welfare measures we introduce to offset the worst injustices of modern society? The problem is one of redistribution rather than of economic growth – of redistributing social resources more evenly – finding satisfying occupations for the redundant, re-training some of the skilled as well as the so-called unskilled, giving more priority to understaffed schools and chronic sick and psychiatric hospitals and restraining extravagant consumption of some resources.

In his book *Challenge to Affluence* Professor Myrdal argues how important it is to re-train or train those who are unemployed or in low productivity occupations and otherwise to carry out redistributive reforms if only for the purpose of 'stabilizing aggregate demand on a high and rising level' (25). But the case for redistribution can be made on ever stronger grounds: first, that poverty is touched at some stage of the life cycle by a majority of a population (it is not a static problem of 'two nations') and that therefore an argument exists in terms of psychological security; and, secondly, when one takes account of individual loyalties to family, community and workmates there is also an argument in terms of social morale. This seems to me to underlie any plan for promoting economic growth. It is not without interest that to create a sense of national purpose in war and stimulate production as well as persuade the population to endure sacrifices, the Coalition Government of 1940-45 approved a number of equalitarian social measures – raising public assistance rates and old-age pensions, introducing welfare schemes for mothers and children and so on. The principle has not been consciously applied in peacetime and yet is very simple. It is one of extending to other areas of social life the basic ethic of medicine, the law and the church, however imperfectly practised, of treating men equally.

Notes and References

1 Rowntree, B. S. and Lavers, G. R., *Poverty and the Welfare State: A Third Social Survey of York dealing with Economic Questions*, Longmans, 1951.

2 Seers, D., *The Levelling of Incomes Since 1938*, Blackwell, 1951; Paish, F. W., 'The Real Incidence of Personal Taxation', *Lloyds Bank Review*, 43, 1957, p. 1; Lydall, H. F., 'The Long-Term Trend in the Size Distribution of Income', *Journal of the Royal Statistical Society*, Series A (General), 122, Part 1, 1959, p. 1.

3 Political and Economic Planning, *Social Security and Unemployment in Lancashire*, December 1952.

4 Shaw, L. A., 'Living on a State-Maintained Income — I', *Case Conference*, March 1958; and Bowerbank, M., 'Living on a State-Maintained Income — II', *Case Conference*, April 1958.

5 Harvey, A., *Casualties of the Welfare State*, Fabian Society, 1959.

6 Ministry of Housing and Local Government, *Caravans as Homes* (A Report by Sir Arton Wilson), Cmnd. 872, H.M.S.O., 1959.

7 Glass, R. and Pollins, H., *Newcomers: the West Indians in London*, Allen & Unwin, 1960.

8 Cole, D., with Utting, J., *The Economic Circumstances of Old People*, Welwyn, The Codicote Press, 1962.

9 Lambert, R. J., *Nutrition in Britain 1950-60*, A Critical Discussion of the Standards and Findings of the National Food Survey, Occasional Papers on Social Administration, no. 6, Welwyn, The Codicote Press, 1964.

10 Miller, S. M., 'Poverty and Inequality in America: Implications for the Social Services', *Child Welfare*, December 1963.

11 Conference on Economic Progress, *Poverty and Deprivation in the United States*, Washington, 1961; the main author of this analysis is Leon Keyserling and it is known as the 'Keyserling Report'; Michael Harrington, *The Other America: Poverty in the United States*, New York, Macmillan & Co., 1962; Penguin, 1968; James N. Morgan *et al., Income and Welfare in the United States*, New York, McGraw Hill & Co., 1962; Epstein, Lenore A., 'Some Effects of Low Income on Children and their Families', *Social Security Bulletin*, February 1961.

12 Kolko, Gabriel, *Wealth and Power in the United States*, New York, Frederick Praeger, 1962; Lampman, Robert J., *The Share of Top Wealth-Holders in National Wealth*, Princeton, Princeton University Press, 1962.

13 Skolnik, A. M., 'Income-Loss Protection Against Short-Term Sickness 1948-62', *Social Security Bulletin*, January 1964.

14 Lynes, T., *National Assistance and National Prosperity*, Occasional Papers on Social Administration, no. 5, Welwyn, The Codicote Press, 1962.

15 Goetz-Girey, R., 'Prestations familiales et salaires des familles dans l'Europe des Six', *Droit Social*, July-August 1963, pp. 426-33.

16 ibid., pp. 427 and 431. See also 'Etude comparée des prestations de sécurité sociale dans les divers pays de la C.E.E.', *Série Politique Sociale*, no. 3, 1962.

17 Paillat, P., 'influence du nombre d'enfants sur le niveau de vie de la famille: evolution de 1950 à 1961', *Population*, no. 3, 1962.

18 Orshansky, M., 'Children of the Poor', *Social Security Bulletin*, July 1963, p. 6.

19 Wynn, M., *Fatherless Families*, Michael Joseph, 1964, p. 18.

20 According to Dr Simon, Ministerialdirektor of the Bundesministerium für Familien und Jugendfragen, about three million children are in fatherless families, one million of whom 'are in the most extreme poverty because their mothers have

too little money or their fathers are failing to support them'. *Bild-Zeitung*, 27 October 1962.

21 Galbraith, J. K., *The Affluent Society*, Hamish Hamilton, p. 258.

22 See, for example, Department of Agriculture, Agricultural Research Service, *Family Food Plans and Food Costs*, Home Economics Research Report, no. 20, November 1962; and Household Food Consumption Service, *Food Consumption and Dietary Levels of Households in the United States*, spring 1955, A.R.S. 62-6, August 1957.

23 The standard adopted by different states varies, as does the full model budget for meeting basic needs under Old-Age Assistance. See 'Meeting Financial Needs', *Welfare in Review*, U.S. Department of Health, Education and Welfare, December 1963.

24 Political and Economic Planning, *Social Security and Unemployment in Lancashire*, December 1952.

25 Myrdal, G., *Challenge to Affluence*, Gollancz, 1964, p. 68.

5 Unemployment and social security in Lancashire*

The success of the post-war scheme of social security in Britain depended on certain fundamental assumptions. One of these was that unemployment must not exceed 8 per cent of the registered population. In fact, for several years unemployment has been around or below 2 per cent and until 1952 there had been no widespread unemployment in any region of the British Isles.

Just before Christmas 1951 a slump in textiles started in Lancashire and Yorkshire. The incidence of unemployment became relatively heavy in those regions in the spring and although the general situation has tended to improve in recent months there still exists a heavy rate of unemployment, particularly in the cotton towns of Lancashire.

Apart from inevitable industrial and employment problems this has raised the question of how the social security scheme is standing up to the slump. Do all the unemployed get insurance benefit? How many seek national assistance? Are many people in poverty? What administrative difficulties have there been? P.E.P. considered that some initial research on the spot would help to answer questions such as these, and would contribute to the detailed assessment of the social security scheme which would have to be made before long. The slump might be thought to provide the first real test of the scheme. Moreover, a study of its effects would give a reasonable idea of what social security problems would arise if there were a more general slump or if a slump occurred in another region.

With these objects in mind research was carried out in Lancashire. Among the people consulted were senior officials of the Ministry of Labour, Employment Exchange managers, officials of the National Assistance Board, the Ministry of National Insurance and the Lancashire and Merseyside Industrial Development Association, trade unionists, personnel and welfare officers of large cotton mills, county and borough councillors, secretaries of local Councils of Social Service and Citizens' Advice Bureaux, officials of local authorities, businessmen and employers. In addition some thirty households were visited at

* This is a shortened version of a draft which formed the basis of *Social Security and Unemployment in Lancashire, Political and Economic Planning*, vol. XIX, no. 349, 1 December 1952.

random in order to gain further knowledge about the effects of the slump, and a number of case-studies, added to the individual cases supplied by local Assistance Boards, will be found in the appendix to this paper (see p. 9). Information was sought particularly from the cotton towns, including Bolton, Burnley, Great Harwood, Nelson, Oldham, Padiham and Rochdale.

The Background of Industry and Population

In 1951 textiles formed the largest industry in Lancashire, employing just under 400,000 workers — almost 15 per cent of the insured population of the county. The engineering and shipbuilding industries employed about 11 per cent of the insured population, and the distributive trades 10 per cent. The industry is concentrated, however, in certain areas, due historically to a number of local factors: the old woollen industry flanking the Pennines, a humid climate, the soft lime-free water carried from the Pennine chain by numerous streams and rivers, the easy access to American cotton through Liverpool, coal for fuel and iron, and, later, steel for machinery. One area, which has been called the 'spinning area', extends from Preston and surrounding districts near the west coast through Chorley, Bolton, Bury and Oldham to Rochdale, and lies across the centre of the county. Nearly half of the Lancashire textile workers are employed here, over 34 per cent of the insured population in the area. The north-east of Lancashire, which has been called the 'weaving area' and which includes Blackburn, Accrington, Burnley, Nelson and Rawtenstall and surrounding districts, has almost another quarter of the Lancashire textile workers, who make up 38 per cent of the insured population of the area. Most of the remaining textile workers are centred in and around Manchester. In particular towns the percentage of the insured population employed in textiles is much higher, over 60 per cent in Nelson and Great Harwood in the weaving area and 50 per cent in Rochdale in the spinning area.

The population in particular areas is therefore greatly dependent on textiles, mostly cotton. This dependence is, in almost all districts, much less than in the years preceding the war. Table 1 gives an idea of the change in emphasis.

In individual towns dependence on textiles was even greater in the 1920s and 1930s. In 1929, over 80 per cent of the insured population of Great Harwood, Nelson, Padiham and Haslingden was employed in textiles, and even in 1939 the percentage in these towns was 70-75 per cent. In Chorley, Rochdale and Oldham in 1929 over 60 per cent of the insured population was employed in textiles.

Between the two world wars there was a general contraction in the textile industry in Britain. There was a fall in cotton production between 1913 and 1924-9 of about one third. Of the volume of cotton

Table 1 Insured population engaged in textiles

| | Spinning area | | Weaving area | |
	Number	Per cent of total insured population	Number	Per cent of total insured population
1929	256,000	58.7	165,000	65.8
1939	202,000	45.7	109,000	49.6
1947	137,000	33.1	68,000	35.6
1950	178,000	34.2	87,000	37.0
1951	184,000	34.0	90,000	38.0

piece goods which entered into world trade Great Britain contributed about two thirds in 1913, one half in 1925 and two fifths in 1929. This contraction was accelerated with the onset of the Great Depression in 1929 and heavy unemployment resulted, particularly in the weaving area. Continued unemployment and the contraction of the industry led to migration in population from the traditional textile centres. The population of the weaving area declined by about 15 per cent between 1911 and 1939 and the spinning area by about 2 per cent in the same period, most of the decline taking place between 1931 and 1939. Between 1931 and 1939 north-east Lancashire, the weaving area, lost over 37,000 people through migration.

Table 2 shows the changes in the size of the insured population in the two main textile areas in Lancashire. Between 1929 and 1947 the insured population in the weaving area declined by about 24 per cent and in the spinning area by 6 per cent, in contrast to the insured population in south-east Lancashire, which increased during the same period by 7 per cent.

The predominance of textiles has always led to the employment of a higher proportion of the total resident population than in the country

Table 2 Insured population (thousands) (a)

	1929	1939	1944	1947	1951
The weaving area	251	220	174	190	237
The spinning area	436	438	391	409	537

(a) The change in these figures is due in part to the inclusion in the insurance schemes of juveniles of 14 and 15 in 1934, of agricultural workers in 1936, and of some non-manual workers in 1941, and the exclusion of women aged 60-64 in 1939 and of juveniles aged 14 in 1947. Finally, when the National Insurance Act of 1946 began operation in 1948 many more workers became insured.

as a whole. This is due mainly to the high proportion of women employed, particularly married women. Table 3 shows the proportions of male and female insured workers.

Table 3 Percentages of male and female insured workers aged 18 years and over

	1929		1947		1951	
	Male	Female	Male	Female	Male	Female
The weaving area	55	45	60	40	57	43
The spinning area	60	40	64	36	59	41
Britain	–	–	71	29	67	33

If the textile industry is considered separately the percentages of insured women exceeds that of insured men, and in 1947 59 per cent of insured workers in the industry in the weaving area were women, and 56 per cent in the spinning area. All these figures of female employment understated the actual situation, for a number of full-time and part-time workers were non-insured married women. The question of non-insured women is important in judging the impact of the present recession.

During and after the Great Depression unemployment in the textile areas of Lancashire was particularly heavy. From 1929 to 1932 about one third of the insured population were unemployed in the spinning and weaving areas, and in certain towns more than half were unemployed in the worst periods. The rate of unemployment continued at about 25 per cent in the weaving area throughout the 1930s and at about 20 per cent in the spinning area, except for two years. In 1938 the rate increased again in the spinning area to 27 per cent and in the weaving area to over 30 per cent.

During the war years unemployment fell to a very low level. Cotton mills were converted to new uses, new industries producing munitions were introduced, and a period of relative prosperity began. The cotton industry in Lancashire contracted by about half, and most of the labour which was released was switched to wartime industries. At the end of the war, when many workers stopped making munitions, a great effort was made by the Government, employers and trade unionists to build up the numbers of people employed in textiles, particularly to take advantage of the demand for textile exports. But the Government war factories in the area were converted mainly to non-textile uses and tended to maintain the more balanced industrial structure that had existed in the war, despite the demands for a great expansion of the textile industry. However, although by 1947 there were only 300,000 people employed in textiles in the north-west, in comparison with over 400,000 in 1939, by 1951 the figure had almost reached 400,000 again.

In view of the need for large exports, particularly to the dollar area, and in view of the diversification of industry that had occurred before and during the war in Lancashire textile areas, the Board of Trade did not accept the view that there still existed too much specialization in textiles in some areas. It preferred to meet the national short-term needs rather than the long-term needs for a more balanced grouping of industry, in view of the full employment existing and the country's economic difficulties. But even during this period of prosperity and expansion fears about future prospects were expressed. For example:

'Post-war Government policy has greatly improved the economic position of South Lancashire, and the scheduling of Merseyside as a Development Area may be expected to have a similar effect. It is the cotton towns, particularly in North-East Lancashire, that have reaped little benefit from measures to foster a more balanced and diversified industrial structure. They remain dependent on a highly specialized industry which is sensitive to changes in world markets and in consumer demand and which faces competition both from reviving and expanding textile industries abroad and from substitute materials at home. Moreover, cotton has not recovered the labour lost during the war and obviously will never recover the labour lost before the war.' (1)

A number of local authorities were anxious to secure a more balanced industrial structure, particularly in the north-east, and the Lancashire and Merseyside Industrial Development Association, in a series of informative surveys, outlined the arguments for this; but the matter was not pressed because of the priority given to exports and the dollar problem by the Government. One example will illustrate the prevailing attitude at the time. In the Economic Survey for 1948 it was stated, 'further measures may be required to restrain the growth of other industries and services in the textile areas and to encourage the transfer of unused textile plant to other areas'.

In discussing the effects of the recent textile slump, then, there are a number of historical considerations that have to be borne in mind: the great dependence of some areas on the industry; the contraction before and during the war; the tendency towards the diversification of industries which was halted after the war by the national need for exports, despite the reservations of the county planning and local authorities; the migration of people, particularly younger people, from the chief textile areas; the tradition of female employment; the history of chronic unemployment and instability in the industry; and the relative prosperity of the war and post-war years.

The Recent Slump

In the autumn of 1951 fears of a recession in the cotton industry became widespread and several thousand workers were temporarily stopped around the Christmas period. Various explanations have been given. The chief acknowledged factors have been the end of the speculative buying throughout the world after the start of the Korean war, the increasing textile production of Germany and Japan (the latter country exporting to countries other than China, its traditional market), and the decline in domestic demand in Britain for textiles, partly because of the new rearmament programme. Other factors, such as the new import restrictions that were imposed in parts of the Commonwealth, contributed to the impact of the recession.

At first many people believed that the recession would last a few weeks at the most but when the mills continued to lay off more and more workers in the spring it became obvious that the set-back was by no means so short-lived.

In the north-west unemployment increased each month, reaching a peak in May 1952 and afterwards declining, but not to a great extent. Although the number of temporarily stopped workers went down the number of wholly unemployed workers rose steadily throughout the year. By August, 25 per cent of the unemployed in the region, or 30,000 workers, had been unemployed more than eight weeks.

Certain key towns are picked out in Table 5. The first three towns in the table are in the spinning area, the second three in the weaving area. In Nelson and Padiham, where 68 per cent and 59 per cent of the insured population respectively are employed in textiles, the rate of unemployment has been particularly heavy, reaching 34 per cent in Padiham in April 1952.

Defects in Unemployment Statistics

The unemployment figures understate actual unemployment however. First, during the summer many workers, although unemployed, will not have registered at their local employment exchange during the holiday period. The true figure would thus have been 10 to 20 per cent higher in July and August.

Secondly, the figures are based on a count made on a particular Monday in each month. This count, for many towns, has not given a true picture of the average amount of unemployment during the month. This is largely because employers adopt different methods of laying off workers. Some mills are open one week in two, or one week in three or four, others are open for three days of the week only; others again may close indefinitely or close down parts of the mill indefinitely. In a particular town the unemployment figure might be 600 on the Monday of the count, but 1,500 on the following Thursday and 3,000

Table 4 Trends in Unemployment (thousands)

	1951 Dec.	1952 Jan.	Feb.	Mar.	Apr.	May	Jun.	Jul.	Aug.	Sep.
Britain	303	379	393	433	468	467	440	393	404	390
Britain (temp. unemployed) (a)	43	64	67	104	143	147	144	101	78	63
N.W. region (b)	43	60	71	111	143	151	145	117	117	106
N.W. (temp. unemployed) (a)	7	16	26	61	89	91	85	56	51	39
N.W. (wholly unemployed)	36	44	45	51	54	59	60	61	66	66
Per cent of employed population unemployed in spinning area	—	1.3	2.3	6.9	10.8	14.0	9.2	7.8	6.5	5.6
Per cent of employed population unemployed in weaving area	—	2.5	3.8	5.2	8.2	10.5	14.7	5.4	9.0	7.1

(a) Temporarily stopped workers: those unemployed who have a definite prospect of returning to their former employment within six weeks and those who are working short-time and are not at work on the day of the count.
(b) The north-west region: Lancashire, Cheshire and the High Peak district of Derbyshire.

Table 5 Unemployment in six Lancashire towns (thousands)

| | 1951 | 1952 | | | | | | | | | |
	Dec.	Jan.	Feb.	Mar.	Apr.	May	Jun.	Jul.	Aug.	Sep.
Bolton No.	*0,7*	*1,6*	*2,4*	*8,4*	*11,8*	*13,1*	*9,5*	*9,7*	*6,4*	*4,7*
per cent of insured population	1	2	3	10	14	16	11	12	8	6
Oldham No.	*0,4*	*11,2*	*1,8*	*8,1*	*11,6*	*12,0*	*11,2*	*11,3*	*10,8*	*8,5*
per cent of insured population	–	1	2	8	11	12	11	11	11	8
Rochdale No.	*0,2*	*0,3*	*0,8*	*3,6*	*10,9*	*9,2*	*6,7*	*4,6*	*0,8*	*4,0*
per cent of insured population	–	–	1	7	20	17	12	9	1	7
Nelson No.	*0,1*	*1,9*	*2,9*	*4,0*	*4,7*	*5,6*	*5,6*	*1,3*	*4,1*	*2,8*
per cent of insured population	–	8	12	17	20	24	24	5	17	12
Gt Harwood No.	–	*0,1*	*0,2*	*0,5*	*0,8*	*1,1*	*0,8*	*0,8*	*0,6*	*0,3*
per cent of insured population	–	2	4	8	13	17	13	13	9	5
Padiham No.	*0,1*	*0,3*	*0,9*	*1,1*	*2,0*	*1,7*	*1,8*	*0,4*	*1,5*	*1,3*
per cent of insured population	2	6	15	19	34	30	31	7	26	22

the next week. Some people argue that the count is in process like a sample and that a figure that is too low for one town's average unemployment in a month will be balanced by a figure from another town which is too high, and the unemployment figure for the region will be roughly correct. But the Ministry of Labour count does not work like a survey sample, simply because the count is taken everywhere on one particular day, and not taken on different days in different areas. In practice, a proportion of people in Lancashire who have been unemployed on Thursday and Friday only of each week have not been included in the unemployment figures. The importance of this count will be seen when unemployment insurance benefits are considered.

Thirdly, there is a long-standing tradition of female employment in Lancashire. About half of these women are married, and married women can opt out of the national insurance scheme. A proportion of these women, who have been unemployed in recent months, are not included in the unemployment figures simply because they are not insured and do not register at the employment exchange. In addition, some women have been in part-time employment, and many of these are the first to become unemployed. (For example, in one group of mills visited there were 250 part-time workers last autumn. By July of this year, no part-time workers remained.)

The unemployment figures for some of the towns predominantly engaged in textile production must, therefore, be considered with caution. The true figure of unemployment in the region, for the above reasons, will have been 15-25 per cent higher than the official figures, and in the summer months will have been 30-40 per cent higher. Accurate figures could be obtained fairly easily by sampling, and there seems to be a good case for enlisting the aid of the Government Social Survey.

Whether or not the employment position improves in the next few months (and most Lancashire people are pessimistic about the future) it is clear that the cotton industry in the county has lost labour that it is unlikely to regain. Some 60,000 workers, 15 per cent, most of them young, have left the industry for good, many of them to take employment in the mines, in engineering, the distributive trades and building. Some trade unions consulted put their own losses as high as 25 per cent. The number of recruits to the industry among boys and girls leaving school has dropped by more than half. The high level of production achieved in 1951 could not be achieved again for at least two or three years. This is partly because of the loss of labour and partly because the work of replacing out-dated machinery has been practically suspended. A smaller labour force could only achieve last year's production given the replacement of most of the existing machinery, much of which is more than fifty years old, and considerable redeployment of labour. And the possibility of building up the number of people employed in textiles again will be frustrated by local sentiment, even if full employment could be guaranteed. Many people with bitter experience of the depression before the war had had their bitterness allayed during the last few years of prosperity. Many more parents (like those in case-study no. 8 at the end of this paper) are determined to keep their children 'out of cotton'. Trade unionists, who said that they had done everything up to this year to encourage people to join the cotton industry, have now said that recruitment efforts should not be expected from them again.

Even should the recent contraction of the industry become permanent some areas in Lancashire would remain greatly dependent on cotton. Old demands for diversification of industry in these areas, particularly the north-east, have been revived in recent months. Representations have been made by the Lancashire and Merseyside Industrial Development Association to the Board of Trade urging the designation of north-east Lancashire as a development area and the introduction of new industries to the area. Local authorities want to end the excessive dependence on textiles in their districts, to stop the migration from the area and to provide more employment opportunities for male workers. Many argue that both population and new industries should be attracted to the area, partly because of its vulnerability to any recession in trade, partly because of the weighting of the age-structure towards the aged through the emigration of younger workers. It might be argued, however, that the north-east is overcrowded as it is and a contraction of the cotton industry would point to a policy of converting some of the older mills to new industries or replacing them with new factories, while increasing production in the remaining mills, perhaps to the 1951 level, with a smaller labour force by replacing out-dated machinery. Such a policy, if pursued vigorously, might be more successful in bringing stability and confidence to the cotton towns than any other.

The Effects of Unemployment on Standards of Living

What have been the effects of the recession on individuals and families, and has social security worked well in the county? In general, the amount of real hardship this year in the cotton towns of Lancashire has been small, despite a rate of unemployment similar to the mid-thirties (though not as high, of course, as in the period 1930-32). This is not attributable so much to the new social security scheme as to the prosperity experienced in the war and post-war years and the fact that the recession has not yet lasted a year. Many families were in a position to tide over a lean period of weeks and perhaps months.

Families with both husband and wife working were often accustomed to a weekly income of from £10 to £14. (Wages average £7-8 for men, and £4-6 for women, although there is a great difference between individual wage packets. A man may get £5 10s. if he is a labourer, £6-7 if he is an assistant spinner, £6-8 if he is a weaver, and £9-10 if he is a mule spinner.) They were fairly well provided with clothes, their houses were mainly in a good condition of repair and, most important of all, many families had savings.

One family of a man and wife, daughter of fourteen and dependent mother, for example (case-study 11), affected by unemployment for several months, were spending £3 a week from their savings although their income through unemployment benefit, a small war pension and a contribution from the mother's old-age pension totalled almost £4. They had economized in a number of ways, but still found that they had to spend from £6 10s. to £7 a week. The man and wife knew from experience before the war how to live on as little as possible (see case-studies 1, 8, 9, 12 and 17 for other examples).

When a family had small or no savings there was of course much greater difficulty in making ends meet. Case-study 3 supplies rather an extreme example. A young married couple (with two small children), previously earning high wages, had committed themselves to a large amount of contractual expenditure — payments on a house mortgage, hire-purchases on furniture, rates, private insurances, etc. In unemployment, when these items were paid for out of unemployment benefit, only about £1 a week was left for food, household and toilet necessities and clothing. The family did not seek national assistance.

Information about deposits and withdrawals of savings in the cotton towns was sparse. There are no regional or local figures of withdrawals from National Savings or Post Office Savings Banks. Information is available only for *new* savings in Lancashire, not *net* savings. These were maintained at a rate similar to 1951. But information provided by Trustee Savings Banks in several cotton towns shows significant changes in the level of savings compared with 1951. In all but one of these towns there was a sharp decrease in the amount of new deposits (over 30 per cent in two towns); and an increase in the amount of withdrawals, especially in recent months.

Likewise there was little information about the volume of weekly payments to building societies, but two of the societies have found that the slump has had no general effect on the development of savings departments and on the advances on mortgage. As regards industrial life assurance, more policies lapsed in the spring and summer of this year in the cotton towns than in the same period last year (in Bolton the number doubled), but the actual number involved was not very large. In general, although there is some evidence to show that it is now more difficult to get new business in the cotton towns, there is little absolute falling-off in the number of payments.

An important factor in keeping up reasonable living standards during unemployment has been the weekly payments made by trade unions to their members, varying from 5s. to 25s. a week (see case-studies 6 and 15). One large union has paid out more than £50,000 in unemployment allowances this year, another over £30,000. Such unions are supplementing the social security scheme. But an increasing number of work-people have now exhausted the amount they are entitled to draw from their unions. Most of the unions that make such payments can do so only for periods ranging from five weeks to six months.

Another factor in diminishing the impact of the slump on individuals has been the varied periods of unemployment. Many people have continued to work short-time (three or four days in the week), or have worked one week and 'played' one, two or more weeks. Less than one person in six in the spring was unemployed for more than a few weeks at a time. Again, in the first weeks of unemployment some people received P.A.Y.E. repayments, but a large number of cotton workers, owing either to relatively low wages or to a number of dependants, did not come into this category. Most cotton workers who became unemployed were often helped in the first week or two of unemployment by the payment of deferred wages (wages earned up to each Friday are usually paid on the following Thursday or Friday). When, however, they started work again they did not receive wages for about ten days and some trade unions argued that some sickness among the unemployed resuming work was due to the full work-load carried on the subsistence income of insurance benefit.

So far there has been little effect on the work of local authorities. The education and welfare services (such as day nurseries and the provision of school meals, the collection of rents and the allocation of new council houses) have all been affected only to a small extent. There have been a few isolated cases of inability to pay the rent of new council houses but in most localities the payment of rates and rent has been as regular as in 1951. However, there seems to have been a falling off in the number of prescriptions sought from doctors. When the shilling charge on prescriptions came into effect in June 1952, 15 per cent fewer prescription forms were made out in England and Wales as a whole, compared with June 1951, but there were 18 per cent fewer in Lancashire, and in cotton towns such as Blackburn and Bolton there was a drop of 23.5 and 19.5 per cent respectively. In July 1952, as compared with July 1951, 5.5 per cent fewer prescription forms were made out in England and Wales, but 8 per cent fewer in Lancashire. But information about prescriptions since the institution of the shilling charge is available only for these two months.

Many of those fortunate enough to continue in employment in the cotton industry during the slump, apart from the unemployed, have experienced difficulties. Mills have had to accept a greater proportion of small orders and orders involving the production of new types of cloth which take longer to prepare, and this, together with the switching of workers to other jobs in the same mills, has led to a reduction in many wage packets (see, for example, case-study no. 8). Trade unions sometimes find they cannot secure the observance of former wage and employment agreements. In particular, other trades offering lower wage-rates have benefited from the slump. Another unfortunate result has been the enforced retirement of some work-people of pensionable age.

Many local shop-keepers have experienced a falling-off in trade, particularly those with businesses close to the mills. It is difficult to name the goods most affected, and by how much they are affected, but clothing, furniture, radio and television sets, footwear, periodicals, meat and groceries are high on the list.

Effects upon the Family Budget

An important question is the change in family budgeting. When the income of a family is seriously curtailed as in unemployment, what is eliminated from the family budget and how is the available money spent? A thorough exploration of this question would give ideas of the standards which ought to be adopted in a social security scheme. While not attempting to deal properly with this some attempt has been made in the present study to find out the effects of a reduction in income among families in Lancashire. Examples of these will be found in the case-studies in the Appendix (p. 91). Some of them are surprising and show that expenditure on the so-called 'luxuries' is by no means reduced first.

It is instructive that part or all of the more highly priced rations, such as meat, bacon and butter, are forgone as readily as cakes, sweets, some periodicals and beer, and that spending on cigarettes and occasional evenings out is often kept up as long as possible. Hire-purchase and private insurance, almost as much as rent and rates, are regarded as first claims upon income (especially the hire-purchase of furniture). No family was encountered which held that it was possible to 'live', even for a few weeks, on unemployment insurance benefit alone. Admittedly, many families would continue to hold this if the rate of benefit were twice what it is, but nevertheless, the degree to which savings are being used up to supplement insurance benefit and the experiences of the few who have practically no other resources (for example, case studies 3, 4, 13 and 18) point to the view that the present rates of benefit do not represent anything like a subsistence minimum. This is mainly because the definitions of such a minimum, considered when the benefit rates of national insurance were being fixed, did not take into account many of the real commitments that families enter into (such as private insurance, club subscriptions and hire-purchase) and the household 'necessities' that are invariably bought (such as washing powders and toilet requisites). It is also possible that rationing and recent improvements in the standard of living have largely ruled out the type of subsistence diet that was possible before the war (see case-study no. 11). The limitations in drawing up a theoretical national 'minimum' can be seen by reference, in particular, to case-study no. 3.

Help from the National Assistance Board

How effective is the system of help during unemployment? In recent months the emphasis has switched from short-term to long-term unemployment. The number of people wholly unemployed, particularly for more than eight weeks, has continued to increase, although the number temporarily stopped has declined. Few people risked views on the rate of unemployment during the coming winter but few were optimistic. If the present level of unemployment continues during the winter then the proportion of people in hardship will increase greatly; for many cotton workers the period of 'getting by' has ended.

The public is apt to assume that the social security scheme protects everyone from hardship. This is not true. Some 15 per cent of those actually unemployed, as against the official figure, are married women formerly in full or part-time employment who have opted out of the national insurance scheme. They are therefore not entitled to unemployment benefit. A further 6 to 8 per cent are people who are disallowed unemployment benefit or who fail to claim benefit. Another 15 per cent of the unemployed are getting reduced benefit payments. It can be said that 35 to 45 per cent of all those actually unemployed are not getting the full subsistence minimum through national insurance which the benefit rates are supposed in unemployment to represent. Some argue that those who do not qualify for a full benefit either depend on their husbands' earnings or insurance but it is not true to say that the remaining unemployed, who do not qualify for the full benefit rate, apply for national assistance. Many people getting reduced benefit or none at all, and even some who are getting full benefit, would qualify for national assistance if they applied; but relatively few people in the cotton towns do in fact apply for assistance.

The reasons for this became clearer during the research in Lancashire. Many local organizations reported the reluctance of people to seek national assistance when in need. At first this seemed to be exaggerated because of the prejudices of people who were not themselves unemployed, or because the reports might have referred to people who, when their circumstances came to be considered, would not have qualified for assistance in any case. But when a number of individual households were visited at random (see case-studies 3, 4, 7, 14 and 17) and when officials, who possessed a detailed knowledge of the circumstances of unemployed people in their localities, continued to assert in private that 30, 40 or 50 per cent of the unemployed were eligible for national assistance, there no longer remained any doubt that the number of people actually getting assistance was much smaller than the number eligible.

An average of 3 to 4 per cent of the official numbers unemployed in several cotton towns have been receiving national assistance in recent months, most of these in supplementation of unemployment benefit. This is proportionately fewer than in either the north-west region or Britain as a whole. Table 6 gives the trend, which can be compared with Table 5.

Table 6 Number of able-bodied receiving National Assistance in five areas (a)

	1952						
	Jan.	Feb.	Mar.	Apr.	May	Jun.	Jul.
Accrington	18	23	24	37	54	80	100
Burnley (b)	48	72	124	222	299	451	520
Oldham	58	56	79	163	194	246	266
Rochdale	24	29	36	82	106	115	112
Bolton	169	190	230	325	408	494	531
N.W. region	9,471	10,215	10,837	11,654	12,446	13,033	14,085

(a) About 60 per cent of those receiving assistance were having unemployment benefit supplemented. It must be remembered that a proportion are people not strictly affected by the textile slump — such as those with temporary or permanent disability. Examples of these will be found among the cases in the Appendix. Part of the increase in the numbers receiving assistance can be attributed to the recent increase in the N.A.B. scale rates.

(b) The Burnley area includes Nelson and Padiham.

Many people were reluctant to go to the local assistance office, partly from experience of poor law relief before the war, partly from an unwillingness to reveal private circumstances to public servants, but also from a misunderstanding or a lack of knowledge of the functions and qualification conditions of the Assistance Board. Few people realize that the funds of the National Assistance Board come partly from taxes they themselves have paid, and few realize that they can apply for assistance if they possess a small amount of savings. Nearly everyone knows of the existence of the N.A.B., it is true, but few know either the scales or the conditions for qualification. Sometimes it is argued that when people are really in need they will in fact seek national assistance. Undoubtedly there is some truth in this, but some in severe poverty resist all efforts to encourage them to apply, and many in Lancashire are in need according to the definition of the Assistance Board, even if they are not in desperate plight (2).

The following is characteristic of the cases encountered in Lancashire cotton towns: a fifty-year-old married man had no resources other than unemployment benefit, which was reduced owing to insufficient contributions in the preceding year. He was advised to apply for assistance but said, 'I'm going to work for any money I get and, anyway, if the assistance people know I'm buying my own house they'll make me sell it.' Examples of people who had not sought advice are given in case-studies 3, 4, 7, 14 and 17.

The number of applications for assistance must also be affected by the reputation of assistance officers in a locality. Because of their wide discretionary powers, assistance officers are bound to vary in their handling of individual claims, particularly when there is heavy pressure of work, as in recent months. Undoubtedly the majority of them are patient and exercise professional restraint, and many borough council-lors and secretaries of trade unions and of Councils of Social Service warmly praised their efforts. But inevitably there are occasional complaints about the treatment of applicants. Sometimes these are due to a misunderstanding. For example, one man persisted in calling at a particular office although he had been told that he could not qualify for assistance because he had not registered for work at the local employment exchange. Careful explanation and persuasion did not have any effect so he was ordered outside in strict tones. The effect on other people in the waiting-room, who did not know the facts of the case and who complained about the behaviour of the officer, can be imagined. There were examples, too, of people who passed on grievances to others just because they themselves had not qualified (deservedly) for assistance. Other complaints are more soundly based and arise mostly because of the behaviour or attitudes of the clerks in offices or 'regulation-minded' officers who are abrupt and unsympathetic when visiting claimants in their homes. There are also cases of people who are refused assistance because they have only recently become un-employed. Local assistance officers apply a rough and ready rule that claimants should not be given assistance until they have been unemployed for four weeks. In theory, a man may be given assistance immediately if he has no other resources, but in practice this does not always happen, because officers, through pressure of work, refuse claims sometimes before they find out whether the individual con-cerned has other resources.

The assumption behind such a rule that a man falling unemployed should be expected to have other resources apart from benefit for four weeks compares oddly with the statutory regulation that some capital assets of an individual are to be disregarded, i.e. the capital value of his house, war savings up to £375 and other capital up to £75, but the assumption has a distinct bearing on the attitudes of many people connected with welfare work of one kind and another in the Lancashire cotton towns. How far should people be expected to have other resources when they fall unemployed? One secretary of a Council of Social Service talked indignantly of unemployed people who came to her office for extra help. 'Most of these people have never cultivated the art of saving when they could. They have had fat incomes and the first week or two they are unemployed they come here saying they are on their beam ends. They say they want help but they do not seem to have cut down much on anything — they are usually smoking.' One example which she quoted of a thriftless man who did not deserve help was followed up elsewhere. The man, formerly a labourer earning under £6 a week with a wife and three children, and receiving slightly reduced unemployment benefit because of insufficient contributions, eventually applied for assistance at a local assistance office and was granted over £2 a week.

This is, of course, an extreme example, but it points to the caution with which people should express views on savings. A proportion of the unemployed, because of their past incomes, their dependants and commitments, cannot be expected to have many savings. But should others be expected to have them for use during unemployment? The proposition that a man should save for unemployment as well as other eventualities is by no means self-evident. Unemployment is rarely an individual responsibility. Moreover, is a man to be condemned if he decides to spend the whole of his wage, week by week, on his home and his family, rather than save for old age or a calamity which might never occur? Saving has to be judged in relation to individual aims and accomplishments and although it may be regarded as socially desirable it cannot be regarded as socially obligatory.

There is another way in which the rigidity of a particular moral outlook may be a disadvantage in handling cases of need. This is the tendency to view all cases with suspicion because a small number of applications have in the past been found to be fraudulent or undeserving.

In the N.A.B. Annual Report for 1951 it was stated that in the country as a whole, 'out of nearly 60,000 recipients who were classified as "unemployed" at the beginning of December, the Board's officers were not prepared to say firmly that more than about 7,000 (5,500 men and 1,500 women) were persons who could be working if they really wanted to work'. This means that the proportion of so-called 'scroungers' is very tiny by any standards. In a period of recession the proportion is necessarily smaller, and there is less reason for suspicious investigation. Yet among some officials, and among those connected with voluntary welfare services rather than among officials of the local Assistance Board, suspicion persists. This inevitably deters some people from applying for financial help.

Some of the local officers of the National Assistance Board would like to give greater time and care to individual cases but cannot do so because of the number of cases with which they have to deal. With the continued increase in the number of applications for assistance dealt with this year, due to changes in assistance rates as well as to the slump, unsatisfactory work cannot be avoided, particularly on days when there are a large number of callers at offices or a large number of people to be visited.

Many of the administrative difficulties of national assistance offices are due, it is true, to inadequate resources and insufficient staff of the right quality. It seems that the National Assistance Board is still regarded as the poor relation of the Ministries of Labour and National Insurance, as can be seen by comparing the amenities of their offices.

The job of most national assistance officers consists largely of case-work and involves a great deal of individual responsibility. They have to win the confidence of the individuals they deal with, inquire tactfully into their personal circumstances and decide in what way and by how much an applicant should get assistance.

Improvements could certainly be made in the publicity given to the qualifying conditions for national assistance, and in the facilities at local offices for waiting and interview. There is little privacy in some interviewing rooms, some of which resemble the dark and tawdry waiting rooms of railway stations. The standing rule of a four-week waiting period upon unemployment should be reconsidered. The assistance regulations are shrouded in mystery and should be published. Finally, staff who tend to view hardship with patronizing charity or undue suspicion should be rooted out and new staff recruited and trained according to more enlightened values.

Other Welfare Services

The methods and outlook of 'poor law' relief in the 1930s have to some extent been retained. On the whole, local assistance officers have successfully adjusted to the more humane principles of the National Assistance Act of 1948, despite the fact that most of them had been relieving officers before the war. But this is not so true of workers in the voluntary welfare services. They vary greatly in outlook, from over-sentimental humanists to strict moralists who would not have been out of place in early Victorian England. At three of six Councils of Social Service visited in Lancashire there was insufficient appreciation of the changed role of voluntary societies since the post-war social security scheme came into force. There was little knowledge of living standards and needs in the localities or of the coverage of the social security scheme; there had been no attempt to find whether unemployment had created any particular needs or had resulted in any legitimate grievances, and there was no recognition that most of the problems arising today cannot be dealt with by the former methods of supplying food and clothing vouchers. They seemed unaware that the soup-kitchen mentality of former public relief is out of date and has no relevance to current social problems.

Workers in the voluntary services in Lancashire have not appreciated the role they could perform in a period of unemployment, in surveying the working of the social security scheme and in smoothing over the individual difficulties that arise. The relationship between independent welfare workers and statutory authorities of the Welfare State has yet to be properly defined.

In only one of the cotton towns visited, Nelson, was there a comprehensive welfare scheme designed to keep track of the problem cases arising in the locality, and this was chiefly concerned with the old and disabled. (This scheme, the Mayor's Welfare Service, involved several full-time welfare workers who regularly visited all the old and the disabled in the town, particularly those living alone. Some domestic services were provided and efforts were being made to give the infirm all the care that was needed.) In Bolton an advice bureau was opened to offer advice on problems connected with unemployment, but this was closed after a time because there were very few requests for advice. Otherwise no other organizations or branches of existing organizations have been created in response to the slump. Local authorities and trade unions, as well as voluntary societies, were often unaware of individual problems connected with social security and unemployment. Some imagined that half the unemployed were getting national assistance. A trade union secretary said he knew of no one in his union who would qualify for national assistance, yet it was found that of ten members of his union visited, five and possibly six would have qualified for assistance.

Administration of Unemployment

The Ministry of Labour acts as the agent for the Ministry of National Insurance in considering claims for unemployment insurance benefit. This means that insured workers who fall unemployed can both register for unemployment and draw benefit at local employment exchanges. When the slump began with little warning around Christmas of 1951 employment exchange managers and staff faced big difficulties. The growth in the number of cases that had to be dealt with is shown in Table 5 (p. 70). At Padiham, for example, there were only three people registered as unemployed during the greater part of 1951. By April 1952 there were more than 2,000. For a time, when unemployment was thought to be a temporary matter, the small staffs had the herculean task of dealing almost unaided with the increased work. There were as many as twenty hours' overtime a week worked. An increase in staff was delayed by a Treasury decision to clamp down on the numbers of civil servants generally in the country, but when unemployment continued temporary staff were sent to the cotton towns. The numbers increased from 5 to 15 at Padiham, from 36 to 70 at Oldham and from 27 to 62 at Rochdale. In the region as a whole the staff of the Ministry of Labour increased by 600.

There existed, then, the problem of the training of temporary staff or staff transferred from other offices or regions, of trying to place workers in areas which are predominantly concerned with textiles, of dealing with an unemployment rate not experienced (except for a few weeks during the fuel crisis of 1947) since before the war. In most of the cotton towns it was found impossible to deal satisfactorily with the increase in claims for unemployment insurance benefit on the ordinary procedure, and emergency schemes were substituted.

The modifications of the ordinary procedure for claiming benefit followed a pattern laid down by the Ministry of Labour. These involved the use of employers' premises to make payments or to take proof of unemployment. Sometimes members of the staff of local exchanges considered claims and made payments at the mills, but usually employers themselves arranged to pay benefit to their work-people using a simple claim form supplied by the exchanges. Scores of thousands of emergency claims were handled each week. When staff were added at exchanges administrative procedures reverted to normal. Examples of the numbers handled are given in Table 7.

In practically all cases, employers have been found to be extremely co-operative in paying benefits. Unemployed workers have been glad to draw benefit at their former place of employment and to dispense with the need of going regularly to queue at the local exchanges. Trade unions welcomed the procedure and generally wanted it to continue. And employers, despite the work entailed, found the procedure useful in holding their workers together and keeping a check on the drift to other jobs. These advantages make it hard for some people to understand why administrative procedures have been reverting to normal, although the absence of queues at exchanges has tended to conceal from public attention the full seriousness of local unemployment. The following reasons were given. The exchanges have difficulties

Table 7 Total benefit payments in two towns (a)

Period and date of payment	Bolton		Padiham	
	Ordinary and extended benefit	Emergency payments	Ordinary and extended benefit	Emergency payments
4 weeks ending 2nd week April 1952	5,271	31,707	1,441	3,736
4 weeks ending 2nd week May 1952	6,570	44,873	1,940	4,504
5 weeks ending 2nd week June 1952	10,622	47,198	2,926	5,219
4 weeks ending 2nd week July 1952	8,120	15,157(b)	2,508	2,548
4 weeks ending 2nd week August 1952	8,649	22,299	3,700	821(b)
5 weeks ending 2nd week September 1952	10,523	19,039	7,026	10

(a) The figures refer to the total for a month, not the weekly average.
(b) Local holidays.

in notifying unemployed people of alternative employment, in verifying claims for benefit and in remaining independent in their actions. The emergency scheme carried the risk that the national insurance regulations would not be satisfied strictly. Officials estimated privately that about 3 per cent would not have qualified in the normal way and another 10-20 per cent (mainly women) would have had their benefit reduced slightly. Against these disadvantages, as seen by the administrators, has to be set the increase in administrative costs that would have been involved, perhaps greater than the amount 'lost', and other advantages of the scheme. There is certainly a case for the payment of unemployment insurance benefit at the place of employment in all areas where there is a large amount of short-term unemployment.

In general, most of the problems involving temporary unemployment which faced exchange managers have now been overcome, and are being replaced by the problem of long-term unemployment. But the existence of temporary unemployment and short-time working in Lancashire has raised the important question of what has been the real figure for unemployment. It is almost impossible for the Ministry of Labour to find out the exact numbers of non-insured married women who become unemployed, but it should be possible to give a more accurate figure for the bulk of those unemployed than those officially released. Table 8 shows the inconsistencies that exist in official local statistics.

Table 8 Average unemployment insurance benefit (U.I.B.) payments per week compared with numbers of registered unemployed (a)

	Mar.	Apr.	May	Jun.	Jul.	Aug.
Bolton						
Unemployed	8,445	11,783	13,111	9,472	9,690	6,424
U.I.B. per week	*9,244*	*12,861*	11,564	5,819	7,737	5,912
Nelson						
Unemployed	4,022	4,702	5,624	5,580	1,274	4,046
U.I.B. per week	3,441	4,445	5,097	3,858	*3,373*	3,101
Padiham						
Unemployed	1,103	2,008	1,744	1,839	402	1,448
U.I.B. per week	*1,294*	1,609	1,627	1,239	*1,127*	1,404
Great Harwood						
Unemployed	456	784	1,123	840	773	595
U.I.B. per week	*685*	*975*	1,064	*940*	549	*733*

(a) The U.I.B. figures are averages over a 5 week or 4 week period and do not correspond exactly with the calendar month.

Unemployment statistics represent the count on one particular day in the month. Attention is called to apparent discrepancies in the figures in italic in the table.

In nine of the sample of twenty-four paired figures, the number of benefit payments exceeded by a substantial amount the number officially said to be 'unemployed', despite the fact that a proportion of the registered unemployed did not and do not get benefit. In these examples, at least, the unemployment figures did not reflect average registered unemployment let alone real unemployment. Where there is a considerable amount of temporary unemployment and short-time working a count should be made in each week of a month in order to find out the average unemployment in the month.

Defects in Unemployment Insurance Statistics

When examining the social security scheme and in particular the coverage of national insurance in an area where there is heavy unemployment a natural course in principle would be to find the number of those unemployed, and the proportions receiving full U.I.B. and reduced U.I.B., the proportion disallowed U.I.B. and not claiming benefit, giving the various reasons for these, and afterwards describing the methods of appeal against decisions and of finding an income where there is no entitlement to benefit. Throughout the research in Lancashire every attempt was made to put into practice this approach.

The outcome is that only rough comparisons but not exact figures can be given. Some reasons for this have already been stated. They include the inaccuracy of official unemployment figures, the impossibility of relating unemployment figures to insurance payment figures with any degree of precision, and the lack of precise information about the number of unemployed people disallowed benefit or not claiming benefit. The methods of collecting unemployment statistics and benefit payment statistics make it difficult to compare the two (3).

Table 9 shows that of the number officially said to be unemployed an average of 74 per cent are said to have received benefit with or without supplementary assistance, and a further 4 per cent to have received national assistance only (4). On the face of it the rest seem to get neither benefit nor assistance. No evidence was found of this in the cotton towns, and indeed employers, trade union secretaries, Labour Exchange managers and others closely acquainted with the recent slump all placed the real proportion below 10 per cent.

Table 9 Unemployment and claims rated for benefit: N.W. region, 1952 (thousands)

	1	2	3	4	5	6
Month	Unemploy-ment (a)	Standard benefit (b)	Additional days (c)	Extended benefit (d)	National Assis-tance (e)	Total 2, 3, 4 and 5
Jan.	59,7	35,1	1,1	4,1	4,4	44,7
Feb.	71,5	44,7	1,1	4,1	4,5	54,4
Mar.	111,3	87	1,2	4,2	4,7	97,4
Apr.	143,4	103,2	1,4	4,2	4,6	113,4
May	150,7	110,9	1,8	4,4	4,8	121,9
Jun.	145,2	90,4	1,9	4,4	4,8	101,5
Jul.	117,2	79.2	2,1	4,6	5,0	91,0
Aug.	117,3	81,0	2,5	4,9	5,3	94,0

(a) The figures refer to a count made on a particular Monday in each month.
(b) Claims rated for the various types of benefit are counted at local employment exchanges on the Monday following the unemployment count in each month.
(c) Benefit granted in excess of the normal period when the contribution record is good.
(d) Benefit paid after unemployment has lasted seven months.
(e) These figures are slightly misleading for they include a small number of applicants who do not qualify for assistance besides those who actually receive assistance.

Reductions and Disallowance of Unemployment Benefit

The extent and meaning of reductions and disallowances of unemployment insurance benefit obviously have an important bearing on the coverage of national insurance and the success of the social security scheme as a whole. It is impossible to give an exact figure for the number of disallowances and reductions (and the extent of the reductions) but local inquiries in several areas established that the proportion of disallowances has been 5-10 per cent, and of reductions 15-25 per cent, mainly affecting unemployed women. The reason for reductions has been usually an insufficient number of contributions in the preceding year.

In June 1952, when unemployment in the north-west region was 145,000, over 13,000 cases were referred for insurance officers' decisions in the course of the month (the insurance officers being the local exchange managers). Just under 10,000, or 75 per cent, were disallowed, because of 'voluntary leaving' (34 per cent), 'contributions' (12 per cent), 'misconduct' (10 per cent), 'receiving wages or compensation' (7 per cent), 'refusal of suitable employment' (3 per cent), 'availability for employment' (2 per cent), and others such as 'subsidiary occupation' and 'holidays' accounted for 7 per cent. In eight selected cotton towns in the region the situation was rather different. Unemployment in these towns in June was 42,000, and in the course of the month over 2,000 cases were referred for insurance officers' decisions. Altogether, 1,500, or 73 per cent, were disallowed, because of 'voluntary leaving' (26 per cent), 'contributions' (20 per cent), 'misconduct' (8 per cent), 'receiving wages or compensation' (6 per cent), 'refusal of suitable employment' (2 per cent), 'subsidiary occupation' (2 per cent), 'availability for employment' (2 per cent), others (9 per cent). The different pattern is attributable to the operation of emergency schemes of payment and to the fact that many unemployed cotton workers have had good insurance contribution records. It is important to add that the numbers of those disallowed benefit does not represent the number not qualifying for benefit, for some people who know they do not qualify do not bother to claim. A small proportion of those disallowed also appeal to local Appeals Tribunals and some of these are subsequently allowed benefit. It is a great drawback to informed discussion of the national insurance scheme that adequate information about disallowances is not published and is not even made available to research organizations or to local Advisory Councils.

Many people in Lancashire drew attention to defects in the insurance regulations and the injustice of a few of them in particular. Establishing the true facts in a case so that the insurance regulations can be applied is sometimes extremely hard, especially in trying to find whether there is disentitlement to benefit owing to industrial miscon-duct, refusal of suitable employment or no availability for employment. A man may be sacked without it being clear whether it was or was not his own fault. The following is one example of a person being refused unemployment insurance benefit because of industrial misconduct.

A cotton labourer with a large family, fearing unemployment, made an attempt to obtain what he thought would be more stable employment. He stayed off work one Monday morning and applied for another job, but failed to get it. It was his intention, if he got the job, to work the requisite week's notice with his original firm. He returned on the Monday afternoon and on being asked where he had been in the morning admitted that he had been to look for another job. He was sacked on the spot and subsequently was refused U.I.B. for six weeks on the grounds of industrial misconduct. The man appealed to the Appeals Tribunal but the tribunal was unable to decide and the case finally reached the National Insurance Commissioner who ruled that the suspension of benefit should be cut down to one week.

Another example is of refusal of benefit for voluntarily leaving employment. A woman was employed as a slubber at a mill and was expected to carry 10-20lb. of slubbings. She sustained an industrial injury in 1948 and now wears a spinal corset. The mill was on short-time and she obtained employment at another mill, where she was expected to carry slubbings weighing 30-40lb. Because of her back injury she could not carry the weights and in addition she had to do more bending than formerly. She became exhausted and after notifying the mill that she could not do the work left after one day. Her claim was disallowed by the local insurance officer but on appeal to the Appeals Tribunal her claim was allowed. Other examples of such cases point to the enormous difficulty of deciding whether a person has given his new job 'a fair trial'.

The insurance regulations which insurance officers have to follow are extremely complex and a great amount of time is spent on doubtful cases. There is no question that improvements could be made in some of the regulations, particularly those which seem to lead to injustices. The latter relate particularly to married women, widows, and persons with subsidiary occupations.

Married women receive 26s. U.I.B. a week as against 32s. 6d. for single women, yet they pay the same contribution rate. If they have paid fewer than fifty contributions in the relevant contribution year their U.I.B. is reduced, and unless they have paid forty-five contributions in preceding years they are ineligible for any benefit (unless arrears in previous years have been paid up and they re-qualify for benefit). Both these regulations are rather harsh on married women who feel compelled to stay at home during school holidays. (In Lancashire, as has been pointed out earlier, a large proportion of married women do not qualify for benefit or they receive a reduced benefit.) The regulations are presumably meant to distinguish between married women who intend to work regularly and those who do not, but this purpose is not achieved.

Widows in employment pay the same contributions as other women but when they are unemployed usually get a much lower benefit because their widows' pensions (sometimes the 10s. pension) are deducted from benefit. This is resented, particularly by widows over the age of sixty, who, although paying full contributions when working, are subject to the deduction of 10s. pension from U.I.B. There are also cases of widows entitled to the new widows' pension of 32s. 6d. whether or not they are entitled to U.I.B. Some of these widows have been paying full insurance contributions for considerable periods and yet, in unemployment, they receive no U.I.B. and have the same income as other widows who have paid no contributions. An example of severe hardship is of a woman who became widowed after 1948. Her husband was not previously insurable. She was ineligible for widows' pension and she secured employment. When she reached sixty years of age she continued in employment but was ineligible to receive sickness or unemployment benefit. Cases have arisen where such persons have been receiving unemployment benefit but were disallowed on reaching sixty years of age.

Persons with subsidiary occupations provide a fair number of anomalous cases when they become unemployed. For example, an elderly married textile operative continued working as an office-cleaner in the evening when she became unemployed. Her earnings for this subsidiary occupation were 22s. 6d. a week. She was ineligible for unemployment benefit because she was earning more than 20s. a week. She thus had a smaller income when doing evening work than she would have done if not working at all. (Her U.I.B. would have been 26s. a week.)

Again, a single woman, when unemployed, continued working in the evenings as a cinema usherette, receiving 28s. 5d. for six evenings' work. She was ineligible for U.I.B. of 32s. 6d. a week. Again she received less when working in the evenings than if she had had no work at all. Neither of these women were credited with a contribution frank, which is normal in periods of unemployment. Several other examples affecting people working part-time as trade-union representatives, caretakers and painters were quoted. It should be noted that the disqualification from benefit if earnings are more than 20s. is a ruling that has existed without change since 1920, and although a pensioner is allowed to earn £2 a week before a progressive reduction in the pension takes place, unemployment benefit is entirely extinguished if earnings exceed £1 a week.

Other regulations that deserve reconsideration are those relating to the payment of U.I.B. during holidays, to late-age entrants into the insurance scheme, and to professional and to non-manual workers not insurable before 1948 who cannot receive benefit after reaching the age of sixty-five. It is also odd that a man cannot draw U.I.B. for his wife if she already has sickness benefit, although this was possible before the war.

Few people are educated in the mysteries of national insurance and although some appeal to local Appeals Tribunals, encouraged sometimes by their unions, when they do not understand why their benefits have been disallowed or reduced, there must be many who do not do this, even though they stand a good chance of winning their appeals. If the national insurance scheme is to go on, there is a strong case for simplifying the bewildering complexity of the regulations and making them more lenient, both because of the administrative trouble and cost in considering doubtful cases and because there seems to be an inherent clash between what may be called the insurance principle, getting a fair reward for payments made, and the subsistence principle, that every citizen should of right get a minimum subsistence income in times of need. At present there is social injustice in the regulations.

Wider Reforms in Social Security

Criticisms have been made of the working of the social security scheme in Lancashire in the present recession. Most have been expressed in relation to the machinery that exists. To question this machinery would be to raise deeper questions. Does experience gained from a study of one area at one particular time provide any evidence for a general change in the social security scheme? The present situation in Lancashire produces certain basic facts:

1. A substantial proportion of people unemployed (perhaps 40 per cent) do not get the full insurance benefit rate which has been said to be the minimum for subsistence, and a large number of people do not apply for the higher subsistence rate of national assistance although they are in a position to do so.

2. A scheme which operates according to some of the principles of private insurance cannot also operate successfully according to the principle of a subsistence minimum in adversity for every citizen as of right.

3. Although only a small proportion of people have experienced real hardship in Lancashire because of the slump this is due not so much to the post-war security scheme as to the degree of dissaving among the population, trade union allowances, recent prosperity and so on (all of which have less effect as the slump goes on).

4. National insurance regulations are extremely complex, sometimes

anomalous, and certainly lead to great administrative trouble and expense.

5. The public in general assumes the social security scheme to be more comprehensive and more successful than it is (partly because it takes more than average effort and education to master even some of the intricacies of the regulations).

The principle of a flat-rate contribution has not been adopted in the schemes of other countries, and is likely to create problems in future. The national insurance scheme is also going to be thrown out of balance in the future by the increasing number and proportion of retirement pensioners.

All these considerations show the need to review the social security scheme. It is worth recalling that Lord Beveridge originally suggested that there should be one Ministry of Social Security, incorporating national insurance and national assistance. Proposals for the replacement of the national insurance scheme by schemes involving a social security tax, an extension of the family allowances scheme to all fields of social security, and the financing of social security out of direct taxation have also been made.

Any effective social security scheme must depend on a good system of employment and well-integrated social relationships. As Lord Beveridge stated in his report ten years ago:

Income security which is all that can be given by social insurance is so inadequate a provision for human happiness that to put it forward by itself as a sole or principal measure of reconstruction hardly seems worth doing. It should be accompanied by an announced determination to use the powers of the State to whatever extent may prove necessary to ensure for all, not indeed absolute continuity of work, but a reasonable chance of productive employment.

Appendix-Case studies*

1. Man (mid forties), married, with two children (10 and 7), a cloth-inspector in a mill. He is the trade union representative for the mill and has just reached his thirtieth week of unemployment this year. One of the worst hit mills in the district. He now gets 32s. 6d. a week for himself, 10s. 6d. for the first child, 2s. 6d. for the second child, unemployment insurance benefit, plus 8s. family allowance for the second child and his wife's earnings of £4 5s. (She has worked continuously and is insured.) His family had cut down on all confectionery at the start of unemployment, stopped buying durable goods such as furniture, reduced spending on rations, and had used savings at the rate of about £1 a week. No reduction in spending on cigarettes or occasional cinema. A small, beautifully kept house, bought before the war on a mortgage which amounts to about 8s. a week. The family, while more careful in their outlay, have not experienced hardship, particularly as the wife was in continuous employment. The man stated that the married women at his mill were mainly insured and that he knew of no one getting national assistance. He was convinced that the few people who seemed to have been hit hardest by the slump were 'too proud' to go to the local assistance office. His chief complaint was his employers' treatment of the workers — not sharing out what work was available.

2. Man (35), wife (37), one child (9). Working as a weaver; wife not in employment. He has worked three days a week for the best part of eight months. Wage, about £4, plus three days' U.I.B. for self, wife and child, now about 32s., total £5 12s. Rent 9s. 6d., life insurance 3s. 6d., hire-purchase 7s. 6d., total 20s. 6d. Finds that fuel and light cost about 7s. a week. Has maintained hire-purchase payments on a wireless, beds and an armchair (22s. a week). Main reduction on meat (about half the ration is bought), bacon, fruit, cigarettes and evenings out. He keeps up a regular visit to a local working men's club, and his weekly 2s. 6d. on football pools, in the hope 'of winning sometime'. No holiday away from home this year.

3. Man (27), wife (23), weavers, two boys (5 and 2). Both formerly employed at the same mill, with a total wage of about £12. Unemployment started in March, and although the husband has now got alternative employment in a dye-works, both were receiving unemployment benefit for twenty consecutive weeks and the wife is still unemployed. They bought the house on a mortgage after the war and are paying it off at the rate of 21s. a week. Hire-purchase payments involve £1 a week, 10s. for a suite of furniture from one firm, and 10s. for beds and lino from a second firm. Rates amount to 6s. a week, water rate about 4d. a week (16s. a year). Life insurances: one at 3s. a week, a second at 6s. 9d. a week. Coal, electricity and gas, formerly about 10s., now 5s. 6d. a week. They had few savings (nothing on marriage and they had been spending a great deal on capital goods and the children). They have kept up all unavoidable payments except

* Selected from interviews carried out at random.

hire-purchase, which has averaged 10s. instead of 20s. a week (this was checked with account books) so that unavoidable outlay during unemployment was about £2 12s. Recently U.I.B. plus one family allowance has totalled £3 14s. so that when unavoidable outlay was accounted for £1 2s. a week was left for food, clothing, household and personal sundries. At the start of unemployment the available savings (about £10) were used to buy tinned food. No meat was bought for four months, no butter, eggs or fresh milk (Ostermilk was given to the two children), part of bacon ration and most of margarine ration, no sweets, practically no fruit and few vegetables, and practically no clothing (the wife patched and made pants and blouses for the children). The family lived mainly on tinned foods and bread and jam. The husband stayed in bed till lunch-time so as to go without breakfast, and the whole family went to bed early to save electricity. The 2s. a week on football pools was abandoned but a small amount on cigarettes was retained. No holiday this year (formerly used to go to London to stay with husband's parents). An occasional visit to the cinema has been maintained. A few articles of clothing were sold. They sought work regularly through the Employment Exchange and tried competitions (newspaper cross-words) to try to win money, without success. They actually helped case no. 4 with tinned food. Main complaints (i) employers, who owned several mills and were said not to have shared what work there was; (ii) hire-purchase firms, said to be too hard in enforcing payments. This family was one of the most cheerful of those encountered. When told they could have applied for national assistance they answered, 'We prefer to manage as we can. They ask too many questions.' And when told of a local Welfare Service (through which it was possible to get assistance, especially clothing) they said, 'That's for people who are *really* poor.'

4. Woman (late twenties), became the mother of a second child just before unemployment, and the father of the children had left her. He has now returned to her, but for a period of four months, during complete unemployment, she supported her two babies on U.I.B., and one family allowance, totalling about 43s. Rent 6s. 6d., life insurance 3s. Parent-family in no position to help her, and her savings were sufficient only to help her in the first month of unemployment. Obviously a little ashamed to go to public authorities for help because of her two illegitimate children. Became desperate on two or three occasions and received tinned food from case no. 3.

5. Widower (58), became unemployed in May after intermittent jobs in cotton mills. He said he had a few pounds saved up and did not apply for U.I.B. for 12-14 weeks. From the end of July he has had 30s. 0d. a week through the local employment exchange (presumably he had an inadequate contribution record or was getting national assistance in supplementation of benefit). He lives in a Salvation Army hostel, paying 10s. a week for lodging. He does not cook, but has one main meal at the hostel each day, costing 2s. The remaining few shillings are spent on bread and jam and tea, razor blades, soap, laundry, mending materials, cotton wool and lint. The last named is bought regularly, because the man has a long history of sickness and infirmity (he spent most of the war in hospital), and following an operation two years ago he has suffered from a leaking rectum. He said he spent no money on drink, cigarettes or gambling. He complained about the payment, once or twice a week, of the 1s. prescription charge for medicaments. His statement that he did not claim benefit for a time because he possessed savings was doubtful, and possibly the man did not go to the Labour Exchange for fear of being directed to work which he did not want or could not perform. He talked of men he knew, also unemployed, who had jam and bread

rather than a meal at the hostel. There was no doubt about his general weakness and poverty, and the long story of the leaking rectum had an air of chilling veracity. There was no opportunity of checking his unemployment and benefit record at the local employment exchange.

6. Man (37), wife (35), no children, man employed as a spinner, woman as assistant spinner. The man has had about fifteen weeks this year on short-time, when he worked three days a week. His wife was temporarily unemployed for a period of six weeks. Both receive 20s. a week from their trade union during unemployment. There has not been a week when both have been unemployed. They do not pretend they have been hard-hit by the slump and apart from being a little more economical in their expenditure during difficult weeks they have not eliminated any regular expenditure item from their budget, although they have been unable to save money for the furniture they want. Payment on a house-mortgage, 25s. No hire-purchase payment. Some spending on behalf of their activities at a local Sunday School (he helps to train a schoolchildren's choir).

7. Woman (38), two daughters (one at school, the other, 15, earning 35s. a week as a shop assistant). She is separated from her husband and hopes to get a divorce before long. Her mother lives with her and contributes a part of her retirement pension to the expenses of the household. The woman has been on short-time since Christmas last, working three days a week for several months. In July she started working three days a fortnight and latterly has been working three days in three weeks. She gets no U.I.B. because, as a married woman, she opted out of the national insurance scheme. She now receives national assistance, about 40s. a week, but delayed seeking it and feels ashamed that she has to have it. 'As soon as I start work fully I'm going to start paying insurance contributions. You have to tell the public assistance people so much of your affairs. It's like charity too.' She has reduced spending on the meat ration, on clothes, coal and household incidentals. She has stopped her former practice of going to the cinema three or four times a week, but refuses to stop going to local football matches (costing her 1s. 9d. a visit plus fares).

8. Man (39), wife (35-6), two boys (14 and 11). Since March the man has had twenty weeks' unemployment. His wife, apart from two weeks, has continued in full-time employment as a weaver. During the man's unemployment the family income had been halved, from about £11 10s. a week to £6 10s. The woman's wage had decreased by 15s. to £1 a week, because she had first worked on a smaller number of looms and now produces less, due to her firm's fulfilment of small orders and orders involving woven cloth previously unfamiliar to her. In her two weeks of unemployment she received no benefit because she had not paid sufficient insurance contributions in the preceding year. She had only paid about forty contributions, instead of forty-five. The weekly payment for the mortgage on the house is 8s. About 3s. for hire-purchase and about 6s. for life insurance. The family had cut down on 'luxuries' — sweets, papers, confectionery, cigarettes — but had maintained piano lessons for the (13-stone) 14-year-old boy and singing lessons for the 11-year-old, amounting to 12s. 6d. a week. Recently £14 was spent on overcoats for the two boys, who attend a nearby grammar school. The two parents have bitter memories of the thirties and said, 'When our children were born we made up our minds that they would never go into cotton.' It was obvious that they had saved and sacrificed much for the boys in recent months. They said that savings had been used up at the rate of £1-1 10s. a week in unemployment,

but that during the years of full employment they had built up a fair amount of savings.

9. Man and wife (mid-thirties), one girl (7). The wife is not in employment and the man works as a weaver. He has had twenty-four weeks' unemployment this year. The house, built in the mid-thirties, was purchased through a building society for £500. The weekly payment on this amounts to 7s. 6d. Rates, about 7s. 6d. a week. Hire-purchase on an electric oven, 5s. a week. Church subscription, about 1s. a week. He said that he had not reduced spending by very much, mainly on cinemas, household goods, laundry and confectionery, but had used up his savings at the rate of about £2 a week during unemployment. These savings have now come to an end and he was very concerned about his prospects this winter, saying that it was completely impossible to live on U.I.B. alone, even if all 'luxuries' were eliminated. He had not stopped having a drink at his local club on Saturdays and Sundays.

10. Man (25), single, formerly engaged in haulage work for cotton firms. An example of the unemployment resulting among ancillary trades. Sole income, U.I.B. 30s. 0d. reduced by 2s. 6d. from 32s. 6d. because he had only 47 stamps instead of 50 on his National Insurance Card. He said that 'the dole is nowt at all for a single man', and that he got by only because he lived with his parents.

11. Man (40), wife (38), girl (14), dependent mother (65-70). Both employed as weavers. Man nineteen weeks' unemployment this year, wife twenty-four weeks. She has just begun work temporarily at a different mill. Income when both were unemployed, £1 11s. 6d. (reduced slightly because of insufficient contributions), plus 26s. for wife, 10s. 6d. for girl, 12s. 6d. (20 per cent war pension), and contribution from the old mother's pension − total about £3 18s. (before recent increase in benefit rates the total was about £3 5s.). Payment on house mortgage 8-9s. a week, regular prescription 1s., rates about 6s., fuel and light about 10s., private insurance 4s. 6d. − total unavoidable outlay about 31s. With unemployment all expenditure stopped on sweets, 'luxuries' such as ham and fresh fruit. The man changed from cigarettes to smoking a pipe and less was spent on meat, bacon, eggs and milk (only part of the rations for the first three were bought). An effort to maintain spending on necessary clothing for the girl at school was made and also on an occasional visit to the cinema. A small amount is spent on a budgerigar and a dog. The man was formerly a T.B. case, and was granted a percentage war pension because his absence from work through sickness in recent years was attributed to the war. A well-kept home, with the family obviously living on a skimpy budget. Both the man and wife had had long experience of unemployment in the thirties, and even when it was pointed out that there had been an increase in benefit rates as well as an increase in prices, they continued to say that it was possible to live on the dole in the thirties but not now. They attributed this to the fact that before the war it was possible to buy ha'p'orths and penn'orths of bits and pieces from local butchers and bakers and second-hand clothing shops, and now rationing and improved standards of living have removed such 'opportunities'. There was no doubt, however, that they had grown accustomed themselves to a higher standard of living during the war and afterwards in full employment. They had been drawing savings at the rate of £3 a week during unemployment − also gained a few shillings occasionally from the local Co-op dividend.

12. Man and wife (53 and 50), no children, both worked for over thirty years in a local cotton mill. Both were unemployed for a period of sixteen weeks and although the man has now found alternative employment his wife is now in her twenty-seventh week of unemployment. House mortgage 8s. 6d. a week, fuel and light 8s., life insurance 5s. 3d. a week. They have experienced no hardship because of accumulated savings (being used up at the rate of £2-3 a week during unemployment), 2s. 6d. a week on football pools, 10s.-12s. 6d. on tobacco, very rare visits to a cinema. They are both teetotallers. Very bitter about employers and lack of future in cotton, though resigned to their own position.

13. Two sisters (57 and 55), both employed in the same mill. Unemployed for five weeks in the spring, and about six weeks' unemployment since then. The elder sister has an average of 2-3 months' sickness each year because of bronchial trouble (this was attributed to over thirty years' work in the card-room of the mill). Practically no savings, U.I.B. for both 52s. (previously 40s.). They pay 8s. 2d. a week rent for a tiny 'back-to-back' house in an area scheduled for clearance, 5s. 6d. life insurance, 4s. coal, 3-4s. electricity and gas. They spend 2s. 6d. a week on a football sweepstake carried on for the funds of a local Catholic church. During unemployment they say they cannot manage on U.I.B. They bought less than half the meat and bacon ration and said that few of their neighbours bought more than half. Their main complaints were (i) the signs of 'tightening up' on wages and more frequent dismissals at the mill; (ii) the decline this year in living standards and in the degree of security in the neighbourhood. Particularly concerned at the hardship that will be caused in the area if the slump goes on during the autumn and winter.

14. Widow (37), child (11), has had three months' unemployment in the last six months. Widow's pension for self and child 15s. (recently went up to £1 0s. 6d.). During unemployment she receives a further 20s. Rent 8s., life insurance 3s. 6d., hire-purchase 5s., fuel and light about 7s. 6d., less in unemployment. No savings. Has received some help from a brother in a neighbouring town. Her spells of unemployment have never been longer than four weeks and although she stated she had experienced great difficulties, particularly because of her child, she admitted that if she had another long spell of unemployment she would have to get 'public assistance', though she would delay it as long as she could.'I'd have to be on my beam-ends before doing that.' Friends of hers said she had gone without proper food herself to ensure that the child had as much as possible. At time of interview her chief difficulty was in getting the child a new mackintosh and pair of shoes at the start of the school term.

15. Male (38), employed as a spinner, wife (about 37), seven children. In the first few months of the year he was employed two weeks in eleven, and then became wholly unemployed. U.I.B. now 32s. 6d., 21s. 6d. for wife, 10s. 6d. for the first child and 2s. 6d. each for six others (£4 0s. 0d.). Family allowances now 48s. (formerly 30s.). Trade union payment 25s. Total £7 12s. 6d. (until the recent increases in benefit rates and family allowances the total was under £6). The man's former wage as a top-grade spinner was £10-11 a week. Rent 6s. 9d. (for an old three-roomed cottage), coal about 3-4s. a week, electricity 2s. 6d., gas 5s. Most of the children get cheap school meals during school terms and free school milk. 10s. a week is spent on the meat ration (cannot afford the full allocation) and he repairs shoes for all the family. The family were obviously never in a position to contemplate much luxury spending, and the reduction in income has

resulted in an all-round scaling down in spending on groceries, fruit and vegetables, and household goods.

16. Man (middle thirties), formerly employed as a taper, wife, two children (under 10). Became unemployed in March and for several weeks his sole income was U.I.B., totalling, with the family allowance for the second child, about 58s. Rent, life insurance, fuel and light amounted to 20s. a week. He had very few savings and because of insufficient money began searching everywhere for a job, in addition to registering regularly at the local employment exchange. After eight weeks' unemployment he found a labouring job on a farm two or three miles outside the town at a low wage. This job ends in the late autumn and he is worried about whether his former mill will be able to employ him then.

17. Widow (late forties), unemployed for thirteen weeks. No entitlement to U.I.B. — she opted out of scheme (and now regrets this). Sole income, widow's pension of 10s. a week, but she lives with a daughter (aged 18), who works as a waitress for about £2 10s. a week. She knew that she might have qualified for national assistance, and although she had no particular objection to applying she had not done so. This was partly because she has been able to use up some of her savings.

18. Single woman (50), only recently became unemployed. Sole income 24s. 6d. U.I.B. (reduced because of insufficient contributions). Practically no savings. Rent 9s., life insurance 2s. 3d. She has forgone her meat, butter and margarine ration in the two weeks of unemployment she has had so far. She has not taken her autumn coal allocation and has given up magazines and newspapers except for one of the latter on Saturdays and Sundays. Her budget had been planned in detail and she found that she could manage on two meals a day. She had not attempted to apply for national assistance, but was afraid she would have to do so if her unemployment continued for long.

Notes and References

1 Lancashire County Council, *A Preliminary Plan for Lancashire*, 1951.

2 'The National Assistance staff who deal with applications are undoubtedly much more understanding than they were a few years ago, but there are still some who make people conscious of their position and there is consequent reluctance to make application. There are also people who have never contemplated applying for National Assistance and cannot bring themselves to do so.'

  'From time to time I meet people who have not applied for assistance when they could do so, and there seem to be the following reasons: (a) lack of knowledge of the provisions made for them; (b) those who feel, rightly or wrongly, that they will not "live on charity" as they term it; (c) those who remember many of the harsh terms of the old "Poor Law" set-up.'

  These two quotations from replies to a questionnaire sent to trade union secretaries, personnel officers of cotton mills, welfare workers and public officials, are typical.

3 It seems that Table 4, *Third Report of the Ministry of National Insurance*, for 1951, p. 7, which gives a contrary impression, is therefore misleading.

4 These percentages are based on a comparison of the average of columns 2, 3, 4 and 5 in Table 9 with the average for column 1.

6 Deprivation of the coloured minority*

In developing policies for racial equality we run the risk of adopting measures which defeat rather than promote our ends. Social services which are aimed specifically at immigrants may degenerate in quality and may in time actually reinforce forms of racial and social discrimination. Therefore I am going to discuss the problem in the wider context of the need to foster social equality. I will offer three arguments. First, that there is a large-scale problem of poverty in Britain into which many immigrants are inevitably drawn. Thus, the Government's negligence over racial integration is merely an instance (even if a major instance) of its negligence over poverty and social inequality. Secondly, that some of the policies which are required to deal with poverty in general will be of particular help to immigrant groups. Thirdly, that the immigrant community should be better integrated with the social services. For example, there should be much greater immigrant representation on committees and boards running the social services. Again, welfare services for immigrants should be organized in conjunction with existing general welfare services rather than set up separately.

Sociologists are beginning to fear that the economic and social circumstances of the immigrant coloured community in Britain will deteriorate in the next years. In the United States a very large proportion of those living in poverty are negroes and three gloomy conclusions have emerged from recent research: '(i) in the years since the Second World War the economic gains of the non-white population have been less than proportional to those of whites; (ii) the gainers in the non-white group itself are in a minority; and (iii) the relative position of a significant majority of non-whites has worsened' (2). Though there have been significant improvements in literacy and years of schooling, for example, the coloured population remains 'educationally disadvantaged. The negro youth encounters poorly prepared teachers and outmoded curricula. He has less access to trained counsellors and guidance. He attends more crowded schools and has less use of new equipment and textbooks. If he graduates from high school

* Paper presented to a Fabian Society seminar in November 1966. (1)

he is less well prepared for college. He is more likely to go to a low-ranking college' (3). In absolute terms conditions have certainly improved, but in relative terms they have deteriorated. This knowledge is crucial for any interpretation of the measures required to combat poverty and encourage racial harmony.

What is the situation in Britain? The immigrant population has certain characteristics which will become less marked as the years pass. They are mainly young and middle-aged with a high ratio of men. At present they include relatively few elderly dependants. They are more dispersed geographically than is often assumed. The educational level is surprisingly high. In 1961 about 60 per cent who had completed their education had done so between the ages of fifteen and twenty; as many as 10 per cent had carried on longer. Although proportionately more were in unskilled and semi-skilled occupations the differences between the immigrant population as a whole and the general population in occupational class were not marked (4). This picture from the 1961 Census was distorted by inclusion of Commonwealth-born Englishmen in the statistics and by deficiencies in enumeration. It has altered since, first because of the entry of large numbers of immigrants in 1961 and 1962 (5), most of them unskilled and semi-skilled workers particularly from Pakistan, who were anxious to enter the country before the Commonwealth Immigrants Act came into force, and secondly because the present selective immigrant policy favours professional and skilled groups. There are big differences between different parts of Britain in the occupational distribution of immigrants and also between different immigrant groups. There are concentrations of immigrants in certain occupations, such as medicine, nursing, teaching and unskilled labouring. But large numbers have higher educational and occupational status than is commonly supposed. For example, a major survey carried out for the Ministry of Labour in 1963 showed that 60 per cent of the Indians and Pakistanis and 52 per cent of the West Indians in the sample, compared with 53 per cent of all people born in Britain, were skilled or held qualifications of some kind. Thirty-nine per cent of the Indians and Pakistanis and 6 per cent of the West Indians held qualifications ranging upwards from O-levels to degrees, compared with 6 per cent of people born in Britain (7). All this helps to distinguish the problem of race relations in Britain from that in the United States.

It is possible that a double process of downward social mobility will develop. Not only may fewer immigrants than native-born citizens maintain jobs commensurate with their qualifications, and housing commensurate with their incomes, but second-generation immigrants may fail to maintain the positions now occupied in the social structure by their parents. Large sections of the coloured minority represent the manual and professional elites of their own countries. Many have had more years of education if not always a 'better' education than the mass of young adults in Britain. Although the occupational status of the coloured minority is in general surprisingly similar to that of the rest of the population, a large number of persons comprising that minority have taken jobs of lower occupational status than those they held in their countries of origin. This is true more of the West Indians than the Indians. For example, Mrs Ruth Glass found in her study of West Indians in London that whereas 41 per cent of the men had the same occupational status as previously, 54 per cent had a lower and only 5 per cent a higher status (8). Again, a national survey carried out in 1963 showed that although 52 per cent of West Indians in employment were skilled or had technical or academic qualifications only 27 per cent had a skilled manual job or a job of higher occupational status (9). It is likely that during the economic difficulties of 1965-7 relatively large numbers of coloured immigrants lost their jobs and were forced to take alternatives with lower pay and status. Certainly there is evidence that the proportion of unemployed among immigrants is higher than the national rate and was, until the steep rise in unemployment in late 1966, about double the national rate (10). Many coloured immigrants lose the jobs held initially in Britain.

Then there are the inequalities of housing. Newcomers to Britain cannot get council housing and their access to private housing is severely limited. Mortgages are difficult to secure and there is prejudice against coloured tenants. Many are forced into lodging-houses. As time goes on there is a tendency for housing to be available to the coloured minority only in particular areas. Development grants are not easy to obtain for properties which are in slum or twilight zones. Councils are unwilling to pull these properties down or to re-house the occupants if the properties are pulled down. Immigrants have to wait for long periods to qualify for council housing and even then tend to be given tenancies in the patched housing rather than the new or even pre-war housing owned by the councils. Colour helps to characterize certain areas of our cities which are not ghettoes in the strict sense of the term because they include isolates and social deviants and older residents belonging to the host society as well as members of other ethnic groups, such as Irish and Cypriots. Rex and Moore call these areas 'zones of transition' (11). Overcrowding in them may increase. Nearly half of all housing is owner-occupied and the proportion of council-owned property is now approaching a third. In number both types of housing are growing. Lettings by private landlords are diminishing. Many houses built before 1919 are included in slum-clearance schemes or re-development schemes and too little new housing for rent is taking the place of the old (12). I want merely to suggest that, given present trends, in time housing standards in such zones are likely to become more sharply differentiated from those elsewhere. There is likely to be relative if not absolute deterioration of the housing occupied by the coloured minority.

Because immigrants have been obliged to settle in those areas of the cities where multi-occupation was possible and where bureaucratic and public opinion was least antagonistic, the schools attended by their children have also been sub-standard. The Plowden Committee has shown that the numbers of immigrant children in areas eligible to become 'educational priority areas' are disproportionately large (13).

Changes of policy could of course affect these trends. But it would be reasonable to assume that the second generation of immigrants is being reared in areas and in schools which fit them to occupy only the lowest levels in the occupational and social hierarchy. The Plowden Committee called attention to the fact that in one borough with a large proportion of immigrants not a single immigrant child had been selected for a grammar school in 1966 (14). The price of accommodation if not assimilation into society for immigrant children may be the acceptance of relatively lower status and income than their parents. Moreover, the previously favourable ratio of dependants to wage-earners is now changing and for many families standards of living will be harder to maintain.

What explains the growth of coloured immigration into Britain in the 1950s and 1960s and the changes in the status of the coloured minority which are now taking place? Rigidities in management-labour relations as well as continuing inflation at a time of 'full' employment in the 1950s must to some extent explain the British need for alternative sources of manpower. Workers from overseas are more willing to accept low wages and less easy to introduce to trade union traditions than workers at home. The flow of immigrants allows firms and those in charge of public services (like health and transport) to hold down costs and postpone structural reforms. Paradoxically, the flow also weakens public pressure for major reform of housing and social services by diverting attention from social problems to strangers within. The poor are augmented. Those who are already poor in British society but who are not the *kind* of poor to stabilize the economy (such as the elderly, the sick and disabled, fatherless and large families) are joined by the migrant coloured poor who *do* perform this function. Because some of the poor are now coloured, the rest of society may find certain aspects of poverty less objectionable and the income and status hierarchy more tolerable. While this process needs to be submitted to longer and more searching sociological analysis, I hope I have suggested some of the social functions performed by the coloured minority. Both consciously and unconsciously societies attempt to meet some of their internal problems by adjusting the kind and amount of migration.

The New Poverty

The circumstances of coloured minorities can be judged only in the context of poverty and inequality in society as a whole. Until recent years it was believed that poverty had been virtually abolished in Britain. Now it is conceded, even by conventional standards, that between seven and eight million, or 14 per cent, live below or just above the subsistence level (15). Coloured immigrants are drawn into an existing social system which is highly stratified according to access to different types and amounts of resources. In some respects the openings for them are the least desirable that society can offer – in areas with poorest housing, and jobs which are low paid and least secure. But even immigrants who – because of skill, educational qualifications, willingness to move or accumulated savings – achieve better living conditions find them continually threatened. Inevitably there are individuals and groups in the host society whose own escape from poverty depends on advancement at the expense of others – whether through individual or social exploitation, industrial action or government intervention. Immigrants join the common struggle to escape depressed living standards and find themselves being pushed into them.

Their deprivation must be understood in relation to wider deprivation. A complex of issues is involved. All societies are continually imposing new needs on their members. Laws which prevent children working in mines and force parents to send them to school impose financial burdens. Emerging social customs create new psychological and social needs which require money to satisfy. In any objective or scientific sense of the term, poverty is relative to the nature and resources of the society in which it is found. It is a serious lack of the resources commanded on average by individuals and families in the society to satisfy the needs and customs defined by that society. Consequently we must be concerned not just with low earnings and low incomes provided through social security, but the redistribution of income through the tax system, the distribution of assets and access to opportunities for material advancement, whether through education, systems of credit or exclusive membership of social groups.

Poverty no longer means sheer lack of income, in the narrow sense of that term. In advanced industrial societies the ownership of wealth and frequent realization of capital assets, the existence of fringe benefits and the differential 'ownership' of public services, including educational 'capital', are important resources which we must take into account. Consequently, poverty may be 'partial' or it may be 'total'. A family may have an approximately average income but live in a slum house, have access only to an overworked G.P. partnership, and send their children to a slum school. Alternatively, it may have a poor income and be ineligible for certain kinds of common fringe benefits, but live in a subsidized new council house in a good environment where there is a new state school.

The implications of such a form of analysis for the coloured immigrant community are fairly obvious. Their problems cannot be considered independently of those of the other disadvantaged groups in the population. The social mechanisms which depress them in status and income and exclude them from important kinds of resources — like eligibility for some forms of social service — have to be examined. Some of the measures in social policy which may help the coloured minority most may therefore be measures which are generally egalitarian. The key concept in this analysis, therefore, is access to resources.

The Importance of General Measures

This brings me to the second stage of the argument. What *general* policies might incidentally promote racial equality? A variety of measures rather than any one single measure will be necessary.

1. Social security. Of the seven to eight million people in Britain known to be living around a subsistence level three million are people living in households which depend primarily on earnings which are low. The number of families with four or more children has increased in the last twenty years. Yet family allowances have been increased only twice since they were introduced in 1946, compared with national insurance benefits which have been increased from eight to ten times. The allowance would have to be raised to about 25s. or 30s. to conform in real terms with the subsistence level advocated by Lord Beveridge in the last war. The system compares unfavourably with that in many other countries. Britain is one of the few countries with family allowances which fail to make a payment for the first child. Again, the allowances paid on behalf of six children comprise, as a proportion of national income per head of working population, 100 per cent in France, 81 per cent in Italy, 81 per cent in Belgium, 44 per cent in Western Germany and 42 per cent in the Netherlands. In Britain, the figure is 23 per cent (16). The case for substantially increasing direct family allowances is unanswerable. They could be financed at least in part by reducing children's tax allowances. Since immigrants' families tend to be larger than average, this would allow more of them to reach the living standards of the mass of the population.

Another urgently needed reform is regular financial support for many kinds of families in which there is a mother but no father. At present there are about 110,000 women with children who are dependent on supplementary benefits. Altogether, their households comprise one third of a million people. Many are divorced or separated wives but about a third are mothers of illegitimate children. Relatively more of the immigrant than of other fatherless families would benefit from the establishment in this country of state maintenance allowances, or, in a proportion of cases, child pensions, as of right. There are probably substantial numbers who choose not to apply to the Supplementary Benefits Commission. More immigrants than others are unemployed. More would benefit therefore if the 'wage-stop' that has been preserved by the new Social Security Act were to be abolished or if extra income produced by the new wage-related scheme for sickness and unemployment were to be used to raise the minimum level of unemployment benefit. One of the defects of the wage-related unemployment and sickness scheme is that it does least for those with the lowest wages.

2. Housing. A concerted housing policy would incidentally aid immigrants. Thus, local authorities could be empowered to take some of the worst privately rented housing into social ownership, and supervise new forms of control and management. A much bigger repairs and modernization programme could be launched and council housing diversified through new forms of management and the definition of tenants' rights. Even an annual total of 500,000 houses (the abortive target for 1969/70) compares unfavourably with that of several European countries. There is a vast problem of slum and sub-standard housing. Unless more effort is made to improve the sub-standard housing which is going to be occupied for the next twenty or thirty years, the rigid hierarchy in accommodation which is now apparent will be preserved. Slums will be created almost as fast as new houses are built. I am arguing therefore for shifting a much larger proportion of our building resources to modernization and repairs, together with the extension of social ownership and a stronger emphasis on tenants' rights, as the most rational approach to more equality of housing.

3. Education. At the present time, there is the enormous problem of allocating resources as between higher, further, secondary and primary education. Those of us who believe that the Government can spend more cannot escape the problem of priorities. I have no doubt that the natural demand for the expansion of the universities has to be restrained in favour of attacking the problems revealed by the Newsom Report, raising the school-leaving age and doing more for the further education of those who have left school at fifteen or sixteen. Within this policy it will be much easier to apply specific measures in areas where there are large numbers of immigrant children. The predominant problem in these areas is language. As the Plowden Committee declared, 'Children should be given special consideration on account of their language and other difficulties and not on account of their colour' (17). The chief need is for general improvements in educational facilities in areas which can be shown to be deficient in such facilities. The subsidiary need is for improvements in language instruction and methods of teaching in areas where there are children of different colour and ethnic origin.

The Principle of Linking Specialist to General Services

This discussion of general strategy leads to the final step in the argument, which is that a policy of integration means better immigrant representation throughout British institutions and also better links between services for immigrants and those for the general public. Not only should there be adequate representation on the Community Relations Commission but also on Regional Hospital Boards, Education and Housing Committees of local authorities, and many other committees, including Government Committees and Royal Commissions which are not necessarily concerned just with matters of particular concern to the immigrant community. The members of the Supplementary Benefits Commission should include a West Indian, an Indian or a Pakistani. Again, not only should the Home Office ensure that some police are coloured, but also that some senior police are coloured. There should be national stock-taking of immigrant participation. We need to know what representation means in practice and also how people in certain occupations and industries respond to the coloured immigrants among them. For example, is the employment of coloured staff in the health services working well, and giving them incentives to improve standards and knowledge, or are they employed on sufferance and without any real powers to take decisions?

Information services afford another illustration. Immigrants from overseas are not the only newcomers. Migrants from different parts of Britain also need advice about housing, schools and doctors. By expanding a national system of Citizens' Advice Bureaux we could link them with a special Newcomers' Advisory Service. A special bureau now exists in Notting Hill. The trouble is that effective Citizens' Advice Bureaux exist in too few areas. Substantial government subsidies are required. They need to be administered independently of local authorities. But information is not only needed by natives or hosts. Through evening and weekend meetings a greater effort could be made to educate local councillors, general practitioners, the employees of the Ministry of Labour, Ministry of Pensions and Home Office, and many others about historical and contemporaneous problems of migration. Similar courses are of the first importance for the police.

The local welfare services are about to be reorganized in the aftermath of the report of the Seebohm Committee. One centre offers simplified administration. It offers concentration of scarce skilled manpower. It prevents the relative deprivation that sometimes springs from administrative fragmentation. Above all, it allows a balance to be struck between general-purpose and specialist services. Social workers would be attached to the general department to help immigrant families with problems of understanding legal requirements and meeting family and cultural problems. More emphasis might be given to straightforward material help services and not just case-work. Much good might come, for example, from a well-endowed house-furnishing loan system.

Separate independent services for immigrants should not be discounted. These must exist and will exist, especially on a voluntary or co-operative basis within immigrant communities themselves. But they should be conceived in relation to services for the general public. There is an argument for some individual projects — such as comfortable residential hostels for unattached individuals working temporarily in Britain — as Rex and Moore argued in their study of Sparkbrook. There is, of course, a powerful argument for the building up of local liaison committees to keep a close watch on the evolution of policy covering a variety of local services. But in general these plans should be conceived in relation to services for the general public. The rather patronizing and too separatist response that is traditionally made in Britain to the problems of minorities should be resisted. Commonwealth immigrants are not just coloured. They are men and women with several young children to support; young adults adjusting to unfamiliar occupations; middle-aged people who are as liable as anyone else to become sick or unemployed or homeless. As such, they have needs as human beings and therefore general rights as citizens.

The White Paper on Immigration from the Commonwealth is not only the most illiberal but also possibly the most inegalitarian statement made by a Labour Government. The section on integration is thinly veiled hypocrisy. Many examples might be given. The difficulties experienced by new immigrants in learning about housing and social services when they first arrive are quoted, but the White Paper proposes neither a new local advisory service nor additions to the staff of housing offices as a solution to this difficulty. 'A number of local authorities already produce leaflets on various subjects in different languages and the Government *are examining the need* for supplementing this material by centrally-produced leaflets or in other ways' (my italics) (18). The White Paper also referred to the extra staff that might be needed by social services to cope with language and other problems. 'The Government propose to give financial help towards *approved* expenditure *in such cases* where *need is shown*' (my italics). Since the main justification given for introducing controls was the need to integrate those already in this country, one might well speculate on the motives underlying this grudging approach to positive integration.

Many people have been working hard since the White Paper was published to undo its harm. They have had small success so far, principally because massive government action is required, not only in countering poverty generally and tackling squalor in housing and schools but in strengthening the Race Relations Act and removing the discriminatory provisions in the present control of immigration. The

106 The social minority

Community Relations Commission must press for general social reform. My fear is that by its inaction in one sphere, and its illiberal posture in the other, the Government will simultaneously increase both poverty and racial inequality.

Notes and References

1 Lester, A., and Deakin, N., *Policies for Racial Equality*, Fabian Research Series, no. 262, July 1967. (Revised and reprinted, November 1969.)

2 Ornati, O., *Poverty amid Affluence*, New York, The Twentieth-Century Fund, 1966.

3 ibid., p. 61.

4 Glass, R., 'The New Minorities: I and II', *The Times*, 30 June 1965, and 1 July 1965.

5 John Goodall found that 52 per cent of male Pakistanis in Halifax in 1964 had arrived between January 1961 and June 1962 and were without exception in unskilled and semi-skilled categories. Goodall, J., *Institute of Race Relations Newsletter*, 1965.

6 [When published in 1969 the 1966 Census data showed that coloured immigrants as a whole have considerably lower status than those born in Britain. Nearly two thirds of Pakistani males and nearly half those from the Caribbean were found to be in semi-skilled or unskilled manual occupations. On the other hand, there was a high proportion of Indians in professional, managerial and other non-manual occupations. See Collison, P., 'Immigrants' Varieties of Experience', *New Society*, 26 June 1969; Sample Census, 1966, Great Britain; Commonwealth Immigrant Tables, H.M.S.O., 1969; Rose, E. J. B., *et al.*, *Colour and Citizenship: A Report on British Race Relations*, Oxford University Press, 1969, Chapter 13.]

7 Harris, A. I., and Clausen, R., *Labour Mobility in Great Britain, 1953-1963*, Government Social Survey, SS343, H.M.S.O., 1966, p. 113.

8 Glass, R., *Newcomers: The West Indians in London*, Allen & Unwin, 1960, pp. 29-32.

9 Harris, A. I., and Clausen, R., op. cit., pp. 112-13.

10 Information kindly supplied by the Home Office. In May 1966, for example, there were 6,200 immigrants registered as unemployed (representing rates of 2.0 and 3.6 per cent respectively among men and women from the New Commonwealth, compared with 1.2 per cent unemployed nationally).

11 Rex, J., and Moore, R., *Race, Community and Conflict: A Study of Sparkbrook*, Oxford University Press, 1967 (see particularly Chapters 1 and 12).

12 Donnison, D., *The Government of Housing*, Penguin Books, 1967.

13 *Children and their Primary Schools*, A Report of the Central Advisory Council for Education (England), (The Plowden Report), H.M.S.O., 1967.

14 ibid., p. 70.

15 Abel-Smith, B., and Townsend, P., *The Poor and the Poorest*, Bell, 1965.

16 For 1961. The figure would now be lower. Hemming, F. W., 'Social Security in Britain and certain other countries', *National Institute Economic Review*, no. 33, August 1965.

17 Plowden Report, p. 72.

18 *Immigration from the Commonwealth*, Cmnd. 2739, H.M.S.O., August 1965, p. 15.

7 The disabled in society*

In Britain about 1½ million people, or 3 per cent of the population, are found in groups *officially* described as disabled or handicapped (2). Over a million live at home. The Ministry of Labour lists 654,000 persons on the Disabled Persons Register (3). There are approximately 450,000 disablement pensioners from the two world wars and nearly 200,000 industrial injury disablement pensioners (4). The local authorities' registers contain the names of 110,000 blind, 30,000 partially-sighted and 205,000 other disabled and handicapped persons, the great majority of whom live at home (5). There are many persons with long-term mental or physical handicaps, probably about 200,000 who reside in hospitals, particularly those for the chronic sick and mentally ill, or in residential homes or hostels (6). They include 65,000 subnormal and severely subnormal patients in psychiatric hospitals. Altogether 90,000 subnormal and severely subnormal and another 71,000 mentally ill or psychopathic persons living at home have mental health services provided by local health authorities (7). The Supplementary Benefits Commission (formerly the National Assistance Board) pays allowances to 138,000 incapacitated persons living at home who are not receiving sickness or other insurance benefits (8). There are 76,000 handicapped children of whom about 32,000 are physically handicapped in special schools or units (9). Other administratively-defined categories might be added. There is considerable duplication in these figures. Their very fragmentation and the confessed inability of the Ministry of Health to give 'comprehensive national statistics' (10) forces us to ask whether we are doing all we should to develop our understanding of handicap and disability and whether the services to meet the needs of the disabled are adequate.

In this paper I shall describe the results of a survey carried out between 1964 and 1966 from the University of Essex. This was carried out in London, Essex and Middlesex by Sally Sainsbury, a research officer at the university, under my guidance. The Greater London Association for the Disabled generously commissioned the work in the

* A lecture given at the Royal College of Surgeons on 5 May 1967 under the auspices of the Greater London Association for the Disabled (1).

belief that it would contribute to the task of re-thinking the roles that should be played respectively by local authority and voluntary organizations as a result of the reorganization of London government. Our data cover one group of the disabled in the three local authority areas — those registered in the 'general classes' of the physically handicapped — that is, excluding the special groups of blind, deaf and hard of hearing. A sample of men and women on the registers was visited and a total of 211 persons were interviewed, the majority being in London. Eight per cent of the original sample refused an interview and another 3 per cent were too ill to give information. The average interview took over two hours.

The survey was thus relatively modest in numbers of persons and of areas covered. This fact should be borne in mind throughout the following report. Moreover, registration with a local authority is voluntary and some kinds of disabled persons do not see why they would benefit by registering. Other disabled persons are not advised by government and local authority departments and voluntary organizations to do so.

Our sample does not adequately represent certain kinds of handicaps such as blindness, deafness and mental illness or subnormality. Only 5 per cent were war or industrial disablement pensioners. Nonetheless, a wide range of people were included, some with multiple handicaps. As many as 45 different kinds of handicaps were represented. There were rather more women than men. Nearly half were married and another third widowed, separated or divorced. Some were in their teens, twenties and thirties but two fifths were middle-aged (45-64) and another two fifths elderly (65+). The main source of income for nearly a fifth was derived from employment; two fifths depended primarily on retirement pensions, nearly a fifth on sickness benefit and the rest on national assistance, disablement pensions and unemployment benefit (11).

The chief conclusion of the study is that there is an imbalance between the impulses of the disabled towards integration into ordinary social and occupational life and the segregative practices of society. One wants what the other largely fails either to recognize or translate into real opportunity. Although a majority of the people registered with the local authorities are severely incapacitated and a majority middle-aged or elderly, most emphasize physical and economic independence and integration in work and society. They are usually realistic about their limitations but believe they could lead an approximately normal life if only they could obtain more help with physical aids, housing, transport and employment. In general they regard special clubs or residential Homes and special workshops as second-best, like other symbols of separate disability status. By contrast, society tends to give weak support to the principles of economic independence and social integration or participation and fairly strong support, some of it unwitting, to the enforced dependence and social segregation of the disabled.

This conclusion naturally requires qualification, for the supporting arguments are by no means entirely consistent. It depends on a wide variety of evidence about the actual situation of the disabled — their environment, work and income and their relationships with family and social services. There is lamentably little factual knowledge. I shall endeavour to present some of the more important strands of evidence in this lecture. A necessary first step is to discuss the underlying concept of disability and explain why new definitions and measures are essential both for knowledge and policy.

The Meaning of Disability

What do we mean when we say that someone is disabled? First, there is anatomical, physiological or psychological abnormality or loss. Thus we think of the disabled as people who have lost a limb or part of the nervous system through surgery or in an accident, become blind or deaf or paralysed, or are physically damaged or abnormal in some particular, usually observable, respect.

Secondly, there is chronic clinical condition altering or interrupting normal physiological or psychological processes, such as bronchitis, arthritis, tuberculosis, epilepsy, schizophrenia and manic depression. These two concepts of loss or abnormality and of chronic disease tend in fact to merge, for although a loss may be sustained without disease, disease long-continued usually has some physiological or anatomical effect (12). Among the people whom we interviewed a wide range of conditions were represented. About 31 per cent specified rheumatoid arthritis, osteo-arthritis or just arthritis and between 4 per cent and 13 per cent in each instance specified the after-effects of poliomyelitis, disseminated sclerosis, bronchitis, epilepsy, coronary thrombosis, or were amputees or hemiplegics. For both meanings of disability the clinical reference-object is the normal human body, of like sex and age.

A third meaning is functional limitation of ordinary activity, whether that activity is carried on alone or with others. The simplest example is incapacity for self-care and management, in the sense of being unable or finding it difficult to walk about, negotiate stairs, wash and dress, for example (13). But this principle of limitation can be applied to other aspects of ordinary life. By reference to the average person of the same sex an estimate can be made of the individual's relative incapacity for household management and performance of both general social roles as husband, father or mother, neighbour or church member, say, and of specific occupational roles.

A fourth meaning is a pattern of behaviour which has particular elements of a socially deviant kind (14). This pattern of behaviour is in part directly attributable to an impairment or pathological condition — such as a regular physical tremor or limp, or an irregularly occurring fit. But it is also attributable to the individual's perception of his condition and his response to others' expectations of him. Thus, activity may not only be limited, but different. And it. may be different as much depending on how it is perceived by the individual and others as on its physiological determination. Two people with an identical physical impairment may differ greatly in their behaviour, one acting up to the limit of his capacities and the other refraining from actions of which he is capable. Alternatively a man with little or no impairment may play the disabled role. Sociologists have recently paid increasing attention to the concepts of the sick role and of illness behaviour (15). Society expects the blind or the deaf or the physically handicapped to behave in certain approved or stereotyped ways. We all know of instances of people assuming deafness or handicap. They may adopt whole patterns of behaviour. Individuals can be motivated towards such behaviour when their physical or neurological condition does not compel it. A family or a sub-culture can condition it. There are cultural differences in disability behaviour. People of different nationality or ethnic group vary in their stoicism in face of pain and handicap (16). All this can be a fascinating focus for inquiry.

Finally, disability means a socially defined position or status. The actor does not just act differently. He occupies a status which attracts a mixture of deference, condescension, consideration and indifference. Irrespective of a disabled individual's *specific* behaviour or condition he attracts certain kinds of attention from the rest of the population by virtue of the 'position' that the disabled, when recognized as such, occupy in that particular society. There are countries and populations which do not recognize or identify mild forms of subnormality, schizophrenia or infirmity, for example. In working-class British society euphemisms for certain handicaps are used. Someone has 'nerves' or is 'hard of hearing' or is 'a bit simple'. So far this would mean that deviance simply is not recognized or clearly distinguished. But the technical, conclusive and stigmatizing labels are avoided. A place is not taken in a rank or a hierarchy. This can, of course, have its advantages. Some people can continue to be treated as ordinary members of the community. To identify or register them as disabled may entitle them to certain special benefits or professional treatment but it may also separate them from society and encourage people to look on them if not as a race apart, like lepers, then with aloof condescension. Disability can imply inferior as well as different status (17). The extent to which an individual belongs to special groups or clubs, has special sets of relationships with doctors and nurses and social workers, relies on particular forms of income and sheltered forms of occupation and is patronized by voluntary organizations will all determine his particular position and status or the extent to which he is integrated into the social fabric. Of much of this doctors, social workers and administrative personnel may be unaware. While the sociologist would not pretend to be able to advance medical knowledge, casework and administration as such, it is his responsibility to develop this aspect of knowledge.

Operational Measures of Disability as a Guide to Action

It would be possible to assemble a large number of data on each of these interpretations of disability. All of them have implications both for our understanding of disability as well as the means with which to offer help and service. Clinical particularizations are essential if pathology is to be investigated or arrested but there can be unfortunate social and administrative consequences. The proliferation of specialist consultants for particular diseases or disabilities and of statutory and voluntary organizations gives emphasis to the separateness rather than the similarity of many disabled conditions with consequential confusion, fragmentation of effort and injustice. Some conditions receive favourable publicity and attention. Others, with worse effects, are neglected. The thalidomide children have attracted vastly more public sympathy than children suffering from subnormality or congenital syphilis. The Spastics Society has an income of around £2 million but the National Society for Mentally Handicapped Children only £40,000 (18).

One consequence is inconsistency of assessment. How do we assess *degree* of disability so as to determine level of pension or of other needs? The McCorquodale Committee on the Assessment of Disablement repeatedly referred in its report to the principle that assessment should be determined by 'means of a comparison between the condition of the disabled person and that of a normal healthy person of the same age' (19), but took no steps to apply the principle empirically. The committee did not obtain information systematically about disabled persons and healthy persons of equivalent age. Nor did the committee try to examine the rationale of current medical assessment. They largely confined their attentions to amputations and loss of limb or eye and did not, even for these minority disabilities, seek empirical justification for percentage assessments. For example, they accepted the loss of four fingers and of a leg below the knee (leaving a stump of between 3½ and 5 inches) each as equivalent to 50 per cent disability. We might question the logic of both rate and equivalence. The loss of three fingers, the amputation of 'one foot resulting in end-bearing stump', the amputation 'through one foot proximal to the metatarpophalangeal joint' and the loss of vision in one eye were all regarded as equivalent to 30 per cent disability. In refraining from exploring the functional, psychological and social effects even of different kinds of limb amputation they failed to take advantage of the growing body of knowledge and research methods developed by the social sciences in the last twenty years. The same kind of criticisms might be made of the more general and rather different definitions of disability currently used by the Ministries of Social Security, Labour and Health (20). Britain is still largely governed in its conduct towards the disabled by the *source* rather than the *effect* of disability. Too little effort has been made to develop *functional* indices, based on questions about individual capacities. Such indices are difficult to develop and have to be treated with caution. But they are implicit in nearly all official definitions and have been partly but unsystematically used in some medical and administrative procedures. For example, the information supplied by doctors on a form used by the Ministry of Labour includes the kind of conditions which doctors believe the disabled person should *avoid* in his employment. The information does not adequately reflect either the general or specific capacities of the disabled person although some 'functional' information is given (21). Britain is not alone in having failed to size up to this problem (22). If we did apply functional measures it is likely that we would identify between 3 per cent and 6 per cent of adults under pensionable age as physically or mentally handicapped. A recent Danish survey established that around 6 per cent of adults were physically handicapped. There was little difference between the rates for men and the rates for women but both rates increased sharply in the fifties. About 3 per cent in the twenties and thirties were disabled and 7 per cent in the forties, but by the late fifties the figure reached 17 per cent, topping 20 per cent in the early sixties (23). In Sweden disability pensions reach 2½ per cent of the adult population. The rate also rises sharply in the fifties and early sixties. But some of the less disabled may not qualify for such pensions.

We developed a crude index of incapacity to manage personal and household activities which involved assessing twenty-three tasks and activities (24). Each activity was scored two if it could not be done at all and one if it could be done only with difficulty. Altogether as many as 17 per cent of the disabled in the three counties were very severely incapacitated (scoring 23 and over). Another 36 per cent were severely incapacitated (scoring 15-22), making 53 per cent altogether. Only 11 per cent were slightly incapacitated (scoring 6 or less). Incapacity tended to increase with age. Only a third of those younger than 45 were severely or very severely incapacitated in our sense, compared with nearly half those aged 45-64 and nearly two thirds of those aged 65 and over.

This kind of approach allows us to compare persons with multiple disabilities. Nearly half the sample had at least two. It also allows us to begin comparing the effects of different disabilities and the ways in which the extent of incapacity changes over time. Very little work has been done on this. Nearly 20 per cent had disabilities which were quickly progressive and another 40 per cent slowly progressive. Many were prone to depression and feared increasing dependence on others. Some people found that their capacities fluctuated according to the nature of their condition and changes in the weather. Even those whose disabilities were quickly progressive found there were periods of recovery or restoration of capacity. In all this I am stressing the relativity of disability, like the relativity of intelligence. There are times, for example in illness or after accidents, when most of us cannot walk or cannot dress or cannot speak. Many of us have a 'permanent' limitation of some kind. It is appropriate therefore to ask to what degree the disabled are more incapacitated than ourselves as a way of asserting a common involvement and preparing the ground for a rational examination of their occupational and social opportunities.

Housing

The first major problem is that of housing. We found that the disabled live in housing which is in some respects worse in basic facilities than the rest of the community. Only a fifth of the sample were owner-occupiers compared with over two fifths of the total population (25). Their incomes were usually small. Half were council tenants. Over time they had qualified for a council flat or house. But some had been recently placed in houses or flats erected between the wars rather than in the last twenty years and a number were in flats not on the ground floor. About a quarter were tenants in private housing and in general these had the worst facilities. Altogether 30 per cent had no hot water supply, 23 per cent no bath and as many as 21 per cent no W.C. indoors. We met people who had to get water from a well or a pump in the garden or a tap in the back yard; who had to share a miserable lavatory with other households or get to one across a yard or to the bottom of a garden along a broken path. Inability to use a W.C. was universally regarded as being the greatest personal indignity. As many as 20 per cent of the persons in the sample lived in homes which were deficient in three or more basic facilities.

Stairs pose a critical difficulty. Seventy-four per cent of the people in the sample had to climb or descend at least one flight of stairs to the entrance of their homes or inside from the W.C. or kitchen to the living room. Thirty-three per cent had to negotiate stairs both outside and inside. One partially-sighted woman who was an epileptic had to mount a flight of steps from her basement flat with no handrail and the fourth step missing. Five per cent had to use lifts to reach their council flats on the upper storeys. This minority all complained that the lifts frequently broke down with sometimes disastrous effects so far as they were concerned. Councils who place disabled and elderly persons on the higher storeys of blocks of flats under the assumption that lifts secure constant access seem to be mistaken.

Against basic structural deficiencies or difficulties such as these the efforts of welfare authorities to introduce adaptations inevitably seem puny. Adaptations had in fact been carried out in just under half the homes of the sample, some by individuals and hospital authorities and a few by voluntary organizations, but the majority by the welfare departments of local authorities. Most of these were of a simple kind: handrails on stairways and in passages and lavatories; ramps up single steps; lavatory seats raised; a few doorways widened and a few electric light switches lowered and electric points raised. There is no doubt that such alterations can make life a lot easier and there is scope for a massive expansion of activity.

Twenty-four per cent specified adaptations which they felt needed to be carried out by the local authority but many others had been told or believed they lived in accommodation which was unsuitable for satisfactory adaptation. We asked the disabled about a variety of facilities which they could not use *because* they were ill-placed or ill-designed. Seventy per cent could not open and shut windows; 42 per cent and 40 per cent respectively could not reach gas and electric meters; 22 per cent were unable to use a cooker and a similar proportion could not use taps, use a sink and reach any cupboards. These are disconcerting statistics.

The problem is partly one of standardizing certain kinds of units so that they can be introduced into homes quickly. But there is a limit to opportunities of standardization. Chairbound people need to have a low sink in the kitchen but an arthritic housewife who cannot stand or bend needs a high stool and a fairly high sink. Moreover, physiotherapists may prefer obstacles to remain for particular persons so that limbs and muscles are properly exercised. Individual solutions will always to some extent be necessary. The problem is also one of devising an effective administrative plan and implementing it quickly. In instances which were all too rare welfare officers had achieved just this. But do local authorities complete a detailed schedule of household deficiencies when a disabled person is newly registered? And can they organize a blitz on the dwelling so that improvements are introduced simultaneously over a very short period and not piecemeal over many months, with all the disruptive and depressing effects this can have on a household? I suspect we are going to need local authority work teams which are seconded to welfare departments by housing departments with the blessing of local trade unions.

Adaptations sometimes achieve much less than they are supposed to achieve. We met persons who used a handrail to help them along a passage and down a couple of steps into a kitchenette but who could not carry a tray of food back and felt obliged to eat meals off a draining board. Nearly all the ramps which had been installed or which could be laid across outside steps could not be used by the disabled individual without help. One woman said that when she tried to go in her wheelchair down a short ramp into her kitchen without help she could not control it and went headlong into the opposite wall. The main problem for wheelchairs, as much in new council flats as old private properties, was manoeuvrability. There was rarely sufficient space in kitchens and living rooms and lavatories to turn round or go easily through doorways and along passageways.

Here the question is how the disabled can be transferred to good housing which first has modern amenities and which secondly does not provide obstacles to persons with limited mobility. The question of special design or adaptation — for that is the real question — is secondary. Some of the people we interviewed wanted to transfer from council homes which were unsuitable structurally or in their siting. Others who rented privately owned homes had applied for council flats. Altogether 16 per cent were on council housing lists, more than half of them for at least two years and a few for over ten years. Half the owner-occupied homes needed major improvements, some of which would be possible to finance or subsidize under existing legislation if only local officials took the initiative to assist applications and organize builders and decorators. I suspect that new scales of priorities have to be drawn up by health and welfare departments on the one hand and housing departments on the other. The former should have responsibility for allocating and administering a high proportion of the accommodation for the disabled and elderly.

Community Care Services

The second major problem is personal and household help. Nearly a fifth of the disabled persons whom we interviewed were unmarried and many others were widowed, divorced or separated. We found that 15 per cent lived alone and had no relatives in the immediate vicinity. Another 10 per cent lived alone and the relatives in the vicinity could not provide all the services that were needed. Finally, around a third of the sample were people who lived with husbands and wives or relatives but who were not employed and were alone for substantial parts of the day. Some had to wait from 8 a.m. to 5 or 6 p.m. for a hot drink and meal. Others reported falls and other accidents which left them lying waiting for help until a relative returned in the evening.

For care in illness and regular care in the household substantially more people relied on family help than on all the health and welfare services put together. For example, during their last illness 66 per cent had been looked after by relatives while 10 per cent had gone into hospital (21 per cent looked after themselves, 2 per cent were looked after by neighbours and 1 per cent by friends). Again, 75 per cent had meals prepared for them by relatives and 9 per cent received them occasionally or often in the week from a meal delivery service. Friends and neighbours furnished valuable, usually supplementary, help to nearly half the sample, mainly by shopping, preparing a meal or cleaning.

The health and welfare services were nonetheless a major source of help. Thirty per cent had a home help, 9 per cent meals delivered to them, 13 per cent were visited regularly by district nurses, 10 per cent had chiropody services at home and another 25 per cent had chiropody elsewhere, and 2 per cent in each instance were helped by the home bathing and borough laundry services. Altogether nearly half the sample had at least one domiciliary service, of whom half had two or more services. In London rather more than a half and in Essex and Middlesex rather less than two fifths of the sample had one or more services. In addition people were in touch with welfare departments and voluntary agencies. Eighty-four per cent said they had been visited at least once, a quarter three or more times, by the welfare officer in the previous twelve months, the other 16 per cent claiming not to have been visited. Three quarters of the visits were said to be routine, lasting from 10 to 30 minutes, but 6 per cent were in connexion with holidays, 8 per cent alterations and 7 per cent aids or gadgets. The welfare departments maintain what is at present mainly a referral service. Thirty per cent were in touch with a voluntary agency of some kind. For two thirds of them this meant membership of a club. For a third or more it meant occasional or regular visits, some routine checks on present circumstances, some inquiries about means, aids, alterations, food parcels and so on. Proportionately more of those who were only slightly or moderately incapacitated were in touch with voluntary agencies.

Doctors and medical social workers in hospital played an important role in referring patients for welfare services. It was not our purpose to investigate medical and hospital care but a substantial number were in close contact with a G.P. Over half had seen one within the previous month and as many as a quarter said they were visited regularly. There was a fifth, however, who had not seen their G.P. in the previous year. A few very incapacitated persons would have liked regular consultations. Others spoke of the problems of getting to hospital out-patient departments.

Despite this range of services we found evidence of considerable need. A third as many disabled people again as were receiving a home help, meals delivered at home and a district nurse expressed a wish for such a service. The majority were very severely or severely incapacitated by the strict standards that were applied. There was a huge latent demand for home bathing, laundry, chiropody and optical and dental services and between 10 and 20 per cent of the entire sample in each instance expressed a desire for these services. Others did not express a desire for such services but by objective assessment seemed to require them. Thus a fifth of those who were severely incapacitated lived alone and did not have a home help. They did not always feel the need for such help. Among those getting the service as many as a fifth (or 6 per cent of the entire sample) received more than eight hours help per week but half received it for only between an hour and three hours and half of them felt the need for more frequent visits.

Some of those living alone did not ask for meals to be delivered because the service had a poor reputation. Only a third of the people having meals said they were hot when they arrived. Many warmed them up though a few could not use the cooker and ate them cold. A third said the meals were usually delivered before 11 a.m. Again, although some received meals five days a week over half received them only twice a week. An inquiry into the diets of a sub-sample suggested that in a quarter to a fifth of instances they were unsatisfactory.

One function of the National Health Service, local authorities and other agencies is to provide aids for the handicapped. A large array of aids, from wheelchairs, tricycles, crutches, sticks and surgical corsets to special eating utensils, long-handled combs and 'permanent' collars and ties, were being used by persons in the sample. The lack of really satisfactory false legs and aids to mobility, despite the far greater numbers having difficulties with legs than with arms, was repeatedly drawn to our attention. Sixty-four per cent of the sample were affected by disability in the lower limbs only and another 28 per cent were affected in both lower and upper limbs. Only 3 per cent were affected in the upper limbs only (26). As many as 65 per cent of the men and 70 per cent of the women in the sample used some aid to get about outdoors and nearly as many indoors. Most of the people with artificial legs who were interviewed had a great deal of trouble either because stumps were sore, or because they suffered from phantom pains. All found walking indoors and outdoors difficult. Leg supports or substitutes such as crutches and wheelchairs are remarkably cumbersome. The value of aids should not be minimized. We made various calculations which showed that average incapacity to undertake a range of tasks was reduced by over a quarter by aids already available. It became possible for people to do more tasks. Incapacity could be further reduced. But there is little doubt that by any rational assessment the top priorities are more good housing, better community services and more generous motorized transport. Ingenuity and research are important but even more important is the willingness to finance services and transport.

In 1956 the Piercy Committee pointed out that expenditure on the disabled by local authorities was not substantial. 'It is clear that only the fringes of the field have yet been touched. The Act gives local authorities very wide permissive powers. to make provision for the welfare of disabled persons, and on the evidence received there is no doubt that there is a need for a fuller and better provision and scope for considerable development' (27). The committee recommended an Exchequer grant for these services but this was not accepted. The Ministry of Health later spoke of steady progress and tried to reassure the public, although from the vantage point of history I believe the attitude adopted by the department will be seen as grudging. It did not even match the cautious and unimaginative approach to reform of the Piercy Committee. In 1963 the Ministry acknowledged that up to a year or so earlier 'the development of local authority welfare services (for the physically handicapped) had been very uneven and a number of authorities had not even made schemes for the deaf or dumb or for the general classes' (28).

The fact that there are far more disabled persons requiring welfare services than are registered has been lamented officially for years. Yet between 1957 and 1965 the numbers of blind, deaf and physically handicapped persons registered with local authorities in England and Wales grew by only 74,000 to 288,000, or six per 1,000 population. The total includes nearly 148,000 physically handicapped other than the blind or deaf, or 3 per 1,000 population. Yet the variations between local authorities are inexplicably wide. The numbers of generally handicapped persons on the registers per 1,000 population range from 0.8 in Chester, 1.2 in Portsmouth, 1.3 in Oxford and Southport, 1.4 in the North Riding, Coventry and Leicestershire, 1.5 in Staffordshire and 1.7 in Kent, at the lower levels, to 6.9 in Lincolnshire (Holland), 7.1 in Glamorgan, 7.2 in Hastings, 7.9 in Bath, 8.2 in West Bromwich and 10.7 in Kingston-upon-Hull, at the higher levels (29). If all authorities were to register proportionately as many as the top ten authorities another 150-200,000 would be added nationally to the registers. It is evident that the problem has scarcely begun to be identified, still less met.

Employment

The third major problem is occupation. Thirteen per cent of the total sample of 211 were in paid open employment and another 4 per cent were employed in a sheltered workshop or at home. More than a quarter of those below pensionable age were in paid employment, some of whom were severely incapacitated. Over half of the thirty-three persons below pension age who were employed were not registered on the Ministry of Labour's Disabled Persons Register. Some who were employed full-time had been told by Disablement Resettlement Officers at the employment exchange that they were unsuitable for work and found work for themselves.

There was an air of near-desperation in the attitudes of many persons below pensionable age to their need for a paid job. As many as 25 per cent expressed a wish for employment. At least half of these did not seem on the face of it to be too incapacitated to obtain a job. If our figures are broadly representative then there are 28,000 on the local authority registers seeking paid employment, 16,000 of them full-time employment. A number in the sample had difficulties in getting work because they could not obtain appropriate transport. The disabled still find it difficult to qualify for specially designed tricycles and adapted cars, especially if their disability is progressive and they have to convince Ministry officials that it is more difficult than it used to be to get to and from work. Some who do qualify find that by contrast with modern vehicles on the roads the tricycles and cars are inferior even in standards of comfort and possibly unsafe. Until recently they were not fitted with heaters, so many of the older vehicles are still grim to drive in winter.

It is difficult in some respects to understand why more of the disabled on the local authority registers who are not at work than who are at work are seeking it, for in status, pay and conditions it is often so unattractive. The disabled tend to be given light assembly work, packing, filing, cleaning and storekeeping. Some are in so-called designated employment, as car park attendants and lift attendants (30). The average wage of the men in the sample in full-time employment in 1965 was £14 compared with £19 at that time in London and the south east.

A disproportionately large number of those in employment were in unskilled and semi-skilled jobs. Some who had accepted paid work at home, making up rosettes or flower-holders and packing toys by the gross, for example, had to work extremely long hours for very little money. In all the instances we came across the average earned was less than three shillings an hour. The local authorities play little role as protective or referral agents for the disabled and most home-work is contracted privately.

The true situation is disturbing: 9 per cent of those on the Ministry of Labour's Disabled Persons Register are unemployed, compared with 2 per cent nationally (31). But this greatly underestimates the scale of the problem. The Ministry declares in effect that many of the long-term unemployed who are not on the Disabled Persons Register have personal handicaps because of age or physical or mental condition (32). There are substantial numbers of disabled on the local authority registers seeking work who are not listed at the local employment exchanges. Some of them will presumably be assessed by the Disablement Resettlement Officers as unsuitable for admission to the Ministry's Disabled Persons Register (33). And no doubt there are substantial numbers of other disabled persons on no official register who are in a similar position. It is time we recognized that this situation is absurd and unjust and should be remedied. The numbers of the genuinely unemployed are being under-represented.

Current activity on behalf of the disabled is not encouraging. Some of the people we interviewed spoke enthusiastically about the efforts made by Disablement Resettlement Officers. But more spoke of discouragement and many had made no use of the special services (34). Training at Industrial Rehabilitation Units is difficult to secure and when secured is not always as up to date as it might be. Little or no help is given in particular to retrain women and older men. Sheltered workshops are few and far between and get too little subsidy and managerial investment to be successful. In any event disabled persons often feel that such employment is to be avoided at all costs. Work in the home would be welcomed by a large proportion of the disabled but depends on skilful organization. Local authorities have permissive powers to operate home-working schemes. Few do so. The disabled need work-finders and transport-organizers and work-flow teams more than occupational therapy as understood in the narrow sense of that term. Some occupational therapists spend a lot of time finding employment for handicapped persons and some uncertainty between them and the D.R.O.s about division of function might well be investigated (35).

The quota of disabled persons is one of the most important instruments of policy. All employers with more than twenty employees must employ 3 per cent of disabled persons. Only 52 per cent of firms in fact satisfy the quota (36). Recently it was also revealed that fewer than 3 per cent of Government employees are disabled. There is no doubt that there are many sympathetic employers who are prepared to go to considerable lengths to help a disabled person. We were given instances of people being given time off and having working hours and conditions adjusted. On the other hand there is no doubt that some employers abuse the provisions of the Disabled Persons (Employment) Acts by persuading some lightly handicapped persons applying to them for jobs to register as disabled persons so that they can meet their quota. Others in practice pay low wages and offer inferior working conditions to the disabled. Discrimination is perhaps practised unconsciously more often than consciously. Nonetheless, the quota is a more effective means of assuring employment than designated employment, Remploy and sheltered workshops. It also encourages ordinary forms of employment, which the disabled prefer.

It seems important to liberalize the conditions under which people can qualify for admission to the register. In broad principle official help should be given to all persons seeking employment, whatever their sex or age and whatever doubts may exist about their capacity to hold employment. This part of the Ministry of Labour's work needs to be imaginatively expanded. The ultimate aim would be the integration of all disabled persons wanting work into open employment. Various forms of subsidy and encouragement to employers might be tried. An immediate step could be the manipulation of Selective Employment Tax in favour of disabled employees.

Income

A fourth problem is low level of resources. We have seen that relatively few disabled persons on local authority registers owned their own homes and that those in paid employment had relatively low earnings. In general the disabled in the sample had low incomes. Altogether 60 per cent of households had a total income of less than £10 a week and another 26 per cent less than £20. (A third of the households, it should be remembered, contained three or more persons.) Three quarters had less than £50 savings. Nearly half depended partly or wholly on national assistance and about 5 per cent might have qualified for supplementary assistance had they applied for it. There is no doubt that a disproportionately large number of the disabled are in poverty or on its margins.

Social security benefits for the long-term disabled are not related to limitation of capacity except secondarily and there is no consistent system of extra allowances for constant attendance or personal support and help. There are anomalies as between different kinds of allowances (37). A man with a wife and two children who is bedfast or chairbound because of multiple sclerosis, say, will receive £8 15s. a week if he is on sickness benefit (including family allowance) or under £10 a week, plus a rent allowance, if he is on national assistance. Yet a man in similar family circumstances who is incapacitated after an industrial injury may receive a pension of £6 15s. plus dependants' and other allowances making a total of £18 5s. Moreover, if this man was once awarded an industrial injury disablement pension of 100 per cent and is rehabilitated so that he can take paid employment again he continues to receive the pension of £6 15s. If he happens to fall sick he receives exactly the same as the first man, that is, £8 15s., plus his pension of £6 15s. A disabled housewife is in the worst plight. If her husband is in full-time work she will usually get nothing, not even national assistance.

Thus disablement for her family can be a disaster, especially if her husband's earnings are small or barely cover the normal day-to-day needs of the household.

The Disablement Income Group is rightly calling for the introduction of a national system of disability pensions. I believe that a generous pension should be introduced for both men and women based on the principle of limitation of capacity, as ascertained by the kind of functional assessment discussed earlier. This would be difficult to work out in practice but seems to be fairer and less arbitrary than any alternative, such as a pension based on the principle of limitation of earning power. The 100 per cent pension might be fixed initially at 30 per cent of average industrial earnings, which would be just over £6 at the present time. There would be additional allowances for dependent adults and children. The pension could be permanent or temporary according to the degree of certainty about the condition, as under the Swedish system (38). These benefits would be supplemented by a system of allowances for constant attendance and personal help. This system of benefits would normally apply upon the termination of six months' earnings-related sickness or unemployment benefit or earlier in instances of undoubted long-term handicap. Earnings-related supplements would continue to be paid to disabled persons over retirement age, as to all other retired persons under the Labour Party's scheme for National Superannuation which is to be introduced before 1970. People disabled in middle or late-middle age would also receive earnings-related supplements to reflect extra contributions made in working life. I would hope that this system would largely overtake special war and industrial pension levels. Discrimination between people disabled in war, industry and civil life is distasteful as well as being an administrator's and a lawyer's nightmare.

The present Government's provisions must surely be regarded as makeshift, because earnings-related benefits cease after six months. The long-term sick will be worse off under the new scheme than the short-term sick. And there is a kind of hiatus implicit in present legislation, earnings-related supplements ceasing after six months of sickness and an unconditional flat-rate allowance of 9s. being awarded by the Supplementary Benefits Commission after two years of sickness. A man who has been unemployed though disabled is not entitled to this extra allowance.

The Problems of Integration

There are of course many other problems and I have touched only on what seem to be the major ones. How acute are they? Have I skirted those which matter even more to severely disabled persons? It is reasonable to suppose that personal relationships with members of the

family and with friends and the physical struggle to participate in many
activities concern the disabled much more than campaigning for more
home help, motorized wheelchairs and even a modern council flat or
house on the ground floor. But politics and the organization of
professional services are not aspects of life which are unconnected with
private relationships. The institutional fabric which we have created and
within which we live shapes our behaviour and values. We would be
unwise to discount it. However much we struggle to avoid allowing the
wider social and political structure to influence our views, it causes us
to treat some people, even in our own families, as inferiors or as
redundant. And it causes the objects of our indifference or of our
self-righteous pity to underestimate their rights. They need to complain
and assert themselves, even more for our sake than their own.

I hope I have sketched sufficient evidence to show that as a society
Britain has what amounts to an elaborate system of discrimination
against the disabled. We do not ensure they have good housing,
adequate community services, employment with dignity or an adequate
income. We do not even think it necessary to count their numbers (39).
I venture to suggest these are facts, not opinions, which we must take
into our reckoning.

What stood out in this largely depressing survey was the warmth and
strength of many of the personal relationships of those who were
disabled. Many of the people whom we interviewed had close friends or
neighbours who were concerned about them. Nearly half were married,
as I have said, and another third were widowed, separated or divorced.
On the one hand, we found evidence of marital strain. Nearly a tenth of
those with a husband or wife who was alive were now separated or
divorced. The rate seems to be a little higher than in the general
population of comparable age. Another tenth, particularly wives, had
marital difficulties of one kind or another. On the other hand, the great
majority seemed to be content or, indeed, richly rewarded in their
marriages. They could count on devoted support and they contributed
a great deal themselves. Much the same is true of relationships with
other members of the family, though it does seem that disability
reduces the scope and therefore the interchangeability of contacts with
the extended family. Relationships are concentrated among a few
people. What is disturbing is the lack of adequate relief for many wives
and husbands and sons and daughters who give personal and household
care. Community services are required to provide a temporary
substitute or a permanent relief for relatives who are under excessive
strain.

How can this principle of participation or involvement in family and
other primary-group relationships be extended to employment, recreation and welfare? There is a gulf, in effect, between private and public

life for the disabled. There must be no illusions. Major improvements in the circumstances of the disabled cannot be secured by modest increments in legislation or services. A gradual reconstruction of the attitudes and values of society is required which can proceed only in relation to the reduction or elimination of many forms of social prejudice and superiority — involving colour, old age and economically unproductive work, for example, as well as handicap or disability. The fundamental difficulty here for individuals and society is one of recognizing diversity without ordering groups of people in superior and inferior social ranks.

I have tried to argue the relatedness of disability to the human condition. There are features of disability such as pain, shyness, awkwardness and abnormality which are known to us all. We have met some of them in our illnesses; we may carry some of them with us in our everyday lives and most of us can expect to encounter them in old age even if we are not thrust face to face with them by ill-luck in youth or middle age. We have to come to terms with the condition, to recognize it frankly and not to banish it from sight and mind. This involves recognizing that there are creative outcomes and original ways of looking at life as disabled persons as well as permanent limitations and idiosyncrasies. As one disabled person who has written sensitively about the problems has said, 'If those of us who are disabled live as fully as we can, while being completely conscious of the tragedy of our situation ... then somehow we can communicate to others an awareness that the value of the human person transcends his social status, attributes and possessions or his lack of them' (40).

This principle of relatedness, integration or participation has to be applied in various ways. The work of many different statutory and voluntary agencies has to be merged or coordinated if the universality of many of the problems of disability are to be recognized and met. Such emphasis as there is on separate organizations, separate services and separate institutions for the blind, the deaf, the epileptic and the subnormal may need to be reduced. Such emphasis as there is on separating the disabled from the non-disabled in sheltered workshops, residential institutions, housing and clubs may need also to be reduced. The possibility of rearranging and consolidating the work of the local authorities in a major new family service in which the disabled can participate, of inviting voluntary agencies to play a vital supplementary role, is one which the present Seebohm Committee could do much to make real. But there must be more central direction and strategy, beginning with a determined attempt to identify numbers and introduce new pensions, employment opportunities and access to good housing. In this, as in many other respects, we require imaginative leadership as well as popular good-will, interest and effort.

Notes and References

1 This lecture owes much to Sally Sainsbury, who carried out the survey on which it is largely based. [See her book, *Registered as Disabled*, Bell, 1970.]

2 The figure is a conservative estimate which allows for double — or multiple — counting of the same persons in some of the categories listed in the rest of this paragraph. Judging from research in other countries, for example, Denmark and Sweden, a figure of 6 per cent of all adults aged 21-64 is likely to be reached when disability is defined broadly. Allowing for a smaller proportion of children but a much larger proportion of the elderly the figure for the whole population would probably be higher. See, for example, Andersen, B. R., *Fysisk Handicappede i Danmark*, Socialforskningsinstittutets Publikationer 16, Copenhagen, 1964, pp. 55-6. [On the basis of a major survey carried out by the Government in 1969, 1.1 million in Britain aged sixteen and over were estimated to be very seriously, severely or appreciably handicapped, and a further 1.9 million were impaired but needed little or no support for normal everyday living activities. Harris, A., *Handicapped and Impaired in Great Britain*, H.M.S.O., 1971.]

3 *Ministry of Labour Gazette*, April 1967, p. 308.

4 *Report of the Ministry of Pensions and National Insurance for the Year 1965*, Cmnd. 3046, H.M.S.O., 1966.

5 For England and Wales, *Report of the Ministry of Health for the Year 1965*, Cmnd. 3039, H.M.S.O., 1966, pp. 127-30. Figures for Scotland obtained from Home and Health Department and added.

6 About 48,000 of those living in council or supported voluntary Homes in England and Wales are described as 'handicapped'. See *Report of the Ministry of Health for 1965*, p. 124.

7 England and Wales, *Report of the Ministry of Health for 1965*, p. 119.

8 In March 1967 the total had reached 144,000 (private communication, Ministry of Social Security). Most of them 'are persons incapacitated since birth or early childhood and living with their parents'. *Report of the National Assistance Board for the Year ended 31 December 1965*, Cmnd. 3042, H.M.S.O., 1966, p. 13.

9 *Education in 1966 — Report of the Department of Education and Science*, Cmnd. 3226, H.M.S.O., 1967, p. 44.

10 *Health and Welfare: the Development of Community Care*, Cmnd. 1973, H.M.S.O., 1963, p. 31.

11 Many of those receiving retirement pensions and unemployment or sickness benefits were also receiving supplementary national assistance. People receiving personal disablement benefits (war or industrial injury) were also eligible to receive national insurance benefits.

12 See also the analysis by Nagi, S. Z., 'Some Conceptual Issues in Disability and Rehabilitation', in Sussman, M. B. (ed.), *Sociology and Rehabilitation*, Washington D.C., American Sociological Association, 1966, particularly pp. 100-103.

13 An attempt to develop a measure of this was made in 'Measuring Incapacity for Self-Care', in Townsend, P., *The Last Refuge*, Routledge, 1962, pp. 464-76.

14 Goffman, E., *Stigma: Notes on the Management of Spoiled Identity*, Englewood Cliffs, N.J., Spectrum Books, 1963; Friedson, E., 'Disability as Social Deviance' in Sussman, M. B., *Sociology and Rehabilitation*, Washington D.C., American

Sociological Association, 1966. More generally see Becker, H. S., *Outsiders: Studies in the Sociology of Deviance*, New York, The Free Press, 1963, particularly Chapters 1 and 2.

15 See, for example, Mechanic, D., 'The Concept of Illness Behaviour', *Journal of Chronic Diseases*, vol. 15, 1962; Mechanic, D., 'Response Factors in Illness: The Study of Illness Behaviour', *Social Psychiatry*, vol. 1, August 1966.

16 See, for example, Zborowski, M., 'Cultural Components in Responses to Pain', *Journal of Social Issues*, vol. 8, 1952; Jaco, E. G. (ed.), *Patients, Physicians and Illness*, New York, The Free Press, 1958.

17 The 'dependent and segregated status [of the disabled] is not an index merely of their physical condition; to an extent only beginning to be recognized it is the product of cultural definition – an assumptive framework of myths, stereotypes, aversive responses, and outright prejudices, together with more rational and scientific evidence'. Ten Broek, J., and Matson, F. W., 'The Disabled and the Law of Welfare', *California Law Review*, vol. 54, no. 2, May 1966, p. 814.

18 According to the Charity Commissioners the Spastics Society received £1.8 million in 1962, and the National Society for Mentally Handicapped Children £39,000 in 1964.

19 *Report of the Committee on the Assessment of Disablement* (the McCorquodale Report), Cmnd. 2847, H.M.S.O., December 1965.

20 In awarding war pensions and industrial injuries disablement pensions the Ministry of Pensions bases assessments on comparison between 'the condition of a disabled person and that of a normal healthy person of the same age. Assessment on this basis measures the general handicap imposed by loss of faculty. Loss of faculty may be defined as the loss of physical or mental capacity to lead a normally occupied life and does not depend on the way in which the disablement affects the particular circumstances of the individual. A normally occupied life includes work as well as household and social activities and leisure pursuits.' *Report of the Committee on the Assessment of Disablement*, p. 4. To be admitted to the Ministry of Labour's Register of Disabled Persons an applicant must (1) 'be substantially handicapped on account of injury, disease (including a physical or mental condition arising from imperfect development of any organ) or congenital deformity, in obtaining or keeping employment or work on his own account otherwise suited to his age, qualification and experience; the disablement being likely to last for twelve months or more; (2) desire to engage in some form of remunerative employment or work ... and have a reasonable prospect of obtaining and keeping such employment or work ...' Finally, local authorities are empowered by Section 29 of the National Assistance Act, 1948, to promote the welfare of persons who are blind, deaf or dumb, and others, 'who are substantially and permanently handicapped by illness, injury or congenital deformity or such other disabilities as may be prescribed by the Minister'. Registers are compiled on this basis from a variety of sources.

21 The Medical Report form includes a section which allows the doctor to indicate whether an individual can use upper limbs (shoulders, arms, hands, fingers and touch) and lower limbs (walking, standing, sitting only, hurrying, balancing, climbing stairs, climbing ladders), and can kneel, stoop, push and pull, and lift and carry. The extent of hearing and vision also can be noted. The need for better functional assessment was recognized by a Working Party of the British Council for Rehabilitation of the Disabled reporting in 1964: *The Handicapped School-Leaver*, British Council for Rehabilitation of the Disabled.

22 See, for example, Hess, A. E., 'Old Age, Survivors and Disability Insurance: Early Problems and Operations of the Disability Provisions', *Social Security Bulletin*, U.S. Department of Health, Education and Welfare, December 1957.

23 Andersen, B. R., *Fysisk Handicappede i Danmark, Bind II*, Socialforskningsinstittutets Publikationer 16, Copenhagen, 1964, pp. 55-6.

24 Including going up and down stairs, getting about the house, washing and bathing, dressing and putting on shoes, cutting toe nails, brushing and combing hair, going to toilet on own, cleaning floors, cooking a hot meal, seeing, speaking and hearing, and organizing thoughts in lucid speech.

25 For national figures of tenure see Donnison, D. V., *The Government of Housing*, Penguin Books, 1967, p. 186.

26 It is interesting to note that, in 1965, 17,163 artificial legs but only 2,736 artificial arms were supplied under the National Health Service. *Annual Report of the Ministry of Health for 1965*, p. 165.

27 *Report of the Committee of Enquiry on the Rehabilitation, Training and Re-Settlement of Disabled Persons*, Cmnd. 9883, H.M.S.O., 1956, p. 26.

28 *Health and Welfare: The Development of Community Care*, p. 31.

29 Calculated on the basis of information kindly supplied by the Ministry of Health.

30 According to the Ministry of Labour's information on designated employment for August 1964, all but a small minority of the 2,769 lift attendants and 2,584 car park attendants were registered disabled.

31 *Ministry of Labour Gazette*, April 1967.

32 This was stated of 80,000 of the 104,000 men unemployed for six months or more in a special inquiry carried out in 1964, 'Second Inquiry into the Characteristics of the Unemployed', *Ministry of Labour Gazette*, April 1966. In a special study of the unemployed who were receiving assistance in June 1956 the National Assistance Board found that a majority had some specific physical handicap. Moreover, they also found that only 72 per cent of the men and 50 per cent of the women with physical handicaps were registered as disabled persons with the employment exchange, *Report of the National Assistance Board for 1956*, Cmnd. 181, H.M.S.O., 1957, p. 42.

33 The history of registration is puzzling. In 1950 the register reached a peak of 936,500 but then declined, in some years rather sharply (the figure for 1966 being 654,000). In 1957 the Ministry explained that only part of this decline was attributable to a falling off in the numbers of disabled servicemen. Many disabled persons did not renew their registration, either because they felt secure enough in their employment, or because the D.R.O.s, supported by the Disablement Advisory Committee Panels, were interpreting disability more strictly 'so as to exclude the lightly handicapped'. There is also the fact that soon after registration started employers persuaded some of their employees to register to help meet the 3 per cent quota. Even if persons who stay with one firm do not re-register they are still counted in the quota. This is plainly unsatisfactory, for some are no longer disabled or have remained no more than marginally disabled. See *Annual Reports of the Ministry of Labour* for 1949-60, particularly for 1949 (Cmnd. 8017), 1957 (Cmnd. 468), and 1960 (Cmnd. 1364).

34 Some have called for an independent review of the work. Members of staff of the Ministry fill the post of D.R.O. by rotation, serving for five years. They then

move on to other work. There is no established training course. Lady Hamilton, 'Integrating the Physically Handicapped', *New Society*, 5 May 1966.

35 Jefferys, M., *An Anatomy of Social Welfare Services*, Michael Joseph, 1966, pp. 68 and 288.

36 The percentage varies from 67 per cent in Wales to 59 per cent in the north west to 49 per cent in the Midlands and 45 per cent in London and the south east. Information for 1 July 1966 kindly supplied in a private communication by the Ministry of Labour.

37 For a clear account of some of these see Willmott, P., 'Social Security in Disablement', in Hunt, P. (ed.), *Stigma: The Experience of Disability*, Geoffrey Chapman, 1966.

38 English translation of *National Insurance Act*, 25 May 1962, Swedish Ministry of Social Affairs, 1963.

39 [In 1968, partly as a consequence of pressure from the Disablement Income Group, the Child Poverty Action Group and other bodies, the Minister of Social Security, Mrs Judith Hart, announced the research which culminated in a survey of the handicapped and impaired in Britain by the Office of Population Censuses and Surveys: Social Survey Division. See Harris, A., *Handicapped and Impaired in Great Britain*, H.M.S.O., 1971.]

40 Hunt, P., 'A Critical Condition', in Hunt, P. (ed.), op. cit., p. 148.

8 Prisoners of neglect: psychiatric hospitals in Britain*

The overall impression in the mental hospitals we saw is one of neglect. It is not just the appearance, the coarseness to the touch, the noise or the impenetrable silence but the smell of neglect that remains imprinted on the mind: the sweet but slightly rotting smell of an assortment of bewildered human beings who exist in claustrophobic proximity like wrinkling apples spaced fractionally apart in a dark cupboard.

But is this fair? Overall impressions are difficult to put into rational perspective. Conditions are by no means uniform. Our study of psychiatric hospitals was designed to produce information about elderly patients (1). Twenty-six hospitals throughout the country were selected at random and visited in 1963 by a specially recruited team of interviewers. We found that conditions were usually worst in the largest hospitals. Over two thirds of the accommodation in psychiatric hospitals in England and Wales and over half that in Scotland is in 97 hospitals, each with 1,000 or more beds. Ten of these were in our sample. Setting aside one which was disorganized because of extensive repairs and redecoration, we visited a total of 168 wards, with 4,456 beds. In 34, with over 1,300 beds, there was no furniture or fittings except beds (no bedmats, chairs, lockers, washbasins, tables or mirrors), and in another 60 there were only a few articles shared by all the patients, or only one article, such as a locker, a wooden box or a mat for each patient. Altogether, three fifths of the wards provided dismal surroundings — by any criterion — for the patients.

One ward, for example, was an attic with sloping eaves and heavy beams at the top of a steep stairway, oppressive even on a bright summer day. The windows were mean and set far apart in grey-white walls, discoloured by large damp patches. Ninety male patients in this attic shared three W.C.s and four washbasins. On the rail of each man's bed hung a wooden coat-hanger — the nearest approach there was to an article of furniture for personal use.

The dormitory of another ward resembled an Edwardian barracks. The beds for fifty women patients were only twelve inches apart and lined the walls and ran in two rows head to head down the middle of the room. The only other furniture was a chair for the night nurse. The

* The full version of an article in the *Observer*, 5 April 1964.

floor was bare and the windows uncurtained. Few of the patients had been visited in the past year or been outside the hospital. The great majority of these fifty women ate and passed their entire days in the one large day-room. Two who on the day of our visit wanted to talk in peace had taken refuge in the bathroom. Several were already seated listlessly at the dinner tables for a meal that was not to be served for another half hour.

The wards of the small hospitals which we visited tended to contain fewer beds and to be slightly better furnished. Although half of them had no furniture or only one article (in addition to the bed) for each patient, half had two or more articles. In several hospitals of all sizes, large sums of money had been spent on modernizing certain wards and introducing amenities, such as pile carpets, footstools, armchairs, lamp standards and potted plants. In some buildings there were comfortably furnished single and double rooms for patients.

But when all this is said there are appalling physical difficulties still to be overcome in most of these hospitals — of corridors running for hundreds of yards like tunnels (one was a quarter of a mile long), of airing courts with high walls and of wards remote from canteens and psychiatric and nursing centres.

These are just some of the problems beginning to be identified. In 1962 the Minister of Health's hospital plan was received with relief and enthusiasm. For almost two decades no more than a handful of hospitals had been newly built and now, at last, capital expenditure was to rise substantially from around £16 million a year in the late 1950s to over £50 million a year in the mid-1960s. Perhaps after another ten years of planning and of increased government spending, many staff in the National Health Service hoped, there might be a reasonable chance of getting a humane and efficient system of hospitals in Britain.

But in the last two years the prospect has begun to recede. Too little research has been commissioned to make the planning less amateurish. Priorities seem wrong. The London and provincial teaching hospitals have 7 per cent of the beds in the country but have been allocated 18 per cent of the capital for new schemes to be started during the sixties. Hospitals for the elderly and the mentally ill have been allocated much less than a proportionate share, although research by J. H. Sheldon, John Wing, George Brown and others has begun to show how much needs to be spent on them. Although many of the 69 hospitals for mental illness with more than 1,000 beds in England and Wales are being reduced in size, only 8 are being closed by 1975. This is not perhaps the most dazzling example of what a prosperous and humane society might achieve.

Nor is there much indication of quickly integrating the hospital population with the outside community, and developing out-patient and day-hospital units, thereby helping to reduce the stigma of mental illness. Efforts are certainly being made to provide units for the mentally ill in general hospitals (and, on a small scale, to provide acute medical and surgical wards in psychiatric hospitals). But although their number will be more than doubled between 1960 and 1975, only 13 per cent of available beds are then planned to be in general hospitals.

Some of the staff cope astonishingly well despite the conditions. As we toured the hospitals we witnessed instances of nurses dealing considerately and imaginatively with individual patients, despite the constant pressure of work in big wards. Two warring women who began to scream at each other were separated gently by two young nurses who then went on to chat to them and hug them affectionately for several minutes to soothe ruffled feelings. In some of the most depressing wards for geriatric patients there were staff who were reconciled to the frequent task of dressing those who were incontinent and clearing up urine and excrement. Some of them were even aware of the therapeutic value of friendly conversation and behaviour towards old men and women whose weeks in this life are numbered.

But when all this too is said, there is still a serious shortage of staff, they are badly paid, have too little training and are mixed in quality. In the large hospitals there is only one nurse or nursing assistant on the staff for every four, five, six or more patients, and this ratio naturally covers three shifts of duty, holiday periods and variations between particular wards. Numbers have remained stationary in recent years or have actually declined (at least in terms of staffing man-hours) to levels far below what is officially sanctioned. At times we encountered two nurses trying to manage as many as 50, 60 or 70 patients in a ward. Sometimes they were, or had to be, indifferent to calls for help. There were nursing assistants who spoke little or no English. One matron justified this by saying, 'You don't need to talk when you can smile, pat them on the cheek and feed them.' There were others who had worked for years in the hospital without receiving any form of training. In some hospitals fewer than a quarter and in most fewer than a third of the nursing staff were trained. While probably only a small minority are harsh and wholly unfitted to be nurses, a substantial proportion are unaware of the therapeutic possibilities of certain kinds of social relations and are forced occasionally by lack of time into acting roughly and impatiently.

They cannot easily stop and listen and talk, especially when someone is deaf, has a speech impediment or is just old. Often we were told that we would 'get nothing out of' a particular patient, yet we met wholly lucid people who for one reason or another had failed to communicate with the staff. A woman in her nineties sitting among severely disturbed geriatric patients was found not to be mentally confused at all. She was simply stone deaf. Although she was partly blind she could read questions printed in capitals by the interviewers and she continued to answer them until she began to tire. Another had a cleft palate, and although in fact she was extremely sensitive and highly educated she was thought to be stupid because no one could make out what she was saying. Our research showed that mental patients are frequently more sensitive and intelligent than they appear to be in a crowd. Moreover, many of them are denied hearing aids, spectacles, dentures and surgical appliances which would help them to be communicative and secure. Staff are too few to supervise the use of some of these aids but paradoxically over-protective in attitude: 'Their glasses (or dentures) would get broken'; 'they would keep taking off the deaf aid'.

Medical staff are also few in number and mixed in quality. The best are responsible for impressive experiments like the district mental health services at Oldham, Bolton, Worthing and Nottingham, but the training of too many others is incomplete and their work sketchy, some of it necessarily so. Some patients described the consultation they had as their 'yearly'. In their recent book, *Mental Hospitals at Work,* Kathleen Jones and Roy Sidebotham showed that the *average* time given to long-stay patients in one mental hospital by clinical staff was 5½ minutes per week. Again and again we found case-records which gave a very deficient account of a patient's history, symptoms and response to treatment. Recent entries were sometimes dated as many as two years apart.

'They ask you what you've done for the hospital, and I think I've done my bit. I used to do sewing at a machine all day and I got a twisted spine. The doctor said I should have stopped that long before. No, I have no therapy to straighten my back, but the doctor got my stick shortened because of me being bent and says it will get better.'

Those in charge of the teaching hospitals have little knowledge of the mental hospital service and psychiatry is given short shrift in the medical curriculum. If only 10 per cent of the grants made to the teaching hospitals could be diverted into teaching projects in provincial mental hospitals there would be a chance of achieving a better balance in the health services and of training doctors better equipped to treat mental illness.

Part of the problem of poor physical conditions and staffing is being met through a shift of emphasis in treatment of the mentally ill from the hospital to the community. Many doctors prefer to admit schizophrenics and patients with affective psychoses, if not those with senile psychoses, for brief periods rather than for a long uninterrupted stay. They favour 'rehabilitation' rather than 'custody'. Fewer restraints are imposed and more activities encouraged. Despite controversy over the numbers of elderly mental patients who will be in hospital in future, the Ministry of Health assumes that the number of staffed beds in mental hospitals will be reduced from 152,000 in 1960 to 92,000 in 1975.

But lip service is sometimes paid to 'community' care. There are physician superintendents who have taken advantage of recent changes in professional and public opinion to discharge long-stay patients without guarantee of adequate alternative care. There are also those who maintain a high proportion of locked wards in their hospitals or who say that the wards are open when staff are in fact left to use wide discretion in locking them at certain times and in certain conditions. The key-ring with its bunch of ten or twenty keys is by no means a thing of the past.

Lip service is also paid sometimes to the principles of intensive therapy. People like Dr D. F. Early at Bristol and Dr Russell Barton at Colchester have introduced experimental industrial as well as occupational therapy schemes in certain hospitals and have also made arrangements with outside firms to employ an increasing number of patients. But such schemes are properly organized in only a few hospitals. In most hospitals the variety of patients and the shortage of funds is felt to be a proper excuse for inertia or lack of ingenuity. Many superintendents and matrons still rely on methods of 'habit-training' and 'discipline', which at one hospital involve gangs of men in such uninspiring tasks as hauling a heavy roller over the lawns.

At all hospitals, however, a number of patients are given jobs as cleaners, laundrymen, seamstresses and gardeners. Suspicious rationalizations are offered to explain why some of these patients have not been returned to the outside community. 'She's my ward worker and very dependable. I don't know what I'd do without her. She's lived here so long that it would be difficult for her to settle down outside again.' But even taking into account those who attend therapy classes, the majority of patients spend most of their time pacing the corridors, sitting in chairs, and gathering around the radiators. The complaint that recurred most frequently in our interviews with elderly patients was, 'I sit here hour after hour not really talking to anyone. Time drags on. There's nothing to occupy my time.' John Wing and George Brown found in an important recent study that the average patient in a large mental hospital spent 5½ hours a day doing nothing. Seventy per cent of the patients did not leave the ward in the day.

When staff are few it is quicker and more efficient to organize the cleaning, serving meals, washing up, cooking and making beds without the patients participating. 'When they do it they make a mess and we have to do it again.' Educating staff to be self-effacing so that highly dependent individuals might make their first faltering steps towards reclaiming their self-respect will take a long time. The trouble at present is that there are so few staff that patients sometimes have to be regularly given sedatives to damp down their unemployed energies.

Perhaps the most crushing indictment of mental hospitals is their disrespect for individual identity. Personal possessions are often non-existent. Dormitories allow small comfort or privacy. There is little variety in meals or the manner of their serving. Ill-fitting and cheaply made hospital clothes hang from human frames which are further derided by clumsy uniform haircuts. Small wonder that internecine warfare rages over apparently trivial issues like the ownership of carrier bags or the right to sit in a particular chair — which are all that are left to the patients.

In short, while there is much that is hopeful and indeed internationally impressive in the development of some hospital services for the mentally ill in Britain — especially for younger patients — the fundamental and inescapable fact about those services generally is neglect, on a huge and discouraging scale. There is nothing to gain from concealing it. Indeed, it must be spelt out in public in remorseless detail, for only then might a relatively wealthy and democratic society willingly allocate the necessary resources to improve pay, conditions, training and staffing — especially in creating small units for fewer than sixty patients to replace the large hospitals. There is sufficient imagination and knowledge among the best psychiatrists and physician superintendents to make one optimistic about the chances of putting a much more ambitious policy into full effect. It is certainly needed. The basic national issue is one of political principle — whether the sick and disabled should have better instead of worse living standards than the well. For the majority they are at present far worse.

Notes and References

1 See, for example, Townsend, P., 'Old People in Psychiatric and Geriatric Hospitals, Nursing Homes and Residential Homes', in Freeman, M. (ed.), *Psychiatric Hospital Care*, Baillère, Tindell and Cassell, 1966.

9 The institution and the individual*

In the last few decades, and especially in the last fifteen years, our methods of caring for the sick, the mentally handicapped and subnormal, the old and the infirm, and children deprived of a normal home life have changed strikingly. We are moving away from a philosophy built on the principle of housing large numbers of these casualties in custodial institutions and have not yet found an alternative philosophy to put in its place. I believe that as society advances in prosperity and becomes increasingly sensitive to the complex needs of the individual, the family, and the community, the justification for retaining more than a few highly specialized institutions gradually disappears.

How have the changes come about? In their long and magnificent history of the English poor law, Sidney and Beatrice Webb frequently expressed exasperation at the resilience of the so-called general mixed workhouse. For several centuries, the chief institutional provision in this country was, broadly speaking, a building in which the young and the old, the sick, the infirm, the blind and the mentally ill, the homeless and the destitute were all given asylum. In those days there must have seemed little alternative to the rather bleak institution. The provision had to be institutional because community services were few and far between, and because that was the neatest and most economical way of dealing with dire need. It had to be bleak because of the social conditions prevailing outside: a large proportion of the population lived in poverty. If the food, amenities and services had been better, and if the staff had been kindly and sympathetic rather than repressive — so the argument seems to have gone — then too many people would have applied for admission and too many would have been inclined to stay there longer than necessary.

With the passing of time, the situation changed. The general mixed institution began to play a diminishing role. Developments in medicine led to demands for more institutions for various classes of sick persons and there was further segregation of the mentally and chronically ill.

* Third Programme broadcast, 31 May 1960, and published in the *Listener*, 23 June 1960.

The growth of the professions, of voluntary associations and of local government produced small armies of physicians, officials and social workers trained to treat special classes of the population in need. Institutions intended only for children or old people began to appear on the scene. The process was a slow one and even today we still have a number of hospitals and local authority institutions housing a medley of people with different needs. But, broadly speaking, by the end of the last war the long battle for classification and specialization had been won. In 1948 the poor law was abandoned in name and to a large extent in practice and the various hospital and other institutional services were rationalized. The history of the institution entered a new phase. For instance, in the hospital services increasing emphasis has been placed not on bigger and more numerous hospitals, with more beds, but on the more efficient use of the beds there are already. In the last ten years waiting lists have diminished and more people have been treated as in-patients. Yet the number of beds occupied has grown by only one in twenty. Periods of hospital stay have shortened and out-patient attendances have increased. The number of day patients is also increasing quickly and, compared with the early post-war years, domiciliary health services have expanded considerably.

A number of new developments and experiments seem to augur changes of an even more dramatic kind. Hospitals are being built to entirely new designs with small, intimate rooms for two, four or six people, grouped in special treatment wards. A few mothers are being allowed to stay in hospital with their children, or to care for them during the day. Unrestricted visiting is more frequently allowed and encouraged. In various ways, hospital patients are treated more like human beings. Attempts are being made to break up the large mental hospital into smaller units with partitioned wards, more furniture, social clubs, workshops and facilities for working outside the hospital precincts. There are pioneering mental health services at Worthing, Nottingham, Oldham and elsewhere. At Worthing, for example, psychiatrists visit the homes of patients or see them at the hospital out-patients clinic; social workers deal with family problems; and physiotherapy and other treatment may be given at home, in the day clinics or in the parent hospital. Four in five patients are treated as out-patients.

Such trends are not all confined to the health service. The care of children deprived of a normal home life has gradually taken a different shape. There are fewer large institutions for boys or girls only, and more small 'family' type Homes for children of both sexes, created on the principle of placing a small group of six to twelve children under the charge of a house-mother. At the same time there has been a big expansion in boarding-out. Ten years ago a third of the children in the care of the local authorities in England and Wales were boarded out; today the proportion is nearly a half.

The trend is the same, though slower, for the infirm aged. Fewer of them are cared for in the big local authority institutions and more in residential Homes for 20-60 persons. As with children, successive governments have regarded the Home with a capital H as second-best, in principle at least, to maintaining them for as long as possible in private households, by the further expansion of domiciliary services. In some areas, such as Hampshire, Plymouth, Exeter and Dorset, experiments in boarding out old people, and in providing special groups of bungalows and flatlets with a warden or housekeeper in charge, have been undertaken as an alternative to institutional care.

It would be wrong, of course, to exaggerate the speed and extent of all these changes. There are still many ugly institutions where conditions are grim and where administrative routines remain strangely unaffected by modern principles of humane management. For example, out-of-date buildings with cavernous dormitories containing 30, 40 or even 50 iron-framed beds and little else are retained, where visiting hours are restricted and patients offered no opportunities of passing the day except by sitting in huge day-rooms.

Yet there is no doubt that two distinct changes are taking place in the social services and are gathering momentum. One is the transformation of the institution by making it more congenial and 'homelike' in its material conditions and by removing many of those characteristics which make it a self-contained entity remote from the outside community. The other is the shift in emphasis from caring for people in institutions towards caring for them in the community. If humanly possible, so it is argued, they should be kept at home.

How do we account for these changes? It is true that they seem to have been motivated partly by the mounting cost of the institution. The cost of caring for a person in hospital can now range from £7 to over £30 a week, and the higher the cost the more those in charge seem to look to the possibilities of keeping some people out of institutions or sending them home at the earliest opportunity. But cost is only part of the story. We are now beginning to obtain new knowledge, by means of systematic research, of the effects on individuals of an institutional environment, particularly when they have been exposed to it for some months or years.

To sum up this recent research would be a difficult task, but there appear to be certain general findings or observations which are common to a number of studies of mental and other hospitals, and institutions for children and handicapped adults. These may be expressed broadly as follows: in the institution, people live communally with a minimum of privacy, and yet their relationships with each other are slender. Many subsist in a kind of defensive shell of isolation. Their mobility is restricted, and they have little access to general society. Their social experiences are limited and the staff lead a rather separate existence from them. They are subtly oriented towards a system in which they submit to orderly routine, lack creative occupation and cannot exercise much self-determination. They are deprived of intimate family relationships and can rarely find substitutes which seem to be more than a pale imitation of those enjoyed by most people in the general community.

The result for the individual seems to be a gradual process of depersonalization. He may become resigned and depressed and may display no interest in the future or in things not immediately personal. He sometimes becomes apathetic, talks little and lacks initiative. His personal habits and toilet may deteriorate. Occasionally he seems to withdraw into a private world of fantasy. In a recent study of 'Institutional Neurosis' Dr Russell Barton even suggested that the mental patient adopts in time a characteristic posture, 'the hands held across the body or tucked behind an apron, the shoulders drooped, and the head held forward'. The gait also has 'a shuffling quality'. The causal process has not been properly disentangled but a number of investigators have argued that it is highly unlikely that individual reactions can be ascribed wholly to factors other than the institutional environment.

In some of the smaller and more humanely administered institutions these various characteristics are less marked but still to be found. They have been noted in prisons, camps for prisoners of war and refugees, and approved schools.

Few studies have yet been made of the relationship between the way the individual behaves in the institution and the absence of family relationships, except in the case of children. Even here the research findings have been suggestive rather than conclusive. Dr John Bowlby has vividly described evidence of the differences between young institutionalized children and those living in their own homes. And in a number of experiments, including a classic instance reported by Dorothy Burlingham and Anna Freud, children in residential nurseries and Homes who were showing unmistakable signs of retarded development made dramatic improvements when they were divided into quasi-family groups of four with a 'substitute' mother to give them her undivided attention each day.

The research in children's institutions has turned on a child's need for dependable love in a family. I suspect that if understood in the wider sense of the need to give as well as receive affection, and to perform reciprocal services within a family (or quasi-family) group, the same may be largely true for individuals of all ages. Recent sociological studies in Western society (following on from anthropological studies elsewhere) have begun to deepen our awareness of the importance to the individual of the family at all stages of his life. Within an organic unit of three generations, largely preserving its identity and independence on the basis of the recognition of biological attachment, the individual achieves a large measure of self-fulfilment, and can satisfy many psychological and social needs, first as a child, and later as adolescent, husband or wife, parent and grandparent.

To a sociologist the absence of close relationships between the three generations is perhaps the most distinctive feature of institutional populations. In a sense the institutional community is one which is relatively closed and artificial. It is closed because it tends to be set apart from the rest of the community as a more-or-less self-contained unit in buildings of an identifiable kind; and artificial because it is not a representative cross-section of the general community: it does not consist of people of both sexes and all ages, or people held together by a network of family, occupational and neighbourhood ties. People have to be admitted from a wide area; they are usually strangers to each other, and their relatives have long distances to travel to see them just so as to spend a few minutes conversing quietly in a public room. Although casual relationships may of course arise, they are usually fragile because, unlike relationships between neighbours or members of a family, they may not last long and cannot be based securely on the reciprocation of services. In a three-generation family living at home a grandmother may prepare meals and look after grandchildren while, for her part, her daughter may do all the heavy washing and shopping. There are many complex arrangements of this kind. In an institution people often have the same disabilities so they cannot do very much for each other. Their behaviour, too, is necessarily overlaid by formal organization and routine. Even when they have the capacity to do many of the things ordinarily undertaken in the course of home life — such as cooking, arranging furniture, repairing clothes and gardening — institutionalized persons have little or no opportunity of exercising such skills.

Many authorities still discount these things and believe that most of the problems posed by the shortcomings of institutional care can be met by two main reforms: by classifying institutions more rigorously according to the different types of inmates, and by creating better physical facilities and material comforts. Thus they would carry even further the present practice of placing children, young adults, the aged, and persons suffering from certain diseases or handicaps in separate types of institutions, sometimes subdividing them also according to sex. This approach may be clinically appropriate or administratively convenient, because trained personnel are scarce and equipment is expensive. But it may not assist the creation of real communities and may make the patients or residents psychologically more insecure.

Whatever its defects, the old Victorian workhouse reproduced a number of the characteristics of the normal community. Some, at least, of the children were able to remain with their parents when they were sick; orphans might find a maternal widow to take an interest in them; and a destitute but not infirm woman could be accepted into the same building as her imbecile sister. I don't want to overstate this argument. No more than anyone else would I like to see the rebirth of the Victorian mixed institution. It was of course a scandal in a civilized society; people lived in miserable conditions on a poor diet, cross-infection was rife, and the same rules were often applied indiscriminately to both the infirm and the work-shy. I merely wish to suggest that the workhouse may have taken so long to die because it possessed *some* of the social and psychological advantages to the individual of living in a general community of three or four generations. And now that we have set it firmly behind us we find ourselves posed with a fundamental dilemma.

How can we reconcile the medical or administrative argument for the specialized institution with the unspoken desire or need of people to live in family groups within a community composed of individuals of both sexes and all ages? In a sense this dilemma has existed, if largely unrecognized, throughout history. But only now, in a society which has the means and — thanks partly to some of the recent work of psychologists and sociologists — a greater inclination to act more tolerantly towards the victims of adversity, has it come to the forefront.

The means of resolving the dilemma may seem to lie in two directions. The first might be to restrict hospital provision to general 'accident' or 'acute' hospitals with highly specialized treatment wards, and with 'recovery' and out-patient annexes adjoining. These would be for people staying for brief periods who require surgery and other forms of treatment which cannot be given to them in their own homes. The second might be gradually to abandon most other types of institution, as we know them, by creating special types of housing and day clinics and by providing a much richer variety of home and welfare services. To me such a policy seems to follow logically from a projection of the trends we are now witnessing in our social services. It would take a long time to achieve and would involve immense difficulties. But once we accept, as in fact we seem to be accepting, the principle that no advanced democratic society should deny the individual the right to a normal home and family life, I doubt whether any other course is open to us.

I once interviewed a man of seventy who, after spending forty years in various hospitals, had recently entered an old people's institution. When I asked whether he wished to stay permanently he said, 'It's comfortable here, of course, and I've seen good and bad. But all my life I've longed for two things — a home of my own and a job of my own.' After forty years of institutional life the little flame still burned.

10 The argument for gradually abandoning communal homes for the aged*

A 'Home' for old people is usually understood to be an establishment in which a number of unrelated people who do not require continuous medical and nursing care sit down to meals together, share other facilities — such as sitting and sleeping accommodation, bathrooms and W.C.s — and obtain certain personal as well as household services from a paid domestic and attendant staff. These personal services often include assistance with dressing and walking and also include occasional nursing since one or more qualified nurses are usually attached to the staff, or, if not, the 'matron' in charge is herself a trained nurse. Although such establishments existed many years ago in different countries, it is only since the war that they have been separately identified from hospitals and nursing Homes as a major instrument of social policy. The word 'Home' appears to be something of a euphemism, however, and any examination of the real functions of the establishments suggests they provide an uneasy compromise between private domestic comforts and public care and supervision in an institutional environment. We would do well to examine their functions closely before too many are built in the coming years. It is the purpose of this paper to show that there are strong grounds for treating such Homes largely as a temporary expedient in the development of policy for the aged in industrial societies which are becoming increasingly prosperous.

At the start it is worth emphasizing that the old people's Home is not the only institution about which uncertainties are expressed at present. In all Western societies there are long-stay institutions of different kinds — psychiatric and chronic sick hospitals, nursing Homes, hostels for the mentally subnormal, and residential institutions and Homes for children and the handicapped as well as for the aged. Are they going to be needed in the next century or should we quickly abandon them and seek alternative ways of caring for the kind of people they accommodate at present? Can the long-term mental hospital be supplanted, in time, by a combination of (i) psychiatric wards in general hospitals, (ii) out-patient and day units, and (iii) care

* First published in the *International Social Science Journal*, vol. XV, no. 3, 1963.

given by psychiatric social workers in the community? Can the children's Home be supplanted by a combination of (i) more use of foster parents and (ii) placing more house-mothers and house-fathers in charge of quasi-families in ordinary houses? Fifty, even ten, years ago these questions might have seemed absurdly impractical. Today I am not so sure. They are uncomfortably real, particularly to those whose work brings them into contact with the patients or residents of such institutions. I believe that these questions are as big as any that can be asked about social policy — involving, as they do, the nature of social control and equality.

In Britain and other countries during the early part of the nineteenth century the principal instrument of social care was the mixed institution for people of both sexes and all ages. The sick were mingled with the infirm aged, orphaned children and unmarried mothers. The evolution of medicine and the primitive experiments which were undertaken in children's and other social work services gradually supplied a basis for a classified system of institutions. Sharper distinctions were made between different conditions and needs. In Britain three main groups of hospitals evolved — general, mental and chronic — but many special hospitals were also opened — for children, for women and for those suffering from tuberculosis and fevers, for example. Similarly, the number of different types of residential, convalescent and nursing Homes also multiplied, some of them for people of a particular age or sex. In theory, each type of institution served a distinct segment of the population and had the purpose of treating a specific and clearly identifiable need which, it was supposed, could not be met in the ordinary community.

In some respects the trend in favour of specialized units has continued since the war. In most countries, so far as I am aware, the number of different kinds of institutions and Homes for old people, for example, has grown. Some authorities would carry this even further. The clinical and administrative arguments are strong, because specialists and trained personnel are scarce and equipment is expensive. Consultants do not have to waste time travelling to see their patients. It is also conceptually neater for fund-raising organizations who have to devise advertisements for the radio and press.

But opposing arguments have come to the fore, which throw doubt on the whole case for having, say, special hospitals for the chronic sick, special Homes for the blind or for spastics, and special institutions for mentally handicapped girls or boys. Modern society is faced with a fundamental dilemma. Put simply, it is torn between the desire to segregate people for treatment according to their physical and social condition and the desire to give them the advantage of living in a 'normal' community.

I am going to attempt to disentangle some of the strands in the argument for gradually replacing many long-stay institutions with alternative accommodation and services. Necessarily I must lean on British experience, though I believe it to be similar, in many important respects, to that of other countries. I am also going to depend, for much of my evidence, on a national survey of old people's Homes recently carried out in England and Wales (1). This was a project undertaken by a small research team from London University during the four years 1957-61, and financed by the Nuffield Foundation. Nearly 200 old people's Homes were visited and information collected, by means of interviews, from hundreds of local administrators, wardens, matrons and nurses and elderly residents.

Residential Institutions and Homes for the Aged in England

In England and Wales there are about 155,000 people aged 65 and over, or about 3 per cent of the population of this age, in mental and other hospitals and nursing Homes. There are a further 100,000, representing another 1½ per cent, in residential institutions and Homes. About a third of them live in Homes owned and managed by religious and voluntary associations or by private individuals. The rest live in Homes managed by the local authorities — in this instance county and county borough councils. The Government exercises general control over the policies of the councils through the Ministry of Health.

At the end of the last war the Labour Government had attempted to remove the final traces of the poor law. Some of the old institutions were re-classified as hospitals under the National Health Service. Others remained with the local authorities and formed the basis of a new residential service for the aged and handicapped who were, in the words of the legislation, 'in need of care and attention'. Speaking of the new service in 1947 the Minister of Health, Aneurin Bevan, stated that the institution was obsolete and was going to be replaced. 'Although many people have tried to humanize it, it was in many respects a very evil institution . . . Bigness is the enemy of humanity.' He went on to describe the new Homes which were to be opened — for a maximum of 25-30 persons, 'so that any old persons who wish to go may go there in exactly the same way as many well-to-do people have been accustomed to go into residential hotels'. Government spokesmen are often contradicted by events and during the next fifteen years few of the old institutions were in fact pulled down. In 1960 they still provided nearly half the accommodation owned by the local authorities — mostly in units with 100, 200 or more beds (2).

But since 1948 well over a thousand Homes have been converted from large houses or newly built by the local authorities. In the early years emphasis was placed on converted premises with up to thirty-five beds, whether in urban or rural surroundings. By the mid-1950s the disadvantages of old buildings and remoteness from urban centres came to be recognized and the Government recommended new buildings with up to sixty beds, mainly in four- and six-bedded rooms, and preferably sited in urban areas. In the last few years, the emphasis has changed again in favour of smaller Homes containing mainly single and double bedrooms. Government policy has therefore followed a chequered course. The post-war Homes compare favourably with the old institutions and by previous standards are comfortable, well furnished and well staffed. Nonetheless, like similar institutions in other countries, they fall short of desirable standards and their function is becoming more and more uncertain.

Are they intended to be for active but lonely people as well as for incapacitated people? And do they serve loneliness and incapacity well? Are old people better off in such a communal environment rather than in independent flats with social services on call and, say, a small restaurant nearby? Moreover, to give one illustration of the way in which these uncertainties affect staff, should the women in charge of communal Homes behave like hospital matrons, hotel manageresses or devoted daughters? There are many questions of this kind which must be asked.

Subject-Matter for Research into Institutional Care

Furnishing evidence so as to answer these questions is not easy. Comparatively little scientific information about communal Homes has so far been collected and published. In order to assess their functions and decide their future place in social policy it is necessary to explore the following major subjects:

1 *Reasons for admission.* The physical, psychological and social factors bringing about the admission of people to Homes. These can be shown by comparing the populations of inmates with the external elderly population, as well as by tracing the background and experience of people admitted.

2 *The quality of the domiciliary welfare services.* The extent to which people admitted to Homes do in fact receive help from public and voluntary welfare services, and from private agencies before their admission (and after their discharge); the general nature and scale of such services.

3 *The quality of the domiciliary health services.* The extent to which people admitted to Homes do in fact receive medical and nursing care, publicly and privately, before their admission (and after their discharge); the general nature and scale of such services.

4 *The quality of facilities and services available in institutions and*

Homes. The extent to which defined standards of physical convenience and comfort (numbers of W.C.s, baths, handbasins, different kinds of furnishings, cubic space and square feet per bed, etc.) are reached in different types of Homes; staffing ratios in relation to degrees of handicap in institutional populations; level of medical, nursing and attendant services and how they compare, in quality and frequency, with similar services available at home.

5 *The degree of incapacity for self-care among the residents.* Assessments of mobility and incapacity, using independent measures and indexes as well as rating scales applied by staff (including medical and psychiatric staff).

6 *The sociology of the institution.* Relationships among residents, staff, and between residents and staff; relationships between residents and families and friends; evaluation of degree to which the institutional population corresponds with an ordinary community. The operation of the organization in relation to the external social system.

7 *The question of institutionalization.* Changes in the physical, psychological and social condition of persons after admission; nutritional level, appearance, demeanour, participation in communal activities and so on; how far such changes might be attributable to institutional environment and regime.

8 *The general attitudes of elderly residents to communal living.* Attitudes towards privacy, material comfort, occupation, independence and dependence, companionship, friendship, family, staff, and loss of home.

These appear to be the eight main subdivisions for investigation. It may be worth summarizing some of the results of the English survey in a form which closely corresponds with these subdivisions, in order to present a clear enough target for later and perhaps more exhaustive research.

A Summary of Evidence about Residential or Communal Homes

First, *the survey showed that a large proportion of elderly residents enter communal institutions and Homes mainly because of homelessness and lack of social and financial resources.* More than a quarter of a sample of residents newly admitted to Homes throughout England and Wales had lost their homes. Most of these were active people. They were evicted or threatened with eviction, were obliged to give up living with others because the statutory tenant was leaving the home or had been warned about overcrowding; were denied access to lodging houses and had been sleeping outdoors or in a variety of temporary shelters; or had lost their homes during a stay in hospital. Most of them were unable to turn to relatives or friends because they had none or because they had become separated from them. Of old people living in residential Homes 59 per cent proved to be unmarried or childless. Many of these did not have, or had little contact with, brothers and sisters and other relatives. Some of them could not find accommodation near the relatives they had. Little evidence was obtained of families being unwilling to help old people, but much evidence of the hardships of those who had no relatives of a younger generation, those who had experienced bereavement, and those whose only available relative had fallen ill or was herself or himself infirm. The bad condition of much housing, as well as poverty, had also undermined people's ability to maintain independence.

Secondly, *the domiciliary welfare and health services are not utilized to the full before admission, nor are they, in all areas, as fully developed for old people generally as they should be.* Fewer than a fifth of those admitted from private households had been receiving home help, meals and other services, beforehand, and only a fraction of these people had received them frequently during the week. Some had not seen their general practitioners in the months preceding admission and many were lacking in aids for disability — modern hearing aids, spectacles, surgical appliances and so on. It is of course arguable that some of them would have been able to maintain independence for longer with such aids. Again, a considerable volume of evidence suggested that while domiciliary services for the aged are much more highly developed in England than in most other countries they are nonetheless inadequate and need to be expanded three-, four- or five-fold during the next decade.

Thirdly, *some services provided in communal Homes are very poor, and many people who are seriously incapacitated, including those with psychiatric disorders, receive comparatively little skilled attention.* The physical condition of many old institutions was found to be bad, and toilet and other facilities in these and in many of the post-war Homes were not satisfactory. They compared unfavourably with the facilities obtainable in the vast majority of private households. Even Homes which were newly built often contained shared rather than individual facilities and furnishings. There were too few staff and scarcely any had received special training. Rarely was there any routine medical surveillance. Fewer opportunities of obtaining physiotherapy, psychotherapy and other forms of treatment were available to the residents than to hospital patients and there was a shortage of aids for disabilities. Staff and residents frequently complained of the uncertain division of responsibility between hospitals and residential Homes. Some old people had experienced several transfers from one to the other.

Fourthly, *a large proportion of the old people living in communal Homes are able to look after themselves in homes of their own.* A sample of several hundred new residents was interviewed and information about their capacities was checked with members of the staff and case-records. By using a specially defined measure of incapacity it was found that over half were physically and mentally capable of leading an independent life. They required little or no help. Some were complementing the work of the staff, cleaning bedrooms, making beds, and preparing and serving meals. Another fifth could live independently if they had considerable assistance but the remaining quarter could do so only if they had a great deal of help every day in the home, for they were extremely frail. When compared with other data, this conclusion was found to apply broadly to the whole population of residential Homes.

Next, *entering a Home has certain critical effects upon the behaviour and attitudes of old people.* The survey showed that in England old people experienced a loss of occupation. Many of them had formerly prepared their own meals, for example. Now none of them did so. They were expected to sit and have most things done for them. Occupational therapy was successful on only a minor scale. They experienced isolation from family, friends and community. Some were living in Homes which were far from urban centres. Others lived considerable distances from relatives and friends. Frequent visits were not feasible. Moreover, such visits as there were tended to dwindle rapidly in number. Visitors could rarely be entertained in privacy, or given tea, for example. Neither were they encouraged to do small services for the residents. They were conscious that this would be regarded as interference with staff routine. External relationships were therefore controlled and limited. The residents' new internal relationships were also tenuous. Only about one in five had made a friend of another resident. Most were reserved in their relationships with residents and also with staff. Some were openly hostile and sought solitude on every opportunity. They showed only too plainly that to live under one roof in the company of a large number of people of the same age does not of itself create a community. Nor does it dispel loneliness. Nearly half the new residents said they were often or sometimes lonely — a much larger fraction than found in surveys of the elderly population at home. Although such feelings could often be attributed to recent bereavement, infirmity or the loss of home and possessions there was some evidence to suggest that they were sometimes reinforced by the shortcomings of institutional life. They also experienced loss of privacy and identity. Many missed not having their own clothing, furniture and other possessions. Three quarters expressed a preference for a single bedroom although only a fifth had one. All these experiences varied in severity from one type of Home to another but seemed to exist in some measure everywhere.

Finally, *the majority of those entering a Home appear not to want to stay permanently in such a place,* although permanent residence is normally assumed to be a condition of admission. Only a sixth of the new residents entering local authority Homes in the English survey had applied for admission on their own initiative. Only a third said they wished to stay in a residential Home, and some of these wished to be in a different one. It is of course extremely difficult to elucidate the true feelings of old persons living in institutions. Some are inscrutable. Others seem to think there is no practicable alternative to entering a Home. Many are understandably ambivalent in their attitudes. They say how contented they are in a Home and how much better off they are than formerly; then they go on to lament the loss of home and friends and say they would do anything to return to where they were again. They make the best they honestly can of conflicting loyalties to their families, to welfare officers, to the staff of the Homes and to their own personal ideals. The data did not suggest that such people are generally querulous and complaining. Some of the residents who were interviewed in the course of the research complained strongly about the staff or the facilities of the Home but they were a minority and even they often balanced their criticisms with praise. The rest were unwilling to make any criticism and, indeed, paid generous tributes to the staff. When many of them went on nonetheless to say how much they wanted to return to a home of their own it was difficult to ignore the intensity of this desire for independence.

The Argument Against the Communal Home

The evidence summarized briefly in this article needs to be elaborated and confirmed. We possess much too little knowledge about the capacities and opinions as well as the social relationships of institutionalized persons, and the eight areas of investigation which are listed above furnish an immense programme of research.

But in the meantime decisions have to be taken and services for old people maintained by governments, local councils and religious and voluntary associations. The latter cannot wait for new surveys to be completed. Sometimes they work with extremely flimsy evidence. Research workers may serve them better by drawing clear if tentative conclusions from such slim evidence as they possess than by drawing no conclusions at all. In this instance the immediate steps in the process of generalization seem to be straightforward. Old people's Homes could themselves be improved in various ways to provide something more closely resembling the kind of environment and life enjoyed by persons living at home. The physical design and facilities, for example, could be better, with single bedrooms, more small lounges, kitchenettes, toilet amenities, workrooms and so on. They could be smaller in size, with up to twenty-five beds. Staff could be given intensive short courses of training. And the residents could be allowed greater freedom of choice in their daily lives. To give a few examples at random: those who take up residence for more than a few weeks might be allowed to furnish their rooms with as many articles of their own furniture as they wish (displacing, if necessary, any publicly-owned furniture in that room). They might be given the chance of preparing and cooking the midday meal, or of bathing themselves without supervision or assistance. But would reforms such as these be enough? I doubt whether they would.

My argument would proceed from the research conclusions described above to the very nature of specialized long-stay institutions. Individuals from diverse localities and backgrounds are brought together under one roof and are expected to share most of the events of daily life. They are often people of one sex who resemble each other in age and physical or mental condition. Paid staff are there to care for them and a common routine is established. The resulting 'community' is in many ways an artificial one. It does not consist of people of both sexes and all ages, linked by overlapping family, occupational and neighbourhood ties, whose relationships are reinforced by the help they can give each other. Their powers of self-expression and self-help are limited. They are not expected, nor are they often allowed, to do much for one another. In a thousand details the matron or superintendent and the staff take over from old people the responsibility for making decisions about everyday life. They are often excessively protective, for example, from a desire to avoid accidents. Or it is quicker and more efficient to do certain tasks themselves than leave them to the old people. Once the process starts it is difficult to stop. It is therefore not surprising to find that most residents yearn for privacy, independence, familiar haunts and some occupation to justify life, even when they appreciate warmth, some degree of comfort, and a good diet.

There are other reasons for having misgivings about the future of long-stay institutions. Old people tend to suffer not from a single but from a number of physical and psychiatric complaints. Their level of health sometimes improves or deteriorates from week to week. It is difficult to classify them into neat administrative categories. To insist that we should is to invite administrative confusion, particularly at a time when the elderly population is growing rapidly, and also to risk some of them not getting skilled medical or psychiatric treatment and supervision when they need it. Individuals cannot be transferred ruthlessly from one type of institution to another as their health improves or deteriorates without them paying some price in psychological security.

Moreover, professional opinion is moving against the incarceration of certain patients for long periods in institutions and in favour of giving them every possible chance of living in the community. The discovery of new drugs and methods of surgery, together with more general developments in psychiatry and geriatrics, has to a large extent made this possible. There is now much more emphasis on active treatment and rehabilitation, even for long-stay patients. The Ministry of Health now assumes that the total population of mental hospitals will decline by more than a third in the next fifteen years and that, *despite* the increase in the number of old people, there will be no need for an increase in the number of geriatric beds in hospital (3). In two or three areas chronic sick patients have been placed successfully in housing which has been specially designed and equipped. But in all countries there is a long way to go. Little has yet been done to develop adequate services at home or in the community. This is a great challenge. The danger is that the rising costs of hospitalization may cause too many patients to be discharged to their own homes or to cheaper welfare accommodation before sufficient efforts have been made to see that they have access to skilled treatment and supervision. The argument that it is cheaper to care for people at home rather than in institutions is often a disreputable one. Usually it amounts to saying, 'It is cheaper to give people practically no services in the home than give them modest services in a state institution.'

All this suggests a radical approach to future policy. At least in densely populated areas it can be argued that all in-patient facilities should be reorganized in truly 'general' hospitals run on multi-purpose lines (4). These hospitals would exist mainly for people staying for brief periods who require surgery and other forms of treatment which cannot be given them in their own homes. They would possess larger out-patient departments and would include certain convalescent units, whether medical, psychiatric or geriatric. The geriatric units would include provisions for *some* of the kind of people who live today in Homes for the aged — those requiring temporary care while they recover from malnutrition, say, those on the borderline of chronic sickness and those needing care during the day.

Most other types of institutions might be gradually abandoned by creating sheltered housing and a much richer variety of home services. Those institutions that remain would have the purpose of assisting individuals through a transition from adversity or dependence to an independent home life. By sheltered housing I mean small groups of flatlets or bungalows in which old or handicapped people can live independently but where there are certain communal services if required and a housekeeper who is on call. Experiments on such lines have been carried out in several countries in recent years. By home services I mean health and family help services. There is an urgent need for the expansion of health and hospital after-care services provided by medical practitioners in the home or in local clinics. The old and handicapped often seem to be at the end of the list of medical priorities. They should receive regular medical visits and examinations and general practitioners might be encouraged to work more often in small groups, so that they can have the ancillary assistance (such as a health visitor and a district nurse) to enable them to do this. There is also an urgent need for the development of a comprehensive local family help service, knitting together the various domiciliary services that already exist in many areas, though usually on a small and improvised scale. One of its objects would be to provide family services for those who have no families. The other would be to provide 'supporting' services for those families who carry a heavy burden in caring for old people at home. It would provide domestic help, shopping, laundry, meals, night attendance and occupational therapy, arrange holidays, supply household aids (such as handrails, wheelchairs, tripod walking-sticks and so on) and in other ways help the aged and handicapped. Its work should be based on the principle of trained social workers paying regular visits to all aged and handicapped persons in the population to assess their needs. This is not a task which can be taken on by religious and voluntary bodies. The population needing help is too large and the kinds of help required too complex. A substantial nucleus of full-time staff with considerable training is required. But voluntary bodies could play a major role by developing supplementary services such as friendly visiting and managing clubs and centres in partnership with the local authorities.

This is no more than a brief sketch of the kind of solution which seems to be implied by the research so far carried out. England is only now awakening to the needs of large sections of its elderly population. The scale of the problem simply was not anticipated in the early post-war years and the domiciliary health and welfare services in particular are grossly inadequate — however well they may compare with what exists in some other industrial countries. Even now those in charge of the social services give the impression of running fast to stay in the same place. In the past ten years the number of people in the British population aged eighty and over has increased by 35 per cent. During the same period the costs of hospitalization — partly due to the rise in the costs of drugs, nursing and surgery — have soared, and the competition for cheap housing for one or two persons has become even more acute. These are just a few of the reasons for the enforced emergence of the communal Home as a major instrument of social policy. There have been similar pressures in other countries.

Yet in Britain there is also an undercurrent of feeling against the long-stay institution which even includes the communal Home, of which recent years have supplied many examples, such as the relaxation of restrictions on mental patients, the improvements in children's Homes and the hopeful emphasis on treatment and rehabilitation. Once the sociology as well as the psychology of institutional care is fully grasped every effort is likely to be made to reduce the length of stay in Homes as well as in hospitals.

The communal Homes which were surveyed in the report summarized here compare favourably with many abroad. Local councils are in some respects justifiably proud of newly built Homes which incorporate good standards of design, comfort and service. I have tended to concentrate on their negative features simply to show the strength of the argument to gradually abandon them. No one would pretend that this can be done in the next few years. But if we look forward twenty years or more it is difficult to believe that society could not develop the sheltered housing and other social services that would make this possible. By doing so I believe the lives of many old people would be enriched and many of their problems averted. In a prosperous society which is also sensitive to individual freedom as well as individual social security the need for communal welfare institutions intermediate between home and hospital should be extremely small.

Notes and References

1 Townsend, P., *The Last Refuge: A Survey of Residential Institutions and Homes for the Aged in England and Wales*, Routledge & Kegan Paul, 1962.

2 [In subsequent years the proportion diminished as new Homes were opened and some of the old institutions were closed. Between 1960 and 1969 the number of places in old institutions was reduced from 37,000 to 21,000.]

3 Ministry of Health, *A Hospital Plan for England and Wales*, Cmnd. 1604, H.M.S.O., 1962.

4 See, for example, McKeown, T., 'The Concept of the Balanced Hospital Community', *The Lancet*, 5 April 1955; McKeown, T., 'Fundamental Problems in Hospital Planning', *The Lancet*, 4 April 1959; Smith, S., 'Psychiatry in General Hospitals', *The Lancet*, 27 May 1961.

11 Nursing homes in England and Wales*

The growth of a system of public health, education, child care or
general welfare is a slow and often confused process. It is not simply
that time and money are needed to build or adapt hospitals, clinics,
schools, residential Homes and so on, and to recruit and train staff —
whether nurses, doctors, teachers or social workers. In giving effect to
the declared aims of policy those in administrative charge must, of
necessity, evolve a thickening web of definitions, regulations and
standards which must somehow be consistent and promote the ends of
policy. Terms and conditions of service for individual employees have
to be devised, areas of public responsibility defined, and resources
distributed in accordance with some principles of equity. It is almost as
if a book of rules has to be compiled to govern the play of various
complex games. This 'book' reflects the moral values of a society and
may seem to be admirably appropriate so long as that society remains
stable in structure and continues to subscribe to certain basic values.
Minor blemishes and inconsistencies can from time to time be
eliminated and refinements added. But it can be a very real handicap in
a period of rapid social change. Even before any plans can be made for
new services to meet emerging needs the hoary assumptions deeply
embedded in the management and organization of existing services have
to be dug out and scrutinized. As a democratic society becomes more
highly organized it is probably harder rather than easier to introduce
sweeping reforms.

   The problem can be illustrated from the history of health and
welfare institutions in Britain. In the nineteenth century it came to be
recognized that there were various groups of individuals with widely
differing needs: those ravaged by infectious disease, the chronic sick
and aged infirm, orphans, unmarried mothers and the workless. They
were unable to cope with their own problems and could not be blamed

* Extracts from Woodroffe, C., and Townsend, P., *Nursing Homes in England
and Wales: A Study of Public Responsibility*. The National Corporation for the
Care of Old People, 1961. The study was treated as a companion (though on a
much smaller scale) to the major national survey of residential Homes for old
people, reported in *The Last Refuge*, 1962.

for not anticipating their adversities. Society had to organize appropriate help and succour. It had to protect them from exploitation as well as misguided philanthropy, not only by setting up an efficient system of public services but by supervising those provided voluntarily or for private gain. The evolution of medicine and the primitive experiments undertaken in child care and social work supplied a basis for a classified system of care. The Poor Law Act of 1834 encouraged a Victorian zeal for classification and it can be argued that the development of a system of highly specialized types of hospitals and other institutions continued almost uninterruptedly for over a hundred years until the early years after the Second World War. The system was by no means perfect but at least it gave the impression of simple logic — of a range of institutions roughly classified according to type of illness and/or individual condition (age, sex and type of deprivation). Thus in time there were tuberculosis, fever, mental and chronic sick hospitals, convalescent and nursing Homes, and different types of residential Homes for children, the handicapped and the aged. In theory each type of institution served a distinct segment of the population and had the purpose of meeting a specific and clearly identifiable need, which, it was supposed, could not be met in the ordinary community. The growth of legislation and administrative regulations by which institutions were organized, managed and supervised was largely based on this fundamental premise.

But two unanticipated developments have confused, and to some extent arrested, this trend. These two are interrelated and mutually reinforcing. First of all, the growth of the elderly population in the last twenty or thirty years has thrown doubt on the differentiation of institutions by function. Old people today comprise the bulk of the patients or residents in many institutions and it is difficult to classify them into neat groups — because they often have a variety of disabilities and complaints. People in roughly the same condition can be found in chronic sick, general and mental hospitals, as well as in nursing Homes, old people's Homes and so on. In a period when the population is ageing the retention of a highly classified list (with 'half-way' Homes and mental 'hostels' added to that list) seems of very doubtful value. The administrative problems become nightmarish but, much more important, the patients or residents are likely to suffer. Many of their needs may not be met, simply because certain forms of treatment or care are not available in the particular types of institutions in which they live, or can be met only at the price of frequent upheavals, by transferring them ruthlessly from one type of institution to another as their physical and mental condition improves or deteriorates.

Secondly, and more generally, human needs are now recognized to be much more complex than formerly assumed. In the light of modern knowledge it is increasingly difficult to place individuals in tidy categories and to take a simple-minded view of the function of institutions. Hospital patients, for example, are now commonly seen to have psychological and social as well as physical and medical needs. It is no longer possible to justify with equanimity their exclusion from the life of the outside community — from people of other ages and the opposite sex, from relatives, neighbours and friends — or to ignore the arguments that, in the interests of their health as well as of their psychological security, they should be helped to return as quickly as possible to their own homes. Thus we have witnessed the introduction of unrestricted visiting; the opening of hospital workshops, day-rooms and cafeterias; the rapid growth of out-patient facilities, day hospitals and specialist consultations at home; the growing emphasis on speedy rehabilitation — even from mental and chronic sick hospitals; and the recent proposals from some quarters to organize in-patient facilities in truly 'general' hospitals run on multi-purpose lines, rather than by maintaining the broad divisions between mental, chronic sick and existing 'general' hospitals. Some of these developments are still in their infancy but the old philosophy of the institution is in the melting pot, and as a result the administrative problems of definition, classification, supervision and inspection have been intensified.

Although this study deals in detail only with nursing Homes attention is drawn to difficulties which are common to many types of institution or Home — such as the problems of meeting social as well as medical needs, of ensuring that both the person in charge and the premises are 'fit' or 'adequate' according to some reasonable criterion, and of safeguarding the interests of individual patients rather than of administrative entities.

Concern has been expressed recently about the treatment of old people and others in private nursing Homes. On 5 December 1960 the Minister of Health stated that he was considering suggestions for strengthening the powers of local authorities in their relations with the proprietors of all these Homes. It is difficult, however, to evolve a new policy or assess an existing one when information is scarce. According to the Ministry of Health there are nearly 1,200 registered nursing Homes in England and Wales, with about 18,700 beds, but little is known publicly about current standards of treatment, staffing, fees, and number and kind of patients. Since 1948, in fact, no systematic research has been carried out into nursing services outside the National Health Service.

A small research project was carried out at the London School of Economics between September 1960 and May 1961. The object of the research was first, to review the practices followed in registering and inspecting nursing Homes, and secondly, to provide preliminary information, of both a statistical and illustrative kind, about the management, functions, and problems of these Homes. To fulfil the second object the proprietors of 227 nursing Homes selected at random were asked to complete a short questionnaire sent to them with an accompanying letter.

The History of Control of Nursing Homes

Nursing Homes are registered today under the Public Health Act of 1936 (1) which replaced without changing in any important respect the original Nursing Homes Registration Act of 1927 (2). This legislation has remained in force without amendment for the past twenty-five years. The Second World War and the birth of the National Health Service have left no mark. To understand many of the difficulties which arise at the present time it is necessary to trace in some detail the history, and the ambiguities, of this legislation.

In the last decades of the nineteenth century the increasing acceptance by the middle classes of the advantages of being nursed away from home as paying patients and the simultaneous reluctance of voluntary hospitals to accommodate them created a demand for private hospitals and nursing Homes (3). From about 1870 they grew rapidly in number. By 1900 there were fifty nursing Homes in London alone. Already by this date there were complaints of abuses. In 1905, urged on by those representing trained nurses, a committee set up to consider the registration of nurses recommended the compulsory registration and inspection of the Homes. From the first, emphasis was placed as much on the qualifications of the nurses as on the condition of the premises.

Bills for the registration of nursing Homes were unsuccessfully presented to Parliament in 1904 and 1925 (4). In March 1926, a Select Committee was appointed 'to consider and inquire into the question of the inspection and supervision of nursing Homes and to report what legislation, if any, is necessary or desirable for this purpose' (5). The committee reported in July of that year.

One of the first concerns of the committee was to include maternity Homes in the definition of nursing Homes. The registration of the former was imminent and had seemed to many people to be a logical development. The state had already 'recognized a special liability in relation to maternity and infant welfare by the passing of the Maternity and Child Welfare Act, and the payments of grants in aid' (6). Experiments in registration had been conducted in London and Manchester, and when the Select Committee presented their report in July 1926, a bill providing for the registration of maternity Homes in all areas was actually before Parliament. The bill was passed in August (7). The way was smoothed for the registration of the others.

The Select Committee reported that 'the Society of Medical Officers of Health are convinced of the urgent need for the registration of maternity Homes — the registration of all nursing Homes is a most necessary corollary' (8). To refrain from taking this next step seemed wrong in principle as well as impractical. There was the danger that medical, surgical and chronic sick patients would be neglected. In the 1920s no less than in other periods of Britain's social history, mothers and children were more effective objects of public pity than the elderly sick. Moreover, the experience of registering only one type of Home in London and Manchester had shown that a reform too narrowly conceived might not even achieve success within its own limits. The principle of public registration might be discredited. A maternity Home with standards falling below those required for registration could readily change itself into a general nursing Home and subject other kinds of patients to undesirable conditions. Finally, partial registration was to a large extent unrealistic since, although some Homes contained maternity patients only, others contained medical, surgical and chronic sick patients too. If only 10 per cent or 20 per cent of the patients in a particular Home were maternity patients how was control to be enforced? The Select Committee strongly recommended that separate registration of maternity Homes should be replaced by the registration of all nursing Homes.

The proposal was discussed largely in terms of whether it was desirable to impose government control on a private enterprise. Non-maternity nursing Homes were still regarded as properly and rightfully independent; the state was reluctant to accept any responsibility. The Government was not particularly enthusiastic about any proposal to restrict the freedom of a business in order to protect consumers. In their statement to the Select Committee, the Ministry of Health said that although 'in favour of registration and inspection of maternity homes in the fulfilment of their functions regarding public health and child welfare, they were not aware of any conditions which would make it advisable to interfere, by means of control or supervision, with what may be regarded as a legitimate industry'.

However, the Select Committee felt both that there was a need for a general reform and that public opinion was ready for it. Despite the claim of the British Medical Association to be 'ignorant of widespread abuses', the College of Nursing and the Society of Medical Officers reported a real and urgent need. The College of Nursing had collected a long list of signatures from matrons and owners of nursing Homes demanding a minimum proportion of registered nurses in every Home. The Society of Medical Officers reported that 'privately managed nursing Homes form the source of constant complaints from all parts of the country'. The committee pointed out that the Ministry had not heard of complaints because there was no channel through which they could come, and because no inquiry or investigation had been made.

Nursing Homes were found by the Select Committee to 'range from a specially built, properly equipped, private hospital, to a totally inadequate, frequently insanitary dwelling house. The person or body of persons in virtual control may be a committee, a medical practitioner, a qualified nurse, or a totally unqualified individual, carrying on the nursing Home as a main or subsidiary business proposition.' The evidence brought before the committee described unsuitable buildings, overcrowded and often insanitary; extreme neglect of patients (9), especially of the 'senile' (10); and small or non-existent nursing staffs. 'Patients are frequently quite unaware that the uniformed individuals in charge of them are in many cases quite unqualified girls with no real training.' The committee concluded from the evidence that classification of existing nursing Homes by the type of patients cared for was not feasible. Medical, maternity, convalescent, and chronic sick patients were all cared for together, and some Homes 'may even combine the taking in of patients with the letting of rooms to lodgers'. Numbers of Homes or of patients were not known.

The detailed recommendations, and the act they produced, were coloured with compromise. There were difficulties in securing adequate legislation. Due to the general shortage of nurses a minimum proportion of trained nurses could not be fixed. Inspection was reduced to a minimum, the attitude of the committee being that patients went into nursing Homes for privacy, and inspection should not be allowed to intrude too rigorously. Moreover, although by recommending registration the Committee had invaded one area of private enterprise, another, the medical profession, was determined to dissociate itself from government control. The doctors, represented by the British Medical Association, would only agree with nursing Home registration if the registering authorities were to delegate their powers to a committee including nurses and doctors, if nursing Homes run by doctors were to be exempt from inspection and if no medical records in nursing Homes could be inspected by the representative of any 'lay body'. The act satisfied the doctors on only the last point.

The committee recommended registration and inspection, but they thought that this was only a partial and temporary expedient. The real problem was the 'senile and chronic sick' among that class of persons who did not 'desire to incur the stigma of a Poor Law institution', but who could not pay at the same rate, and did not need the same equipment, as acutely ill patients. This was 1926; the remedy suggested was the separation of the two groups, and for the senile and chronic sick 'the provision of proper paying accommodation by the local authorities'.

The Nursing Homes Registration Act was passed in 1927, to be replaced, with only small alterations, by the Public Health Act of 1936, under which nursing Homes are registered today (11). A nursing Home is defined as 'any premises . . . for the reception of, and the providing of nursing for, persons suffering from any sickness, injury, or infirmity', and includes a maternity Home (12), but excludes any public authority or Royal Charter hospital or any mental hospital or Home (13).

Under the act any person who 'carries on' a nursing Home without being registered by the local authority commits an offence (14). The local authority is a county council, a county borough, or (where the county council delegates its powers) a county district council.

Registration may be refused for the following reasons:

1 if the proprietor or an employee is not a 'fit' person to run that particular Home or to work in it;
2 if the premises are not 'fit' or will be improperly used;
3 if, in a Home that is not a maternity Home, there is not in charge and resident a registered medical practitioner or a 'qualified' nurse, or if there is not a 'proper' proportion of qualified nurses on the staff;
4 if in a maternity Home the superintendent of nursing is not a qualified nurse or a certified midwife, or if any person employed 'in attending any woman in the home in childbirth or in nursing any patient in the home is not either a registered medical practitioner, a certified midwife, a pupil midwife, or a qualified nurse'.

The same grounds may be used for cancelling registration, and when registration is refused or cancelled the proprietor may appeal to the courts against a local authority's decision. The ambiguity of these conditions has crippled the power of the local authorities, as will be shown later. Proprietors may take the case to court and, since there is no standard definition of 'fit' or 'proper', usually win.

An inspector, appointed by the local authority, may enter and inspect any nursing Home or suspected nursing Home, and if the authority requires records to be kept he may inspect these. (The act empowers local authorities to pass by-laws prescribing the records to be kept of patients admitted or children born, and the notice to be given of deaths.) But — the concession to privacy and the B.M.A. — the act specifically does not authorize the representative of the local authority to 'inspect any medical record relating to a patient in a nursing home' (15). This has been taken also to mean no medical examination of patients.

Local authorities may grant exemption from registration and inspection to 'any hospital or institution not carried on for profit', or to what is generally known as a voluntary Home, usually run by a voluntary society. Exemption may be refused or withdrawn and may be made conditional. The act gives no guidance as to legitimate grounds for refusing exemption but the intention is presumably that voluntary Homes with low standards of care should be inspected. The proprietor of a voluntary nursing Home may appeal to the Minister if aggrieved by refusal or withdrawal of exemption, or by the conditions attached by the local authority.

Under the Mental Health Act of 1959 mental nursing Homes are now also registered with general nursing Homes, although special provisions have been added.

The Problems of Definition

Several crucial terms in the act are ill-defined. The definition of a nursing Home is inadequate, and depends largely on the vague words 'the providing of nursing'. Does 'nursing' include personal and housekeeping services? Should hotels and guest houses with a few elderly residents who receive some attention from a nurse be included? And is a retired nurse who takes an elderly infirm friend into her home and looks after her running a nursing Home? These questions indicate some of the present difficulties.

Other examples can be given. A higher standard of nursing qualifications is required in a maternity than in a general nursing Home, but the designation of a Home with both maternity and other patients is not made clear. The legal definition of a maternity Home is 'any premises ... for the reception of pregnant women, or of women immediately after childbirth'. The intention of the act seems to be that a maternity Home may have other patients as well; the nursing requirements specifically apply both to 'any woman in the home in childbirth' and to 'any patient in the home'. The result of this interpretation would be that an elderly patient in a 'maternity Home' must be nursed by a qualified nurse, while an elderly patient in a Home with no maternity patients may be nursed by an unqualified one. The London County Council, on the other hand, interprets a maternity Home as one 'into which maternity cases only are received'. 'Any patient in the Home' is taken to mean any maternity patient not actually 'in childbirth'. Maternity patients in general nursing Homes in London are protected by a special instruction conveyed to proprietors (16).

The definition of a 'qualified nurse' is usually limited by the act to a state registered nurse (17). However, nurses listed elsewhere than in the general part of the register (male nurses, mental nurses, and children's nurses) may count as qualified 'in premises solely for a class of patients in whose case the requisite nursing can be suitably and adequately provided by' them. If this means anything it is that a male nurse, for example, may not be in charge or count towards the proportion of qualified nurses in a Home unless all the patients are men. And a mental nurse is similarly disqualified unless the Home is 'solely' for mentally disordered patients. Moreover, no amendment has been made, as a result of the Nurses Act of 1943, to include state enrolled nurses among those designated as qualified. Therefore S.E.N.s may not count towards the proper proportion of qualified nurses in a general nursing Home, and may not be employed in 'nursing' any patient in a maternity Home. It is clear that in practice local authorities do consider S.E.N.s to be 'qualified', at least as regards being members of the nursing staff. However, these various problems are overshadowed by the absence of any definition in the act of a 'proper' proportion of qualified nurses.

The act provides for the compulsory registration of anyone who 'carries on' a nursing Home, but again the term is ambiguous. Does the person with the controlling financial interest 'carry on' a Home, or the person who manages it day by day? There is some administrative confusion (18).

Finally, two of the four grounds for refusing or cancelling registration depend on the undefined word 'fit'. Some guidance is given. A person may be unfit 'by reason of age or otherwise', and premises may be unfit 'by reasons connected with situation, construction, state of repair, accommodation, staffing, or equipment'. This is extremely vague, and in practice much is left to the discretion of the local authority. In the case of an appeal, however, there is no room for discretion; the person or premises must be proved 'unfit' before a jury, and official regulations give no precise guidance as to the interpretation of the legislation.

By the legal definition nearly all institutions providing nursing care and accommodation outside the National Health Service *could* be classified as nursing Homes (19). This is not the practice. Local authorities have taken a definition which roughly excludes three groups — convalescent, disabled persons' and old people's Homes, and some large voluntary hospitals. The distinctions are somewhat arbitrary and artificial and appear to be based to some extent on the qualifications of the staff, rather than the requirements of the patients or residents. A private nursing Home where, as is often the case, all patients are elderly and only some are bed-fast, may be almost indistinguishable from a private old people's Home, and a seaside nursing Home catering for 'all types convalescent — no heavy nursing', from a nearby convalescent Home. And yet the method of control varies; the nursing Homes are registered under the Public Health Act of 1936, the old people's Home comes under the National Assistance Act of 1948, and the convalescent Home is not registered at all.

Legal niceties cannot meet all or even most of the problems posed in the exercise of public responsibility for private and voluntary Homes which provide refuge for the sick, the infirm, and those unable to lead a normal life in homes of their own. But the confusion and ambiguity in current legislation inevitably add to the problems of suffering.

The National Picture

There were 1,188 registered nursing Homes in England and Wales in 1960, with a total of 18,666 beds (1,620 maternity and 17,046 other) (20). Since 1938, the first year for which information was obtained, the trend has been towards fewer and larger nursing Homes, with a much smaller proportion of maternity beds. Between 1938 and 1960 the number of all Homes fell by 55 per cent (21) while the number of all beds dropped by only 17 per cent. The number of maternity beds fell by 74 per cent while, despite the fall in the total number of beds, the number of beds reserved for purposes other than maternity rose by 5 per cent. In the past ten years the total number of beds has fluctuated between 18,500 and 20,000, but while there are now less than half as many maternity beds as in 1950 the number of beds used for other purposes has tended to increase, being about 2,500, or 17 per cent more, than in 1950. Table 1 shows the figures in more detail.

Table 1 Registered nursing homes and beds in England and Wales: 1938-60 (a)

Year	Homes	Beds			Maternity beds as % of total	Average size of homes
		Maternity	Other	Total		
1938	2,663	6,271	16,276	22,547	27.8	8.5
.....	.....	.....	......	......	....	....
1948	2,190	6,921	15,855	22,776	29.7	10.4
1949	1,991	5,419	15,192	20,611	26.3	10.4
1950	1,742	4,106	14,580	18,686	22.0	10.7
1951	1,650	3,490	16,347	19,837	17.6	12.0
1952	1,606	3,504	15,784	19,288	18.2	12.0
1953	1,578	3,178	16,152	19,330	16.4	12.2
1954	1,467	2,599	16,098	18,697	13.9	12.7
1955	1,456	2,567	17,007	19,574	13.1	13.5
1956	1,417	2,325	17,456	19,837	11.7	14.0
1957	1,340	2,110	16,880	18,990	11.1	14.1
1958	1,271	1,858	16,834	18,692	9.9	14.7
1959	1,245	1,764	17,219	18,983	9.3	15.2
1960	1,188	1,620	17,046	18,666	8.7	15.7

(a) Source: Ministry of Health.

Nursing Homes are concentrated mainly in the home counties, the dormitory areas around London, and in middle-class or 'retirement' areas along the coast and in the south west of England. Like hotels they tend to cluster in pleasant and therefore profitable places, drawing patients from beyond local boundaries. In 1960 Kent, Sussex, Surrey, London and Hampshire had 41 per cent of all nursing Home beds between them, whereas in many parts of the country, particularly in Wales and parts of the Midlands and of the north of England there were no nursing Homes at all (22).

Most patients in nursing Homes are old people. In 1959 in England and Wales, for every 1,000 people over 65 there were 3.2 nursing Home beds for other than maternity cases. Hastings had 25.8 per 1,000 population over 65, Bournemouth 19.4, Croydon 15.9, Eastbourne 14.6, Southport 12.9, and West Sussex 13.5. By contrast with the national figure of 3.2 for nursing Homes, there were approximately 7.0 beds per 1,000 population over 65 in voluntary and private old people's Homes and 10.7 in chronic sick and geriatric departments of N.H.S. hospitals. As would be expected, those areas with a relatively large number of nursing Homes often had a relatively large number of voluntary and private old people's Homes as well.

The *registered* nursing Homes which we have described do not account for all the nursing Home accommodation outside the Health Service in England and Wales. For the first time in 1959 and 1960 the Ministry of Health collected statistics from the local authorities for voluntary nursing Homes which *had been granted exemption.* (These are not included in Table 1.) In 1960 there were 114 such Homes with a total of 5,496 beds, of which 234 (4.3 per cent) were for maternity purposes. Besides the voluntary Homes granted exemption there are numbers of other voluntary nursing Homes and hospitals which are in fact exempt because they have never been considered liable for registration by local authorities. No one knows quite how many of these there are, but in 1960 in the area of the South-West Metropolitan Regional Hospital Board alone there were at least 18 such Homes, 16 of which contained 1,119 beds. In the same area there were also at least 15 private or voluntary convalescent and recuperative holiday Homes, 9 of which contained 254 beds (23). Such Homes are not registered and statistics regarding them are not collected by the Ministry. This is a matter for public concern.

From 1961 the total of registered nursing Homes will be increased by the inclusion of mental nursing Homes. Several different categories of private and voluntary institution for the 'mentally disordered' will be reclassified and registered as mental nursing Homes, with voluntary Homes not having the possibility of exemption. In 1959 in England and

Wales there were approximately 96 such institutions with a total of 4,390 patients on 30 December 1959. Only 11 of these were actually called Mental Nursing Homes; the others included Licensed Houses, Approved Homes and Certified Institutions for mental defectives, Registered Hospitals, and 'Deemed' Hospitals for the mentally ill or mental defectives.

The Survey

The information sought from the proprietors of nursing Homes was deliberately limited in its scope. There were no previous studies on which to build and it seemed preferable to obtain a preliminary outline of the number and characteristics of such Homes, and their patients, in different parts of the country, before considering the desirability and scope of more intensive research. A short postal questionnaire was therefore drawn up in the hope that it would be completed by those in charge of a cross-section of nursing Homes throughout the country. It included questions about numbers, sex and age of patients, number and qualifications of nursing staff, weekly charges, frequency of inspection by local authorities and role of medical practitioners. Special information was sought about the number of elderly patients who were bedfast, incontinent, required help with dressing and were unable to walk outside without assistance. Proprietors were also invited to make comments about the difficulties of managing nursing Homes (to which many of them generously responded). As a check a small cross-section of Homes was also visited.

Information about patients was supplied by 130 proprietors of private nursing Homes. In 63 per cent all the patients were of pensionable age, in another 14 per cent all but one, and in a further 11 per cent more than half: 87 per cent of these Homes therefore catered entirely or mainly for elderly patients. The remaining 13 per cent were occupied by children and by maternity and younger surgical or convalescent patients. There were sixteen of these Homes. Two were for convalescent children, two were residential nurseries and one was for mentally or physically handicapped children under the age of twelve. Four more were exclusively for maternity patients, another four housed acute sick and surgical patients and the remaining three contained a mixed group of maternity, young surgical and both young and elderly convalescent patients.

Eighty-five per cent of all the patients in this sample of private nursing Homes were of pensionable age. Most of these were women and most were over 80 years of age. In fact nearly half the patients in these private nursing Homes were women of 80 years of age and over. Only

14.5 per cent of the patients of pensionable age were men, compared with 31.4 per cent in the entire elderly population of England and Wales. Nearly half these nursing Homes were occupied entirely by elderly women or contained only one elderly man among the women patients.

A second striking feature of the elderly patients is that the majority, namely 57 per cent, were unmarried or had no surviving children. This compares with a proportion of approximately 25 per cent in the elderly population of England and Wales and suggests that those with families are less liable to enter nursing Homes in old age.

The third striking feature of these elderly patients is the substantial numbers among them who were said not to be immobile or severely incapacitated. This requires some explanation. Proprietors were asked for information about the numbers of their patients who were permanently or temporarily bedfast, could not walk alone outside and needed at least some help in dressing. Approximately 26 per cent were said to need no help in dressing and altogether 23 per cent were said to be capable of walking outside the Home unaided. These are likely to be under-estimates rather than over-estimates (24). The proportions varied widely. In 7 per cent of the Homes all the patients were bedfast; yet in 17 per cent the majority were able to walk outside without help.

But the frailty of the majority of the elderly patients must also be emphasized. Nearly 20 per cent had been admitted direct from hospital. Sixty-eight per cent of the women and 57 per cent of the men were over 80 years of age. Several matrons drew attention to women in their nineties or even over 100 years old. Nearly 26 per cent of the patients were permanently in bed (25) and a further 11½ per cent temporarily so at the time of the inquiry. Another 36 per cent were said to require at least some help in dressing. Altogether 23 per cent were said to be incontinent.

These data imply certain consequences. They suggest, for example, that staffing provisions in nursing Homes serving old people need to be reviewed in relation to the capacities of the patients and also that there may be some problems affecting registration and inspection which have hitherto gone unrecognized. Broadly speaking, the large number of private nursing Homes in the sample which catered mainly or entirely for old people fell into three categories according to the capacities of their patients: (i) those in which there were a large number of bedfast chronic sick requiring a large amount of nursing care; (ii) those in which the very infirm, as distinct from either the chronic sick or the relatively active, predominated, and where a large amount of care and attention, but not a great deal of skilled nursing, was required; and (iii) those in which 'patients' who were able to do most things for themselves predominated, and where household, rather than personal or nursing services, were chiefly required. The following are examples of the three types:

> One nursing Home had 32 patients, 5 men and 27 women, all over 80. 24 were permanently bedfast, and 28 incontinent. The 8 patients not in bed all needed help dressing, and were unable to walk outside alone. There was one nurse for every 5 patients.
>
> In another Home all 37 patients were elderly. The three men were under 80, and of the women 5 were under 80, 25 between 80 and 90, and 4 were over 90. Only 3 patients were permanently bedfast, and none were temporarily in bed, but 10 patients were incontinent, 25 needed help dressing, and 28 were unable to walk outside alone. There was one nurse for every 7.4 patients.
>
> In a third Home, the 26 patients were all women over 80. None were in bed, only 3 were incontinent, 13 could dress themselves without help, and 23 could walk outside alone. There was one nurse for every 2.5 patients.

On the basis of our incomplete evidence, it seemed that rather less than half the Homes fell into the first category, a quarter in the second and over a quarter in the third. In the actual functions they performed a substantial number of nursing Homes appeared to be little different from many private old people's Homes. The descriptions given by medical officers, such as 'medical and chronic' or 'convalescent and medical' did not appear to be of much help in differentiating the various Homes.

Individual Homes ranged from a convalescent Home with 45 beds to a country farmhouse taking in two convalescent children during the summer. The average Home had 14 beds, and nearly 80 per cent of the total had between 5 and 30 beds.

Standards of accommodation varied widely. The proprietor of a small Home in Wales, with three elderly women as patients, wrote:

> The Home is situated in a tiny village in a rural area. Each patient has her own room which is furnished as a bed-sitter. I have myself decorated the rooms in pastel pink, grey, and blue. Covers, etc., are washable and of a dainty chintz material. I personally think a pretty, restful room is of great importance, especially for elderly people. I have a TV lounge, also radios for each room. My own garden supplies all my vegetables, fresh fruit, and flowers, and a neighbouring farm supplies my milk and eggs.

One of the Homes visited in South London was in marked contrast:

> The Home consists of a small dark brick house divided into two. The two parts have been clumsily joined, leaving sudden steps and

doors in the narrow corridors inside. Of the 16 patients — all elderly — three are in single rooms, ten in double rooms, and three share one room. The bedrooms are small and dark, with dingy paint and curtains, iron beds with hair mattresses, and a few armchairs and bedside tables. There are no pictures or flowers. The patients spend all day in their rooms, in bed or in chairs beside their beds. There is a small sitting room downstairs with a TV set, but although the proprietor said the staff have no sitting room, they eat here, the night nurse sleeps here, and since 'the patients don't seem to want to use it' they have made it their own. One or two patients still venture in to watch TV. There is no dining room; the patients eat off trays in their rooms.

No specific information was obtained about the number of patients having single rooms but 15 per cent of the proprietors (with 8 per cent of all beds) spontaneously mentioned that they had single rooms only, and others indicated that some of their patients were in such rooms. Private rooms appear to be a common and desirable feature of nursing Homes and yet they are rarely favoured in National Health Service hospitals. This difference appears to be one worthy of detailed study. In the postal inquiry many comments were made by proprietors. Most of these were in favour of single rooms, at least from the viewpoint of the psychological needs of the patient, and a few proprietors even preferred to leave one bed empty in a double room. 'Four of our rooms are large enough for two beds but the type of people who come here are not willing to share with a stranger.'

Two matrons mentioned particular difficulty with double rooms. One wrote, 'They are an intolerable strain on the occupants'; and the second, 'For this double room I choose my patients carefully — either both convalescent or both bedridden.'

Some arguments, however, were put forward against single rooms. They might isolate the patient from the activities going on in the Home.

Our two four-bedded wards are splendid for long-term cases — somehow the personal element is missing, yet there is always something to watch.

I find it is better for elderly patients to be *with others*, and not in *single* rooms — hence all my patients see a number of staff and plenty of visitors daily who chat with them even if not relatives or friends.

To accommodate several patients in a room could mean economy in work, and therefore an opportunity to reduce costs or to increase income from a larger number of patients. 'Shared rooms are a great help in caring for the moribund or very ill cases who no longer care.' In one Home nine mentally deteriorated and incontinent patients lived

together in one room. For nursing Homes (no less than for other types
of institutions) the arguments for and against the use of single rooms —
whether medical, nursing, social or psychological — seem to be worth
testing against empirical evidence.

Another important feature of nursing Homes is the lack of sitting
and dining rooms for ambulant patients. This provides a sharp contrast
with nearly all registered old people's Homes. The assumption seems to
be that a nursing Home is like a hospital; the people are called patients
(almost half the proprietors used the abbreviation 'pats.'), and their
lives are assumed to centre round their beds. In an old people's Home
there are 'residents' instead of 'patients' who are assumed to have
additional needs for 'sitting' accommodation. But in the sample of
nursing Homes 63 per cent of the elderly patients were not bedfast, and
could get out of bed on their own. Only ten proprietors mentioned that
a sitting room was provided for their patients. In one of the visited
Homes there was no sitting room, in another the sitting room had been
taken over by the staff, and in a third the sitting room was a narrow
conservatory, facing the wall of the next door house, and with chairs
for only a third of the patients in a straight row along either side. The
patients' feet touched in the middle, and the TV could be seen only
from the few chairs directly opposite it. Most of the patients were
sitting in their rooms. Besides the expense of using a room that might
have been a bedroom as a sitting room, some proprietors also felt it was
undesirable because it brought together patients whom it was wrong to
mix. One wrote: 'I think having a lounge for all up patients is difficult
unless you have one for confused patients and one for normal patients,
as the confused patients tend to get normal patients confused, if not
annoyed.' When registering a nursing Home most local authorities do
not expect sitting and dining rooms to be provided.

Social Life of People in Nursing Homes

The proprietors drew our attention to the length of time many elderly
patients spent in the Homes before they died (periods as long as nine
and ten years were mentioned). Such patients were often unmarried or,
if married or widowed, childless, and did not often have visitors.
Concern was expressed about their social isolation. Even when they had
relatives the latter sometimes lost interest 'once they find they are
settled and well cared for'. The proprietors often linked the question of
isolation with that of payment of fees. Old people who were really
isolated seemed to be those with no relatives helping to pay.

> One of the greatest curses of growing old is that one's circle grows
> less, and someone has to be the last, and I feel so utterly sorry for
> these poor old souls who are either mentally lost or physically
> paralysed, with nothing and no one but a solicitor or similar person

to pay the fees. It saddens me to see so many old folks abandoned (no matter how kind we are it's still not your own) or else with no one. To die knowing no one cares.

I think it is very sad to watch these poor old people worrying as to whether their money will run out. It is astonishing how few get any help from their children. In fact I can think of three of my six who would be able to live very comfortably if their family were not constantly asking for money, and in return pay a 'duty' visit once a month.

Having little contact with the outside world the patients turned to their nurses, and here the proprietors depicted frustrated affection.

The patients are usually lonely, always grateful for fond loving kindness and affection, appreciate gifts and special attention from me. They become very attached to staff who attend them over a period. A big problem is deafness. Staff find old people very trying at times, nervous due to modern living, and unable to contain themselves. This causes friction between the staff and the old folk. So much patience together with lots of love is required, as they all seem to lack security.

Control of generous impulses: this is not a great worry with the staff who have been here for years, but we watch out for relief nurses and domestic workers. Old people will offer their possessions if these are admired, and a rule has to be made that nothing must be accepted without reference to the nurse in charge. Care is taken to consult the patient's relatives, or solicitor, or bank manager.

The amount of contact between nursing Homes and local voluntary and statutory organizations is not known. One proprietor had arranged for the rector to visit socially, and for 'ladies to come and visit and read'. A second wrote: 'The other great problem is not having a "bottomless stocking of gold" to pay enough people to bear company to those elderlies with no relatives.' But these were the only indications of outside help. The majority of patients seemed to depend for regular social contact on each other, the doctor, the matron or proprietor, and the staff.

There are clearly a number of crucial matters worth detailed investigation. To what extent do patients in nursing Homes have contacts with other patients? How often are they unnecessarily restricted to their rooms? How far are they isolated from the local community? Should society do more to safeguard the interests of those who have no relatives to visit them? How far is psychological and social security dependent on a diminishing bank balance? These are some of the disturbing questions threading the written comments offered by proprietors.

The Social Characteristics of Staff

According to the postal information the nursing Homes in the sample had an average of one full-time nurse — qualified or unqualified and including a nursing orderly — to every 2.5 beds. This average is lower than that regarded as desirable by some authorities (26). It includes the full-time equivalent (defined as 40 hours or more a week) of part-time nurses and the matrons in charge. A 'qualified' nurse was usually a state registered nurse, a state certified midwife, or a state enrolled nurse. Staffing ratios ranged from slightly more than one nurse for each bed, to one for every nine beds, and in one small Home there was no nurse at all. Some proprietors may have exaggerated the number of nursing staff employed. Even so, more than a quarter of the Homes (accounting for nearly a third of the beds) had a staffing ratio of 1 : 3 or poorer.

The Homes with a large proportion of patients in bed or unable to walk out alone tended to be those with the best staffing ratios, but the correlation was not a striking one. There were a number of Homes with roughly the same incidence of infirmity among the patients but widely different staffing ratios.

Staff problems seemed to provide the biggest headache for the proprietors. Of the 72 who made written comments at the end of the questionnaire, 55 per cent mentioned staffing difficulties, and a quarter of these wrote of nothing else. One wrote across the page, 'Inability to find suitable staff causes complete frustration!' Nurses who are single, young and qualified are scarce, and if they have professional ambitions they are unwilling to work in a nursing Home with no prospects of promotion. Young married nurses, even when they work full-time, have their minds on their children, and older nurses may not be able to do strenuous work. Night nurses are extremely difficult to find. 'A good night nurse is a jewel worth pampering,' said one matron. The smallness of the Homes as compared with hospitals may mean that nursing staff have to help with domestic work. 'Sometimes there is very little nursing to be done and the nurses complain of too much housework.' And the nursing work itself may be both strenuous, if there are many patients who need lifting or who are incontinent, and medically uninteresting and depressing, since most of the old people will not get any better.

> Staffing is difficult. Married or elderly nurses are the rule in medical or chronic Homes. Married women have home and family troubles. The elderly ones may be slow, and unable to lift heavy patients.
>
> Work tends to be with elderly people on the verge of senility. The younger nurses want work which shows more results, but they have a better 'tonic' effect on the old people.
>
> The average nursing assistant is in the 35-50 age group, and the work is depressing as it represents the future to them as gloomy and frightening.

Some proprietors were particularly pleased with their unqualified nurses.

> These nursing auxiliaries are generally sensible married women who, when they have their families off their hands, return to the kind of work they have always wished to do. They have proved in my experience more kind, reliable, loyal, and interested in the nursing of elderly patients, than the average S.R.N. looking after them as though they were their own relatives, regardless of time and energy.

For many proprietors a nurse's ability to sympathize with old people was more important than her nursing qualifications. 'Any nurse who does not understand that an elderly may be difficult, strange in speech, or wear her corset upside down if she wishes to, and should not be called a mental patient, is little or no use in this life.'

Proprietors complained of the high salaries expected by nurses and of nurses thinking only of money. Some said they could only afford fairly low wages. It would therefore be of some interest to find why, nonetheless, a considerable number of qualified nurses have been attracted into nursing Homes. A few proprietors felt they had exceptionally satisfactory arrangements with staff who had become a permanent part of their 'family'.

> My staff have been with me for years but we are all getting older and satisfactory replacements will be hard to find. The staff are satisfied with a lower salary than they could get elsewhere in return for a feeling of all working together, and a give and take with regard to hours and time off.

These social factors may be important. But whatever the staffing arrangements a good deal of work seemed to fall on the matron herself.

There appears to be some ambiguity in the use of the term 'proprietor'. In considering applications for registration from proprietors of nursing Homes the local authorities are conscious of the practical needs of doctors and elderly persons in the district for information about the addresses of Homes and the names of persons actually managing them. In drawing up a list the name and address of the owner, when different from the name and address of the resident matron, may not always be given. In the duplicated lists received from local authorities the column of names was headed variously 'Owner', 'Matron', 'Proprietor', 'Run By', or 'Person in Charge'. Very rarely was a distinction made between matron-proprietors and employed matrons. The replies to our postal questionnaire from those managing Homes were not always precise enough to provide definite knowledge about ownership. (Field visits to different areas would probably be needed.) However, it seemed that at least 9 per cent of the Homes, containing 15 per cent of the beds, were owned by medical practitioners and managed by their wives, jointly by themselves and their wives, or by employed matrons. Another 3 per cent or 4 per cent of Homes seemed to be owned by limited companies and managed by employed matrons. While these figures are subject to a margin of error, there is little doubt that the vast majority of private nursing Homes in the sample were owned and managed by individual matrons.

Eighty-nine per cent of those in charge were women, two thirds of them being married or widowed and one third spinsters (a few of whom shared responsibility with another spinster). A further 9 per cent were married couples and the remaining 2 per cent unmarried men.

Some of these people described themselves and their careers. There were those who had just bought their Homes, and those who had been registered for twenty or thirty years. Some mentioned they were getting old, and two were on the point of retiring. A large number said they were overworked. One wrote, 'I am on call day and night, seven days a week' and another, 'I have not had a holiday for two years, seldom have a day off, and usually work 12-14 hours a day.' Two had been hospital matrons, and another two, without nursing qualifications, had been obliged to assume full responsibility by the unexpected death of the wife or daughter who had been the proprietor. One woman wrote, 'I gave up my hospital career to look after my invalid parents. After their death I converted my own house into a registered nursing Home for three patients. I am able to nurse, cook, and do the necessary housework myself.' Another said, 'I only take two patients here in my own home, and I am single-handed and do everything myself except for a little domestic help. I have a partially-disabled husband and I have to do this for a living. I only take elderly ladies who are more or less permanent and can do some things for themselves.' In contrast to these small Homes, the husband of a couple running a maternity Home with 25 beds said:

> My wife [the matron] and myself own and run the Home. My wife has been nursing for 35 years; she was the night sister at — Hospital. I am an ordinary person with a fund of experience. It is essential to have someone resident who is a jack of all trades. My wife is not only the matron but also she is prepared to step in to any position when staff let us down, and believe me they do these days. We have been open for fifteen years.

The matron or proprietor (who is, with comparatively few exceptions, as we have seen, the same person) wields considerable power. Usually she is not responsible to any kind of committee or board of directors, and has been selected for her post by no one but herself. She may be attracted to the idea of running a nursing Home from a sense of professional independence and vocation. She can practise her craft in a way she feels is in the best interests of certain kinds of patients and which is free from the arbitrary restrictions imposed by a superior authority. There is little doubt that some matrons apply the highest standards in their work. But these standards are to a large extent self-imposed, and. freedom from control (other than informally through doctors and relatives) may also result in the adoption of low standards in many places. There is little doubt that some matrons find their way into nursing Homes because they have not made a success of a hospital career or, more particularly, because by temperament and personality they are not fitted to co-operative nursing of the kind undertaken in most public institutions. In short, some of the matrons managing nursing Homes are extremely able women, but others, it would seem, are incompetent or authoritarian. This is of vital concern to their patients — particularly to those who have no relatives and who are bedfast or otherwise immobilized. Even when they become insecure and unhappy some patients may be unwilling to leave. Their resources may have diminished, they may be paying reduced fees and they may be unaware of the existence of more congenial voluntary, local authority or hospital institutions. A proprietor described some of the problems as follows: 'So many are quite alone in the world, with perhaps a couple of friends as old as themselves, and if unhappy in a Home they sometimes can do nothing about it but stick it out until the end.'

In their written comments on the questionnaire the proprietors in the sample revealed, often without meaning to, the range of attitudes they had to their patients. There were wide divergencies, for instance, on the practical matters of making all patients have a bath each day, of making all patients get out of bed, and of allowing them to determine their own activities and occupations.

On the face of it the majority seemed to have a kindly attitude to their patients. One proprietor demonstrated her sympathy in practical terms:

We find the most important thing with elderly patients is to make them feel still useful and wanted by someone. Even the rich patients are frequently just a nuisance to their relatives. We took on this work to educate our three sons, and we make a point of thanking the patients for enabling us to do so, and the boys themselves show gratitude and courtesy to them and run errands for them, etc. Another thing that makes elderly patients happy is to be allowed something from the home they have had to give up. This may utterly ruin your nice orderly, carefully matched up room but *it really does count to the patient*. We have had ghastly brass bedsteads, a chiffonier, and one brought forty-nine pictures with her — but she was happy here for years until she died. Old people cannot be 'drilled' into rules and regulations. They need gentle and friendly persuasion. We do not force daily baths on them, and some have only two baths weekly and a daily wash over. Warmth is of extreme importance, and simple plain meals, nicely served on trays (if in bed) ... We try to remember that most of them are from an age very different from ours, and to make allowances. A little gesture of affection, a goodnight kiss or a little hug, mean a great deal to them.

Proprietors who lack sympathy and tolerance are probably exceptional, but the point is that there is nothing to prevent them from carrying on their jobs. Postal information is certainly not the best way of elucidating their attitudes but in our small inquiry even this was sometimes found to be revealing.

In time I hope to have this Home as good as can be found, then I will alter the category of pats. and take in a lower age group and make it more interesting. I look on these old pats. as insurance policies for my bread and butter ...

The following is a description of the matron-proprietor of one of the Homes actually visited:

Mrs Parkinson is about forty, portly, pleasant looking, and was dressed in neat navy blue, very nearly a matron's uniform. Her competence and efficiency seem to leave her relatively unharassed. She has four weeks' holiday a year, a car, is hoping to retire in a few years, and as we sat talking in her elegant sitting-room, tea was brought to us in fine china. The patients' rooms, in contrast, were crowded and dismal. There was no sitting-room, and the front door was fastened by three bolts during the day. In one room there were two old men sitting with their backs to each other, their faces close to opposite walls. Mrs Parkinson, who had knocked at none of the doors, said in a loud voice that one was unsociable. 'He keeps having strokes and coming back in. He ought to be thankful he has the use of an arm and a leg, but he won't speak to anyone.' The other man was doubly incontinent. She asked, as to a child, 'Have you been naughty again?', and while he confessed that he had, told me not to come too near because of the smell.

So far as they could be discerned, the main divisions seemed to be between those proprietors who emulated hospital standards and routine, emphasizing hygiene and high standards of nursing, and those who saw themselves as providing a comfortable home for old people; or, alternatively, between business women attempting to make a financial profit from their own work and elderly women who were content with a modest living so long as they could maintain their professional status by looking after a few old and permanent patients.

Social Control

Local authorities varied in the frequency with which they inspected nursing Homes in the sample. A third of the Homes were visited only once or twice a year but a quarter four or more times. Most authorities inspected some Homes in their areas more frequently than others. In one fairly typical county, for example, the number of inspections a year ranged from one to five. But authorities varied in their general policies — some carrying out two or three times as many inspections as others. A proprietor in one county said her Home had been open for nearly a year and not yet inspected. Proprietors said that the inspections were carried out by the Medical Officer of Health, his deputy, or the district health visitors. Sometimes the visit was extremely brief and the inspection amounted to little more than a discussion with the proprietor in his or her room.

The problem for many local authorities is the small scale of the work involved. In 1960, 22 per cent of all authorities responsible for registered Homes had only one on their lists. A further 34 per cent had no more than five. Altogether 75 per cent of the authorities were each responsible for twelve Homes or fewer. It is difficult to see how they could be expected to develop a really strong and informed inspectorate. And although the Public Health Act allows different authorities to combine, few or none of them have done so (27).

In nearly all Homes those in charge seemed to have a close relationship with the local doctors, much more so, at least, than appears to be the case with those in charge of private old people's Homes. The consultation rate in nursing Homes may be much higher than in geriatric units of National Health Service hospitals and residential accommodation provided under the National Assistance Act. This close relationship seemed to be with several doctors rather than one. The only Homes entirely under the care of one doctor were three Homes for children (of the four replying) and there were only five more with one doctor visiting regularly but with others on call. In the remaining Homes several doctors were visiting different patients regularly, i.e., at least once a month, though often much more frequently.

There was evidence also of the encouragement given by doctors to proprietors opening a nursing Home. A few proprietors mentioned that their Homes had been started or kept going at the suggestion of the local doctors. Another was 'supported by all the specialists in the town'. The proprietor of one of the visited Homes had been offered financial help by a local doctor to buy another Home for sale in the area. 'He wants somewhere to put his patients.'

The Fees for Nursing Homes

Fees varied widely between Homes, and often between patients in an individual Home as well. All patients appeared to pay at the same rate in only 10 per cent of the Homes. In the others the fees were expressed as a range, and in some Homes the difference between the highest and the lowest fee was as much as 11 guineas a week. Fees were partly determined by the function of the Home. The lowest weekly fee paid in a Home with elderly patients was 2½ guineas, the highest was 25 guineas, but these were exceptional. Most of the Homes at the top and bottom of the scale had no elderly patients. Although our information was imprecise, it seemed that the average fee paid in the children's Homes was about 5 guineas a week; in Homes with no elderly patients 18 to 20 guineas and in Homes with elderly patients only, from 10 to 12 guineas (28).

Taking all the Homes together, there seemed to be some correspondence between staffing ratios and the fees charged. But there were many exceptions to this general trend. In one Home with less than two beds for each nurse patients paid as little as £5 15s. 0d. a week, whereas in another with the same staffing ratio patients paid as much as 24 guineas, and both these Homes had elderly patients. Similarly, the lowest and the highest fees in Homes with elderly patients and between two and three beds for each nurse were 6 guineas and 25 guineas respectively. It appears that the fee charged by a Home cannot invariably be taken as an indication of the amount of nursing attention a patient will receive.

When fees varied among different patients of the same Home they seemed to be determined by the amenities of a room, the number of patients sharing a room, the length of time a patient had been in the Home, and sometimes the size of a patient's income. The Homes with only single rooms had a fairly high average fee of 16 guineas a week (although again they varied between 8 and 25 guineas) and front rooms and large rooms were sometimes more costly than others. In Homes with both single and shared rooms the former cost on average about 3 guineas a week more. A few proprietors mentioned that long-term patients, or patients who had been in the Home before the last increase in fees, were charged less. At least six proprietors were retaining some patients at reduced fees because the patients could not afford more. One proprietor wrote:

> In the 13 years since we came to this area we have never parted with anyone whose means or capital has been used up. Our County M.O.H. would be willing to find beds for those without means, but we live in an odd corner of the county and it would make it difficult for visitors to visit even the nearest hospitals. It is a good thing that

none of those with 'pensioners' beds realize it, and therefore are under no 'compliment'.

By contrast other proprietors indicated that when an old person's money ran out she had to leave and go into an old people's Home, or more usually a hospital. The extent to which one or other of these two policies is adopted must make a very great difference to the sense of security of the patients concerned. And yet from one point of view the display of too much sentiment or sympathy can lead to severe financial difficulties and threaten the future of a Home. Information was not obtained about the numbers of old people leaving nursing Homes, and in particular those leaving for financial reasons (29).

Charging for 'extras' appears to be a source of embarrassment to nursing Home proprietors. One, who may have been exaggerating, wrote, 'In some Homes patients are charged as much as 7s. 6d. for a single injection, rubber bedpan, and other equipment.' Others replied with pride that they made no extra charge and that *their* patients knew how they stood. A proprietor who would have liked more extra charges wrote: 'I have difficulty in charging extra for damage, i.e., stains on linen, damage to furniture by wheelchairs and lotions, bedside rugs and pillows wet by incontinence, linoleum ruined by too much washing.'

Proprietors were asked specifically whether they made extra charges for heavy nursing or for special diets. Twenty-seven per cent charged for heavy nursing (3 per cent specified that by heavy nursing they meant employing an extra nurse), and 7 per cent for special diets. Other proprietors volunteered the information that they charged incontinent patients extra for their laundry, had coin meters for gas and electricity in the rooms, or charged for heating in other ways.

It is therefore difficult to know how far the figures supplied by proprietors truly represent the fees actually paid by the patients. They may have given the rates now advertised, and some of their older patients may have been paying less, or they may have given the basic charges without including the 'extras' normally paid by all or most patients. How often is an elderly person misled about the existence of extra charges when he or she applies to enter a Home?

In those Homes with low or average fees, several proprietors said they were in financial difficulties. Nine said they were making no profit or very little, and were barely able to cover their costs, and a further four recently had to raise their fees or the number of extra charges. They pointed out that with a small Home a few empty beds mean a large cut in income. 'One's margin of profit is so small it soon turns to a loss if several rooms are empty,' wrote one. Another had 'a constant worry to keep the beds full'. These proprietors expressed resentment at the lack of recognition by the Government of the service performed by this private sector. Nursing Homes, they said, relieved the pressure on the insufficient supply of hospital beds for the chronic sick within the Health Service. There were some old people, too ill to go into an old people's Home, not ill enough to go into hospital, and without the money to pay for a nursing Home, who remained alone in their houses although badly needing attention. And thirdly, nursing Homes enabled old people to avoid the workhouse. The proprietors of seven Homes in different parts of the country suggested there should be some form of Government subsidy to enable more old people to enter nursing Homes and to stay in them, if they wished, until they died.

> Many long-term patients with fixed income of say £6 6s. 0d. wish to remain at the nursing Home but the Welfare will not allow them the £2 2s. 0d. but will give them beds in old people's Homes, or even give a hospital bed at great cost to the Health Service. The M.O.H. should deal with this. I have already asked my M.P. When we need beds for urgent cases they have no beds.

> It is a pity that the Government has not sufficient foresight to supplement fees. Some patients have 5-6 guineas income and when their capital is exhausted are taken into hospital. Having been here probably two or three years, *three* have died within two weeks of the move.

> I should like to expand; there has not been a profit to date. Our local geriatric hospital is full and has a long waiting list. The geriatric consultant for the area is very keen on the lines on which we run — homely atmosphere and occupational therapy. I receive most of my patients from the hospital. Therefore why could not the local authority advance a loan to small nursing Homes so that they can expand and relieve the strain on the Geriatric Hospital beds?

> In this area [Cornwall] we find old people averse to what they will always think of as the Workhouse but their savings will not enable them to come to us. It would help these old folk considerably if they could have part paid for them by the State. Besides saving the State their full keep it would make them happy in their old age (30).

But in fact, far from subsidizing the Homes proprietors said some local authorities and Regional Hospital Boards were providing ruinous competition. A proprietor with 14 beds and only 5 patients wrote:

> Normally I am registered for 14 patients but now the local authority have opened a Home for the aged in the same road. Sick patients are sent to the local infirmary whether they like it or not, and the cottage hospital now takes the elderly sick . . . From being of great use I now find no one wants a private Home.

Another Home had had to close down because of 'difficulty in obtaining fee-paying patients due to local Councils having opened old people's Homes, and the fees charged by them being much lower than in a private nursing Home'. If these proprietors are to be believed it would seem that some nursing Homes are being squeezed out of existence, and their function usurped, on one side by the National Health Service hospitals, and on the other by the local authority old people's Homes. However, while this may be true of some Homes, there appears to be no general trend in this direction. Over the last ten years, as pointed out earlier, there has been a slow increase in the number of nursing Home beds not used for maternity purposes. The increase has not kept pace with the growth of the number of persons in the population aged 75 and over (which is 27 per cent greater than ten years ago) nor has it kept pace with the growth in the amount of accommodation in private old people's Homes registered under the National Assistance Act (31). But although, compared with ten years ago, a larger proportion of infirm and sick elderly persons may now be cared for in hospitals or in residential accommodation instead of in nursing Homes, the role of the latter is still considerable.

Conclusion: Problems of Public Responsibility
The information obtained from nursing Home proprietors, which has been described in the foregoing pages, is not comprehensive. Many important questions have still to be answered. But when taken with evidence from other sources there seems to be some basis at least from which to approach the problem of devising future policy.

Why are the present methods of supervision unsatisfactory? First of all, there is no doubt that some establishments are run as nursing Homes and yet escape registration and inspection. Medical Officers of Health, Chief Welfare Officers and social workers have quoted instances to us, and some nursing Home proprietors themselves expressed misgivings.

I suggest that your report emphasize most strongly the need for local authorities to investigate all non-registered Homes, and those who advertise as 'Home of a Nurse'. These have not the amenities of registered Homes of good repute and do not comply with the minimum in fire protection. This applies also to Hotels which cut into the trade of nursing Homes illegally. Attention to these points by local authorities would strengthen the position of reputable Homes which maintain high standards.

A few proprietors pointed out that the problem involved all kinds of Homes for old people and not just nursing Homes. 'Elderly people are in these Homes, often without proper care and attention, in Homes that have no fire escapes, insufficient bathrooms and toilets, etc. When they get ill and incontinent they are sent on to us, alas mostly to die.'

Secondly, many non-profit making voluntary Homes are exempted from registration and inspection. Local authorities appear to adopt different practices, some following the letter of the law, others disregarding the provision for making exemptions unless appeals are lodged. There does not seem to be any reason, other than that arising from a desire to preserve separate status and identity, for allowing voluntary nursing Homes exemption from registration and inspection. Once entombed in legislation an assumption is hard to dig out. Voluntary nursing Homes must be known to the local authority, and shown each year to be non-profit making, before exemption can be granted. What is the difference between being listed and investigated, or registered and inspected? The voluntary Homes are not saved any inconvenience by their privilege; some have been put to considerable trouble to claim it. Ministry of Health Annual Reports between 1927 and the Second World War record a few appeals each year — some allowed and some not — from nursing Homes and hospitals which had not been granted exemption. But in 1960 there were some voluntary nursing Homes, perhaps a considerable number, which did not bother to claim exemption at all. This helps to explain the fact mentioned earlier in this report — that Ministry of Health statistics about nursing Homes are incomplete and also merge voluntary with private registered Homes. As long ago as 1930 Professor E. G. Gardiner concluded from a review of nursing Homes in Great Britain that voluntary Homes should be included in inspection. 'Some of the benefits of governmental supervision could be fairly easily obtained by a slight amendment of the Nursing Homes Registration Act 1927, removing the possibility of exemption for institutions carried on not for profit.' (32)

Thirdly, it would seem that few of the patients in private registered Homes have any regular contacts with organizations and individuals in the local community. As we have seen, many of them are in their eighties and nineties, many are extremely frail and many do not have children or other close relatives to visit them. Although the staff of some Homes may maintain high standards others seem not to do so. Few of the formal and informal controls exercised in many public and voluntary hospitals and other institutions exist. Relationships with doctors and ministers of religion may be maintained but there are no responsible members of a visiting committee who call regularly and there are few contacts with local voluntary associations or local authority officials. The dangers of individual isolation and defence-lessness are only too likely to arise.

Fourthly, there is no formal method of ensuring, within reasonable limits, that the proprietor or matron is fit to care for the infirm and chronic sick. She is not appointed by a committee of a hospital, local authority, or voluntary organization and with the exception of ensuring that she has a nursing qualification little can be done by the local authority to prevent an unsuitable person from managing a Home.

Fifthly, desirable minimum standards for nursing Homes (involving physical amenities and staffing) have not been laid down by the Ministry. As we have seen, the Public Health Act is vague and as a result local authorities not only vary in their interpretation of requirements but also find difficulty in securing that their standards are adopted before registration. They are conscious of the weakness of their powers, not only when first considering applications but after registration.

Far too frequently, nursing Homes have been registered and for some time maintained a satisfactory standard, and later their standards have deteriorated. Cancellation of a registration once given is far from easy, and it is felt there is need for some alteration in the law to require annual registration, and for more precise standards of staffing to be laid down by the Ministry (33).

The act has never been effective. In 1937, distressed by the 'circumstances attending two recent deaths' in a regularly inspected maternity Home, the Minister emphasized the importance of adequate supervision (34). In 1938, perhaps partly as a consequence, the registrations of twenty-four nursing Homes were cancelled. But except for an occasional tightening of procedure following a public scandal local authorities have been reluctant in the past to take action. They are no less reluctant today. They fear that the patients might be worse off as a consequence; they are conscious of shortages of beds in hospitals and residential Homes, and they realize that if an appeal is made against cancellation the proprietor is more than likely to win. The authority must prove the proprietor, the staff or the premises to be unsatisfactory. Handicapped by the vagueness of the act, the lack of defined standards, and the inability to subject patients to medical examination, this can be a hazardous operation. The court has supported a local authority only once (in Essex) in the whole history of nursing Homes legislation. The proprietor, his livelihood at stake, tends to be the object of the court's compassion.

Short of closing a Home there is little a local authority can do to raise or maintain standards once registration is granted, beyond offering tactful advice. Counsel's opinion, given in 1939, is that a certificate of registration, once issued, remains valid for a Home even though drastic changes may take place in the number and composition of staff and patients and in the Home's amenities. (Before 1939 conditions were often specified in the certificate or covering letter.) This explains the interest of the Society of Medical Officers and other bodies in conditional registration.

The basic reason for dissatisfaction with existing definitions and regulations is the low standards found in many Homes and the powerlessness of the local authorities to do much about them. As Dr Glyn Hughes reported in a survey of terminal care in the United Kingdom:

> What is clear is that a large proportion of these Homes are quite unsuited to provide the terminal care of patients who, in their last stages, require the most skilled nursing attention; in fact, in many of them the conditions are bad, in some cases amounting to actual neglect when measured by standards that can reasonably be expected. In so many cases it was obvious that the patients in their last days were existing under tragic conditions . . . the only fully trained nurse may be the owner, and in a large number [of Homes] there is no night staff at all. Means of communication are often non-existent or quite inadequate to ensure immediate attention; normal nursing facilities are conspicuous by their absence, rooms are often overcrowded . . . Although a large proportion of terminal cases may be ambulant almost to the end there is often no day-room accommodation or even comfortable chairs in the wards. (35)

Although little detailed evidence could be collected in the postal survey, some of the written comments of proprietors (in addition to our personal visits and interviews) bear out the accuracy of this summary. One proprietor wrote, for example:

> I had seen about 12-15 nursing Homes with a view to purchase, but I was horrified at some of them from the point of view that very little was provided in the way of extra comforts for the long-term patients. Only the bare essentials in furnishing were provided. Fees varied and an awful lot of extras were added, items which I would have expected to be provided. In this Home I was horrified to find that the rooms were very crowded, and working was difficult, i.e., one bed had to be moved before you could get in to make the second, and drip-feed oil heaters were used in spite of the fact that the average age of the patients was 70. Washing of soiled linen was done in the sluice, dried outside, and aired in the kitchen. I had 7 patients who were doubly incontinent, so you can visualize what the state of things was.

These five immediate reasons for dissatisfaction with present arrangements for registering and inspecting nursing Homes suggest ways in which an alternative policy might be developed. At the least there seems to be a strong argument for new legislation introducing conditional registration. Local authorities have been pressing the Ministry for twelve years to promote it. In 1948 West Bromwich

County Borough suggested revision of the law. Southampton County Borough, with the support of the Association of Municipal Corporations, asked in 1950 for annual licences and conditional registration. But the Ministry felt reform was unnecessary since similar powers, to enable local authorities to specify requirements for old people's Homes, had been given to the Minister in the 1948 National Assistance Act, and he had not felt it necessary to use them. The argument continued. In 1957 the Society of Medical Officers of Health produced a memorandum advocating stronger powers for the local authorities, and in particular conditional registration. The Ministry stated that there were few complaints and the existing statutory provision seemed to be adequate, but said they were prepared to reconsider the matter when the opportunity for legislation arose in due course. In 1960 the Association of Municipal Corporations again proposed ministerial powers similar to those in the National Assistance Act. The Minister was by then about to make regulations for old people's Homes under the provisions of this act; when he did so, however, he limited himself to fixing the number of persons who could be accommodated in an old people's Home.

Progress was slow and some local authorities became restive. Two of them decided to adopt new tactics and move the argument into Parliament. Hertfordshire County Council promoted a private bill, which was passed, giving them greater control over their private nursing Homes and old people's Homes. Devon followed suit in introducing a similar bill. In the absence of national reform it appears that a number of local authorities will be prepared to change the law piecemeal. This new evidence of public concern seems to have brought the Minister to the brink of action. In answer to a private question on 5 December 1960, he said he was considering suggestions for strengthening local authorities' power over nursing Homes. He also undertook, in reply to a supplementary question, to look at the complaints made in the annual report of the Medical Officer of Health of Bournemouth.

The Hertfordshire Act might well be a model for new legislation. It provides for conditional registration of both nursing Homes and old people's Homes, the standards of premises, diet, and the numbers of patients and staff being specified on the certificate of registration. For infringement of the conditions fines may be imposed. In other ways the powers of inspectors are extended. Patients may be interviewed in private, and medical practitioners may examine medical records. There is therefore a chance of an authority's decision being supported in the courts against a proprietor's appeal, a chance which the alternative remedy of annual licensing would not give.

But a second and more important precedent for new legislation is contained in the Mental Health Act of 1959. The act provides for the registration and inspection of mental nursing Homes under more stringent rules than the Public Health Act of 1936. Whereas the latter does not specify how many patients must reside in a building before it has to be registered as a nursing Home, the Mental Health Act specifies that 'one or more mentally disordered patients (whether exclusively or in common with other patients),' constitutes a mental nursing Home. The Minister has powers to prescribe what information has to be supplied by mental nursing Home proprietors applying for registration, and in July 1960 such regulations were issued. Applicants must now supply details of 'the company, society, association, or body making the application', accommodation for patients and staff, ages, qualifications, and experience of any employed manager, number and grades of other staff, number, sex, type, and age group of patients, arrangements for their treatment and occupation, and finally details of the applicant's interest in any other Home (36). The number of patients must be specified in the certificate of registration, and the local authority may make registration conditional in other ways they 'consider appropriate' regarding the patients to be received.

The Minister is also given general powers by the act to 'make regulations as to the conduct of mental nursing Homes'. For infringement either of conditions of registration made by the local authority, or of national regulations made by the Minister, a series of fines may be imposed before final resort to the power of cancelling registration. As for inspection, a representative appointed by the local authority is authorized to 'visit and interview in private any mentally disordered patient . . . to investigate any complaint about his treatment' or wherever the inspector 'has reasonable cause to believe that the patient is not receiving proper care'. Inspectors who are also medical practitioners have the right to conduct medical examinations of these patients in private, and to inspect medical records, although only 'relating to the treatment of the patient in the nursing Home' (37). Moreover, the Minister also has the power to specify the frequency of inspection, and in the regulations already quoted has laid down that it must be at least once in every six months. Finally, voluntary mental nursing Homes cannot be exempt from the provisions of the act.

It would clearly be wrong and absurd if other nursing Homes were not to benefit from similar legislation. Mental disorder is difficult to define, particularly in old age, and there is no reason why infirm, chronic sick, surgical and medical patients should have a lesser right to statutory protection. If the act is applied strictly, patients in the same Home would have different rights to protection by the local authority. The presence of mentally disordered elderly patients, and the category of the Home, might vary from month to month. The position might even arise whereby a Medical Officer of Health, suspecting that the patients in a Home are not well treated, would have first to establish that at least one of the patients was suffering from mental disorder to procure the right to interview any patients in private, and then would be able to interview only those who, being mentally disordered, could give him least information.

It is doubtful, however, whether legislation drawn up along these lines could be successful unless the Ministry is also prepared to give a much more precise definition of all the various types of Homes and the standards expected of them (with at least the same assiduousness as the Home Office has devoted to the task of issuing regulations and memoranda about children's Homes) (38). Definitions are of course extremely tricky to devise but they are necessary if society is to take proper responsibility for frail and sick persons. There is not simply the need to uphold the powers of a registering authority in the courts but also to locate some Homes which at present escape public supervision.

There is no doubt that if all nursing Homes were subject to the same legislation as the mental nursing Homes this would be a welcome reform. But it would be a limited one, and this fact should be recognized. Some major problems would not be solved. How far, for example, could local authorities ensure that the proprietor or matron of a Home was suitable for the task? To insist on a nursing or medical qualification does not appear to be enough, simply because the pecuniary rewards of running some nursing Homes may attract the wrong kind of people, and particularly those who have not been found suited to a career in the statutory health services. The question of the financial independence of a nursing Home is hard to separate from its administrative independence. Although there appear to be some Homes in which the proprietor secures a fairly large income and the staff have expectations of financial rewards greater than those obtainable in public service (either from salaries or from tips and legacies) most are not 'profit-making' in the customary sense of the word. Fees are often fixed at a level which makes the Homes barely viable as financial concerns and, by today's standards, the matron or proprietor makes no more than a comparatively modest living. The main practical objection to privately run nursing Homes is therefore not that profits can too easily be made at the expense of the sick, but that those who manage them are free from public appointment and regular supervision. There seem to be at least two possible solutions. Could an independent committee (consisting, perhaps, of local doctors and nurses as well as local authority representatives) interview any prospective matron of a nursing Home and admit her to a special form of nurse registration? Or, more fundamentally, should Society rule that no establishment containing several sick or infirm persons be run by a private individual, but only by the employee or appointee of a charitable trust or local committee of management (39)? Many private nursing Homes would not have to close. Negotiations between proprietors and local charitable organizations or statutory authorities could result in their being placed under a voluntary committee of management.

Another problem which would not be solved by simply widening the scope of the more specific measure introduced for mental nursing Homes is that of the relationship between nursing Homes and other types of private health and welfare institutions operating outside the main health and residential services of the country. In the pilot survey we found that a large number of nursing Homes seemed to be indistinguishable from private Homes registered under the National Assistance Act in respect, at least, of the capacities of their residents or patients. To what extent, therefore, should they be supervised by different departments of a local authority? This, however, is not the only question. A given establishment housing elderly people, a few of them bedfast and the others in varying degrees infirm, could easily be a convalescent, recuperative, or rehabilitation Home, a private or a voluntary nursing Home (and within either of these categories a mental nursing Home), a private old people's Home, or a 'Royal Charter' Voluntary Home. Depending on its status it could come under any one of six separate legislative requirements and be inspected or visited either by representatives of the Regional Hospital Board, the local authority Medical Officer of Health, the local authority Chief Welfare Officer, or by no one. Present legislation is pitted with anomalies.

There is an urgent need for a thorough study of all kinds of health and welfare establishments which accommodate three or more sick or housebound persons and which are not run by local hospital management committees or local authorities. There is no comprehensive and very little illustrative information of any kind which is publicly available. While the population of nursing Homes is growing very slowly the population of private old people's Homes is rapidly increasing. Many persons have reported that this is because it is easier to obtain registration under the National Assistance Act when facilities are poor and the prospective proprietor has no nursing qualifications. Certainly it would seem that while Medical Officers of Health, for example, carefully investigate nursing qualifications and the existence of sluices, Chief Welfare Officers are more concerned with sitting-rooms, warmth and furnishings. The former would appear to be preoccupied with health and hygiene; the latter with comfort.

Although a comprehensive study would be required to produce really precise evidence for a national reform it may be useful to indicate provisional conclusions on the basis of our limited research. It seems desirable for Britain to adopt more uniform methods of registration and inspection. It is impossible to see any reason for the exemption of any institution caring for the sick, the handicapped or the infirm from public registration, inspection and accountability. Those running an institution where the standards are high should be proud to pass on their knowledge and experience both to the public authority as well as to those struggling to achieve minimum standards. All would gain from closer contact and knowledge of each others' existence.

It is also hard to see how an authority in whose area there are only from one to a dozen Homes can register and inspect responsibly. In 1960 22 per cent of all councils with nursing Homes in their areas were inspecting only one and a further 34 per cent between two and five Homes. As many as 75 per cent were inspecting from one to twelve. There are therefore many local authorities where no more than a few hours of the time of any member of the staff is taken up with the problems of registered Homes and where there is little opportunity to develop an experienced knowledge of how standards can be enforced or raised. The solution may be to set up a regional inspectorate under the Ministry of Health with powers to register and visit all types of voluntary and private Homes for the sick and infirm (40). The inspectors would be a mixed group of people qualified in medicine, public health or social administration and though they would have primary responsibility for registration and inspection their work would be supplemented by the health and welfare departments of each local authority, which would collect and pass on local information.

There are of course dangers in devoting so much attention to the achievement of reasonable minimum standards in all voluntary and private institutions that the shortcomings of public institutions may be neglected. Unsatisfactory standards in public hospitals and residential Homes are too often condoned and there should be a strong inspectorate independent of the managing authority. This could work under the control of a Health and Welfare Commission — consisting of representatives of the public as well as of interested charitable and professional organizations appointed by the Government — which would be empowered to publish reports at regular intervals. Reforms of such a kind — for the public as well as the 'voluntary' or 'private' sector — would make a substantial contribution to the liberty, and security, of the individual citizen.

One final problem should be posed. The object of registration and inspection is to protect sick and infirm patients or residents by enforcing minimum standards of care and treatment. For establishments which accommodate at least three or four sick, handicapped or infirm persons and in which staff are employed for nursing or attendant duties, questions of public responsibility are fairly straightforward. But what is to be done about an establishment advertised as an hotel or guest house where there may be one, two or three elderly persons among the residents who, because of infirmity, spend much of their time in bed? Or what is to be done about a former nurse who provides board and lodging in her home to one or two frail elderly persons, or who acts as a companion help to a single old lady? Should these households be registered as nursing or old people's Homes and be inspected accordingly? Many people would hesitate to see rigorous rules applied and indeed there is a good deal of understandable equivocation on the part of the Ministry and the local authorities. In defining an old people's Home some local authorities will not register unless there are at least three old people accommodated; others are prepared to register if there is only one. In the case of hotels and guest houses even this approach is usually abandoned. So long as accommodation is advertised for temporary paying guests an hotel can often have as many as a dozen elderly residents without being subject to registration. To insist on classifying such establishments as nursing or old people's Homes would seem to flout commonsense and threaten individual liberty (41). Old people themselves might suffer. Rather than tolerate the presumed indignities of registration many hotel managers and companion nurses might compel their elderly residents to leave.

Is the problem one that can never be satisfactorily solved? It will seem so as long as legislation is framed primarily in terms of institutions rather than also in terms of people. The principle on which modern society should insist is that of public responsibility for individuals who are sick, handicapped and infirm. How can this be put into practice? A duty should be laid on general practitioners to notify the local authority health and welfare departments of any individual living in a private or non-private household other than a public institution who suffers from a particular long-term disability or has been bedfast for at least one month, or housebound for at least three months. Inability to walk outside a building without aid supplies a useful working definition of 'housebound'. (This would apply, for example, to about 10 per cent of persons of pensionable age.) Existing registers of the handicapped (such as the blind and the deaf and dumb) could be extended to cover individuals of all ages (though particularly those aged seventy and over) who have some marked incapacity (42). The duty of the local authority would be to visit regularly all individuals so notified to find whether certain of their basic needs are being met and, if not, to offer and provide appropriate care and assistance (a home help or district nurse, delivery of meals, collection of laundry, alternative housing, physiotherapy, occupational therapy, and so on). Any proposal for the care of an individual elsewhere than at his present address would of course be subject to his consent. In the last analysis the principles of registration and inspection of voluntary and private nursing and residential Homes cannot be successfully applied unless some complementary measure of this kind is introduced. After all, legislation of a somewhat similar kind already exists for children deprived of a normal home life, and Home Office Regulations cover the conditions under which individual children are cared for by foster parents as well as the facilities and conduct of institutions (43).

It is difficult to follow established administrative traditions and consider the problems of nursing Homes in isolation from those of other categories of health and welfare institutions. To do so would be to perpetuate artificial distinctions and to overlook the importance of developing general principles according to which the sick and the infirm should be treated — wherever they may be housed. It is this basic fault which explains the uneven development of policy in recent years. Today, for example, services for children are much more closely supervised than those for old people. Historically this can be explained by the special attention that was given to children's services by the Curtis Committee and the comparative lack of attention given in the years since the war to services for old people. But from an administrative or humanitarian viewpoint this is clearly wrong and absurd.

Effective national policies also cannot be formed unless detailed account is taken of the quality of the administration of local, voluntary, and private social services. Improvements in the one must be accompanied by realistic provisions for improvements in the other. And this happy marriage will never be arranged without more deliberate attempts by the Government both to produce a better supply of basic information and to stimulate a larger volume of public discussion and criticism.

Notes and References

1 *Public Health Act,* 1936, 20 Geo. 5 and 1 Edw. 8, Ch. 49, Part VI. Nursing Homes in London are registered under the Public Health (London) Act, 1936, 26 Geo. 5 and 1 Edw. 8, Ch. 50.

2 *Nursing Homes Registration Act,* 1927, 17 and 18 Geo. 5, Ch. 38.

3 See Abel-Smith, B., *The Hospitals 1800-1848,* Heinemann, 1964.

4 *Nurses and Private Nursing Homes (Registration) Bill,* 1904, and *Nursing Homes (Registration and Inspection) Bill,* 1924-5. The former proposed the voluntary registration of private nursing Homes.

5 *Report of Select Committee on Nursing Homes (Registration),* House of Commons, 1926, p. i.

6 *Select Committee,* op. cit., p. vi.

7 *Midwives and Maternity Homes Act,* 1926, 16 and 17 Geo. 5, Ch. 32.

8 *Select Committee,* op. cit., p. vi. The registration of midwives in 1902 provided an important precedent for the registration of other nurses seventeen years later. Abel-Smith, B., *A History of the Nursing Profession,* p. 77.

9 For example, two witnesses described a Home with 15-20 patients, where an untrained nurse, her husband, and a single housemaid comprised the nursing staff. A doctor had a monopoly of the patients in this Home and two others nearby. Other doctors were never called in. The proprietor and her husband were both alcoholics. They slept in a room with some of the patients, or, if all the beds were occupied by patients, in the kitchen. Most of the patients were elderly and bedfast. 'I would like to mention one old woman who was not senile enough not to notice what was being done to her. She was incontinent and to save trouble with her at night she was put into the bath and left there for the whole night. She was brought out when her people came, and put on a bed ... Some of the patients have died in the night and other patients have banged on the door and on the floor to bring help and nobody has come until the morning.' One of the two witnesses, a clergyman, always advised the old people to go to the workhouse instead. *Select Committee,* op. cit., Qs 725-80.

10 'Your Committee find that abuses do exist and are sufficiently prevalent, particularly in the cheaper class of home catering for senile chronic cases, to render some form of supervision and inspection essential.' ibid., p. ix.

11 The 1936 Act brought the 1927 Act into line with other legislation passed in the intervening years. For example, in describing medical practitioners the words 'duly qualified' were replaced by the word 'registered', 'lunatics' became 'persons of unsound mind', and 'local authorities' were more precisely described throughout as 'county councils, county borough councils' etc. The later act gave local authorities slightly more power over exempted nursing Homes, enabling them to attach conditions to exemption and stressing that exemption 'may be withdrawn at any time'. It also added slightly to the power of registration by including 'state of repair' as a subject for 'fitness' and offence against a relevant by-law as a ground for cancellation.

12 ' "Maternity home" means any premises used or intended to be used for the reception of pregnant women, or of women immediately after childbirth.' *Public Health Act,* 1936, Section 199.

13 ' "Nursing home" does not include:
   (i) any hospital or other premises maintained or controlled by a government department, county council (including the London County Council), or metropolitan borough council, or by any other authority or body constituted by special Act of Parliament or incorporated by the Royal Charter.
   (ii) any institution for persons of unsound mind within the meaning of the Lunacy and Mental Treatment Acts, 1890 to 1930.
   (iii) any institution, house or home certified or approved by the Board of Control under the Mental Deficiency Acts, 1913 to 1927.'
   Public Health Act, 1936, Section 199.

14 A proprietor is registered in respect of a particular Home. When a nursing Home is sold registration does not pass automatically to the new proprietor.

15 *Public Health Act,* 1936, Section 191. The confidentiality of medical records is not invariably preserved in legislation regarding inspection. In a nursing Home having at least one mentally disordered patient the medical records of all patients may be inspected by the local authority inspector if he is also a medical practitioner.

16 'No other person than a legally qualified medical practitioner, qualified midwife, pupil midwife or qualified nurse may attend any woman in the home in

childbirth, or nurse any maternity patient accommodated therein.' See London County Council, *Statement Issued for the Information of Persons Carrying On or Intending to Carry On Nursing Homes in the County of London,* 1936 (in process of revision, para. 40).

17 A state registered nurse is a woman registered in the general part of the register kept under the Nurses Registration Act of 1919, or one who has not registered but who had, before 1928, completed a three-year course in a training school approved, or later approved, by the General Nursing Councils. *Public Health Act,* 1936, Section 199.

18 Some authorities, such as the London and Middlesex County Councils, have attempted to clarify the position by registering both persons. In London the following regulation has been adopted: 'If the applicant for registration is not resident in the home, it will be necessary to nominate for the Council's approval a person who is resident in the home and who should give a written undertaking to be responsible for the following duties (the name of the person when approved will be entered by the Council on the certificate of registration, in addition to that of the applicant, as the person in charge).' The duties are specified and amount to being responsible for running the Home. London County Council, op. cit.

19 The National Assistance Act, 1948, provides for the registration of Homes for disabled persons and old people, and specifically excludes those Homes that come within the definition of a nursing Home in the Public Health Act, 1936 — those Homes that provide nursing. But disabled persons are defined as 'persons who are blind, deaf, or dumb, and other persons who are substantially or permanently handicapped by illness, injury or congenital deformity'. Many of those living in Homes need nursing care from time to time. Nursing is often provided in old people's Homes as well, or at least the sort of caretaker nursing provided in many nursing Homes for old people. Strictly, then, many of the Homes registered under the National Assistance Act may be little different from many nursing Homes.

20 In 1960 in Scotland there were 606 beds (136 maternity and 470 other) in Homes registered under the *Nursing Homes (Registration) Scotland Act,* of 1938.

21 The net decrease conceals the fact that a number of new Homes are registered every year. In 1960 about 60 new proprietors were registered and 109 registrations withdrawn. Some of these are changes in ownership of existing Homes.

22 There were no Homes in 10 small counties (6 of these were in Wales), and in 21 county boroughs, for example, Sunderland, Oldham, Preston, Stoke-on-Trent, and West Ham.

23 Compiled from the *King Edward's Hospital Fund Directory of Convalescent Homes,* 1960, the *Annual Charities Register* for 1960 published by the Family Welfare Association, and from information regarding contractual arrangements obtained from the South-West Metropolitan Regional Hospital Board.

24 Some research studies have shown that nurses working in institutions tend to underestimate the capacities of patients in their care. For example, Sommer, R., 'Patients Who Grow Old in a Mental Hospital', *Geriatrics,* 14 September 1959, pp. 581-90.

25 Patients lifted or helped out of bed and propped in a chair for part of the day were counted as bedfast.

26 The London County Council requires a staffing ratio of 1 : 2 in nursing Homes, with at least one night nurse when there are four or more patients or when any patient is acutely ill. 'This requirement may be modified where senile-infirm patients only are accommodated.' London County Council, op. cit. Middlesex County Council has stricter requirements: 1 : 1.5 with a night nurse to every six patients in Homes admitting acute cases, and 1 : 2 with a night nurse to every eight patients in Homes admitting chronic cases. *Statement Issued for the Information of Persons Carrying on Nursing Homes in the County of Middlesex*, 1961. There are difficulties in comparing nursing Homes with hospitals. In small Homes strict division of labour is not possible. A full-time nurse, particularly the matron, may spend a considerable part of the day in domestic chores, including shopping, or in administration. On the other hand resident staff, again especially the matron, often work more than forty hours a week. With these reservations the ratio of 1 : 2.5 for the Homes in the sample may be compared with 1 : 2.9 in Health Service hospitals in England and Wales having 90 per cent chronic sick patients. (Source: Ministry of Health.)

27 Provision was made for local authorities to combine 'for the purposes of any of their functions under this Act'. *Public Health Act*, 1936, Section 272.

28 For the year ending 31 March 1960, the cost per bed per week in N.H.S. hospitals with 90 per cent or more chronic sick patients was £10 18s. 7d. (Source: Ministry of Health.)

29 No information is made available by the National Assistance Board about the number of nursing Home patients receiving national assistance.

30 Point is given to the proprietors' suggestion by the fact that a small number of patients in private nursing Homes *are* paid for by the Regional Hospital Boards. For example, of all beds in institutions outside the N.H.S. under contract to the South-West Metropolitan Regional Hospital Board for 1961, 12.5 per cent are in private nursing Homes (Regional Hospital Board). In 1955 hospital authorities in England and Wales had contractual arrangements involving 1,273 beds for the chronic sick in voluntary and private nursing Homes. Boucher, C. A., *Survey of Services Available to the Chronic Sick and Elderly*, 1954-5, H.M.S.O., 1957.

31 'On 1 January of this year there were nearly 1,100 private Homes registered by local authorities in England and Wales for the handicapped and aged. The total has grown by over 150 in the past two years.' Townsend, P., 'Private Homes for Old People, I', *The Times*, 17 May 1960.

32 Gardiner, E. G., *Convalescent Care in Great Britain*, Chicago, 1935, p. 101.

33 *Annual Report of the Medical Officer of Health for Bournemouth, for the Year 1959*, Public Health Department, Bournemouth, p. 9.

34 *Annual Report of the Ministry of Health for 1937/8*, p. 45.

35 Glyn Hughes, H. L., *Peace at the Last*, a Survey of Terminal Care in the United Kingdom; United Kingdom and British Commonwealth Branch of the Calouste Gulbenkian Foundation, 1960, pp. 24-5.

36 Statutory Instruments 1960, no. 1272.

37 *Mental Health Act*, 1959, Part III, Sections 14, 16 and 17.

38 See, for example, *The Administration of Children's Homes Regulations*, 1951 (Statutory Instruments 1951, no. 1217) and the memorandum by the Home Office, circulated in July 1951, on the *Conduct of Children's Homes (Seventh*

Report on the Work of the Children's Department, November 1955), H.M.S.O., 1955, pp. 104-16.

39 There are of course many different ways in which various responsibilities could be specified and advantage might be taken of existing legislation covering other types of institution. Good examples are voluntary children's Homes and approved schools, where the committees of management are not appointed by the Home Office but are responsible to the Secretary of State for the welfare of children and are required to undertake certain minimum supervisory tasks.

40 The provision for registration and inspection of independent schools offers a precedent which may be worth detailed study. Such schools for example can be 'recognized as efficient' and a similar designation may be appropriate for some nursing Homes. Her Majesty's Inspectors are full-time specialist advisers, not employees, of the Ministry of Education, and the sanction of refusal or cancellation of registration is made effective by the provision of appeal to an independent tribunal of experts. *Education Act*, 1944, Part III.

41 In drawing up legislation for mental nursing Homes the Ministry felt impelled to specify that 'one or more mentally disordered patients (whether exclusively or in common with other patients)' constituted such a Home. Theoretically hundreds or perhaps thousands of private households containing at least one such person could be classified as mental nursing Homes but it is very doubtful whether local authorities will interpret their responsibilities so strictly.

42 Section 29(1) of the National Assistance Act already gives the Minister powers to prescribe a wider definition of incapacity and (4)g of the same section gives the local authority powers to compile and maintain registers. Section 29(1) states that 'A local authority shall have power to make arrangements for promoting the welfare of persons ... who are blind, deaf or dumb and other persons who are substantially and permanently handicapped by illness, injury or congenital deformity or such other disabilities as may be prescribed by the Minister.' Sections 25 and 28 of the National Health Service Act are also relevant. Section 25 states, for example, that 'it shall be the duty of every local health authority to make provision in their area ... for securing the attendance of nurses on persons who require nursing in their own homes'.

43 *The Boarding-Out of Children Regulations, 1955* (Statutory Instruments 1955, no. 1377) and *The Administration of Children's Homes Regulations, 1951*.

12 The political sociology of mental handicap

A case-study of failure in policy*

It is commonly agreed that there is a crisis in Britain in the services for the mentally handicapped. Instances of bad treatment of patients in hospital, poor conditions, and understaffing in many wards have been revealed and have attracted wide publicity. Different solutions to the problems have been canvassed. None has yet been put into effect. This may be surprising to some people in view of the seriousness of the problems, the concern of the public and of medical, nursing and other staff, and the avowed intentions of Ministers in successive governments to put things right. How can our failure to do more in the last two years and to adopt an unambiguously specific policy be explained? My purpose is to analyse some of the structural and political factors standing in the way of a swift improvement of services and of the quality of life enjoyed by the handicapped. Political sociology has come to be differentiated from political science principally because of the sociologist's emphasis on the social aspects, both informal and formal, of political behaviour and political institutions. Political acts are those which determine the fate of men other than the actors. They are sanctioned not only by law but by custom and structural situation. The fate of the mentally handicapped is determined not just by Parliament, Ministers of State and local councils, but by the powers entrusted in or assumed by all those caring for them. The sociologist's interest in 'bureaucracy' and 'organization' leads him to investigate special problems like those of rough treatment in hospitals. But he tends to review social control in terms both of internal structure and external relationships.

The problem of understanding the gap between aims and performance is not, of course, peculiar to Britain. The deprivation which many of the handicapped experience, relative to the living standards in the societies to which they belong, is an international phenomenon. This continues to be so, even when powerful lobbies gradually arise to press for improvements. At the same time it is important to understand that conditions may not be uniformly bad. There is considerable

* Paper presented to an international conference organized by the World Federation for Mental Health in association with the National Society for Mentally Handicapped Children, University College, Dublin, March 1971.

variation in quality in many different systems, whether of firms, schools or hospitals. There are new hospitals as at Northgate in England as well as those 50 or 100 years old. Similarly, there are new hospitals in Denmark, such as Vangede and Lillemosegard, with high standards of material provision, but other hospitals like Ebborodgard, in North Zeeland, which are 75 years old (1). In any national system there are elements which tend to become showpieces for international display or placatory gestures to the best elements among the professional staff, rather than models of what can be and are designed to become standard practice within a very short span of time. Variation in conditions is perhaps wider in Britain than in some countries. For instance, more buildings seem to have been adapted from other uses and embellished with annexes and architects' follies. This gives the sub-communities who live in them a certain distinctiveness from the rest of the hospital population. I have been in hospitals and other institutions in the United States and on the Continent with worse living quarters and stricter custodial regimes than any I have seen in Britain.

Ministerial Initiative to Deal with a Scandal

Britain's experience in the last two years, then, is an instructive example to study in order to understand why the problems of the mentally handicapped are so difficult to solve in any society. For it was two years ago this month that the report of an independent committee of inquiry into allegations of ill-treatment of patients in a Welsh hospital was published, and provoked immediate public anxiety (2). Official inquiries are conducted from time to time but rarely made public. After allegations had been published in a Sunday newspaper in 1967 a committee was set up under Sir Geoffrey Howe, Q.C. (now Solicitor General in the Conservative Government) towards the end of that year. The committee completed its hearing early in 1968 and though the date of submission of the report for the Minister of Health is not specified there is internal evidence which makes it likely that it went to the Ministry in the middle of 1968 (3). While there it must clearly have become the subject of acute controversy. To his credit, Mr R. H. S. Crossman, the Secretary of State for Social Services, who became responsible for the amalgamated Department of Health and Social Security in the late summer of 1968, decided that the report should be published. It appeared in March 1969. The nature of the report should be clearly understood. It did not just find certain members of staff at fault in their treatment of patients but traced responsibility through the senior nursing staff to the chief male nurse, the physician superintendent, the Hospital Management Committee and its officers, the Regional Hospital Board and, finally, the administrative structure of the National Health Service itself, including the authority exercised by the Minister. Junior staff were to some extent the victims of an inadequate system and of inadequate resources provided by the Government, the Boards and local authorities to that system.

> The present tripartite administrative structure of the National Health Service has failed, so far as Ely is concerned, to produce a sufficiently integrated service and pattern of care for the mentally subnormal. The concept of community care has been insufficiently developed. (4)

The Secretary of State then began to develop this theme with great energy. Recently I have studied afresh many of the press reports for 1969, 1970 and 1971. I would be surprised if there is any period in the history of Britain or any other country, even in the United States during President Kennedy's patronage of the issue, when the needs of the mentally handicapped have attracted greater public attention and sympathy. Having established a public bridgehead why was this advance not then consolidated?

It would, of course, be possible to give a narrative history at length. Mr Crossman visited hospitals, gave speeches and held press conferences throughout the country. He was applauded in Parliament for demonstrating in detail what he called the 'underprivilege' of the mentally handicapped inside and outside hospitals (5). In April 1969 he set up a working party to advise him on policy. By coincidence, soon afterwards Dr Pauline Morris's national survey of hospitals, which had been financed by the National Society for Mentally Handicapped Children, was published. It reinforced with a wealth of factual evidence the case for reorganization of services (6). Valuable information was becoming available also from Professor Tizard's and Dr Kushlick's research studies (7). Instances of ill-treatment at other hospitals came to light and were the subject of court cases. It will, of course, be many years before the full history of this period can be written. The Official Secrets Act prevents part of the story from being given. However, it is evident that the momentum was not sustained. A detailed statement of policy was delayed, first during the final six months of the Labour Government and then for the first nine months (so far) of the new Tory Government (8).

Early Contradiction in Policy

In retrospect I think it can be shown that under both Governments, and very early in the crisis, a fundamental contradiction in policy emerged. Both Mr Crossman and Sir Keith Joseph have pursued simultaneously two policies, on the one hand diminishing and on the other increasing the already large role played by hospitals in the total system of services for the handicapped. On 18 June 1969, for example, Mr Crossman said,

'My own top priority in the hospital service at present is to divert more resources to the long-stay hospitals which, I fear, have in the past often been a deprived sector of the hospital service' (9). However, on 25 September 1969, for example, he said, 'The basic policy will have to be that never again do we pile up human rejects behind these high walls' (10), and on other occasions added that there were thousands of the 60,000 long-stay patients who could live outside if there were places for them (11). Although no doubt Mr Crossman, Sir Keith Joseph and others would argue that it is possible to reconcile both objectives I do not believe they have insisted on spelling out the implications in full. Had they done so the contradiction would have become more apparent.

This contradiction has its roots in the structural contradictions of the management of the health and welfare services and in society itself. We have to draw on both political sociology and the sociology of communities for aid in constructing explanations. There are formal limitations on the powers of the Secretary of State which can largely obstruct him from putting into effect certain policies. To these can be added informal limitations as well — in terms of personnel, procedures and communications. There is a long chain of command down through the Regional Boards, Hospital Management Committees and hospitals, buttressed by Exchequer control of finance. The length of the chain and the weaknesses in some of its links make difficult the adoption and implementation in hospitals of new policies. The management committees badly need strengthening. Resolute policies can evaporate halfway down the hierarchy (12). Moreover, a country which sets considerable store in the principles of local democracy and family self-determination is bound to find it difficult to accommodate a hierarchical system of this kind.

Secondly, control over the local authorities is indirect. Ministers can enforce statutory regulations, inspect, exhort and tempt in a variety of ways. But their powers are emasculated in part by the lack of authority over staff, by lack of forms of specific grant and subsidy (especially since the percentage grant system was withdrawn) and by the cultural convention that local councils are supposed to have a very large measure of independence. Moreover, when all or nearly all local services can be shown to be starved of resources a Minister is likely to be inhibited from pressing his own particular claim too strongly. It would not have been surprising if Mr Crossman had been forced to conclude that the most important part of any new policy needing to be developed was ruled out because he was powerless to put it into execution. Even exhortation may have seemed impossible. During the campaign Mr Crossman was reported to have called all the Regional Hospital Board chairmen to meetings. To call together the representatives of nearly 200 local authorities in England and Wales must have seemed much less manageable. In any analysis of the distribution of power to determine the fate of men the cumulative effect of leaving out a key element at many stages of discussion and policy-making has to be remembered. Throughout 1969 and 1970 neither of the successive Secretaries of State could have been fully apprised of the importance of the community care services in any strategy. Even in the Department of Health itself the Secretary of State cannot be said to have an administrative staff which includes powerful representation in numbers and expertise of their interests. The same might be said of research. Those conducting research for the Hospital Boards are bound to have a different orientation to the mentally handicapped than if they had been working for the local authorities.

Thirdly, any proposed change of policy which appears to threaten the interests of bodies holding considerable power is likely to be resisted and to be diverted to those interests. The Secretary of State was indicating changes which might weaken the far-ranging authority of the nursing and medical professions, particularly those branches of the professions concerned with the long-stay hospitals for the mentally handicapped. Politicians and others called attention to the social and occupational needs of pat.ents and therefore to the appointment of far more specialist staff, such as social workers, and occupational therapists, the introduction of volunteers from the community and the encouragement of patients to visit and work in the outside community. The call to reduce hospital numbers came not only from the Government benches but also from the Opposition (13). There was a classical reaction on the part of nursing staff and medical superintendents. They closed ranks. All that was required, they said, was better resources and an end to the hurtful smears which sapped morale and endangered staff recruitment. Far from being run down the hospitals should be re-created and developed as centres of excellence, upon which the services for the community as well as the inmates could be based. Because so few staff work for the handicapped outside hospital and are also poorly organized, and because the nursing and medical staffs are dominant inside these hospitals and can bring pressure to bear on the Department of Health through a range of committees, it is not surprising that they were so successful in opposing the announcement of a new kind of policy.

Fourthly, the act of isolating mentally handicapped people, usually in large institutions, is also a political act. It confers greater power than perhaps we suspect on certain people but also certain ideas and values. The staff determine every detail of life of patients to an extent which is unrivalled in, say, the most paternalistic firm. This creates special problems for staff as well as patients. But this conferment of power has other effects. Physically we create populations which are fundamentally different from any local community. In structure they do not consist of three or four generations, with very small family units, and complex social and occupational networks, which are in personal contact with a wide range of different public services. It would be misleading to suggest that they are 'communities' in any ordinary sense of that term. Scientifically they do not satisfy certain conditions which might be laid down for rural or urban communities (14). As a consequence the system of political authority is much more oppressive for the patients. Compared with members of rural or urban communities they have fewer alternative groups to which to escape if the one in which they spend most of their time makes them feel unwanted or uncomfortable. There are fewer alternative channels of complaint, fewer alternative political agents to proselytize their interests and fewer possessions and less space in which to manoeuvre to show personal authority and independence. The individual patient is politically weak and vulnerable. It is important for us to understand that the very existence of the long-stay hospital shapes our concepts of mental handicap itself, our values, our fears and even our willingness to assume that the problem is one primarily for medicine and nursing (15).

The Structural Factors Obstructing Reform

These four structural factors in the distribution of power over the fates of the mentally handicapped — the despotic but also fragile chain of command from Government and Secretary of State to individual hospital and ward; the restricted powers of the central Government over the local authority; the concentration of real power over the handicapped upon hospital medical and nursing staffs, and the separation in space of ghettoes for the mentally handicapped — seem to me to be the crucial factors in explaining the failure of policy to match needs. For nothing effective to alter them was introduced during 1969-70. They are the fundamental political obstacles to improvement of services. These four factors in the political sociology of mental handicap help to explain why the radical policy which might have emerged in 1969 shows even less signs of emerging now. A more subtle and powerfully planned strategy to overcome each obstacle would be required. Instead, they were reinforced. At the end of 1969, for example, the Government announced certain stop-gap measures to spend money on food and furnishings in hospitals and build pre-fabricated units. The sums committed were not large by national standards (16) and do not seem to have resulted in other than minor improvements (17). The statement unfortunately weakened the demand for major measures to meet the crisis, and the pre-fabricated units have clearly been a mixed blessing. The need to reduce the hospital service in scale by rapidly building up local authority services and change its nature, by developing occupational and social therapy and introducing a new system of staffing, was quietly forgotten or at least postponed. As a consequence, policy was distorted into something almost the opposite of what was intended and radical reforms became much harder to introduce. This was a strategic mistake of the first order.

Nor should we ignore the impact that these changes might have wrought on the images of mental handicap held by first the medical and associated professions and secondly by other key groups in society — politicians, senior civil servants in the Department of Health and Social Security and organizations representing the interests of the mentally handicapped. By excluding mental handicap from having any substantial part in the medical curriculum the teaching hospitals have done notable disservice to the interest of the handicapped. The lack of adequate study and research has helped to perpetuate images of the mentally handicapped as incomplete persons and hence exposed them to custodial and authoritarian attitudes. All this can only gradually be undermined and replaced. Action on the four structural factors can accelerate the process.

Three Solutions
Various attempts to rationalize the crisis are still being made. I shall refer briefly to three — the fake 'normalization' solution, the Central Board solution and the hostel solution. In Britain, as in other countries, great emphasis has been placed in recent years on policies which allow the mentally handicapped to lead a normal life. Thus 'normalization' has been defined as 'making available to the mentally retarded patterns and conditions of everyday life which are as close as possible to the norms and patterns of the mainstream of society'. This would allow them to sleep in a private bedroom, mix easily with people of both sexes, eat breakfast in a small group, have considerable choice in clothing and leisure-time pursuits and leave home each day for a place of work where they earned wages (18). The Government has broadly supported this thesis (19). But much depends on how it is interpreted and worked out. It can, of course, be distorted.

Dr H. C. Gunzberg and others have seized on the concept of 'normalization' and invested it with a peculiar meaning partly, it would seem, to justify power being left with the hospitals. The term is, of course, a dreadful piece of jargon used to express an idea almost as old as man himself, namely that he should lead as normal a life as possible. But the elaboration of the concept seems to bear little relationship to our knowledge of human relationships. For example, no attempt is made to discuss the kinds of group within which individuals learn and practise the ordinary skills of living and whether the hospital can even in principle create the conditions necessary to offer the same opportunities. The family and the private household are, after all, very intimate units in social and emotional terms and their complex qualities are not easy to reproduce. If we were to attempt to investigate how to do so we would have to draw extensively upon social psychology and sociology. But the huge literature on family relationships, community behaviour and the socialization of the child is almost ignored by latter-day adherents of the view that the hospital is omnipotent. Dr Gunzberg argues that the hospital 'should be reorganized to become a preparatory stage before placement in normal conditions'. He asserts that it can 'normalize' people although he admits that it is 'not normal in itself' (20). This seems to me to be a very damaging admission. It is rather like suggesting that if you want to teach a child what it is to follow a normal family life you cannot do better than commit him to the care of parents who are far from being normal. One wonders why it is necessary in the first place to remove many handicapped people from the family and the community if the hospital would find it so difficult to reproduce their benefits. Dr Gunzberg does not pursue the implications of introducing more training, employment and social education for a 'hospital', its staffing and staff training, nor does he analyse numbers of patients involved in the different activities. This is especially important since he admits that there will continue to be many patients who will have to be protected from 'the mainstream of society'. Throughout history the rehabilitation ward, the therapeutic community, and similar experiments have in part served as distractions from the fact that most long-stay institutions have essentially negative functions. The study by Julius Roth and Elizabeth Eddy of the myth of rehabilitation in the institution on Welfare Island in New York stands as a warning to all who suppose that a form of institutional service fulfils a laudable function when in reality that function applies to a tiny minority of patients and amounts to an elaborate deceit not properly grasped by the public or even by all the staff. Unless words are to be drained of all meaning, 'normalization' can only mean the gradual abandonment of the hospital as the principal agent of caring for the handicapped. This is in fact the central idea of some experts overseas whose conception of 'normalization' is very different from that discussed by Dr Gunzberg (21).

A Central Board for the mentally handicapped on the model of those in Denmark and Sweden is currently regarded by some people in Britain as offering an alternative solution to all problems. They believe it would help to release much bigger resources for the mentally handicapped. But similar administrative forms play different functions in different countries. There are arguments from principle against such a change — for example that this would almost automatically give too much reliance to institutions in the overall system of care, make more difficult the sharing of responsibility with parents and the community, strengthen the already considerable powers of the professions, and reduce efficiency by hiving off certain kinds of services which are needed as much for the physically handicapped and elderly as the mentally handicapped. Some problems would therefore be solved at the expense of creating others. There are also arguments from history. Britain had a Central Board of Control which was wound up by stages in 1948 and 1959 — although with the benefit of hindsight it might have been preferable to place the service, like residential and welfare services for old people and the disabled, under the entire jurisdiction of local authorities. Moreover, the Kilbrandon and Seebohm Reports have led to acts of Parliament integrating the local personal social services. No country would easily contemplate the dismantling of legislation so soon after enacting it.

The argument for hostels as a substitute for hospitals has to be developed carefully and questioned critically at each stage. If hostels are remote from urban centres, unintegrated with any local community and managed in an authoritarian way they can suffer from most of the disadvantages of existing hospitals together with other disadvantages as well. It is social structure and organization that is important. Private households, sheltered housing, local authority hostels, hospital hostels and large hospitals form a continuum of domestic and social organization. Measures of intelligence and other abilities among the mentally handicapped show that the majority do not fall far short of the mean in the normal distribution. My implication is that the domestic unit in which they live should also be close to the private household. The development of small children's Homes, with six or seven children and houseparents, is a model which comes close to the ordinary family household. It is this which Dr Grunewald has in mind for the mentally handicapped (22). In British cultural terms this would be an extension to the mental handicap series of practice not only in large parts of the children's service but the services for old people and the disabled. In recent years local authorities have rapidly developed sheltered housing for small groups of elderly and disabled people. They can be placed in localities with which they are familiar and within easy distance of family and friends. Adapted or new flatlets or converted houses could be developed on the same model for mentally handicapped adults. The danger of the hostel of say 25 or 50 places, from a strictly sociological or social psychological point of view, is that it is not a household, a hospital, a family or a community.

This is not the place to elaborate alternative policy. If we were to confront the major obstacles which I have tried to identify we would need to adopt a programme of reducing overcrowding in hospitals, rapidly increasing sheltered housing, day centres and workshops in the community, by introducing a new percentage grant, or a five-year centrally financed community care programme to balance the reduction of the subnormality hospitals' share of the total costs of the National Health Service. Many other strategies would have to be pursued — such as the association of parents and local representatives with management of hospitals and hostels, and the training of new types of community work staff to support and advise the family. This amounts to a complicated redistribution of power. I have argued that the forces accounting for the present impasse lie deep. But the Government is now exhibiting moral cowardice. Only by putting its considerable weight unambiguously behind this central policy can the nation begin to resolve the crisis of the last two years.

Notes and References

1 See Shearer, A., *The Quality of Care. Report of A Study Tour in Denmark,* National Society for Mentally Handicapped Children, 1971. Whether there are similar variations in, say, the U.S.S.R., is problematical. Certainly there are first-hand international accounts of very good standards of treatment and staffing in 'children's houses' for the severely subnormal. See Boom, A. B., 'Children's House No. 15 for Severely Subnormal Children', in Segal, S. S., *Backward Children in the U.S.S.R.,* Leeds, Arnold, 1966.

2 *Report of the Committee of Inquiry into Allegations of Ill-Treatment of Patients and Other Irregularities at the Ely Hospital, Cardiff,* Cmnd. 3957, H.M.S.O., March 1969.

3 The proceedings were clearly treated as a matter of urgency and evidence was last heard on 23 February 1968 (Report, p. 8). Reference is made (Report, p. 105) to the fact that 'the recommendations of a Special Sub-Committee have been adopted (*to come* into effect on 1 April 1968)' [my italics], which suggests that the report was completed in the spring. I also understand that the Department of Health requested the committee more than once to shorten its report.

4 *Report of the Committee of Inquiry into Allegations of Ill-Treatment of Patients and Other Irregularities at the Ely Hospital, Cardiff,* Cmnd. 3957, H.M.S.O., March 1969, p. 128.

5 For example, on 11 February 1970: 'In 1968 43 per cent of patients in hospitals for the mentally handicapped were in wards of more than 50 beds and 58 per cent had less than 58 square feet of bedspace. Thirty-one per cent had no lockers . . . The minimum standard is far below the minimum standard we set ourselves long before I was Minister . . .' The difference in costs for acute and mentally handicapped patients was 'inexplicable except on grounds of underprivilege'. *The Times,* 12 February 1970.

6 Morris, P., *Put Away,* Routledge & Kegan Paul, 1969.

7 Tizard, J., *Community Services for the Mentally Handicapped,* Oxford University Press, 1964; Tizard, J., King, R. D., Raynes, N. V., and Yule, W., 'The Care and Treatment of Subnormal Children in Residential Institutions', *Proceedings Association for Special Education,* 1966; Kushlick, A. and Cox, G., 'The

Ascertained Prevalence of Mental Subnormality in the Wessex Region on 1 July 1963', *Proceedings of the First Congress of the International Association for the Scientific Study of Mental Deficiency*, Montpelier, September 1967.

8 [A Government White Paper was published in June 1971. For a comment see the Postscript below, p. 208.]

9 In a speech (in the event read for him) to the Annual Conference of the Association of Hospital Management Committees at Weston-Super-Mare.

10 The *Guardian*, 25 September 1969.

11 ibid., 16 April 1970.

12 The Ely Report gives instances of the local H.M.C. failing even to *see* major Government circulars about policy, op. cit., p. 106.

13 For example, Lord Balniel, the Opposition spokesman on health and social security, stated in Parliament on 11 February that 'At least half of the 60,000 patients in subnormality hospitals are not in need of constant nursing care at all although they need some kind of residential care. The emphasis should be on development of domiciliary services.'

14 See the review of meanings of 'community' by Stacey, M., 'The Myth of Community Studies', *British Journal of Sociology*, June 1969.

15 The point has not escaped research workers. For example, 'Treating the institution as if it were primarily a hospital introduces at the outset an obstacle to thinking about how it may be best used to serve the inmates', Roth, J. A., and Eddy, E. M., *Rehabilitation for the Unwanted*, New York, Atherton, 1967, p. 205.

16 In the financial year 1969-70 Regional Hospital Boards were believed to have been persuaded to re-allocate £2 million to long-stay hospitals from other uses. For the financial year 1970-71 the Government announced a further £3 million for these hospitals (or 7.3 per cent) but more than half of this would have been allocated in any case, since health service expenditure increases regularly each year, and current expenditure on all kinds of hospitals was planned to increase by 3.7 per cent at 1969 prices anyway. See Serota, Baroness, in *Subnormality in the Seventies, The Road to Community Care*, National Society for Mentally Handicapped Children, 1970, p. 5; and also *Public Expenditure 1968-9 to 1973-4*, Cmnd. 4234, H.M.S.O., December 1969, p. 52.

17 For example, press reports on the first pre-fabricated units to relieve over-crowding have called attention to the relatively ungenerous space and facilities. See also the reservation by Kushlick, A., 'Residential Care for the Mentally Subnormal', *Royal Society of Health Journal*, September/October 1970, pp. 260-61.

18 Nirje, B., 'Normalization', *The Journal of Mental Subnormality*, December 1970, p. 62, and Nirje, B., 'The Normalization Principle and its Human Management Implications', in Kugel, R., and Wolfersberger, W., *Changing Patterns in Residential Services for the Mentally Retarded*, Presidential Commission on Mental Retardation, Washington, 1969.

19 Most recently in the White Paper, *Better Services for the Mentally Handicapped*, Cmnd. 4683, H.M.S.O., 1971. For example, the White Paper asks for help and understanding to give the mentally handicapped person 'as nearly normal a life as his handicap or handicaps permit' as one of the principles on which services should be based (para. 40).

20 Gunzberg, H. C., 'The Hospital as a Normalizing Training Environment', *The Journal of Mental Subnormality*, December 1970, pp. 71-2.

21 See, for example, the work of Dr Grunewald from Sweden. In particular, he stresses the small group home for an average of seven people. Grunewald, K., 'The Guiding Environment: The Dynamic of Residential Living', Conference on *Action for the Retarded*, 28 March 1971 (publication forthcoming).

22 Conditions in Sweden are in any case much more favourable to the handicapped than in Britain. For example, only 11 per cent of those in any form of residential care are in hospitals. Practically half of the mentally handicapped sleep in single rooms and altogether 97 per cent are in bedrooms with four beds or fewer.

Postscript*

A White Paper published last week affords a decisive test of the Government's ability to comprehend a major human and social problem and do something effective about it. In 1969 the scandal of the ill-treatment of many patients in hospitals for the mentally handicapped broke upon an unsuspecting public. The report of a Committee of Inquiry, headed by a Q.C. who is now the Solicitor-General, revealed desperate overcrowding, primitive institutional amenities, insufficient occupation, lack of clothing and furniture and 'old-fashioned, unduly rough and undesirably low standards of nursing care' in one large hospital in Wales. Similar revelations about hospitals in Somerset, Essex and elsewhere were also made in the press, on television and in the courts.

The then Secretary of State for Social Services, Mr R. H. S. Crossman, deliberately fostered public concern. But when Labour lost the election in June 1970 it had taken only a few ill-considered interim measures and a White Paper was stuck in the pipeline.

The Tory Government has taken a whole year to ruminate over its predecessor's unpublished proposals and the decisions that have now been reached are tragically disappointing in nature and scale. The Government proposes a reduction of hospital numbers and a shift to a more balanced division of services between community care and hospitals but does so in a half-hearted and confused fashion which may result in a pattern of services little better than they are now.

For example, the question whether hospitals are an appropriate form of care for people who are not ill, but whose intelligence is limited, is not coolly and logically pursued. After all, it was only as a result of the administrative reorganization of the National Health Service in 1948 that many existing institutions were called hospitals.

That seems in retrospect to have been the wrong decision. All the statistical evidence (including some in the White Paper collected on behalf of the D.H.S.S.) shows that the great majority of people in such hospitals are not in need of continuous medical or nursing care, do not need 'assistance to feed, wash or dress' and even have 'no physical handicap or severe behaviour difficulties'.

This carries the inescapable conclusion that the basic forms of care required are social, occupational and educational and that except for very handicapped people who are also physically or mentally ill, and who might be cared for in general hospitals or units attached to general hospitals, these hospitals should be phased out. A date could have been worked out with hospital and local authorities, say 1981-2. The numbers are not so large and financial resources so restricted as to make such a programme unrealistic. Instead the Government has decided not only to spend money on improving old hospitals for temporary periods (how long will they last?) but erect new, small hospitals.

* Published in the *Sunday Times*, 27 June 1971.

It carries the conclusion that priority should be given to the build-up of community over the hospital services. Instead the Government has chosen to allocate most of the proposed increases in revenue and capital expenditure in the next few years to the hospitals.

It also carries the conclusion that much more money should be devoted in the immediate future to community services — family support services, such as home helps, workshops, day centres and group housing. A special rate support grant would be quite feasible as an emergency measure for a few years. Instead the Government accepts rates of growth of expenditure over 15-20 years which are only a little higher, and in some cases lower, than for other types of public expenditure.

Finally, it carries the conclusion that the alternative forms of residential care for the mentally handicapped should be worked out carefully, particularly in relation to the responsibilities of housing and social service departments for the elderly and physically disabled. Instead, the Government offers no sustained analysis of the social and residential needs of the mentally handicapped, although it asks hospitals and local authorities to fix dates 'after which the hospitals will not be expected to admit any more people needing residential rather than hospital care'.

The need for residential care is left undefined. Yet any dispassionate examination of the 'care and attention' clauses in the National Assistance Act about residential care in relation to the capacities of the mentally handicapped suggests that the need for sheltered housing (like children's homes for six children with houseparents, and group housing for elderly and disabled) will be substantial.

Although the Government suggests that the hospital population might eventually diminish to 56 per cent of its present size, the difference is more than made up by a proposed increase of residential Homes, with up to 25 people per Home. Much depends on whether or not this resembles private housing in urban localities. What the nation does not want is a system of minor isolated barracks put up by local authorities in pale imitation of the larger Victorian barracks which are at present run by the hospital authorities. Yet the White Paper makes this an all too likely possibility.

Britain can do a lot better, and more quickly, for this underprivileged minority. Living conditions in hospitals must of course be improved temporarily while the alternative in the community is created. But the real drive must be to build up opportunities for the mentally handicapped to lead an ordinary life like other people, go to work and school, attend day centres and physiotherapy sessions, and live in conditions of decency and privacy. That can be done only with the help of the new local social service departments, a sensitive appreciation of the needs of the family and imaginative leadership from Government.

13 Human need in Ulster *

There are other strategies open to a government in developing a course of policy than passing coercive legislation or implementing it widely and punitively. The Northern Ireland Payments for Debt (Emergency Provisions) Bill, 1971, became law on 14 October 1971 and was rushed through the Northern Ireland Parliament without a single amendment. The act is designed to counter civil disobedience and the rent strikes in particular. While no one would question the lawful right of a housing authority to receive rents from its tenants, the act raises serious issues, some of them unprecedented in the United Kingdom, about civil rights. For example, it is retrospective to 1 April 1971 even though Britain is a signatory to the European Commission of Human Rights, which prohibits retrospective legislation. Because it is retrospective and because the Northern Ireland Government and not the court is left to determine the rate of repayment, the weekly deductions from earnings and social security benefits for rent, rates and water rates could be (and have been) excessive. Moreover, section 2 of the act empowers the Government not just to force families to pay council rents by cutting off incomes at source, but to charge additionally for interest (at a rate to be determined by the Government) and for the costs of collection.

The act makes it possible for the Government to seize national insurance benefits, including retirement pensions and sickness benefits, which have been previously treated as inalienable rights secured by virtue of contributions paid by the individual over many years. Indeed, the list of benefits which can be seized — which includes invalidity and industrial injury pensions, attendance allowances (for the most severely disabled people in society) and even the death grant — constitutes one strand of evidence making it difficult to believe that the intentions of the act are 'reasonable'.

The act also restricts the powers of the courts to safeguard the individual's rights. Contrary to previous legislation about debts, the court cannot make an order for a repayment of less than the amount due; nor is it empowered to hear the individual, take account of his means and issue an order governing the amount of repayment. The

---

* First published in *New Society*, 25 November 1971.

scope for any appeal is restricted only to liability, and cannot cover the rate of repayment or any administrative lapse. There is no appeal against the allocation of social security payments towards the clearance of debt.

Finally, the act pays little regard to the general objective of social security legislation to meet human need. No principle guaranteeing a subsistence income for children, the chronic sick or old people is invoked. Amounts of debt are to be deducted from income without regard to family circumstances. Subsection 4 of section 1 specifies that in cases of reduction of benefit to pay debt no payment shall be made by the Supplementary Benefits Commission to meet exceptional need, but the commission 'may in their absolute discretion, specially determine under this subsection to pay such benefit'. A printed form circulated by the Government states that a debtor 'or his wife will not normally be entitled to supplementary benefit on account of exceptional need'.

When the act was passed in mid-October it went virtually unreported in the British press and there appears to have been no editorial comment. On 11 November the Child Poverty Action Group attempted to get the issues discussed publicly. On 12 November the Northern Ireland Government reacted defensively. Up to that date no public pronouncement had been made about the way the Government intended to interpret and apply the act, although families were already finding that their benefits were reduced. The Government now said it was applying the legislation reasonably, deducting up to a maximum of £1.50 per week in some cases, and up to £3.50 in others. Orders for repayment up to these maxima began to be issued on that day and some orders for repayment which had been issued previously were changed. But before 12 November punitive deductions were being made. This is demonstrated by photocopy evidence of deductions in the possession of the Child Poverty Action Group, for example, of £8.50 and £9.50 per week.

Public opinion in Britain seems to have forced the Government to begin applying the act less severely. But many questions remain unanswered. Some affect the narrow application of the act. Thus, is it reasonable to deduct as much for the repayment of rent from a family which is heavily wage-stopped as from another family? Are the severely disabled and elderly really going to have their pensions withdrawn, as the act allows?

The fundamental issues are even wider. In terms of the needs of the poor as well as of social progress, the act must be seen as unnecessary in the first place and likely only to worsen poverty and social relations. Although many families only began to withhold their rent after the introduction of internment (a measure which is itself not difficult to represent as a departure from fair legal process) some had already struck in protest at the failure of the housing authorities to mend roofs, windows, doors and lavatories. Environmental services, like street lighting, cleaning and repairs have deteriorated. The rate of unemployment is just under 10 per cent among men, and is much higher among the Catholic than the Protestant population. Families are living in constant fear of arson, military searches in the middle of the night, injury and death. The administration is under great strain and, quite apart from the act, the C.P.A.G. is getting reports that some households fail to receive social security payments regularly. All this means severe deprivation in a region which already has an incidence of poverty two or three times higher than Britain.

Emergency legislation of a negative kind is therefore no answer. What is required is a broad social policy which is immediate, generous and just. It must cover temporary housing for the homeless and an urgent repairs programme as well as the fair allocation of permanent housing; a public employment policy as well as incentives to boost employment generally; a bold programme to improve environmental and welfare facilities, particularly for children, and to make immediate payments through social security to meet family needs arising from the crisis. The act suggests that the Northern Ireland Government no longer has the capacity or imagination to develop such a policy, and plainly massive resources are required from the British Government.

14 Home and welfare services for old people*

In the 1930s the unemployed posed, by common consent, the biggest social problem for Britain; since the war this unenviable position has been occupied by the elderly. Why should this be so? Why, after twelve or thirteen years' experience of the post-war legislation, are the problems of the aged so insistent, so disturbing, and, generally speaking, so far from amelioration, still less solution? To answer these questions one would have to delve deep into the history of policy formation, taking careful note of the influence of economic crises, of the pressures, professional and otherwise, laid upon the Government, and of the values subscribed to by planners and politicians, into the separate and not always complementary functions of different services concerned with the aged, into the paucity of certain kinds of information from Government and independent sources, and into the experiences of old people themselves in their day-to-day lives, including their contacts with local and central administration. I cannot attempt to deal properly with these fascinating issues. All I can do is to try to keep the major questions before you and to select a few of the facts bearing upon them. I shall confine myself to tracing some of the developments in the home and welfare services for the aged — by which I mean the local health authority services (home help, district nursing and health visiting), housing and residential accommodation, and a diverse group of voluntary and local authority services, ranging from chiropody, laundry, visiting and meals services to social clubs and day and occupation centres.

How are shortcomings assessed? One method is individual illustration. Just over two years ago an unmarried man of seventy-four was living in one room in a house scheduled for clearance in north London. No repairs had been carried out for many years. There was one tap for all the occupants in the basement and no electricity. The old man had £2 14s. 6d. national assistance, plus, from November to May, a coal allowance of 4s. 6d. He paid 5s. 3d. rent. He had a heart attack and was in hospital for three weeks. He then came home but found it increasingly difficult to get to the shops and look after himself. He had

* An address given on Friday, 12 May 1961, at the annual general meeting of the Association of Directors of Welfare Services in the City of Bath.

no surviving relatives. He went to his doctor, who gave him a prescription for sleeping tablets and embrocation and told him he should go into a Home.

A neighbour took pity on him and started giving him meals and getting his shopping. As she had small children to look after this began to prove difficult and she got in touch with the local old people's welfare association. After a visit the secretary came to the same conclusion as the doctor. Reluctantly the old man was persuaded to see one of the L.C.C. welfare officers. The welfare officer thought that he urgently required admission and suggested Luxborough Lodge, three miles away, a former workhouse with 1,250 beds and the largest residential establishment for old people in the country, and then two other former workhouses south of the river. The old man stuck out against this. His brother had died in Luxborough Lodge a few years before and he did not think much of the place. Could he be admitted into a small Home locally, the neighbour asked? There were four or five in the borough, which was particularly favoured in London, and she and others would be able to visit him. The welfare officer said no. The old man could not be looked after properly except in a large Home and, anyway, he was not 'the type of person' who would fit into a small Home. What he did not say was that only a quarter of the old people entering L.C.C. accommodation go into anything but the former workhouses. The old man stuck to his guns even when the welfare officer argued that the former workhouses had completely changed in their character. 'Leopards never change their spots and them leopards are still here.' A second welfare officer called and could not persuade him to change his mind. Neither of them could suggest practicable alternatives.

The neighbour went back to the old people's welfare association and found, despite genuine sympathy and understanding, that No, services in the home were not provided. She began to learn about the variety of different organizations, contacted the Town Hall and got the Home Help Organizer along. 'It's difficult for my home helps to work in places like this,' the organizer said, 'and anyway, they're in short supply. If we got one we couldn't promise more than an hour a week.' The neighbour 'phoned the L.C.C. again and eventually it was agreed to put the old man on a waiting list for a small Home, but he would have to wait at least six months and probably indefinitely. 'It will be a miracle,' said one of the officers. So there we were. The man seemed to be dying of cancer. He had an inadequate income. The doctor would not recommend him for hospital because there was a shortage of beds and he did not require continuous nursing care. He had no prospect of getting a flatlet with better amenities or of getting the services of an adequate home help service. He got meals from a mobile meals service, but only twice a week. In practice he had no choice but to live where he was or go into a former workhouse. This would have been miles from the few friends he had and would have meant final separation from the big ginger tom cat on which he doted. The welfare officer did not visit him again although a representative of the old people's welfare association called two or three times. Who, in any event, was responsible for seeing that his needs were met? His neighbour visited him daily, at considerable cost to herself, to get his shopping, empty his slops, clean his room and give him meals, because there was no one else.

This might have been the end of the story. In fact he took a turn for the worse and his doctor secured his admission to a chronic sick ward of a nearby hospital. He stayed there for two weeks over Christmas and spoke up courageously about the poor facilities. One W.C. was shared by two wards of men and in the early morning there was always a queue, including patients in wheel-chairs. He said there was no handbasin which the men could use for shaving and washing and that the patients were expected to be out of bed at 5.20 a.m. for a cursory wash of their faces and hands. He was sent home without any attempt apparently being made to find what kind of home he was going to, and no follow-up visit was arranged by the hospital. He was rapidly going down-hill and had dysentery. His neighbour went in daily to perform the herculean task of nursing him in bed. She herself contacted the district nursing and home help services and finally a nurse and a home help began to visit daily. But this lasted only three days, for he died early one Saturday evening. Even in death he was neglected, for, despite requests, the doctor did not come to see him and, because it was a weekend, no one was sent to remove the body until 4.30 p.m. on the following Monday. He lay quite unattended for forty-six hours in a house occupied by three other people, except that his ginger cat was still perched on his chest.

Perhaps I do not need to apologize for describing this example at length. It simply bears out so many of the shortcomings in our services which can be documented at length. How can they be explained? In the first place we must remember that a good deal of the 1945-8 legislation was backward-looking, meaning that it was framed largely in terms of the problems encountered in the 1930s, and in terms of some of the problems encountered in the war. The issue of old age, as we know it, was not really faced. We have only to remember how the Beveridge Report was preoccupied with the subsistence standard — a measure taken over from pre-war surveys of poverty — and how it neglected (perhaps understandably) the implications of the growth in occupational pension schemes, to realize how quickly social change can make social provisions look archaic. Or take the home help service, which was expanded in the war largely as a means of aiding the mother during childbirth and yet which has become increasingly concerned with the needs of old people. One wonders now whether its originators would have been so insistent, if they had been able to foresee developments, on making it a service administered by the Medical Officers of Health.

In tracing since the war the origins of many of the services for the aged one looks in vain for signs of imaginative foresight of what might be required, for any semblance of long-term strategy in the development of the services. Instead we have a rather odd arrangement of services which have grown up piecemeal, which some are glad to explain away as the British 'genius' for improvisation. Nothing could better illustrate this than the sections of the National Assistance Act dealing with handicapped and old people's welfare, which have hardly encouraged the rapid expansion of adequate schemes and which have led to an uneven and confused pattern of existing services. Legislation cannot be wholly attuned to modern needs if, in order to provide necessary laundry and meal facilities, some local authorities have to disguise themselves as voluntary associations.

In legislating for the 1950s, then, society did not sufficiently anticipate needs. But what in fact has happened since 1948? The switch in social priorities to increasing provision for the aged has not been as rapid as so many people have tended to assume. I shall briefly consider domiciliary, housing and residential services in turn.

Services in the Home

The most encouraging development has been the increase in the number of people entering the domestic help service. Over the last five years the number of domestic helps in England and Wales has increased by the equivalent of 1,300 full-time workers a year (the rate of increase being very much faster from 1948 to 1952). There are now the full-time equivalent of roughly 25,000 (assuming that two part-time workers equal one full-time worker). We must remember, however, that this number is only about half that of domestic staff working in hospital wards and rather less than 6 per cent of the total number of people in private domestic service in the country. We must also remember that only about two thirds of those aided are elderly persons; that they comprise only about 3-3½ per cent of people over sixty-five, and that two or three hours' cleaning a week is the usual quota. So here we have a gradual but scarcely remarkable expansion.

The shortcomings of the service can to a partial extent be indicated by the variations from district to district. Some research in which I have recently been involved shows that in places like Lancashire, Nottinghamshire, London, Barnsley, Newcastle, Wigan, Rotherham, Reading and South Shields between 6 per cent and 10 per cent of people aged sixty-five and over had a home help. In many other places, such as Cornwall, Derbyshire, Herefordshire, Huntingdonshire, Sussex, Chester, Hastings, Liverpool, and Manchester, fewer than 2 per cent did so. From knowledge of the circumstances of old people up and down the country nothing suggests that their needs vary so widely as this. 'In many areas,' states the report on a Ministry of Health survey of services available to the elderly (the Boucher Report), 'the service was thinly spread. In Tynemouth a help was rarely supplied for more than two weeks for any one person and never for longer than six weeks. In Carmarthenshire, on the other hand, although the home help's duties were limited to domestic cleaning, she could if necessary devote up to 24 hours a week to the care of any one individual.' And in Hartlepool the service was restricted to once a fortnight. Thus, according to where they live, infirm old people living alone with identical needs may get one or two hours' cleaning once a day, once a fortnight, or not at all. Sometimes all kinds of household services seem to be available, including shopping, washing, and cooking as well as cleaning; more often there is cleaning only. A lot depends on whether or not the Medical Officer of Health takes the view that giving a small number of people considerable help is preferable to giving the maximum number of people a little.

There is less ground for satisfaction, if that is the word, with home nursing. The equivalent of about sixty or seventy extra full-time nurses a year have been recruited to the home nursing services since 1956. The rate of increase has steadily diminished in the last five years. Again, there was a much quicker expansion in the years after 1948. We are better off by only 2,500 nurses in this service than we were before 1948 (the hospitals being over 43,000 better off — I would remind you that the nursing staff of the hospitals numbers about 200,000 — compared with 10,000 district nurses). These nurses pay about half of their visits to old people. So here we have witnessed little expansion and, for reasons which I shall touch on later, may be facing an urgent problem.

The third local health authority service we may consider is health visiting. If we count two part-time workers as one full-time worker, there are now fewer health visitors than there were between 1948 and 1952. The proportion of visits paid to old people has remained at less than 10 per cent throughout the last decade, despite recent exhortations to give more time to the aged. Although the figures do not disclose the situation exactly, I think it would be true to say that a smaller proportion of old people are visited by health visitors than ten years ago.

It is difficult to judge what expansion has taken place in the mobile meals services and some of the other services provided entirely or mainly by voluntary organizations. There is no hard evidence of a rapid increase in recent years. A very rough picture emerges from study of the annual reports of old people's welfare committees and of bodies such as the W.V.S. In Barnet, for example, about 21 meals are served twice a week. In Poplar the W.V.S. cooks and serves 130 meals a week, in Ipswich 80-90 and in Newcastle 150 (fifty people getting meals three times a week). These are typical examples from areas where a service exists. In some places the meals are supplied by civic restaurants, in others by factory canteens or by a central kitchen of the welfare department, and in still others by the school meals service. At Stoke-on-Trent two meals are delivered on each visit in the hope that one will be heated and eaten the following day. Most of the mobile meals services operate on a once, twice or thrice weekly basis and hardly any serve a meal each day of the week. The service thus varies widely in its organization and scope but usually seems to be concerned with 20-30 people and rarely more than 50 or 100 in a locality with an elderly population of a few thousands.

A recent inquiry undertaken by the Government Social Survey for the National Corporation for the Care of Old People showed that only just over 20,000 old people in the country, or less than half of one per cent, are aided by mobile meals services. An attempt was made in this inquiry to estimate what the true needs are. The first step was to calculate how many people would be aided if existing services were extended to areas where there is as yet no provision. Eighteen thousand, or 85 per cent, more people would be added to the figure of 20,000. The second step was to ask those receiving meals whether they wanted more. The average person received less than two meals per week and expressed a wish for rather more than three. Altogether it seemed that the services should be expanded at least three- or four-fold if current needs are to be met. Even this estimate is a conservative one, for it is based on the assumption that in the areas where meals are served there are no other old people requiring them.

This is a somewhat chastening conclusion, especially when we place it in the context of other developments. Home helps may be helping more people to get adequate midday meals but there is no general evidence of their work being directed towards this function. And when we learn of recent experiments with day centres and luncheon clubs we would do well to recall the closing of civic restaurants since the war. In 1945 there were 1,600 civic restaurants in the country, which were a great help to the aged. By 1953 the number had fallen to 250.

The search for evidence can be instructive. Anyone attempting to form a general view about the progress that has been made since the war in domiciliary services which are unsupported, or only partly supported, by public funds will be disappointed by the lack of information on a national scale; he will be confused by conflicting statements about adequacy, and bewildered by the immense variety of provision and types of administration; and, if he is not careful, he will gain a false impression of the scale of activity from the publicity that is given to a few notable experiments going on in the country. This last is of particular interest. Some of the experiments in day centres, occupation centres, boarding-out schemes, night-attendance schemes and so on for the elderly have been under way for ten years. They have attracted a good deal of approbation, and books and articles on the welfare of the aged contain many references to them; but none, so far as I am aware, have been studied critically in the appropriate detail and none could be said to have caught on like the prairie fire. To local authorities and voluntary organizations no less than to individuals a place loses some of its attractions when others have been there before. Sometimes, therefore, there are deceptively few parts of the country possessing certain services.

Housing Services

No survey of post-war developments, however sketchy, would be complete without some reference to housing and residential services. Only in the last few years has a special interest been taken in old people's housing. In the years immediately following the war the chief problem was the overall housing shortage, and efforts were mainly directed towards building homes for young families. Today we are beginning to recognize that old people have special housing needs. An analysis of the 1951 Census revealed that proportionately more elderly persons living alone were deprived of certain basic household amenities, such as piped water, cooking stoves and water closets, than the rest of the population.

But the problem is a more subtle one than this. A growing proportion of the elderly seems to be living alone and there is much too little compact accommodation, consisting of small flatlets or bungalows with one or two bedrooms, to serve their needs. The Ministry of Housing has not attempted to obtain and publish detailed information about new housing occupied by old people and the figures issued about completed one-bedroom dwellings are not impressive. Since 1945 about 175,000 such dwellings have been built by local authorities. The annual total rose from about 17,000 to only 22,000 in the seven years between 1952 and 1959. Although it is extremely difficult to make estimates of need it can be shown that the number of households comprising one or two persons aged sixty-five and over is increasing by at least 40,000 per year. Quite apart from the question of making up previous deficiencies this comparison seems to supply a rough measure of the extent to which housing policy is failing to meet emerging needs.

Another special feature of the housing problems of the elderly is that produced by disability or handicap. Various surveys suggest that about 10 per cent of the elderly living at home are housebound or bedfast and others are restricted in their mobility and physical capacity. There appears to be therefore a *prima facie* case for building a large proportion of houses specially designed to cater for different levels of infirmity and handicap, where effective use can be made of local welfare services. The most promising method of meeting this need is through 'grouped dwellings' schemes. Mr S. K. Ruck recently undertook a survey in which he found that less than one elderly person in every 1,000 had so far benefited from such schemes put into operation by local authorities. The distribution, he said, was 'patchy'. Both Middlesex and Lancashire, for example, have an elderly population of about 250,000 and the inquiry showed that the former had 39 grouped dwellings and the latter 443. More than half the county and county borough councils had no schemes at all.

Residential Services

Residential accommodation has also suffered from lack of money and drive in the last ten years. In his speech on the second reading of the National Assistance Bill at the end of 1947 the Minister of Health, Aneurin Bevan, said that the workhouse was to go and that it was a very evil institution. Later on the Parliamentary Secretary to the Ministry of Health, Mr John Edwards, said, 'even if nothing else happens . . . the Poor Law is dead'. The annual report of the Ministry for the year ended 31 March 1949 added, 'The workhouse is doomed'. The plan was to close down the former public assistance institutions as fast as possible and to make a break with the past. These statements have found an echo in some of the remarks recently made about old mental hospitals by the present Minister of Health, Enoch Powell.

In 1950 there were, as shown by the Ministry of Health, 38,000 or 39,000 residents living in former workhouses and other old institutions; on 31 December 1957 there were 34,000. Although the Ministry has not supplied later information this figure cannot have changed much in the last few years.

I do not want to give the impression that substantial improvements have not taken place in residential services. Many new Homes have been built since 1950. Many others have been converted from large houses, where the amenities and standards of comfort are satisfactory. Moreover, good use is being made of Homes run by voluntary associations, such as the Red Cross, the W.V.S. and the Salvation Army. Neither would it be realistic to ignore the influence of a long series of economic crises in delaying building projects and of the difficulties of accommodating very frail people. When all such qualifications are made the stark conclusion remains that the 1947 aims have not been realized.

Most local authorities are reconciled to keeping the old workhouses for the foreseeable future. It can be, and is, argued that the workhouses can be modernized out of all recognition, and that, for the very frail, these large premises serve a useful function. But this argument has not been discussed fully in public. The issues are not debated in Parliament. The facts are not known. I would add, by way of justification for putting the matter in such a simple frame — and thereby risking the real possibility of misunderstanding — that evidence of a *general* transformation of the conditions of the old workhouses does not exist. The Ministry itself has stated that there are 'institutions which have shown little change since 1948'.

Developments in Government Strategy

What principles lie at the basis of present policy? What has been the overall strategy adopted by both Labour and Conservative Governments since 1948? Despite their simplicity these questions are not at all easy to answer. In a parliamentary debate, the previous Minister of Health expressed the Government's policy as follows: 'First, more effective liaison is required between the various agencies providing the services; secondly, the key to problems stemming from an ageing population lies with the preventive and home services, for the extension of communal accommodation can never of itself be enough.' This was not a new pronouncement. These two principles — good liaison and keeping old people in their homes — have been advocated down the years by different Government spokesmen.

To what extent is the problem one of achieving better liaison and co-ordination? Let me quote one authority on the subject who refers to medical as well as other services for the aged.

A review of the reports left the impression that the liaison between the general and the mental hospitals was often poor, and the co-operation between the hospitals, Medical Officers of Health and general practitioners was not usually satisfactory. Even the liaison between the health and welfare department of a local authority, where they were separate, was sometimes inadequate. In a few places the hospital and the local health authority appeared to ignore each other's existence. Co-operation between the various authorities at officer level was usually stated to be cordial and satisfactory, but the results did not always confirm this belief ... The existence and activities of a long established Old People's Welfare Committee in one County Borough were unknown to the Medical Officer of Health ... It was frequently asserted that a separation of the health and welfare departments had not always worked to the advantage of either department or of the old people.

There are further statements of a similar kind.

The person speaking here is not Mr Guillebaud. It is not the chairman of the National Old People's Welfare Council or the Secretary of the National Corporation for the Care of Old People. It is not even Professor Titmuss. It is Dr Boucher, a Senior Medical Officer of the Ministry of Health, in a semi-official report of a Ministry survey of the services for the chronic sick and elderly. We have no reason to suppose that a purely independent inquiry would be less critical. Those of us who have carried out research on any of these services could provide many more examples. Some have been supplied recently by Miss Slack for the County of London in a fascinating and cogent report. Exhortations by cabinet ministers over the past ten years do not appear to have achieved a great deal. The domiciliary services are unco-ordinated, many of those in charge of old people's Homes do not appear to be in harmony with those in charge of hospital accommodation; preventive and after-care services for the elderly barely exist in many areas, and generally it is clear that many professional workers operate in complete isolation of one another, despite their overlapping of interests. With the rapidly increasing number of old people and with more and more specialization in the various social services, the difficulties are likely to increase rather than diminish. This is a very serious situation. It is worth recalling that the Guillebaud Committee argued strongly that the inadequacy of the hospital and residential services for the aged was more important than their lack of co-ordination. Nevertheless, the committee took a rather different line about the preventive health and after-care services and suggested that proper integration was more important than spending larger sums of money. A detailed study of the text reveals a number of inconsistencies, but they were able to qualify what they said by referring to the Ministry of Health survey, which was then under way and which I have just quoted. The survey, said the committee, would 'enable the authorities to judge how far, and in what respects, the provision now being made under the National Health Service Acts and the National Assistance Act is failing to meet the needs'.

The survey is in fact more revealing than some people are inclined to believe. It points to the conclusion, first, that comparatively little progress has been made in improving co-ordination between the different services; but secondly, that the need for better co-ordination is of much less importance than the need for a reform of the administrative structure and for a big expansion in the various services.

Adequacy of Services

This brings us to the second object of Government policy since the war — to help old people to stay in their own homes for as long as possible. This is wholly worthy and has been supported by the findings of social surveys from 1945 onwards. But how much should be spent on home services and how much on the residential or institutional services? So far as the figures can be interpreted it seems that in 1959-60 the gross expenditure on the aged by the home help, district nursing, and health visiting services was in the region of £10-11 million. Allowing for all kinds of other local authority and voluntary expenditure on meals in the home, chiropody, laundry and the rest, the total spent on domiciliary services for the aged may have been over £12 million. Gross expenditure on Part III residential accommodation alone was over £25 million in the same year. The figures are necessarily rough but the relativity does not seem to have changed much in the past ten years. Is this what we mean by giving priority to the preventive and home services? Does the figure of about £12 million spent on meeting the needs of the elderly at home seem adequate in relation to the sum being spent on, say, the ambulance services, the care of mothers and young children, or the executive council's share of superannuation for G.P.s? Does the figure sound very realistic in a period when there is growing insistence on the quick turnover of geriatric beds and on the importance of avoiding institutionalization, whether for children, young adults or old people? Should we perhaps remind ourselves that in ten years the number of people in the population aged seventy-five and over has increased by several hundred thousands, or about 27 per cent, and that there are now nearly 2 million of them? Most of the old people served by home helps and district nurses are of this age.

One of the reasons for the present lack of public concern about the needs of the aged is the lack of high-level inquiry and investigation. The Guillebaud Committee devoted 5½ of its 310 pages to the care of the aged. The Phillips Committee had previously given up 6½ of its 120 pages to roughly the same subject. No other Government committee or commission has examined the problems since the war. The Government, and indeed the Opposition, seems to have little interest in investigating the welfare and social needs of the elderly. There was the spectacle recently, for example, of the National Advisory Committee on the Employment of Old People being wound up without undertaking the research that had been advocated in its two preliminary reports. The committee had not even met for the last 2½ years of its existence.

I have come back to this central matter of the need for investigation and the paucity of information because it makes difficult any general assessment of policy trends since 1948, particularly in relation to services which vary so widely in their objects, their administration, their financing and their scope. With this major qualification we are obliged to conclude that the major social issue of the 1950s, and now the 1960s, was not properly foreseen in the early post-war discussions and legislation; that some of the most important aims affecting the elderly have not been put into practice; that the development of many services has scarcely kept pace with the rising numbers of old people, still less met their needs; that despite the most strenuous and imaginative efforts on the part of many voluntary and statutory bodies the pattern of services is extraordinarily fragmented and unco-ordinated, and that despite public advocacy of the principle of, wherever possible, maintaining the elderly in their own homes there is no evidence of the switch in priorities which would be necessary if this principle were to be applied. In short, the challenge has not been posed or met. A future social historian may well select this as the most striking failure of social policy in the last decade.

The Approach to Policy

Without having more detailed information it is difficult to be confident about the exact form that future policy should take. But a few possibilities can be posed, on the basis of present knowledge.

The more we consider the fragmentation of existing services and the ways in which, as in the example of the old man I quoted earlier, needs are unmet and undetected, the more we are led to the conclusion that one department in each local area should be primarily responsible for the social and welfare needs of handicapped and aged individuals living in their own homes. Some people argue that this responsibility should be exercised by the health department of the local authority. My own research studies, however, suggest that this is not likely to be the best solution. In principle it would seem advantageous in the future to make a clearer distinction between the administration of health and welfare services. On present information and experience there is a strong argument for the enlargement of the local authority welfare department. The argument would start from the need to pay systematic visits to the handicapped and aged. The crucial step may be to make it a duty for each local authority to compile and maintain a list of isolated and homebound people, with simple information about each individual. Until that is done no local authority will be convinced of the extent of its responsibilities. Lists have sometimes been drawn up in various areas but usually in a haphazard way with no precise idea of purpose and with no conception of the problems of keeping them up to date. Voluntary organizations which have sometimes attempted this have found the job of doing it properly far beyond their resources. In time I think the aim should be to visit new single or widowed pensioners with the intention of building up a list of the 10 per cent to 20 per cent of people requiring regular visiting or help by the various domiciliary services. The list would serve purposes similar to the registers of other handicapped groups — the blind and partially sighted and the younger disabled. Perhaps a start could be made through the Ministry of Pensions and the National Assistance Board with pensioners over seventy-five.

Who should do the visiting? The strongest argument is in favour of people with social work training being attached to the welfare department. They might do the initial or 'assessment' visits and local voluntary services could play a valuable role in carrying out supplementary 'friendly' visits.

The next major function of the welfare department might be to manage the home help service. The demands upon this service have in fact been growing fast and although in some areas its functions are limited almost entirely to house-cleaning, in others washing and shopping are done and meals prepared. Moreover, the home help is extremely popular. This suggests that the service should have responsibility for all household jobs which for one reason or another the old person (or his family) cannot provide. It would make sense for the service to undertake delivery of meals and provide facilities for laundry. If each welfare department had a nucleus of full-time visiting staff, with social work training, and also had control of the domestic help service, a basis would exist for a comprehensive family help service, with the very definite purpose of keeping the isolated and homebound aged in touch with society. I have deliberately referred to a 'family' rather than a 'home' help service to imply the two chief purposes of any comprehensive home service: (i) to provide normal family services for those who have no families; (ii) to provide 'support' services for those families of old people which carry a heavy burden of care. Its functions would be visiting, household jobs (such as cleaning, shopping and washing), night attendance, and delivery of meals. This service might also manage specially designed dwellings for the aged and handicapped and be able to put a person's home into a good state of repair. I do not think we can meet all the problems without new legislation. Far too little use has so far been made by the local authorities of the permissive powers in the National Assistance and Health Service Acts. This is one possible means of integrating existing services.

Another is the possible secondment of a district nurse and a health visitor or a psychiatric social worker to a group of general practitioners, who aim to examine regularly all their elderly patients over a certain age, say seventy-five or eighty. I doubt whether general practitioners will be able to play a full part in the development of preventive health services and after-care unless there is a deliberate attempt to encourage groups of them to work more often together, with the proper assistance of ancillary workers. This argument is reinforced by any consideration of emerging needs in the community mental health services.

This is no more than an inadequate indication of a policy which would have to be worked over in every detail before it could be realistically presented. However, it suggests the two major reforms which may be necessary if old people as well as other handicapped and infirm persons are to be offered the right to go on living in their own homes.

15 Integration and segregation of the aged in industrial societies *

Before the end of the Second World War few studies of ageing or the aged in industrial societies had been carried out by social scientists. In Britain, for example, little information on the aged at home or in institutions was published between 1900 and the mid-1940s. Yet in this period the number of people aged sixty-five and over grew from under 2 to 5 million. It was left to a doctor, J. H. Sheldon (later to become president of the International Association of Gerontology), to produce, as late as 1947, the first really perceptive account of the social problems of the elderly (1). Since then, in the short span of less than twenty years, the number of studies has swollen rapidly, from a trickle to a modest stream and, at least in the United States, to an impressive flood. The proceedings of the 1960 Congress of the International Association of Gerontology were recorded with difficulty in four large volumes costing $47.50 cents.

Public interest has followed a somewhat parallel course with official inquiries being started, networks of government, municipal and voluntary committees being created and discussions in the press, on radio and television recurring frequently in most industrial countries, particularly during the last ten years. A remarkable publicity campaign was mounted in the United States where for example, after the Council of State Governments in 1955 recommended an intricate pattern of inter-departmental and citizens' advisory committees supported by paid staffs at state level (2), all fifty states put committees to work in preparation for a giant White House Conference on Ageing, which was held in 1961.

This explosion of interest must not be applauded uncritically. The setting up of elaborate research studies and of committees sometimes diverts public attention from government unwillingness to spend money on services. This is a risk which is particularly liable to affect old people since, unlike professional, trade union and even some unemployed groups of younger age, they are unable to prosecute their own interests indefatigably. Another risk is that the multiplication of voluntary committees is of little or no help to old people if these committees are

* The plenary address at the First Canadian Conference on Ageing, Toronto, 24 January 1966.

unconcerned with training, good organization and the careful selection of priorities. Just when the public may feel comforted by the growth in the number of agencies concerned with the aged, their problems may in fact be getting worse. In the bitter winter of 1962/3 in London I knew of the desperate plight of a widow in her eighties living with a disabled son of sixty in a flat in an old tenement block. After leaving hospital she had become ill again with pneumonia and for some days a hospital bed could not be found for her. Her son had bronchitis and could not get out. Sewage spilled over the floor from burst pipes in the flats above them and had frozen solid. There was no coal and, despite help from neighbours, there were problems about drawing money, obtaining food, finding someone to clean, chasing the doctor and so on. A representative of the old people's welfare committee was informed and called to find what was wrong. A sub-committee was called to discuss the case and three or four days passed before four middle-aged ladies visited the flat one evening. They stayed for half an hour, raised their hands in horror at the lack of toilet facilities, made the old woman's bed between them and left half a bottle of disinfectant on the mantelpiece. This was all. Voluntary agencies are an indispensable feature of social service in Western democracies. Yet we need to keep a sense of realism about the quality and scale of the contribution they sometimes make.

Conflicting Theories of Integration and Segregation
These two examples of old people being treated by government, in the first case, and by voluntary agencies in the second, with sentimental condescension pose the basic problem of the present day. Should old people be integrated into society or segregated from it? Would they prefer to work and be treated like everyone else in society, irrespective of age; or would they prefer the retired status of a section of the population which is gently removed from the mainstreams and cross-currents of ordinary life, even to the extent of living independently of their families in retirement 'communities' — such as caravan camps, groups of seaside bungalows or country flatlets, and residential institutions? The answer to this question could make a big difference to the way governments interpret the needs of old people or go about meeting them.

There are a number of theories based on the theme of the segregation of the aged. These take three forms — of postulating that in modern industrial society the elderly are segregated from the young; that an increasing degree of segregation is the normal experience of the final phase of the individual life-cycle, and that whereas formerly the elderly were integrated into the family and society they are now increasingly segregated. The first is concerned with contemporary structural relationships between old and young, particularly within the family. The second is concerned with individual ageing during the life span. The third is concerned with historical changes in the relationships, roles and attitudes of the elderly in society. The three obviously have points of correspondence but are frequently confused.

The Theory of the Contemporary Segregation of Young and Old

This theory is least developed. Do old people mix chiefly with people their own age rather than with younger generations? Are the bonds of kinship of little or no consequence, especially in urban areas? In Europe and America there is now strong evidence from a series of local and national studies that contacts between the generations within the family are usually frequent and emotionally close (3). I have been involved in a cross-national study of people aged sixty-five and over in Denmark, Britain and the United States, and this shows that about two thirds of those with children see at least one of them every day or nearly every day (4). Although there is evidence from some countries of more of the aged being segregated from their married children in separate dwellings, there is also considerable evidence of them living near and exchanging services every day — 'intimacy at a distance' is the phrase coined by Rosenmayr and Kockeis (5). The British evidence is particularly voluminous and also shows that middle-class family patterns are not so very different from working-class family patterns (6).

But while there is support for the broad contention that about two thirds of the elderly are in touch every day or nearly every day with younger members of their families a substantial minority of the others are isolated from their families either because they do not have children or other surviving relatives or see little of them. Some of these people are also further isolated because they are no longer in paid employment, have no friends and do not belong to clubs. Among instances of those who are extremely isolated, in the sense of living alone and not having fairly frequent contacts each week with either relatives or friends, are bachelors who have moved from job to job in their lifetime and never retained a continuous social identity, women who have given up jobs in domestic or hotel service and have neither family nor local home, and widows and widowers who have lingered on in the family home instead of, say, going to join an only child living abroad or in a distant part of the same country. There has been comparatively little study of extreme isolation among the elderly but the number seems to be small (around or below 5 per cent) (7). There has also been little study of the comparative extent and quality of intergenerational contact *outside* the family compared to that *within* it but such contact seems usually to be small.

Engagement and Disengagement at the End of the Life-Cycle

The second theory is that in the last stages of the life-cycle and irrespective of growing infirmity or falling income the individual 'disengages' from society and society from him (8). The theory has led to considerable controversy because its critics suppose it condones a policy of indifference towards the problems of the aged. ('They are alone, because they want it that way, and therefore they should be left alone.') There is little evidence of old people taking the initiative to 'disengage' or withdraw and a good deal to suggest they are distressed by the loss of roles and relationships, for example, upon retirement and bereavement. Not everyone reaches a high plateau of involvement or activity in middle life from which there is a gradual fall in later life. For one thing, the fall is rarely graduated or smooth. It consists of irregularly spaced steps of varying depth. For another, many individuals never reach a high plateau; they cannot be said to have become 'engaged' or to have got farther than the peripheries of social involvement. All their lives they have been isolated or semi-isolated. Even when disengagement appears to be gradual, as when an elderly housewife gives up first the shopping, then the heavy cleaning and washing, and only last of all the cooking and the payment of rent and other outgoings, there is a marked unwillingness to surrender these functions. Women of extreme age often retain important roles as housewives, mothers and grandmothers. Final retirement from the role of housewife is rare and steps towards it are taken only in consequence of infirmity and bereavement.

Insufficient attention has also been given to forms of compensation, replacement and substitution when there are losses of roles and of relationships in old age. Widowed people remarry or rejoin their married children, or develop more intensive relationships with one or more of their children. They may see more of their neighbours. *Extensive* social interaction may be gradually replaced by *intensive* local social interaction, involving many fewer people. Loss of roles may heighten the subjective importance, and increase the effectiveness of execution, of those that remain. It may also lead to a search for substitute occupational roles. These adjustments are not peculiar to old age, though they occur rather more often then.

In consequence of the uneven process of loss and replacement the overall difference in social activities and relationships between people in their eighties, say, and those in their sixties is found to be much smaller than might be expected. A high proportion of people in their eighties and nineties maintain a large number of activities. In a recent national study in Britain, for example, nearly three quarters of even those aged eighty and over who were living alone had paid visits to relatives or friends or had met them in a pub or club on the day before the interview, quite apart from more than half receiving visits from relatives, friends and neighbours at home (9). Many people die before they reach the eighties, of course, and a large number of those who do survive to an advanced age are found to be active. But so long as health is reasonably well maintained the evidence is that the great majority of the aged do not 'disengage' from society in number of contacts or common types of activities (10). However, some individuals do disengage in other senses (11), and there may be proportionately more of them than at other ages — as is suggested by the rise in suicide rates with age in most industrial countries — probably partly because of grief after bereavement.

Historical Trends in the Integration or Segregation of the Elderly

There is the third type of segregation, of historical detachment of the elderly from society. Sociological theorists have alleged the disintegrating effects on settled rural communities and extended families of industrialization, and have argued there was a loss of functions by the family and a shift to nuclear or immediate families, to looser social networks and the isolation of the aged (12). Such assumptions are certainly still made today and are taken over in official statements of policy. One assumption made by the recent Canadian Royal Commission on Health Services was that 'The family occupies a place of shrinking importance in the field of social relationships ... The composite functions of the kinship structure have been whittled away and assumed by specialized bodies outside the family.' (13) This is a mis-statement which does not correspond with the evidence. We have already found that recent studies of modern society show in fact that the majority of the elderly have important roles and are fairly well integrated into both family and society, and by this is meant the *extended* family of three or four generations, although a minority of up to a fifth or a quarter are relatively isolated. Were fewer isolated a hundred or more years ago? Really good information from the past is lacking. But such information as there is does not support the theories of the social changes induced by industrialization. In pre-industrial times three-generation households were rare and a large number of old people lived alone, in villages and towns alike (14). It is unlikely that even when living in different dwellings all or nearly all of them were as intimately involved in everyday family life as some sociologists have suggested.

What we *can* identify are two important social changes — in the structure of the population and in occupational status. Profound changes have been taking place in the structure of the population. In Britain, for example, after growing from under 2 million at the beginning of the century to 5 million by the mid-1940s, the number of persons aged sixty-five and over grew to 6½ million by 1965 and is expected to reach 8 million in the late 1970s. In Canada the numbers are expected to grow from about 1½ million this year to over 3 million by the end of the 1980s (15).

Other structural changes are less well known. More old people have small families than did their predecessors. More of the younger ones among them are married rather than widowed. More of their children's than of their own generation are marrying, and marrying earlier. Because of early marriage and the compression of the child-bearing years, mainly into the twenties, the difference in years between the generations is, on average, being reduced (16). There is a corresponding trend in favour of greater longevity. More people are reaching the sixties and seventies and although the expectation of life of men in some countries at the age of sixty has not lengthened very much, women's expectation of life has been lengthening steadily, if not dramatically, during the century (17). Among persons over 65 the number of those aged 80 and over is increasing disproportionately. In Britain they increased by about 40 per cent between 1951 and 1961. In Denmark, to consider a small industrial country, they are expected to increase by about 30 per cent during the next ten years, and in Canada the numbers of those aged 75 and over are expected to increase by nearly 42 per cent between 1961 and 1971 (18). All this means that quite apart from the mounting pressures being placed on the social services a four-generation social structure has now emerged in most industrial societies. As many as 23 per cent of the elderly with children in both Denmark and Britain and 40 per cent in the United States have great-grandchildren. This change is having profound repercussions upon the latter stages of the life-cycle. Old people are dividing into those who belong to the third and those who belong to the fourth generation. Their functions and problems are becoming more distinct.

Retirement

The second major change, historically, is in the socio-economic status of the elderly, relative both to the preceding generations of the elderly and to their younger contemporaries. More are retiring, and are obliged to retire, early (19). Yet many of the elderly can expect to live for at least ten years after retirement. A quarter of all men over the age of 65 in Britain have been retired for at least nine years. Again, more of their children's than of their own generation have had a longer formal education and, because of shorter working hours and advancing prosperity, have had greater opportunities to take advantage of 'informal' kinds of education in society. This tends to make worse the problems of communication and of the maintenance of respect between older men and their younger contemporaries, which earlier retirement has already revealed.

There are strong forces favouring the early retirement of older people and the belief that they are and should be economically dependent. It is argued that the value of their work is minimal, and that their presence in industry obstructs modernization and the achievement of efficiency, because younger people seeking promotion are frustrated at the lack of opportunities. There is a good deal of support, especially among trade unions, for the right to a long period of rest after a lifetime's service. All these favour a policy of segregation. However, it could be argued that it is in the interests both of the elderly themselves and of society to prolong working life and maintain physical and social rhythms. Despite the beliefs of the younger generation there is evidence from a number of countries that those approaching the normal retirement ages intensely dislike the prospect of changing from full-time work to complete retirement and large numbers would prefer to continue in some form of employment, including part-time or light work (20). Men in particular are reluctant to lose the satisfactions and associations that work supplies. Although substantial numbers of the retired appear to be content with their status, there are also substantial numbers who are still fairly active and would like to return to some form of employment. In a national study recently in Britain 49 per cent of retired men aged 65-9 and 29 per cent of retired men aged 70-74 said they felt able to do some sort of paid job; altogether 28 per cent and 16 per cent had little or no incapacity and *wanted* some form of paid job. They represented a third of a million men in the population (21). There seems to be a similar huge reserve demand for alternative work among retired men in the United States.

Although an increasing number of women are entering paid employment in late middle age (with the possibility that in the future more women aged sixty and over than at present will be in gainful employment) the problem broadly divides into one involving women and one involving men. It is important to abandon any idea that the majority of older women are economically 'dependent' in any real sense. They contribute enormously to production in two ways. First, many of them make it possible for husbands to go out to work. Secondly, by the work they carry out for their families and particularly their grandchildren (such as by caring for sons, daughters and grandchildren during illness and by caring every day for young grandchildren) they contribute to the work-performance of their children, and in particular, at least if they are in their sixties, make it possible for their daughters to go out to work. The rise in the employment of married women is closely connected with the role played by grandmothers in the extended family (22).

The attachment of men to the activities and associations of a lifetime, and to the status derived from them, is not surprising. Reference group theory alone would lead us to expect it. But if the social or human arguments favour, as I believe they do, a greater measure of occupational 'integration' of the aged then we require no less than a revolution in current industrial policies. Like many younger disabled people older retired people do not want to work in segregated sheltered workshops. They want employment in ordinary conditions. One of the tragedies since the war has been our perverse refusal to recognize the occupational needs of the aged and develop new methods, as by the setting up of special employment offices and the appointment of job replacement and liaison officers, to reintegrate many elderly people into industry and commerce.

Income Security

I have discussed segregation from family and social relationships and from employment. Another form of segregation is income segregation. It could be argued that a retired population with separate and relatively low status might not require a standard of living higher than minimum 'subsistence', and pension or public assistance payments should be based on this minimum. Alternatively, it could be argued that an older section of the population which has been encouraged to work until the onset of infirmity rather than to an early chronological limit, which still has access to some forms of occupation (including part-time employment of a light nature) and which otherwise contributes to social life, deserves a standard of living related to the standards of those at work. Otherwise there is the risk of widening the gulf which already separates the two nations of elderly poor and young well-to-do. Pension and public assistance payments might then be related in principle to (i) previous individual wage-levels; (ii) period of postponement of drawing pensions; and (iii) annual changes in national income per head. Adoption of the principles of 'integration' or 'segregation' would make a major difference to the social security policies followed by governments. Both Britain and Canada have pension schemes of a predominantly 'segregationist' (subsistence) type though both have made concessions in recent years to the principle of wage-related pensions (23). Both have a long way to go to begin to catch up with the more far-sighted schemes which exist in countries such as Sweden and Germany.

Housing and Welfare

Another example of the conflict between policies of integration and segregation is in housing and welfare. It could be argued that a generation which has been absolved from making any further contribution to national production, which has completed its parental function of rearing the next generation and which obtains basic psychological and social satisfactions from elderly peers rather than from younger generations would prefer residential segregation — in a local as well as in a household sense. Moreover, some of them would require domestic and professional services which it is difficult and costly to supply in certain kinds of areas and in scattered households. Large groups of flatlets or bungalows all occupied by elderly persons might then be provided. For the same kind of reasons substantial numbers of residential Homes and institutions for old people, as a kind of second stage of defence against the advance of infirmity, might also be provided. But, alternatively, if many older people continue to work or to keep house for younger people and if they not only maintain close contact with their children and grandchildren but derive more intense emotional satisfaction from these contacts than from those with their peers, then it would be logical to integrate their housing or their residential care with that for other age groups. Indeed, zealous pursuit of the former alternative may unwittingly cut old people off from their 'natural' contacts and sources of help during illness and infirmity and force governments to develop more organized forms of domiciliary and institutional help than would otherwise be necessary.

In a book reporting a study of residential institutions and homes for old people in England and Wales I concluded that in their present form such institutions failed to meet the psychological and social needs of old people and should be replaced by alternative forms of care as quickly as possible. I argued as follows. At one extreme are the most infirm residents, between 15 per cent and 25 per cent, who would be better placed in geriatric hospital facilities. At the other extreme are a large minority of active residents, about 20 per cent, who are admitted to institutions primarily because they are evicted from or otherwise lose their own homes. They need not be there if different kinds of housing with decent amenities — ordinary bungalows or flatlets — were available through welfare and housing agencies in the right places. Between these two extremes are a large number of moderately infirm old people who are capable of doing most, but not all, personal and household tasks for themselves. I have little doubt that the majority of these could live in groups of flatlets or bungalows, so long as home help and meal services are available and a housekeeper in each group is on call. In Britain these groups of 'sheltered' housing are at last being built on a modest if still not sufficient scale.

This kind of change in policy cannot be brought about overnight. A big improvement in geriatric hospitals and a rapid expansion of sheltered housing for groups of, say, 6 to 20 old people, is required in every locality before residential institutions and Homes are replaced. In

Canada and Britain, this could be supported by an extension of group medical practice and the concentration of local health services in such groups. In many societies this may take a number of years. But the arguments against residential institutions (24), particularly arguments drawing on evidence which reveals the social and occupational limitations of the segregated community of the elderly, are far more powerful than those administering the institutions and Homes care to admit. This seems to be true of this type of institution in all industrial societies and seems to be true, though to a lesser extent, even of the most comfortable modern Homes of the communal kind.

Many governments are poised at a critical juncture in the development of policy, suddenly aware of the rise in numbers of the aged. The percentage in residential institutions and Homes is tiny in comparison with the total population aged sixty-five and over (25). Is segregation the right policy for them or would they benefit from integration into a local (usually *their* previous local) community? This is the first and most critical question in the development of welfare policies for the aged. The answer will lead to a long chain of consequences in housing and capital costs generally, the training and distribution of personnel, the relationships between the generations and the value that society gives to old age. The evidence is far from complete, but it shows we should improve and strengthen geriatric facilities and preventive measures in medicine, partly through the extension of group practice, for the really frail and disabled on the one hand, and build up the various home services together with small groups of sheltered housing for the moderately infirm on the other, and lay less and less emphasis on the halfway institution. While trying to ape both hospital and community, the residential institution or Home succeeds in being neither. The real challenge to the ingenuity and resourcefulness of governments and voluntary services alike is to strengthen the network of services which make it possible for the elderly to live with comfort and dignity in their own homes and retain the perspectives of a lifetime. Most industrial societies have begun to experiment tentatively on a small scale. No society has yet risen properly to the challenge.

Notes and References

1 Sheldon, J. H., *The Social Medicine of Old Age,* Oxford University Press, 1948.

2 The Council of State Governments, *The States and Their Older Citizens,* Chicago, The Council, 1955.

3 For example, Shanas, E., and Streib, G. (eds.), *The Family, Intergenerational Relationships and Social Structure,* New York, Prentice Hall, 1965; Townsend, P., 'Comment on Family and Kinship in Industrial Society', *Sociological Review Monograph,* no. 8, October 1964.

4 Shanas, E., Townsend, P., Wedderburn, D., Stehouwer, S., Milhøj, P., and Friis, H., *Old People in Three Industrial Societies*, New York and London, Atherton and Routledge, 1968. The study was financed by the National Institute of Mental Health and later the Division of Community Health Services of the United States Public Health Service. (British grant-designation MH-05511 and CH-00053.)

5 Rosenmayr, L., and Kockeis, E., 'Propositions for a Sociological Theory of Ageing and the Family', *International Social Science Journal*, vol. XV, no. 3, 1963.

6 Rosser, C., and Harris, C., *The Family and Social Change*, Routledge, 1965.

7 In San Francisco a figure of 5 per cent not having contacts with other relatives or friends was arrived at. Lowenthal, M. Fiske, 'Social Isolation and Mental Illness in Old Age', *American Sociological Review*, vol. 29, no. 1, February 1964. See also Shanas, E., *et al.*, op. cit. Tunstall identifies a similar minority in his study of social isolation among the elderly in four areas of England. Tunstall, J., *Old and Alone*, Routledge, 1966.

8 Cumming, E., and Henry, W. E., *Growing Old: the Process of Disengagement*, New York, Basic Books, 1961; Cumming, E., 'Further Thoughts on the Theory of Disengagement', *International Social Science Journal*, vol. XV, no. 3, 1963. There are many direct and indirect statements in reports of studies of the aged throughout the world which suggest disengagement. For example, 'for the mass of older people increasing age carries with it a decreasing association with the younger generations. In the . . . social sense the conjugal family is the sole unit of intimate relationships. With the withering of this unit the surviving members must, on the whole, expect to continue their lives as individuals.' Hutchinson, B., *Old People in a Modern Australian Community*, Victoria, Melbourne University Press, 1954, p. 63. See also, Parsons, T., 'Old Age as a Consummatory Phase', in *The Gerontologist*, vol 3, 1963; and for critical reviews of the disengagement hypothesis, Rose, A. M., 'A Current Theoretical Issue in Social Gerontology', *The Gerontologist*, vol. 4, no. 1, March 1964, and Talmon, Y., 'Dimensions of Disengagement: Ageing in Collective Settlements', unpublished paper read at the International Gerontological Research Seminar, Markaryd, Sweden, 1963.

9 Shanas, E., *et al.*, op. cit.

10 In a national study of the aged in Britain in 1962 a number of comparisons were made between people in their late sixties and those aged seventy-five and over who (a) lived alone and (b) showed no incapacity according to a specially applied incapacity index. Thirty-four per cent of the former compared with 32 per cent of the latter had visited friends on the previous day; 44 per cent compared with 43 per cent had gone shopping; 56 per cent compared with 46 per cent had gone for a walk; 33 per cent compared with 23 per cent had met friends outside the home; and 40 per cent compared with 38 per cent had had visitors at home.

11 Various kinds of psychological or personality withdrawal are described in Reichard, S., Livson, F., and Peterson, P., *Ageing and Personality*, New York, John Wiley, 1962.

12 Parsons has written: 'By comparison with other societies the United States assumes an extreme position in the isolation of old age from participation in the most important social structures and interests.' Parsons, T., *Essays in Sociological Theory*, revised edition, New York, the Free Press of Glencoe, 1954, p. 102. Many sociologists of an earlier generation had developed the same themes, e.g., Ogburn, W. F., *Social Change*, New York, Viking, 1922 (revised edition, 1952), and *Technology and the Changing Family*, New York, Houghton, Mifflin, 1955; and Burgess, E. W., and Locke, H. J., *The Family*, New York, American Book Co.,

1945. There are many recent examples. Of Germany, Baumert has written of 'the increasing tendency towards exclusion of ageing parents from the families of their married children', and of America, Nimkoff has said, 'In 1900, in an era still agricultural, the aged were generally persons of considerable power in the family because they controlled property and occupations and they were greatly respected for their knowledge and ability. Since then, with the growth of our industrial society, property and jobs have moved away from the family control. Increased physical mobility separates the aged more often from their children and other kin.' Baumert, G., 'Changes in the Family and the Position of Older Persons in Germany', and Nimkoff, M. F., 'Changing Family Relationships of Older People in the United States during the last Fifty Years', in Tibbits, C., and Donahue, W. (eds.), *Social and Psychological Aspects of Ageing*, New York and London, Columbia University Press, 1962.

13 *Report of the Royal Commission on Health Services*, vol. I, Ottawa, Queen's Printer, 1964, p. 103.

14 Ogburn himself showed that the large household of many persons was not typical even in the mid-nineteenth century. *Technology and the Changing Family*, pp. 99-100. In 1865 in New York State only 3 per cent of households contained three generations, and even in 1703 in New York only 4 per cent 'could be considered three-generational'. Friedmann, E., 'The Impact of Ageing on the Social Structure', in Tibbitts, C. (ed.), *Handbook of Social Gerontology*, Chicago, University of Chicago Press, 1960. In a number of English villages the number of households having resident in-laws in the seventeenth century varied from 0 to less than 20 per cent. Large numbers of middle-aged and elderly widows lived alone. Laslett, P., *The World We Have Lost*, Methuen (University Paperbacks), 1965, pp. 89-99.

15 Stukel, A., 'Population Projections 1966-1991', Appendix E in Brown, T. M., *Canadian Economic Growth*, a study prepared for the Royal Commission on Health Services, Ottawa, Queen's Printer, 1964.

16 Between 1941 and 1961 the average age at marriage for spinsters in Canada, for example, declined from 24.4 to 22.9 and for bachelors from 27.6 to 25.8. There was a marked rise in fertility in the 1950s followed by slightly lower rates in the early 1960s. Dominion Bureau of Statistics, *Vital Statistics 1961*, Ottawa, Queen's Printer, 1963, p. 99. Compared with the early years of the century in the United States. 'The youngest women marry one to two years younger and complete their child-bearing two or three years younger, and their length of married life is about nine years longer.' Glick, P. C., and Parke, R., 'New Approaches in Studying the Life-Cycle of the Family', *Demography*, vol. II, 1965, pp. 187-202.

17 In the United States, for example, the expectation of life of white males aged sixty increased by only 1.6 years between 1900 and 1962, while the expectation of life of white females of that age increased by 4.7 years. Brotman, B. B., 'Trends in Life Expectancy, 1900-1962', *Welfare in Review*, U.S. Department of Health, Education and Welfare, vol. 3, no. 5, May 1965.

18 Stukel, A., op. cit.

19 In Britain, for example, Census reports show that whereas 79 per cent of men aged 65-9 and 53 per cent of men aged 70-74 were gainfully occupied in 1921, the figures had dwindled to 47 per cent and 27 per cent by 1951. There are reasons for doubting the entire reliability of the 1921 figures but the trend is clear.

20 For example, among studies completed in Britain are *Workers Nearing Retirement: Studies Based upon Interviews with Older Employees in the Industrial Town of Slough*, The Nuffield Foundation, 1963. Among American studies are Thompson, W. E., 'Pre-Retirement Anticipation and Adjustment in Retirement', *The Journal of Social Issues*, vol. XIV, no. 2, 1958.

21 Townsend, P., and Wedderburn, D., op. cit. See also Pearson, M., 'The Transition from Work to Retirement', *Occupational Psychology*, vol. 31, 1957; Ministry of Pensions and National Insurance, *Reasons for Retiring or Continuing to Work*, H.M.S.O, 1954.

22 Jephcott, P., Sears, N., and Smith, J. H., *Married Women Working*, Allen & Unwin, 1963.

23 Among others, Professor Robert Clark has argued for the maintenance of a flat-rate programme in Canada. Clark, R. M., *Economic Security for the Aged in the United States and Canada*, Ottawa, Queen's Printer, 1960; and 'Some Reflections on Economic Security for the Aged in Canada', in Clark, R. M. (ed.), *Canadian Issues: Essays in Honour of Henry E. Argus*, Toronto, University of Toronto Press, 1961.

24 Townsend, P., *The Last Refuge: a Survey of Residential Institutions for the Aged in England and Wales*, Routledge, 1962. 'The Argument for Gradually Abandoning Communal Homes for the Aged', *International Social Science Journal*, vol. XV, no. 3, 1963.

25 In few industrial societies are there as many as 4 per cent. In Britain there are 2 per cent, in Denmark nearly 4 per cent, in the United States 2 per cent and in Canada rather less than 3 per cent. The figure for Canada is derived from statistics referring to the numbers of beds in 'Homes for Special Care' not specifically designated as 'nursing' beds but as 'domiciliary' and 'unspecified' beds. *Statistical Data on Homes for Special Care*, Health Services Section, Research and Statistics Division, Department of National Health and Welfare, Ottawa, February 1965. For the other three countries see Shanas, E., *et al.*, op. cit., Chapters 4 and 5.

16 Sociological explanations of the lonely*

Among the population, particularly old people, isolation and loneliness are thought to be common problems. How many lead solitary lives? Why do they do so? What does it mean emotionally? This paper offers a provisional account of isolation and loneliness among old people in Britain. It is based on data collected in two stages of a survey carried out in 1962. Two separate national random samples of people aged sixty-five and over were interviewed in the spring, the late autumn, and early winter of 1962, numbering over 4,000 altogether. The survey was primarily designed to contribute to a cross-national study of the aged in Britain, Denmark and the United States but also to offer evidence on certain important questions affecting the aged only in Britain (2). The paper starts by discussing 'isolation' and related concepts and goes on to describe how many old people are isolated, at least in relation to their contemporaries, and to ask whether loneliness is explained by such isolation or whether it has a more complicated aetiology. Although no information has been collected from persons at successive dates as they grow older the whole frame of argument and explanation is couched in terms of interaction between the individual and society during the last stage of the life-cycle. Otherwise it is impossible to understand what are the social and psychological processes at work.

The Concept of Isolation

By 'social isolation' some people mean the universal and necessary lack of communion between man and his fellows. The isolate is an individual who cannot properly communicate his feelings and experiences — even when he is totally and continuously immersed in social activities. As Halmos vividly describes it, 'He is shut up amidst the fellow-members of his community into a cubicle where he is engaged in a life-long conversation with himself' (3). The title of Riesman's book, *The Lonely Crowd*, conveys this meaning precisely (4). Others use the term 'isolation' to describe the lack of integration of a particular group, such

* First presented as a joint paper with Sylvia Tunstall (formerly Korte) at the Seventh Congress of the International Association of Gerontology, Vienna, June 1966 (1).

as an ethnic minority, into society, *even when individual members of the group enjoy a great deal of interaction.* They can nonetheless be said to be 'socially isolated'. Sometimes isolation is taken to refer to members of a group (such as those in certain work-groups or suburban neighbourhood groups) who have virtually no social relationships with other members of the group, *even when they enjoy other kinds of social interaction.* There are other uses of the term. Thus, individuals may have few relationships and activities — by comparison with other persons in society, or with their predecessors, their age-contemporaries, or even themselves at an earlier stage of life.

In the social sciences these different possibilities are rarely allowed and distinguished. Some have received a lot more attention than others. As a result of the interest in theories of social evolution and the social consequences of industrialization, there is a large amount in the literature about 'de-socialized' modern society and the impersonality and solitude of urban life. With the coming of the Industrial Revolution, it is supposed, 'We see the emergence of a mass society in which the individual is thoroughly weaned from his community and begins to live either in solitude or in mobs and audiences . . . Certainly, ours is a desocialized society in which social isolation is widespread' (5). But whatever the accuracy of such inferences about the direction of social change few serious attempts have been made to specify and measure various kinds of isolation. This applies particularly to the diversity of individual experience. Just as economists have been concerned primarily with aggregates of income in different sectors of the economy rather than with its distribution among individuals and families, so sociologists have been concerned with general levels of social participation and interaction rather than with *its* distribution among individuals.

In considering social isolation in old age we can usefully start by distinguishing between objective and subjective states. Questions about the extent to which the individual interacts with society can be answered objectively, at least in principle. His behaviour can be observed and plotted. How he *feels* is another matter. Although we can often make accurate inferences from behaviour to feeling we are sometimes wrong. There are all kinds of objective cues to subjective states of happiness, depression and loneliness, for example, but at times the pattern of cues is inconsistent and at others they are flatly contradicted by the assertions to the contrary of the individuals concerned. Someone who has a full social life, a happy family and a brilliantly successful career may claim he is perpetually unhappy or lonely. Equally, someone living in poverty who leads the life of a vagabond and has no contact with friends or relatives may claim he is happy and never feels lonely. It is the sociologist's task to explore the contiguity of objective and subjective states to find recurring patterns. Old people may be isolated from society in the following senses:

(i)   by comparison with their contemporaries; this might be termed *peer-contrasted isolation*;

(ii)   by comparison with younger people; this might be termed *generation-contrasted isolation*;

(iii)   by comparison with the social relationships and activities enjoyed by the same people at an earlier stage of the life-cycle, in youth or middle age; this might be termed *age-related isolation* or *desolation*;

(iv)   by comparison with the preceding generation of old people; this might be termed *preceding cohort isolation.*

This paper is concerned primarily with the first of these four types of isolation. It should be remembered that social isolation can be *partial* in each of the senses listed. An old person may be isolated from his peers but fully integrated into his family; he may belong to fewer associations than does the average member of the younger generation but may spend more time with different members of his family, with neighbours and with fellow-members of the principal club or association to which he belongs; and finally, he may lose a wife and the associations of work but not children and friends. Again, isolation can be *lifelong, intermittent, initial* or *terminal* in relation to the individual life-cycle.

The Difficulty of Providing an Operational Definition
If we seek to define the degree of isolation there are difficulties of measuring the duration, range and kind of social participation. First, *duration.* One man may visit a pub for two minutes or two hours; one woman may live with a son; another may be visited by a son for two hours every evening; and another may be visited fleetingly by a son every day on his way to work. How far is it possible to discriminate between these situations in any 'measure' of the extent of social participation?

Second, *range.* One man may belong to a club and visit it five times a week; another may belong to five different clubs and visit each of them once a week. One widow may see one of her five sons five days a week but the others not at all; another may see each of her five sons on one day a week. Should their level of social participation be treated as broadly the same?

Third, *kind.* Some old people may be seen frequently by their married children but excluded, say, from the grandparent roles. A son may pay a courtesy call on his widowed mother and sit with her for an hour or two watching television; or they may talk together at length and exchange all manner of services. Are these contacts of equal 'value'? More broadly, should work and family contacts and social contacts other than with relatives be accorded equal weight? For example, one man living alone may visit a married daughter and spend holidays with her and her family; he may also meet one or two of his former workmates every day at a habitual meeting-place. Another man living alone may have no contact with relatives or former workmates, but he may belong to a football spectators' club and an old people's club, attend various functions arranged by welfare agencies and spend holidays in a special hotel for the elderly. If the number, range and duration of social contacts were broadly the same, should their level of social participation also be treated as the same, even if the latter lacks two of the main types of social interaction enjoyed by the elderly?

Among old people especially there are major differences in kind of participation. Some see a lot of relatives but have no friends and few acquaintances, and vice versa. Some lead both a rich familial life and rich extra-familial life; others have neither. A fourfold classification of the kind set out in Fig. 1 would seem to be justified. However, matrices need to be developed which cover a variety of structural situations within the family as well as outside the family.

Figure 1 The dimensions of social participation

		Family participation	
		Strong	Weak
Extra-familial	Strong	Double integrate	Extra-familial integrate
social participation	Weak	Family integrate	Isolate

There have been a number of attempts to develop a general scale of social participation. Most are unsatisfactory because investigators have tried to find a short-cut through the laborious task of collecting information about the huge range of human social activities. One general scale is unsatisfactory because it simply counts the number of individual affiliations to associations and tends to ignore individual membership of primary groups (6). For the old a simple index of isolation has been used in one investigation. Account was taken of (i) seeing children at least once a month, (ii) seeing relatives at least once a month, (iii) having very close friends living, (iv) having personal friends, and (v) having made new friends (7). The trouble is that this is inconsistent and crude. The scale switches from a certain frequency of associations to the mere existence of certain associations, and the chosen frequency can accommodate widely different experiences. A man in full-time employment leading a rich life with his family could be classified as socially isolated because he does not satisfy three of the five criteria of the scale; whereas a retired man living alone who sees a daughter and a brother only once a month and friends who only see him once or twice in the year may yet count as fully integrated. A more elaborate index has been developed in a series of British studies (8). As much information as possible is collected about every kind of social activity for the purpose of estimating the average number of social 'contacts' per week (9). This method takes no account of intensity and kind of contact but seems reliable enough to distinguish those who are relatively isolated in the elderly population. The broad approach and variations in method are discussed carefully by Tunstall (10).

Measures Used in the Survey

It was not possible to develop a precise index of isolation in the national survey. To do so would have meant including a large number of questions on social activities, probably at the expense of obtaining data on retirement, income and incapacity. Instead, we sought to develop three simple categorizations and one which was slightly more complex but not by any means ideal. The first three were:

1 *Living alone*
2 Persons declaring themselves to be *often alone*
3 Persons who were *isolated from family,* that is, they had no surviving children, siblings or relatives, and if they had one or more of these relatives had not had contact with them in the previous seven days. The categorization was based on a summary of answers to a series of questions about family contacts.

In the fourth category persons were classified as extremely isolated, partly isolated and not isolated according to certain simple indicators. Five items of information were sought:

(a) whether persons lived alone, with one other person or with more than one other person
(b) whether or not there was contact the same day or the previous day with a child
(c) whether or not there was contact the same day or the previous day with a sibling living elsewhere than in the household
(d) whether the old person had worked full- or part-time or not at all in the previous week
(e) whether or not persons living alone had had visitors, met friends or visited friends or relatives the previous day.

On the basis of this information, people were allocated to one of three groups:

1 *Extremely isolated* persons living alone, who had had none of the four types of contact (b)-(e) listed above, that is, they had not seen a child or a brother or sister the same or the previous day, had not worked in the previous week, and had neither received visitors nor met or visited friends or relatives the previous day

2 *Partly isolated* persons living alone, who had had only one of the types of contact (b)-(e). Also, persons living with one other person who had had none of the four types of contact (b)-(e)

3 *Not isolated.* All other persons.

Various rough assumptions underlie this classification. We assumed that extreme isolation would be experienced rarely by anyone except those living alone and that partial isolation would be experienced rarely by anyone living with more than one other person. These are plainly shaky assumptions but some intensive studies suggest that they are approximately correct (11). By persons *living alone* is meant persons who share a room, flat or house with no one else, who sleep alone and by implication rather than accredited fact eat alone in such an 'independent' dwelling. There are old people living alone who spend all their days at work or with friends or relatives and who only sleep at their permanent addresses. But so long as these exceptions are borne in mind it remains true that those occupying a household alone tend to be limited in their 'bridge' contacts with society and include among their numbers *most* of the persons who are severely isolated.

Whether an old person who lives with one other person is isolated or not depends upon the relationship between the individuals concerned. It is possible for two individuals, elderly friends, or an old person and an unmarried child, to keep house and take meals together, while maintaining separate rooms in the dwelling and having few contacts. In other 'typical' two-person households such as those consisting of elderly married couples or two siblings, the two may share every room in the dwelling and be constantly in each other's company. There are of course some individual old people who live in larger households and yet spend all but a few minutes each day alone in their own rooms. But such cases are probably exceptional (12).

We also assumed that contacts within the 'immediate' family, that is, with children and siblings were decisive in determining whether or not individuals were isolated or integrated. Very recent contacts alone were considered. We ruled out those which were less recent than the previous day. Nearly 80 per cent of old people in Britain who report seeing a child the same day or the previous day report that they *usually* see a child daily, and most of the other old people report seeing one weekly. In the absence of any data on the number of contacts in a given period, such as a week, recent contacts provide the best available indicator.

We assumed, too, that work of any kind, even a few hours' part-time work, provided significant social contacts for the great majority of people. This remains to be tested, however. Different work situations afford the individual different opportunities for social contact and there are certainly some work situations which provide a minimum of social contact, for example, a night watchman or domestic cleaner in a private house whose occupants are out at work.

This index of social isolation is not precise. It is roughly approximate for the purpose of producing certain national estimates and describing the characteristics of isolated old people.

The Overall Degree of Isolation

Table 1 shows that only a small minority of the old, 3 per cent, lived in extreme isolation as defined. These old people were living alone. They had passed the previous day without seeing a child, or sibling, and had not had any visitors, paid any visits or met any friends. They had not had paid employment for any hours at all in the previous week. For a few the previous day may have been exceptional but for most there was little doubt that they led a barren social existence. A further 29 per cent were partly isolated – made up of 9 per cent living alone and another 20 per cent living with one other person. Thus we can conclude that while *extreme* isolation seems to be relatively rare in old age, partial isolation is relatively common.

Nevertheless, it should be stressed that the majority of old people, 67 per cent, had frequent sources of contact in the household, family and community. They included more than two fifths of those living alone.

Table 1 also shows other kinds of 'aloneness'. Those lacking relatives altogether or who had had no recent contact with them accounted for 3 per cent and 13 per cent of the elderly respectively. As many as 27 per cent of the old people reported that they were often alone.

The Characteristics of the Isolated

Women were found to be more isolated than men, except in their contacts with relatives, as Table 1 shows. Thirty per cent, compared with 11 per cent, lived alone. Thirty-five per cent, compared with 16 per cent, said they were often alone. Thirty-five per cent, compared with 28 per cent, were extremely or partly isolated. How can this be explained?

First, a much larger proportion of women than of men are widowed

Table 1 Percentage of people aged 65 and over in Britain living in isolation (a)

Category of social isolation	Men	Women	All persons
Living alone			
Extremely isolated	2	4	3
Partly isolated	4	13	9
Not isolated	5	12	9
Total alone	11	30	22
Living with one other person			
Partly isolated	22	18	20
Not isolated	32	24	27
Living with two or more persons			
Not isolated	34	29	31
Total	100	100	100
Number in sample	1,004	1,493	2,497
Often alone			
Often alone	16	35	27
Not often alone	84	65	73
Total	100	100	100
Number in sample	1,002	1,487	2,489
No family or isolated from family			
No relatives at all	2	4	3
Relatives, none seen in last week	16	11	13
Relatives, one or more seen in last week	82	85	84
Total	100	100	100
Number in sample	1,004	1,496	2,500

(a) Based on Stage 1 of the survey only (i.e. a total of 2,500 interviewed), itself a nationally representative sample.

and single. More widowed than married men and women live alone and are thus more likely to be socially isolated. But marital status does not entirely explain differences in the social integration of men and women. For, as Table 2 shows, more widowed women than men in the sample lived alone, and slightly more of the widowed women than men were isolated. But even among the married, a slightly larger proportion of the women than of the men lived in partial isolation — partly because more of the men went out to work. Secondly, once widowed, the individual's chances of living alone and of living in isolation are highest for those without children and lowest for those with several children, particularly if daughters are strongly represented. They are still higher for those who lack not only children but also siblings. More women than men are single or otherwise childless. There is a strong correlation between the structure and density of an individual's immediate family network and his chances of living alone and in isolation. Thirdly, women are expected to fulfil the role of housewife, even at an advanced age, and are therefore more often expected to live alone when widowed.

Table 2 Percentage of men and women of different marital status living in isolation

	Men			Women			
Social relations	Married	Widowed divorced or separated	All	Married	Widowed divorced or separated	Single	All
Living alone							
Extremely isolated	—	5	2	—	6	10	4
Partly isolated	—	14	4	—	18	27	13
Not isolated	—	19	5	—	21	10	12
Total alone	—	*38*	*11*	—	*45*	*46*	*30*
Living with one other person							
Partly isolated	29	4	22	34	4	27	18
Not isolated	39	18	32	35	20	9	24
Living with two or more persons							
Not isolated	32	39	34	30	31	17	29
Total	100	100	100	100	100	100	100
Number in sample	701	256	1,004 (a)	510 (b)	770 (b)	213	1,493

(a) Including 47 single men.
(b) Differences occur in the totals owing to variation in the classification of the informally separated.

Table 3 relates the two main types of isolation that we have been concerned with so far: social isolation and isolation from family. It indicates how strong is the correlation between these two types of isolation. Of course the correlation in part derives from the way in which we have defined social isolation: mainly in terms of recent contact with a child or sibling. But the table does provide additional descriptive evidence. Thirteen per cent of the tiny group of extremely isolated old people had no relatives at all; a further 37 per cent had had no contact with children, siblings, or other relatives in the previous week. Thus half of the extremely isolated old people were isolated from family. The rest had had contacts with their family in the previous

Table 3 Percentage of extremely isolated, partly isolated and non-isolated persons who have certain characteristics

Different characteristics	Extremely isolated (a)	Partly isolated		Not isolated		
		Living alone (a)	Not living alone	Living alone (a)	Living with 1 other person	Living with more than 1 person
Married	—	—	77	—	67	49
Widowed and divorced	78	77	9	88	30	44
Single	21	23	14	11	4	7
Having children	53	47	57	79	89	88
Childless	47	53	43	21	11	12
Sons only	31	34	27	27	20	14
Daughters only	22	22	32	22	26	21
Children of both sexes	46	44	40	51	54	65
No personal incapacity	41	49	56	56	60	41
Moderate or severe personal incapacity	19	14	11	9	10	12
No relatives	13	12	6	2	0	
Relatives, none seen in last week	37	27	32	3	5	
Relatives, seen in last week	50	61	62	95	95	
Number in sample	126	375	493	403	1,452	

(a) Percentages for those living alone based on Stages I and II of the national survey. Other percentages based on Stage I only.

week. For those who were partly isolated, nearly 40 per cent lacked relatives or had not seen any during the previous week.

Table 3 also brings out the other principal characteristics of those who were extremely or partly isolated. There was a relatively high proportion who were widowed and an even higher proportion who were single; a high proportion were childless and had sons only. Despite the fact that incapacitated *infirm* old people are more likely to be widowed and therefore more likely to be isolated, the proportion of isolated persons in the sample who were severely incapacitated was only slightly higher than of those who were not isolated. Among women the proportion was in fact a shade smaller. Many infirm people had moved to join married children or other relatives after being widowed.

Activities and Those Living Alone

Those living alone accounted for most of the isolated among the elderly. How do they pass their time? We asked old people which of a list of seven activities they had engaged in during the previous day. The average old person named three. Listening to the radio was the most common activity (63 per cent). Watching television accounted for 37 per cent. Broadcasting services are plainly important for those living alone. Of the social activities listed, having visitors, mentioned by 42 per cent, was the most common. Social contacts outside the home — visiting friends or relatives or meeting friends somewhere — were less frequently mentioned.

Table 4 Percentage of persons living alone, according to personal incapacity, who had engaged in certain activities on the previous day (a)

Activities	Personal incapacity				Men	Women	All persons
	0	1-2	3-4	5+			
Listening to radio	65	61	60	66	61	65	63
Watching TV	40	37	33	21	38	37	37
Going for a walk	49	47	25	9	52	38	41
Shopping	46	45	31	16	44	39	40
Having visitors	38	43	54	47	37	43	42
Visiting friends	31	27	23	13	24	27	27
Meeting friends	31	27	19	10	27	26	26
None	2	1	2	6	–	2	2
Mean number of activities	3.0	2.9	2.4	1.9	2.8	2.8	2.8
Number of persons in sample	264	150	52	68	109	432	541

(a) Based on Stage I of the national survey.

There were few differences between men and women and differences in mobility account for some of the variations observed. However, going for a walk was more common among men than women even when those without any incapacity were considered.

The data presented in Table 4 provide evidence of the way in which infirmity restricts the range of activities even of an old person living alone. With increasing incapacity far fewer people reported going out for a walk, shopping, visiting or meeting friends. Even watching TV decreased among the incapacitated, although radio listening was mentioned. However, visitors compensated a little. A slightly larger proportion of the moderately and severely incapacitated than of those with little or no incapacity had had a visitor on the previous day.

We found that a smaller proportion of the extremely and partly isolated than of the non-isolated had been shopping, walking and watching TV on the day previous to interview, as Table 5 shows. Probably infirmity provides the main explanation for the difference; the isolated had exposed themselves less to the casual social contacts that occur when out walking and shopping.

Table 5 Percentage of extremely, partly and not isolated persons living alone who engaged in certain activities on the previous day

Activities	Living alone		
	Extremely isolated	Partly isolated	Not isolated
Listening to radio	63	64	65
Watching TV	24	38	44
Going for a walk	29	35	48
Shopping	37	37	45
Number in sample	124	364	401

Often Alone in the Day

The great majority, but not all, of those living alone said they were often alone. But a minority of persons living with others, and in fact a substantial minority of persons living with their children, said they were often alone. Table 6 shows how far subjective assessment corresponded with structural designation. Two particularly interesting conclusions can be drawn from this table. First, fewer persons who live with a spouse than persons who live with children or with others said they were often alone. Although many elderly married couples live very self-contained lives, the figures testify to the companionship that marriage provides in old age. Secondly, except for those living alone, more women than men in different types of households tended to say that they were often alone.

People who had a moderate or severe degree of incapacity were more likely to say that they were often alone than those with little or no incapacity. This correlation is not very marked, however, when household arrangements are standardized, and there is one exception. Few severely incapacitated and bedfast persons who lived with a spouse said they were often alone. It looks as if married couples tend to be drawn together when one of them becomes severely incapacitated. The crucial determinants of old people's feelings of aloneness seem to be sleeping in a structurally separate dwelling alone; the loss of the

Table 6 Percentage of persons living in different types of household who say they are often alone (a)

Social isolation	Per cent			Number		
	Men	Women	All persons	Men	Women	All persons
Living alone	73	73	73	187	715	902
Extremely isolated	(b)	86	86	30	96	126
Partly isolated	83	78	79	64	311	375
Not isolated	65	66	66	93	308	401
Living with spouse only	7	15	10	785	602	1,387
Living with children						
Widowed or single	19	27	25	125	354	479
Married	5	14	9	191	130	321
Living with others						
Widowed or single	15	17	14	68	184	252
Married	(b)	(b)	11	37	32	69
All persons	16	35	27	1,002	1,487	2,489

(a) Figures for those living alone and those living with spouse only based on Stages I and II of the national survey. The remaining figures are based on Stage I only.
(b) Percentages not computed on a base of less than 50.

physical proximity of a spouse; and several hours spent alone in the day — in that order.

Family Activities in Relation to Other Social Activities
So far particular attention has been paid to family relationships in the social integration of old people. Have we exaggerated the importance of these relationships? Are social activities, such as visits to clubs or churches, and friendships as important or more important? More information than was collected in the national survey is needed for these questions to be answered satisfactorily. But enough information was obtained for a first approximate answer.

Only a small minority of the sample were active members of old people's clubs, though a somewhat larger minority belonged to other types of clubs, as Table 7 shows. Most of the men belonged to sporting and recreational clubs but 5 per cent to working men's clubs and 3 per cent to political clubs and societies. Among women 8 per cent belonged to church clubs and over 6 per cent to other organizations, such as townswomen's guilds. A third of the men and nearly a half of the women were members of a church, although a considerable fraction of those claiming membership had not attended during the past month.

Table 7 Percentage who were members of clubs and churches

Last attendance	Old people's clubs (a)		Other clubs (a)		Church	
	Men	Women	Men	Women	Men	Women
Within last month	5.8	11.2	18.1	11.2	19.5	30.1
Not within last month	0.9	1.7	4.9	4.1	12.7	15.7
Not a member	93.3	87.1	77.0	84.7	67.8	54.2
Total	100	100	100	100	100	100
Number in sample	1,004	1,493	1,004	1,493	1,626	2,433

(a) Based on Stage I of the national survey only.

The important point is that the great majority of old people were not members of any club and a majority, too, even of women, did not claim to be members of any church.

Table 7 shows that far more women than men attended church and old people's clubs but more men than women attended clubs other than those specifically for old people. A special analysis of the characteristics of those who were members of clubs and churches helps to explain this.

A disproportionately large number of those who were members of old people's clubs were widowed men and women and a strikingly small number were single women, as Table 8 shows. A disproportionately large number of women but not of men who were living alone belonged to them. The women tended to be mobile and in age they did not differ strikingly from those who were not members of clubs. We may conclude that although there is an expected correlation between 'aloneness' and membership of old people's clubs, it is not marked. Considerable proportions of those in the sample who were members were married; lived with children or others; were still in their sixties; were mobile and were still at work.

So far as the development of welfare policies is concerned it is surely important that old people's clubs do not generally cater for the older and less active people. Nor do they cater to a marked extent with those who are isolated.

Is membership of a club or of a church a substitute for membership of a family in old age? We tried a number of statistical analyses but found little difference between those who belonged to clubs and those who attended church in the extent to which they were integrated into the family. The proportions having no relatives at all and having no contact with relatives during the previous week were almost identical. So, too, were the proportions seeing a child the previous day. Perhaps

Table 8 Percentage of persons belonging and not belonging to clubs who had certain characteristics (a)

Characteristics	Men			Women		
	Old people's club member	Other club member	Non-club member	Old people's club member	Other club member	Non-club member
Married	60	70	71	31	34	35
Widowed, divorced or separated	34	25	25	66	44	50
Single	6	5	4	3	21	15
Living alone	7	13	11	42	33	27
Living with spouse only	38	53	46	21	26	23
Living with children	43	24	33	29	23	35
Living with others	11	10	10	9	18	15
Living alone and extremely isolated	2	1	2	4	3	4
Living alone and partly isolated	4	5	3	21	14	11
Living alone and not isolated	7	6	5	18	13	13
Aged 65-9	29	50	36	33	40	32
Aged 70-74	35	28	28	32	30	29
Aged 75+	22	14	22	17	17	20
Working	15	36	26	7	9	9
Fully mobile	88	96	86	88	89	72
Mobile with difficulty	12	4	6	8	7	9
Housebound or bedfast	—	—	7	4	3	19
Total	100	100	100	100	100	100
Number in sample	68	230	706	192	228	1,073

(a) Figures based on Stage I of the national survey except for the figures on isolation of those living alone. These figures are based on both stages and the base numbers are as follows: men: old people's club member 122; other club member 364; non-member 1,244. Women: 322; 382; and 1,733 respectively.

the most telling statement that might be made is that three quarters of the persons who had no relatives at all or had not seen any relative for at least a week did not belong to a club. One fact which stands out is the substantial proportion of single women who were found to be church members and yet who had also had frequent contacts with members of their families — particularly with brothers and sisters. While we must conclude that some individuals find compensation for their lack of close relatives in club and church activities, others add these activities as well as friendships to a family life that is rich already.

Did persons living alone and lacking contact with the family have substitute relations with neighbours and friends? Our data are incomplete but offer a few pointers. We have described above the numbers of people living alone who received visitors on the day previous to interview. Table 9 shows that relatives predominated among these. This in itself is a noteworthy fact but also noteworthy is the small overlap between visits from neighbours, friends and relatives. A markedly higher proportion of those lacking than of those having children had been visited by neighbours and friends and it therefore seems that the associations implied by such visits substitute to some extent for those which might otherwise be maintained with children. However, this remains a provisional and incomplete indication of the operation of a principle of compensation or substitution until a more rigorous study into the interrelationship of social structure and social isolation is undertaken.

Table 9 Percentage of persons living alone who were visited by a neighbour, friend or relative on the previous day

Visitor	With children	Without children	All
Neighbour	12	18	14
Friend	8	17	12
Relative	29	12	22
All	41	40	41
Number in sample	561	344	905

Loneliness in Old Age

So far the circumstances of isolated persons, but not their reactions to those circumstances, have been described. In the national survey we asked old people whether they felt lonely often, sometimes or never.

Loneliness is usually understood to be an unwelcome feeling of lack or loss of companionship. The degree of loneliness felt by an old person is not easy to determine, but most people understand the question 'Are you lonely?' readily enough and, judging by their manner, have plainly reflected upon it many times. When relatives are present during an interview there is a danger of getting an answer that is different from the one that would be given by the old person alone. There are old people who tell their children they are lonely to encourage them to call as often as possible. Yet they recognize that they do not *feel* lonely in a profound sense of that term. Interviewers were urged to check answers given in such conditions whenever possible; but it should be emphasized that although the answers are generally regarded as reliable they were given at a particular time and should not be regarded as representing uniformly *permanent* individual attitudes.

Relatively few old people feel lonely often. Table 10 shows how wide of the mark has been much of the pessimistic and misleading speculation about the loneliness of the elderly in industrialized countries. Here there is evidence of the subjective integration of the majority of the aged, adding to the evidence of their objective integration. But extreme loneliness is not a rare phenomenon and occasional loneliness is quite a common one. In general a substantial minority of the elderly say they experience some degree of loneliness.

Table 10 Percentage of men and women of different marital status who say they feel lonely

Degree of Loneliness	Men				Women			
	Married	Widowed divorced or separated	Single	All	Married	Widowed divorced or separated	Single	All
Often	3	11	7	5	4	13	4	8
Sometimes	11	24	14	14	17	30	23	26
Not lonely	86	65	79	80	79	57	73	66
Total	100	100	100	100	100	100	100	100
Number in sample	1,128	420	71	1,619	843	1,246	336	2,425

Loneliness and Isolation

Who are the people who feel lonely? Earlier we found that the widowed and the single tended to be the most isolated, and indeed we now find that more of them experienced loneliness, as Table 10 shows. Earlier, too, we found that more women than men lived alone and were extremely or partly isolated and, again, we now find that more women than men of the same marital status experienced loneliness. An illustration will help to suggest the pattern of isolation for some people.

A widow aged eighty lives alone in a bungalow in a Yorkshire dale. Her husband, who was a platelayer working for British Railways, died four months ago. A son lives nearby and she sees him and his family every day. Her only other child, also a son, lives more than an hour's journey away and last saw her a month ago. She sees little of other relatives and does not belong to a club or attend church. On the day before the interview she went for a walk, listened to the radio and was visited by her son's family. She says she prefers living alone but says she is often alone and that time often passes slowly. She also says she is often lonely.

The isolated and the lonely may seem to be composed of broadly the same people. However, this is not so. One of the most important findings of the national survey was that those living alone and in relative isolation from family and community did not always say they were lonely. Isolation and loneliness were not coincident.

Table 11 shows that a large proportion of those living alone experienced some feelings of loneliness. But over two fifths of the extremely isolated persons living alone, who had had no contacts on the previous day with children, siblings, other relatives and others, and no paid employment in the previous week, maintained that they were never lonely.

Table 11 Percentage of persons living alone and all persons who were lonely

| Degree of loneliness | Living alone | | | | All old people |
	Extremely isolated	Partly isolated	Not isolated	All	
Men					
Often	(a)	23	14	20	5
Sometimes	(a)	35	34	32	14
Not lonely	(a)	42	52	47	80
Total	100	100	100	100	100
Number in sample	30	62	93	185	1,619
Women					
Often	24	19	15	18	8
Sometimes	34	38	38	38	26
Not lonely	42	43	47	45	66
Total	100	100	100	100	100
Number in sample	96	311	308	715	2,425
All persons					
Often	26	19	14	18	7
Sometimes	32	38	37	37	21
Not lonely	42	43	48	45	72
Total	100	100	100	100	100
Number in sample	126	373	401	900	4,044

(a) Base less than 50.

Just as we found substantial numbers of isolated people who did not feel lonely, we also found some 'integrated' people who did feel lonely. For example, a fifth of the widowed men and 30 per cent of the widowed women living with a child felt lonely sometimes or often but only 15 per cent of the married couples living on their own. In fact, of those saying that they were often lonely, only just over half were living alone. About a fifth lived with their spouse only but just over a third were living with children and others.

At first sight these results are puzzling. How do we explain them? It may be helpful to give illustrations from individual circumstances. First, an isolated man and an isolated woman who were not lonely.

One man, aged 75, lives alone in an English town in the Midlands. He used to be a mole-catcher. He is married but has been separated from his wife since the First World War, and has not seen his two children since she took them away with her. None of his siblings are alive and he does not belong to clubs and societies or attend church. He has not had any visitors in the past seven days and claims to have had no conversations with anyone. He says he is often alone but never lonely. He does not find that time passes slowly. He watches television and the garden is a credit to him (though the house is very untidy and bedecked with cobwebs). 'I'm as happy as can be.' He now walks a little unsteadily and has difficulty in climbing stairs. In the spring and summer he visits friends in a neighbouring village every week or so and helps them with their gardening.

A single woman of 70 lives alone in a terraced cottage on the outskirts of a small county town in the south of England. She has not had a paid job for ten years and used to serve in a shop. She has no brothers or sisters — 'I'm the last one of my family' — and her closest relative, a niece, lives a hundred miles away. She says she is often alone but that time never passes slowly and she is never lonely. 'I like being alone. I think there's nothing like it. My clocks go so fast. All my visitors say so.' She has brief visits from a friend on most days and her vicar calls once a month. Once a week she pays privately for domestic help.

Secondly, a person who does not live alone but *is* lonely.

A widow of 82 lives with her single daughter of 50. She has not worked for more than twenty-five years but despite some infirmity (she suffers from arthritis and is limited in walking and climbing stairs) leads an active social life, belonging to two women's guilds and the local Methodist sisterhood. She attends meetings or goes shopping most afternoons of the week, occasionally visits cinemas and theatres and sees two or three of her brothers and sisters every week and other relatives less often. She also has friends living locally. Her husband died a few years previously. She is conscious that her sight has been getting worse lately but still prepares all the meals for the household and does most of the housework. Her daughter is plainly solicitous. 'She buys me presents, treats me to the pictures and theatres, and takes me out for bus rides and on holiday.' But her daughter is at work in the week and despite her activity in the home and outside she says she is often alone, that time often passes slowly, and that she is often lonely.

We can move towards an explanation in negative terms. Although our measures of social interaction and integration are neither as full nor as specific as we should prefer them to be, the evidence presented here demonstrates that loneliness is not conditioned exclusively by physical or social segregation, or rather, to use the terminology tentatively suggested earlier, it is not conditioned by contrasted isolation. In particular, people who are, by comparison with their peers, life-long isolates, are not usually lonely. As Mrs Fiske Lowenthal has affirmed, many people who are extremely isolated are not lonely. She found one major group of the extremely isolated to be self-sufficient and self-possessed. They were alienated from society: 'male, single, and rather likely to be foreign born, with a history of considerable occupational and geographic mobility; more often than not, they wind up as alcoholics and live on Skid Row or its environs . . . Interviewers often found them courtly, charming and satisfied with their way of life' (13). The other major group of extreme isolates consisted of nearly as many women as men. Many had achieved a high occupational level, had married but had usually been separated or widowed. Few had had children, and had been estranged from them if they had. 'Problems having to do with personal losses in childhood or early adulthood figure frequently in their life stories – the death of a parent, usually the mother, or a sibling, for example . . . They give the impression of having tried but failed and the bulk of their adult lives is characterized by marginal if not precarious social adjustment. We have called them the *defeated*' (14).

Loneliness is not, therefore, a necessary reaction of those who are extremely isolated. Some students have gone on to point to a multiplicity of causes. Shortly after the Second World War Sheldon showed for old people in the town of Wolverhampton that the lonely tended to be widowed and single people, living alone, in their eighties rather than in their sixties, and relatively infirm. The 1962 national study has in these respects confirmed his study and other local studies. Sheldon also found that not all the people in these conditions were lonely and he concluded, 'Loneliness cannot be regarded as the simple direct result of social circumstances, but is rather an individual response to an external situation to which other old people may react quite differently' (15). There seemed to be no single 'cause' of severe loneliness.

But once the question is studied in the context of the life-cycle rather than in the context of scattered social conditions and affiliations it is possible to see a more consistent and comprehensive explanation.

Desolation and Loneliness

A persuasive hypothesis is that loneliness is attributable to age-related isolation or *social desolation*. A person who has lost a social intimate, usually someone he or she loves, such as a husband or wife, a relative or a close friend, is isolated by reference to a previous situation. For younger people time 'heals' in the sense that there is a chance of re-marriage or of the replacement of a close relative or friend who has been lost by another relative in the extended family or a friend. For older people this process of healing also occurs, but it is normally less rapid and substitutes tend to fall short of former intimates in the roles they play in the lives and affections of old people.

The crucial social losses sustained by old people seem to be the following: spouse, child, sibling, grandchild, friend or acquaintance at work or in the neighbourhood. If they are deprived of the company of a close relative, usually a husband, wife or child through death, illness or migration, they will complain of loneliness. If they have no family or if relationships with family are relatively weak they will tend to be lonely, especially once also deprived of the company of friends. The national survey provided three examples of the importance of loss or deprivation in understanding loneliness. First, fewer persons who had never been married than persons who had been married and were now widowed felt lonely. The old people who still had the company of a spouse were rarely lonely, although some of them had very limited social activities.

Secondly, whereas married but childless old people were no more likely to be lonely than married people who had seen a child very recently, the position was quite different for the widowed. Many more of them were lonely if they had no children. Widowed women were even more likely to be lonely if they had a surviving child that they had not seen recently. These women seemed to experience a double deprivation — the loss of husband and of children's company. These findings are given in Table 12.

Thirdly, a significantly larger proportion of those widowed within the last five years than of those widowed some ten or twenty years previously reported that they were often or sometimes lonely

Table 12 Percentage of married and widowed persons with different kinds of contact with a child, who were lonely (a)

Degree of loneliness	Men			Women			All persons		
	Child seen yesterday or today	Child not seen yesterday or today	No child	Child seen yesterday or today	Child not seen yesterday or today	No child	Child seen yesterday or today	Child not seen yesterday or today	No child
Married									
Often	3	2	4	3	7	4	3	4	4
Sometimes	11	14	8	17	21	16	13	17	12
Not lonely	87	84	88	80	72	79	84	79	84
Total	100	100	100	100	100	100	100	100	100
Number in sample	370	221	108	269	164	82	639	385	190
Widowed, separated or divorced									
Often	4	14	(b)	8	20	19	7	18	19
Sometimes	22	27	(b)	30	36	30	28	34	30
Not lonely	73	58	(b)	62	44	51	65	48	51
Total	100	100	100	100	100	100	100	100	100
Number in sample	161	51	40	511	147	102	672	198	142

(a) Based on Stage I of the national survey only.
(b) Percentages not computed on a base of less than 50.

(Table 13). In some respects those who were recently widowed tended to be more isolated than other widowed persons. They had not yet adjusted themselves to new circumstances and were transitionally rather than permanently living alone. After a time some of them would arrange for another person or family to share the home or they would move to live with a child.

Table 13 Percentage of widows (and of widows who had seen a child the same or the previous day) who were lonely

Degree of loneliness	Years of widowhood									
	0-4		5-9		10-19		20 or more years		All	
Often	18	*14*	13	*9*	8	*7*	13	*8*	12	*9*
Sometimes	36	*34*	30	*28*	31	*30*	27	*25*	30	*29*
Not lonely	46	*52*	37	*63*	61	*63*	61	*66*	67	*62*
Total	100	*100*	100	*100*	100	*100*	100	*100*	100	*100*
Number in sample	232	*140*	239	*166*	260	*250*	377	*225*	1,277[a]	*790*

Figures in italics refer only to those among the widows who had seen a child on the same or on the previous day.
(a) Total includes 19 persons unclassifiable on duration of widowhood.

Recent contact with a child provided some consolation to the widowed, including the recently widowed. But even when contact with a child is taken into account, those widowed in the last five years still stand out as the most lonely. Much the same was true of infirmity. The widows who had lost their husbands many years previously were older and more infirm than the others. While time allows the wounds of bereavement to heal, it also progressively deprives widows of the physical ability to take initiatives in sustaining substitute relationships. So here would be another reason for expecting the extent of loneliness to vary with length of widowhood. We found, however, that when we allowed both for incapacity and contact with family, a correlation between duration of widowhood and loneliness still remained. Table 14, for example, shows that among persons without incapacity substantially fewer of those widowed for ten or more years than of other widows were lonely.

Social loss is inextricably bound up with physical decrescence. More of the widowed were incapacitated. But among the widowed, loneliness increased with increasing personal and household incapacity. The correlation between loneliness and incapacity was independent of

Table 14 Percentage of widows without personal incapacity who were lonely (a)

Degree of loneliness	Years of widowhood				
	0-4	5-9	10-19	20+	All
Often	10	12	2	7	9
Sometimes	32	29	24	15	24
Not lonely	58	59	74	78	67
Total	100	100	100	100	100
Number in sample	60	68	77	96	301

(a) Based on Stage I of the national survey only.

marital status. Widowhood and incapacity had a cumulative effect upon loneliness. The majority of the severely incapacitated and bedfast widowed reported that they were lonely often or sometimes. One of the interesting features of Table 15, which shows the relation between incapacity and loneliness, is that more of the married men than of the married women who were incapacitated and bedfast reported that they were often or sometimes lonely. This is yet another reminder of the apparent greater emotional impact upon men than upon women of physical incapacity. The strong correlation between loneliness and incapacity for the married is particularly surprising since few of them complained of being often alone.

Mitigation of Loneliness

Since the most important determinants of feelings of loneliness appear to be (i) the loss of a husband, wife or child, or any other person with whom the old person has a significant relationship, and (ii) infirmity, it may be difficult to see how it can be relieved through any form of social policy. But how far can company mitigate acute feelings of loneliness? Our data are not detailed enough to enable us to examine the part that neighbours, friends, welfare schemes, clubs and churches might play in reducing feelings of loneliness. It is not easy in a cross-sectional type of study to distinguish cause and effect. But our data do suggest that the feelings of some of those who experienced a severe social loss were relieved by other contacts and relationships. The widowed who had seen a child yesterday or today were less likely to feel lonely than other widowed persons — though they were still more likely to feel lonely than married persons. The widowed who lived alone but had had recent contact with a child were less likely to feel lonely than other widowed persons living alone. It seems therefore that

Table 15 Percentage of married and unmarried persons with different degrees of personal and household incapacity who felt lonely

Degree of loneliness	Men			Women			All persons		
	Little or none	Moderate	Severe incapacity (and bedfast)	Little or none	Moderate	Severe incapacity (and bedfast)	Little or none	Moderate	Severe incapacity (and bedfast)
Married									
Often	1	3	16	2	7	12	1	5	14
Sometimes	8	16	32	13	28	23	10	21	28
Not lonely	91	81	52	85	65	65	90	74	58
Total	100	100	100	100	100	100	100	100	100
Number in sample	835	205	68	562	191	66	1,397	396	134
Widowed and single									
Often	10	12	(a)	8	14	20	8	13	20
Sometimes	21	24	(a)	26	34	34	24	32	33
Not lonely	69	64	(a)	66	53	46	68	55	47
Total	100	100	100	100	100	100	100	100	100
Number in sample	320	127	29	871	473	171	1,191	600	200

(a) Percentage not computed on a base of less than 50.

the relationship with a child can provide some compensation to those who have lost, even recently, a marriage partner. But we cannot pursue this question far. Our analysis takes no account of other compensatory social relationships and activities. Some of those not seeing children every day see other friends daily. Some of those seeing children every day see them only fleetingly, and because of infirmity spend much of their day alone. Information in greater depth is required and for larger numbers before realistic social continua can be devised and theory elaborated.

Nonetheless, we can conclude that desolation, in particular the loss of someone who is loved, explains the loneliness of old people more appropriately than peer-contrasted social isolation. But we can also conclude that substitute or compensating social involvement can be an important mitigating factor.

Notes and References

1 A few passages were published in Chapter 9 of Shanas, E., *et al.*, *Old People in Three Industrial Societies*, New York and London, Atherton and Routledge, 1968.

2 The interviewing and some of the analysis was carried out by the Government Social Survey. The survey was generously financed first by the National Institute of Mental Health (grant M 05511) and then by the Community Health Services of the United States Public Health Service (grant CM 000 53). The Ministry of Health in Britain financed the final stages of the national survey. See Shanas, E., *et al.*, *Old People in Three Industrial Societies*, and Townsend, P., and Wedderburn, D., *The Aged in the Welfare State*, Bell, 1965.

3 Halmos, P., *Solitude and Privacy*: A Study of Social Isolation: Its Causes and Therapy, Routledge & Kegan Paul, 1952, p. xv.

4 Riesman, D., *The Lonely Crowd*, New Haven, Yale University Press, 1950.

5 Halmos, P., op. cit., pp. 44 and 89.

6 Chapin, F. Stuart, *Experimental Designs in Sociological Research*, New York, Harper Brothers, 1947, and Chapin, F. Stuart, *Social Participation Scale*, Minneapolis, University of Minnesota Press, 1952.

7 Kutner, B., *Five Hundred over Sixty*, New York, Russel Sage Foundation, 1956.

8 Townsend, P., *The Family Life of Old People*, pp. 166-72; Willmott, P., and Young, M., *Family and Class in a London Suburb*, Routledge, 1960; and Tunstall, J., *Old and Alone*, Routledge, 1966.

9 'By "contact" is meant a meeting with another person, usually prearranged or customary at home or outside, which involves more than a casual exchange of greetings between, say, two neighbours in the street', Townsend, P., op. cit., p. 167.

10 Tunstall, J., op. cit., Chapter 3. See also appendix 3.

11 Tunstall in a survey in four areas in England reported that 92 per cent of the isolated lived alone. All the extremely isolated — persons reporting five or fewer contacts in the week — were living alone at the time of the interview. Tunstall, J., op. cit., pp. 70, 82.

12 Tunstall found only one isolated person living in a household of more than four people. His survey revealed a big difference between one-person households and all other households. An old person was not significantly more likely to be socially isolated (according to his definition) if he lived in a household of two, rather than one of three, four or more persons. However, persons living with one other person only were more likely to have an intermediate contact score and less likely to have a high contact score than those living in households consisting of three or more persons. Tunstall, J., op. cit., p. 70.

13 Lowenthal, M. Fiske, 'Social Isolation and Mental Illness in Old Age', in Hansen, P. From (ed.), *Age with a Future*, Proceedings of the Sixth International Congress of Gerontology, Copenhagen, 1963, Munksgaard, 1964, p. 467.

14 ibid.

15 Sheldon, J. H., *The Social Medicine of Old Age*, Report of an Inquiry in Wolverhampton, Oxford University Press, 1948, p. 130.

17 Sociology and the relationship between husband and wife *

This book (1) is likely to be the subject of much controversy among sociologists, not only because of its matter and presentation but because of the method of research upon which it was based. Shortly after the war the Tavistock Institute of Human Relations and the Family Welfare Association jointly sponsored a programme of research on the 'normal' family, aided over the years by three of the Foundations. In addition to Miss Bott, a social anthropologist, the research team consisted of a medical psycho-analyst, a lay psycho-analyst and a social psychologist. Altogether, interviews were held during the early 1950s with twenty families consisting of man and wife and from one to four children. They lived in various parts of London and the husbands ranged in occupation from a plumber and a boot-finisher to a business manager, and a statistician in a welfare agency. They were seen in their own homes from 8 to 19 times, averaging 13, and most agreed to visit the institute for a further two or three clinical interviews. The research aimed to understand the social and psychological organization of some urban families.

Miss Bott's study is concerned principally with the relationship of the family to their relatives, friends and neighbours and with the relationship between husband and wife (although there is also a good chapter on class). Each family was treated as a distinct social system so that detailed comparisons could be made. The couples varied in their relationships, some helping each other about the house, making joint decisions about financial and other matters and spending much of their leisure-time together, others having a fairly marked division of labour between them, dividing financial responsibilities and rarely going out together. They could be placed on a scale according to the degree of segregation in their role-relationship. How could the overall differences be explained? Not by social class, because although some professional couples inclined towards partnership in their activities, there were some who shared little with one another and, indeed, there were some working-class couples who shared far more. Miss Bott says that she found it easier to understand the differences when she came to examine the couples' relationships with friends, neighbours, relatives, clubs,

* First published as a review article in *Case Conference*, April 1958, vol. 4, no. 10.

shops, places of work and so on. The external social relationships of all the families seemed to form a *network* rather than a closely interrelated or organized group. Moreover, there was considerable variation in the 'connectedness', as Miss Bott put it, of their networks — or the extent to which the people known by a family knew and met one another independently of the family. This variation seemed to correspond to the variation in the relationship between man and wife. The author therefore put forward the hypothesis which is central to her book: *'The degree of segregation in the role-relationship of husband and wife varies directly with the connectedness of the family's social network.'*

The relationship between husband and wife tends to be neglected by sociologists and it is good to be reminded of its importance in this provocative book. Although written for a small group of specialists and likely to be found solemn, if not difficult, reading by the layman, it has some new things to say about sociological method and theory. Miss Bott has made no bones about the difficulties of a theoretical analysis and states quite clearly, 'the contribution of this book must be in its interpretations, not in the facts described'. Just because she has said this I think we must follow her cautiously and investigate her progress from data to theory. The social worker, as much as the sociologist, is anxious to learn more about the means whereby social 'facts' can be established, and the means whereby one can reason from the facts. In this paper I shall therefore concentrate on one, if the major, aspect of *Family and Social Network,* and concern myself chiefly with research method and the interpretation of research data in furthering our knowledge about the relationship between man and wife.

In the first place the reader of this book is troubled by the way the evidence has been collected. The author has risked a good deal of criticism by giving a very long and honest account of the research methods and quite apart from its relevance to the results this deserves to be compulsory reading for anyone embarking on social research. So many problems and hesitations are revealed. Rather unconvincingly, Miss Bott explains that knocking on doors at random was thought to be inappropriate and a laborious system of finding families was invented. An approach to forty-two agencies — general practitioners, tenants' associations, schools, hospital almoners and so on — eventually produced twenty families to be interviewed. Families contacted by this method may be rather exceptional, and although their occupational status varied greatly it is perhaps important to note that no unskilled manual worker was among them. In the interviews, Miss Bott and her colleagues seem to have been unnecessarily self-conscious in raising matters about which they imagined their informants would be reticent, to have been haphazard sometimes in collecting data and in the early stages even avoided taking notes until afterwards. Despite the prolonged interviewing the data are frequently said to be 'insufficient' or too 'inconsistent' for crucial analyses.

In the second place the reader does not have his curiosity allayed by the way the evidence is presented. The twenty families are inadequately described. Although they are in the same 'phase of family development' in that the couples each have a child under ten, have been married four to eleven years and are, it seems, mainly in their thirties, the details are not given and the families are hard to visualize. Sometimes the text comes alive with a concrete detail or quotation – as when one man remarked, 'Men have friends. Women have relatives' and later, 'Women don't have friends. They have Mum.' But more often the findings are presented separately from the theoretical analysis as generalized reportage, and not used to sharpen definition and classification.

Thus, in the sections on 'network connectedness' Miss Bott describes the activities and relationships of the only family with a 'close-knit' network and makes statements such as 'they knew a considerable number of local people and many of these people were acquainted with one another', and also, 'several of his friends knew one another'. As such information is central to the analysis, one is anxious to know how many, and how often they saw each other. Too often very general statements are made about collectives – lumping together friends, neighbours and relatives, or parents, brothers and sisters, children and in-laws.

It is this attention to detail which seems to be absent from the Tavistock inquiry: not just the finicky detail of the over-scrupulous sociologist or the distracting detail of the author who likes a good story, but the detail which should be (though rarely is) the stock-in-trade of every sociological inquiry – such as ages, age-differences, group or family sizes and structures, distances and frequencies of contact. In a real sense these are all measurable, and it is mainly by the imaginative use and description of forms of measurement, I believe, that sociology can proceed.

The problem, however, is not only of collecting detail, so as to substitute precision for vagueness in the statement of fact. It is one of interpretation, or of sorting out the data and relating them to definitions and the use of terms. Take the example again of 'the connectedness of a family's social network'. It is clear that many of the relationships of a man and wife and young children are individual rather than family relationships. The wife may see little or nothing of the husband's intimate friends or acquaintances at work; the husband may see little or nothing of the wife's more friendly neighbours and relatives or the people she sees while shopping; and both may see little of the children's friends at school. Each individual's network may be 'connected' but there may be little overlapping. The careful sorting out of the mass of research data into categories would help us to understand whether a couple have few activities in common or to what extent immediate families can be treated as 'social systems'. To put my point in a different way, if man and wife are segregated in their role-relationship it is a bit difficult to see how the *family* network can be connected.

A different example might be taken. Miss Bott makes what seems at first sight a valuable distinction between 'complementary', 'independent' and 'joint' organization of family activities (using the first two in defining the phrase 'segregated conjugal role-relationship').

> In *complementary organization* the activities of husband and wife are different and separate but fitted together to form a whole. In *independent organization* activities are carried out separately by husband and wife without reference to each other, in so far as this is possible. In *joint organization* activities are carried out by husband and wife together, or the same activity is carried out by either partner at different times.

This is all right until we think of classifying behaviour. Usually I take the dog for a walk — usually my wife irons the clothes. When I am ill or out of London she will take him out — say ten days in 365. Similarly there are times, say three times a year, when I will do some of the ironing. Normally we carry out these activities without consulting each other, though I suppose we both assume the other does his or her job sometime, somehow. When my wife and I do these things simultaneously, or sometimes simultaneously and sometimes independently, are they joint, complementary or independent? So much of the behaviour observed by a sociologist is like this and simply to avoid ambiguity and open the way to measurement he must lay down his interpretations much more strictly. In laying them down he is often obliged to return to his data or to the people he has been interviewing to seek fresh insights into their relationships.

Many of these difficulties in method and interpretation are due to a muddled idea of what the sociologist should be trying to 'explain' or, rather, what *kind* of explanation for social behaviour he should be trying to provide. One of the most interesting features of Miss Bott's book is the revelation of the effects both on her and on the report she has written of 'inter-disciplinary' research, of working with analysts and social psychologists. At the start she said she had a preference for an environmental or social rather than psychological explanation for social behaviour. She argued with other members of the team about fitting together psychological and sociological or anthropological analyses. A sort of brain-washing went on, and in the end Miss Bott says a change took place in her own mind and she now believed that actual behaviour was somehow a synthesis of personality on the one hand and a 'fixed immutable social environment on the other'.

I think Miss Bott's first instincts were the right ones. But her conversion explains, I believe, why so little emphasis has been put on the measurement of detail or on precise interpretation and why behaviour and feeling are so often confused in this book. (Examples are p. 78 — obligation towards siblings; p. 81 — favouritism; pp. 129, 131 and 140 — relations with parents and other kin; pp. 144-5 — status; and p. 240 — classification of conjugal organizations.) Put quite crudely, there are different levels or kinds of scientific explanation for any one event. The observation of a boy eating several green apples and then being sick will be given different kinds of explanation by a biochemist, a physician and a psycho-analyst. Each explanation is appropriate in its own context and to combine them in one comprehensive explanation is likely to be muddling rather than helpful.

In the present state of affairs it is hard enough finding out what each of the social sciences is about without being told that each one should be fully integrated with every other and that different social scientists would do better to work together on a project than pursue their interests separately. People who do say this often forget the enormous range of interests among the different academic disciplines. The economist may be chiefly interested in people because he wants, among other things, to understand the subtle relationships between their wages, their savings, their production and their consumption. The sociologist may be more interested in social structure and the relationships between various social groups. (The social anthropologist is interested in many of the same things as the sociologist but tends to have confined himself to non-industrialized societies, with the consequence that his methods and techniques of study are more individual, more descriptive and less specialized.) The social psychologist may be primarily interested in the personality of the individual as it is affected by the group and in mass feelings, opinions and attitudes, the psychologist in man's mental processes, and the psychiatrist in the conscious and unconscious motives of individual action. All of them find plenty to do for their interests are by no means narrow.

It would be perfectly true to say that if we sat each of these specialists in a cinema to watch the Gorki trilogy, say, or de Sica's *Umberto D,* and afterwards asked them, as specialists, to give an 'explanation' of what they had seen, they would differ remarkably. That may not be because one of them would be right and the others wrong, but simply because each would have different interests in what he had seen. To combine their explanations into one would be tantamount to eliminating all individual insights and interests and writing an official communiqué of uniform dullness. We have to declare our interests if we are to see problems and find answers to the problems. If we say we are interested in everything then explanation becomes diffuse and unmanageable. It is one thing to have an interchange of information between the disciplines; it is another to compromise about aims, methods and the character of hypotheses.

How does this preceding discussion affect both our general under-standing of what sociology should be about, and our understanding of the relationship between man and wife? Sociology has frequently been discredited for producing sweeping (and often meaningless) generaliza-tions and interpretations whose basis in fact is concealed by a metaphysical use of jargon. One does not have to be a positivist to believe that far too little attention has been given to the questions of precise definition and verification. It is usually more difficult to observe and interview people than to draw up questionnaires and direct teams of interviewers, and more valuable to relate research findings to categories, definitions and classifications than to devise elaborate explanations at the most general level (and often in several languages) about the facts that are supposed to have come to light.

The more immediate, and perhaps more difficult, task of sociology is to concentrate on the intermediate processes in any empirical inquiry, on the systematic collection and evaluation of information about people's behaviour and on the formulation and testing of what may be called 'second-order' hypotheses. By second-order hypotheses I mean hypotheses linking or explaining two sets of observations which, if confirmed, pave the way for hypotheses of a higher order of abstraction. Thus, to give a simple illustration, during some recent research on old people in Bethnal Green I found that most were very reserved in their relationships with their daughters' husbands. When living nearby few saw them more than once a week, although they usually saw their daughters every day. But there were a number of puzzling exceptions. Some old people had relatively close and fond relationships with their daughters' husbands. Among the explanations that could be given for the variations in contact were two that appeared to be inherently interesting — one which I could check statistically and one which I could only illustrate from some of the interview data. (A statistical check would of course be possible if enough information were collected for a large sample.) These were: (i) old people with daughters but not sons see more of their daughters' husbands than do people with sons; (ii) old people see more of their daughters' husbands when the husbands' parents are dead. (Or, to put it round another way: husbands see more of their parents-in-law when their own parents are dead.) These are very elementary examples but they seem to bear within them a line of thought about the effect of family structure on individual relationships and behaviour which may be important.

This general, if tentative, line of thinking about sociology suggests how we might approach the difficult question of the relationship between man and wife. We need to know, in much greater detail, what actually goes on in society. We know extraordinarily little about the number of evenings a week husbands in different social classes spend with their wives; how the wage or salary is divided between them and whether any details of income or expenditure are kept from the other; and who does exactly what job, and how often, in the home and with the children. In a particularly interesting study carried out in the war Charles Madge showed that some parts of the country, notably Lancashire, were peculiar in that many husbands gave their wives their entire wage-packet. In Blackburn the proportion was 49 per cent; in Slough 5 per cent. Reports have frequently been given in social surveys of husbands not telling their wives how much they earn or what problems they have met at work, and of wives pinching and scraping to give a squarer meal to the wage-earner than anyone else. Many observations of this kind have not been followed up by more systematic and intensive study. They are applicable to all social classes. I have interviewed middle-class and professional wives who have known far less about their husbands' earnings and occupations than many working-class wives.

We want to know not only what goes on between man and wife, but what goes on in their other relationships. The sociologist has to disentangle the relationships entered into by man and wife separately and together and somehow measure the intensity of each. He also needs to examine how the relationships vary according to structural variations in the family. It seems likely, for example, that differences in age, length of a couple's marriage, the number of children and sex and age differences between them may each have an influence on the extent to which there is a division of labour and on whether or not the couple share their leisure-time.

It also seems likely that the marriage may be influenced by whether or not there are parents (or brothers and sisters) on both the husband's and wife's side, particularly those who live near and are seen frequently. In contrasting one extreme example of segregation of role and another of partnership Miss Bott does not appear to attach much importance to the fact that in one the wife's parents were alive and lived near and in the other they were dead. I would argue that close contact with nearby relatives, particularly parents, is perhaps the major reason for segregation in role between man and wife. At one point, in describing the only family with a 'close-knit' network, Miss Bott says 'Mrs Newbolt was responsible for most of the housework although Mr Newbolt did household repairs and she expected him to do some of the housework if she became ill. *This was usually unnecessary because her mother or sister or one of her cousins came to her aid. These female relatives helped her greatly even with the everyday tasks of housework and child care.'* (My italics.) It is worth pondering on this extract for what it tells us about the family. How meaningful is it to think here of the immediate family — consisting of Mr and Mrs Newbolt and their children — as an independent entity?

Good social theory about marriage can grow only out of good information and my argument amounts to saying that we have not spent enough time on the job of getting more exact, more detailed and more reliable information. Neither have we spent enough time on the job of saying exactly what we mean, and how what we mean is related to what we have observed, when we use words like 'contacts', 'separation', 'segregation', 'consultation', 'independence', 'cohabitation' and 'isolation' in interpreting people's activities and relationships.

Reference

1 Bott, Elizabeth, *Family and Social Network,* Tavistock, 1957, pp. xi, 252.

18 Family and kinship in industrial society*

Sociologists have for generations toyed with comprehensive theories of the relationship between industrialization and family change. In contrast to a wealth of speculation there has been an astonishing absence of hard evidence. How common was it in the eighteenth century for parents to live with or near their married children and share a joint domestic economy? How common was it even in 1950? What systematic study has there been in Britain or in any other Western society of the relationship between grandparent and grandchild, brother and sister, mother's brother and sister's child – or even between husband and wife? To what extent does the immediate or nuclear family in fact live as a nuclear family? These are primarily rhetorical questions. But they serve as reminders of the bold presumptions of Simmel, Weber, Tonnies, Durkheim, Ogburn, Burgess, Linton, Parsons, Homans and a host of other distinguished sociologists who have developed elaborate theories on the subject. A large number of sociological texts have been published which contain sweeping generalizations. It is as if a chancellor's dispatch box had been brandished triumphantly almost every year; but rattling about inside there have proved to be only a few dried peas.

In the history of sociology there has been remarkably little relationship between the development of elaborate theories and the collection of data. Quite why this should have been so is a subject worth study in its own right. There are scientists whose best ideas come from hours spent at their desks writing rather than from routine work in a laboratory. The good ones probably do both. The social scientist's laboratory must normally be the environment in which a human group or community lives. If he works there and tries to develop major theories he will normally be aware of the need to show how they are dependent on certain 'middle-range' (or 'second-order') hypotheses which are empirically testable.

But, secondly, we may be a long way farther out of the wood of ignorance than Professor Firth suggests (1). Like Professor Goode in his recent analysis of changing family patterns (2), he is sceptical of much previous theory and is sensitively aware of the need for sophisticated

* First published in *The Sociological Review Monograph*, no. 8, October 1964.

revisions. Nevertheless, he comes out in favour of the emergence, with industrialization, of the nuclear or elementary family – even if some wider kin ties are preserved. He refers to the extended family 'giving way' to some variety of the nuclear family. While recognizing that changes in structure and organization have taken place, I find it difficult to accept this conclusion either as a precise descriptive summary of the evidence relating, say, to the last hundred or two hundred years in Britain or as an explanation of how society necessarily adjusts to the needs of industrialization. I cannot do more here than suggest my reasons.

One side of the equation is what forms of the family existed in the past. O. R. MacGregor and others have pointed out the possible use that might be made of historical sources (3). Sufficient has certainly emerged from work by Eugene Friedmann (4), Smelser (5), Braun (6), Greenfield (7), Goode and others to show that the three-generation household was relatively uncommon in previous centuries in both the United States and many parts of Europe. Early mortality also kept low the proportion of persons who were members of cohesive three-generation descent groups.

The other side of the equation is evidence about the family in contemporary society. There are now a large number of data about close functional relationships between relatives other than the members of the nuclear family. There are local studies from North America and many parts of Europe. In the last few years there have been studies by Sussman and Burchinal (8), Key (9), Dotson (10), Reiss (11), Sharp and Axelrod (12), Litwak (13), Ayoub (14), Mitchell (15), Streib (16) and others covering metropolitan areas like New York, Chicago and San Francisco as well as rural areas like Cleveland and South-West Ohio, and covering the upper and lower middle classes as well as the working classes. In Britain there exists the work in rural areas of, among others, Williams (17) and Rees (18) and in urban areas of Young and Willmott (19), Rosser and Harris (20), Shaw (21), and Kerr (22).

Perhaps the fullest information available involves the aged. Gerontology has contributed a vast amount of field data on family contacts and relations. It may not be generally known that since 1945 reports of more than forty field studies of old people have been published in Britain, many of which give information about the family. Old people in areas as different as the Orkneys, Anglesey, Aberdeen, Shropshire, Lewisham, Woodford and East Ham have been surveyed (23). At least ten such local or regional studies have been carried out in the United States (24) and several in France, Germany, Italy, Sweden and Norway (25). In Vienna, a series of studies have been carried out by Rosenmayr and Kockeis (26).

These studies vary, of course, in scope and quality but perhaps I may quote from the latest study, which is a cross-national survey carried out simultaneously in the United States, Denmark and Britain to emphasize the conclusion to which they all point. This survey was based on comparable questionnaires and involves national probability samples of approximately 2,500 persons aged sixty-five and over in the three countries (27). A series of questions was asked about the children, grandchildren, siblings and other relatives in the course of the interview. In each of the countries between 62 per cent and 69 per cent of those with surviving children had seen one or more on the day of interview or on the previous day, and most of the others had seen one or more of their children within the previous week (28). Of those who saw their children less often, some spent several weeks with them each year. The majority of old people in the United States with children live with or within ten minutes' journey of at least one of them. Isolation because of social and geographical mobility is a minority phenomenon.

The data now available allow certain conclusions to be drawn. First, as in other international research, such as that on social mobility, the similarities between countries are more striking than the differences. Perhaps we have allowed ourselves in the past to exaggerate the influence, at least upon the organization of the family, of contrasting physical environments, technical institutions and cultural heritages.

Secondly, the extended family, by which I mean the group of from 3 to 20 or more relatives who are in daily or almost daily contact and who include at least two individuals who stand in a relationship different from that of any two members of the *immediate* or *nuclear* family of parents and unmarried dependent children, exists as a cohesive organization for the majority of the population (29). This is no longer a wayward belief of a few eccentric sociologists and anthropologists working in areas which are supposed to contain quaint cultural survivals. Despite the risk of making such statements before an academic audience without the space to develop all necessary qualifications, it seems right to discourage colleagues from going on using the tired hypotheses of the turn of the century. Some sociologists seem as reluctant to accept evidence of the existence of the extended family as some moralists and theologians are to accept evidence of extra-marital sexual relationships. They prefer to deny the reality of what they consider to be an improper primitive survival.

The extended family is indeed *the* primary group for a substantial proportion — we don't yet know exactly what proportion — of the populations of industrial societies. This family is not a well-defined segment of a network of kin. It usually spans three or four generations. However, there are nearly always relatives such as married siblings who live far away and play little part in the affairs of the group. This group *may* be smaller than it was in pre-industrial societies. I estimate that the number of grandparents and great-grandparents must have increased in this country from 4 or 4½ million at the turn of the century to around 10 million today, and this relative increase has encouraged a vertical splitting of the network of kin, whereas a century ago there was often only a sole surviving grandparent trying to hold together, however loosely, the pyramid-like network or structure.

This gives hints of the ways in which a theory of family change might be developed. There is need for rigorous definition of the different family groups that exist, whether functional, associational or formal, and for comparative study of the behaviour of family groups of different structure and organization. The relationship between two individuals in a family group will be affected, for example, by their sex, their marital status, their difference in age, the generation to which they belong, whether they have a biological or an affinal relationship and what that relationship is. When we consider not two individuals but a largish family group the individual characteristics might be combined in many different ways. It will be a huge task to delineate the chief groups, investigate irregularities in the statistical frequency of, say, the eldest sibling or mother's brother playing a crucial role in the upbringing of the individual, explain some of the differences in behaviour and examine the influences of social and occupational mobility. Multi-variate analysis of populations is probably our nearest profitable approach to the experimental situation.

I cannot pursue the possibilities of structural theory save to point out that if we can explain why some family groups interrelate closely while others of similar structure do not, then we will throw up empirical clues for a theory of family change. Secondly, if we use demographic data intelligently and take account of variations over time of mortality rates, frequency and age of marriage, family size and so on, we will begin to eliminate some of the variables which may, in addition to industrialization (whatever that means), account for changes in family behaviour. For example, the principal demographic trends of greater expectation of life, earlier and more marriage, and families completed at an earlier age, have plainly altered the structural complex of family relationships — (i) giving more emphasis to descendent and perhaps affinal relationships as compared with collateral relationships, (ii) narrowing the distance in years between the generations while increasing the number or span of generations surviving at any time, and (iii) generally reducing to a smaller number of common types or forms of family which exist in society.

Sociologists are sometimes reluctant to accept or even examine the facts about the wider family because it is assumed to be antithetical to progress, contradicting the political ideals of equality, democracy, fellowship, social mobility and prosperity. It is supposed to obstruct occupational mobility and hence occupational and technical change. But even if some of its forms have changed, it has survived. There must be some senses therefore in which it *promotes* occupational mobility, in which the loss of authority by the parental generation actually results in a *strengthening* of the relationship between fathers and sons. Moreover, wives often offset occupational rivalry between their husbands and sons by promoting the aspirations of their sons and act as a check to divisions which might otherwise occur. Status differences between the generations and the effects of these on family relationships are rarely discussed in terms which discriminate carefully between husbands and wives, and sons and daughters. These are merely provisional lines of thought towards a revision of theory.

Notes and References

1 Firth, R., in the *Sociological Review Monograph*, no. 8, October 1964.

2 Goode, William J., *World Revolution and Family Patterns*, New York, The Free Press, 1963.

3 MacGregor, O. R., 'Some Research Possibilities and Historical Materials for Family and Kinship Study in Britain', *British Journal of Sociology*, XII, 1961.

4 Friedmann, E. A., 'The Impact of Ageing on the Social Structure', in Tibbitts, C. (ed.), *Handbook of Social Gerontology*, Chicago, University of Chicago Press, 1960.

5 Smelser, Neil, *Social Change in the Industrial Revolution*, Chicago, University of Chicago Press, 1959.

6 Braun, Rudolph, *Industrialisierung Volksleben*, Erbenback-Zierrich, Reutsch, 1960.

7 Greenfield, S. M., 'Industrialization and the Family', *American Journal of Sociology*, LXVII, 1961, pp. 312-22.

8 Sussman, M., 'Relationships of Adult Children with their Parents in the United States', in Shanas, E., and Streib, G. (eds.), *Family, Intergenerational Relationships and Social Structure*, Prentice-Hall. Sussman, M., and Burchinal, L., 'Kin Family Networks: Unheralded Structure in Current Conceptualizations of Family Functioning', *Marriage and Family Living*, XXIV, 1962, pp. 231-40, and 'Parental Aid to Married Children: Implications for Family Functioning', *Marriage and Family Living*, XXIV, 1962, pp. 320-32. Sussman, M., and White, R. C., *Hough: A Study of Social Life and Change*, Cleveland, Western Reserve University Press, 1959.

9 Key, William H., 'Rural-Urban Differences and the Family', *Sociological Quarterly*, II, 1961, pp. 49-56.

10 Dotson, F., 'Patterns of Voluntary Association Among Urban Working Class Families', *American Sociological Review*, XVI, 1951, pp. 689-93.

11 Reiss, Paul J., 'The Extended Kinship System of the Urban Middle Class', Ph.D. Dissertation, Harvard University, 1959.

12 Sharp, M., and Axelrod, M., 'Mutual Aid Among Relatives in an Urban Population', in Freedman, R. *et al.* (eds.), *Principles of Sociology*, New York, Holt, 1956, pp. 433-9.

13 Litwak, E., 'Extended Kin Relations in an Industrial Democratic Society', in Shanas, E., and Streib, G., op. cit. See also 'Occupational Mobility and Extended Family Cohesion' and 'Geographic Mobility and Family Cohesion', *American Journal of Sociology*, 1960, pp. 9-21 and 385-94.

14 Ayoub, Millicent, 'American Child and His Relatives: Kindred in South-West Ohio', project supported by Public Health Service, 1961. Reported by Sussman, M., op. cit.

15 Mitchell, William E., 'Descent Groups Among New York City Jews', *The Jewish Journal of Sociology*, III, 1961, pp. 121-8. 'Lineality and Laterability in Urban Jewish Ambilineages', read at 60th Annual Meeting of the American Anthropological Association in Philadelphia, Pennsylvania, 16 November 1961.

16 Streib, Gordon F., 'Family Patterns in Retirement', *Journal of Social Issues*, XIV, 1958, pp. 46-60.

17 Williams, W. M., *The Sociology of an English Village: Gosforth*, Routledge & Kegan Paul; Glencoe, The Free Press, 1956.

18 Rees, A. D., *Life in a Welsh Countryside*, Cardiff, University of Wales Press, 1951.

19 Young, M., and Willmott, P., *Family and Kinship in East London*, Routledge & Kegan Paul; Glencoe, The Free Press, 1957; Penguin Books, 1962; Willmott, P., and Young, M., *Family and Class in a London Suburb*, Routledge & Kegan Paul, 1960; Willmott, P., *The Evolution of a Community*, Routledge & Kegan Paul, 1963.

20 Rosser, C., and Harris, C. C., 'Relationships through Marriage in a Welsh Urban Area', *The Sociological Review*, vol. 9, no. 3, November 1961, pp. 293-321.

21 Shaw, L. A., 'Impressions of Family Life in a London Suburb', *The Sociological Review*, New Series, vol. 2, no. 2, December 1954.

22 Kerr, Madeleine, *The People of Ship Street*, Routledge & Kegan Paul, 1958.

23 For references see Townsend, P., *The Family Life of Old People*, Penguin Books edition, 1963, particularly p. 237.

24 See, for example, Longford, M., *Community Aspects of Housing for the Aged*, New York, Cornell University Center for Housing and Environmental Studies, 1962; Young, M., and Geertz, H., 'Old Age in London and San Francisco: Some Families Compared', *British Journal of Sociology*, vol. 12, no. 2, June 1961, pp. 124-41; Varchauer, C., *Older People in the Detroit Areas and the Retirement Age*, Eerdmans, 1956.

25 For a number of references see Burgess, E. W. (ed.), *Ageing in Western Societies*, Chicago, University of Chicago Press, 1961.

26 Rosenmayr, L., and Kockeis, E., *Leben und Alter Menschen in Heimstatten*, Vienna, Sozialwissenschaftliche Forschungstelle, Institut fur Soziologie, Universität Wien, 1960; *Umwelt und Familie alter Menschen*, Neuwied and Berlin, Hermann Lichterhand Verlag, 1963; and 'Propositions for a Sociological Theory of Ageing and the Family', *International Social Science Journal*, XV, no. 3, 1963, pp. 410-37.

27 The research in each country was made possible by generous grants from the N.I.M.H. and other branches of the United States Public Health Service. In Britain the Treasury made it possible for the Government Social Survey to carry out the important role of sampling, interviewing and tabulating. Also see, Friis, H., 'Cross-National Research on Old Age', *International Social Science Journal*, XV, no. 3, 1963.

28 This is a convenient way of collecting information. There are research studies showing that answers to questions about last contacts correspond, in the main, with those about frequency of usual contacts.

29 Usually, but not necessarily, the family lives in one household or two or more households in a single locality and usually but again not necessarily, it consists of individuals belonging to three or four generations. When the members live in two, three or more households not all may be in daily association but only the 'connecting' members of each household. The *immediate* family can be defined as one or both parents and their unmarried children living in one household. Any two of its members stand in one of three relationships to each other: wife/husband, parent/unmarried child, unmarried sibling/unmarried sibling. A single person, two unmarried siblings, or a married couple living in a single household are not described as a family. See Townsend, P., *The Family Life of Old People*, Chapter 9.

19 Marx and the Soviet family after 1917 *

Most sociological writing about the family in modern society has been unreal. The founding fathers saw it as an elaborate institution which was gradually being shorn of its membership and functions. The functionalist tradition of the United States represented particularly by William Ogburn, Ernest Burgess, and Talcott Parsons has been to assume that industrialization required the extended farm family to be transformed into the mobile urban unit of married couple and young children. From being a clan whose ramifications penetrated the political, economic and cultural systems of society, it was reduced to a pattern of interpersonal relations — still important in rearing children and satisfying sexual needs but very much diminished from its former importance. Hence the tedious multiplication of American studies of dating on the campus and of marital adjustment. In the last decade a number of American sociologists have begun to break away from this myopic tradition and to find that the extended family counts in modern politics and economic and social life. But there is still astonishingly little that bears comparison with British studies of kinship by the Institute of Community Studies, Raymond Firth, Rosser and Harris. By and large, the American sociologist has still to discover that, say, the phenomenon of the Kennedy family represents many facets of family at every level of American society.

The limitations of this American standpoint are found in Kent Geiger's study of *The Family in Soviet Russia* (1) in which he summarizes the writing of Marx and Engels on the family and goes on to discuss the recent history of the Soviet family, basing much of his analysis on four main sources of information — Soviet refugees in Germany, Germans who had been prisoners of war in Russia, Soviet publications and other writing. He concentrates on fertility, marriage, divorce and child upbringing in Soviet Russia and tends to neglect the transmission of wealth and educational opportunity, political influence and continuity, the network of domestic and emergency services, including the care of the old, and the communication of social change

---

* A lecture delivered at the University of Essex in 1968, an extract of which was published in the *New Statesman,* 13 December 1968.

through the contacts of the generations within the family. But in fairness, the Soviet literature could hardly be said to call his attention to such matters and he describes very well the attempts of the Government to apply Marxist theory on the family to the problems of Soviet society after 1917.

Marx's and Engels's Four Stages of Family Development

Marx wrote of the family much as he wrote of capitalist society. He saw the two as mutually supportive and treated both as historically ephemeral. He and Engels were preoccupied with the relation of husband and wife and the way it was affected by property relations and other aspects of the economic system. The fullest outline of their theory can be found in Engels's book, *The Origin of the Family, Private Property and the State, in the Light of the Researches of Lewis H. Morgan* (2), which was published in 1884 after Marx's death, but which is recognized to contain the fruits of a lifetime's collaboration.

Marx and Engels seized upon Morgan's evolutionary scheme and argued that the family assumed different forms in historical development. In the first stage men and women lived as a *promiscuous horde*. In the second stage *group marriage* evolved in different sub-types, mainly determined by the gradual introduction of different forms of incest taboo. Thus the moiety system of the Australian aborigines implied a wide range of sexual choice and meant that entire groups were married, moiety with moiety. Then there was the consanguine family in which mating between the generations was taboo but not between brothers and sisters and first, second and third cousins, and the 'punaluan' family, in which the incest taboo was now extended to brothers and sisters and cousins of the opposite sex. In the third stage came the *monogamous family*, which Marx and Engels were to discuss at length, and in the fourth and final stage would arrive a *new form of group relations* under Communism. This is a simplification of the typology and in struggling to fit the findings from studies of different societies within it Marx and Engels had to elaborate various transitional forms. But essentially their approach is governed by the principle of natural selection and of the central role of economic development and private property in introducing social change.

The different stages of family evolution were hypothesized to correspond with different stages of social evolution — from primitive Communism, slavery, feudalism and capitalism to Socialism. Between primitive Communism and slavery the transitional form of the pairing family (bridging group marriage on the one hand and monogamy on the other) evolved. In this one man lived with one woman, but the marriage tie could easily be dissolved by either partner. Polygamy and infidelity could be practised by the man but not the woman. With the increasing importance in society of private productive property stricter control of the family unit was required. Property had to be protected and heirs provided. The patriarchal family as the first family-form in written history came on the scene. Women were increasingly subjugated by men.

The bourgeois family was corrupted by property relations and by thoughts about money and exchange. Everyone dwelt on dowries and inheritance and true love became impossible. In one purple passage Engels wrote that the bourgeois wife 'only differs from the ordinary courtesan in that she does not let out her body on piece-work as a wage-worker, but sells it once and for all into slavery' (3). She became a domestic slave, the mere producer of an heir and the satisfier of loveless lust. Both adultery and prostitution were an offshoot of this bourgeois family life. Within the social microcosm of the family the husband was the bourgeois and the wife the proletarian. The family merely reflected the inequalities of power in the wider society.

The proletarian family of course was free of the corrupting influence of private property. But it could not achieve happiness because exploitation arose not from within the family circle but from outside it. The ruthless demands of modern industry ruined domestic and family relations. Women and children were exploited mercilessly with low wages and bad conditions of work. In self-defence against extreme poverty the proletarian married early and produced many children to gain a supplementary pittance in factories and mines. He turned to the pleasures of drink and sexual indulgence as a form of escape. Yet the proletarian family contained some of the features of true love, marital equality and freedom to divorce or separate which approach Marx's and Engels's image of the family under Communism.

Here then is perhaps the basic flaw or at least ambiguity in the Marxist analysis of the relation between private property or capitalism and the family. In one case the ownership of private property corrupts. In the other lack of it does not secure freedom from corruption. The maldistribution of property in the wider society and the corrosive effects of sweated labour and poverty take over as determining agents of behaviour and relationships within the family. Or rather, everything that is approved is attributed to the lack of property. Everything that is disapproved is attributed to ownership of property and, when it is lacking, to the evil machinations of external society.

Under Communism the family as previously known would disappear. Property, consumption, work and the rearing of children would be taken over by society at large. The union between man and woman would continue to be close. Women would be freed from domestic slavery and would play their part in the wider social units of society. Quite what would happen to relations between parents and children and between other members of the wider family was not made clear. The Communist society would 'transform the relations between the sexes into a purely private matter which concerns only the persons involved and into which society has no occasion to intervene. It can do this since it does away with private property and educates children on a communal basis, and in this way removes the two bases of traditional marriage, the dependence, rooted in private property, of woman on the man and of the children on the parents' (4).

Were Marx's Prophecies Fulfilled?

What in fact happened in the Soviet Union after 1917? Inheritance was not abolished. Even in a first decree in 1918 immediate relatives who had been living with the deceased could inherit an estate of up to 10,000 roubles. But in 1919 this limit was lifted on peasants' farmsteads and in 1926 it was abandoned entirely. Although a strongly progressive inheritance tax was maintained until 1943 even this tax was then abolished. The 1918 decree recognized a legal responsibility for the care of relatives and in 1926 the list of possible relatives to whom there was a legal obligation was actually extended. There were powerful attempts to persuade the population to give their first loyalties to society, and only secondly to the family and personal life. There were many actions and resolutions serving to discredit the older generation and give greater status and power to youth. Campaigns were launched to release women from domestic and maternal slavery. But the transfer of women to productive employment was very slow. There was unemployment in the 1920s and too few communal kitchens and dining halls, laundries and day nurseries were opened. There were sharp differences between ideology and practice. Geiger quotes party members who made thunderous speeches about the role of women in the revolution and behaved in a reactionary way in their own homes. The problem of double standards was certainly one that permeated Soviet life — or at least the life of party workers — at this time. Some women were not so much released from enslavement to the family as also introduced to the enslavement of the factory.

Legal restraints on married couples were reduced. Mutual consent was the main requirement for marriage. Divorce became much easier. Abortions were made legal and were free. The original family code of 1918 prohibited adoption on the ground, among others, that the State could bring up children who would otherwise be adopted and lost to the derided institution of the family. But the realities of poverty and homelessness (estimated to affect 9 million children in 1922) forced adoption to be legalized in the Soviet Code of Marriage, Divorce, Family and Guardianship of November 1926. That code also created reciprocal obligations for maintenance not only between the married pair but between parent and child, grandparent and grandchild and between siblings. Even at this stage the law recognized the fact of family organization.

The struggle to present Marx's and Engels's theory still continued, but a change came in the 1930s when, partly due to the influence of the writing of such people as Makarenko, who had worked for many years with homeless children and who gained the patronage of Stalin, the family was reinstated as a desirable institution in Soviet society. Makarenko wrote of it as a Communist collective or cell in which the parents set their children good examples of Communist values and prepared them for useful work in society. Housework was discovered to be socially useful labour. Stable family life became important. In 1934, in a blaze of publicity, Stalin visited his old mother in the Caucasus.

By 1944 the legal status that had been given to *de facto* common law marriage was withdrawn. Illegitimacy was reinstituted: a child born outside marriage did not have the right to claim the name or the estate of his biological father. Homosexuality became a criminal offence in 1934. Discouragements to divorce were introduced in 1935-6 and 1944. After being made legal in 1920 abortions became illegal again in 1936. Co-education was abolished in 1943 and renewed emphasis placed on domestic training for girls. The family was back in favour — in some ways with a vehemence that made it resemble in authority and status the family of central Europe.

But there is still a final turn of the wheel. Since the death of Stalin some of the measures re-introduced in the 1930s and particularly in 1944 have been vigorously questioned. In 1955 the law re-introducing penalties for abortion was rescinded. The heavy administrative and financial barriers to divorce and the stigmatization of the mother of the illegitimate child were the targets of attack. In 1968 a law decreed that children born outside marriage have the right to the father's name if paternity can be established — either by a joint statement or through a court.

But the institution itself was very much alive. Khrushchev declared in 1961, 'People who say that the significance of the family drops during the transition to Communism, and that it disappears with time, are absolutely wrong. In fact, the family will grow stronger under Communism. Completely disencumbered of property considerations, family relations will become pure and lasting.' Extended family relations persist and David Lane has discussed evidence of larger proportions of three-generation households in various areas of the Soviet Union than, say, of Britain (5).

In all this we must not underestimate the role of research in showing that organizations other than the family were not, at least in some respects, doing their job so well. The findings of social psychologists and sociologists in the Soviet Union and other parts of Eastern Europe as well as the West, which show that there tends to be a higher incidence of mental and speech retardation and of behavioural disorders among children in day nurseries and institutions than other children, have been taken very seriously.

Criticisms of Theory

The Marxist can only reconcile these developments with the edicts of historical materialism either by categorizing certain phenomena as natural or biological and therefore independent of the main concerns of Marxist analysis, or by admitting that the family is as much affected by the cultural and social superstructure as by the economic base.

He is then opening the way to a more pluralistic theory. To Marx and Engels the acquisition of property was the central explanation of the rise of the monogamous bourgeois family and its loss would therefore remove the need for such a family. The ownership of property must therefore have been the overriding factor controlling the internal constitution, organization and system of role-relationships of the family. Yet in their theory this is not applied consistently. Lack of property among the proletariat leads to a tendency towards marital equality and love but the overriding factor now becomes the external economic and industrial system.

I am not pretending that Soviet experience provides a fair test of the central Marxist proposition that the monogamous family is a bourgeois institution which is the product of the property relations of society. The ownership and inheritance of wealth was not abolished, and inequalities of power remained. But the practical steps that were taken in fulfilment of the theory did not lead to consequences in the predicted directions. In political, economic and social terms there was a strong move, for example, towards the emancipation of women. Many women were able to take paid employment. But corresponding facilities to ease the drudgery of the home (dining halls and day nurseries, for example) were provided in inadequate numbers and the evidence that part of the drudgery has shifted swiftly to men is slight. In a sociological study in Leningrad there were only 48 among a total of 160 working-class families in which the housework was done with the help of the husband. Time budget analyses have shown that men have more free time and more time for sleep than women. Compared with a full-time housewife with a family, a woman who also has a job is busy for three hours more per day, has two hours less of relaxation and leisure and over an hour less sleep.

We could argue in fact that the partial 'emancipation' of women in Soviet society was due less to a change in the property relations of society than to a change in population structure combined with the need to reduce real cost per unit of industrial output. Their status vis-à-vis men has undergone very slow change. In the 1920s three quarters of all women between 20 and 55 were in the labour force, a figure which has been maintained to the present day and which compares with about two fifths in the United States. But the male population of the Soviet Union had been decimated in the two world wars. At the 1959 Census there were 20 million more females than males, and, among persons aged thirty-two and over, twice as many. In the circumstances any society might react by stressing the value of woman's work outside the home — with all that accompanies such a change in her status in society.

The Soviet family policy has been of a cyclical nature since the revolution. Certainly it seems to be oscillating between counterposed forces which are little understood. There are social problems of illegitimacy, abortion and divorce as in other societies and reactions to these seem to be subject more to the varying tides of public opinion than to a thorough understanding of their relationship to family structure and behaviour. One contention I would make is that sociologists in the Marxist tradition have failed to plumb the sophisticated functions served by the family in political, economic and social life. These are not all nepotistic and corrupting. Some of the inspiration of Socialist values, as in the use of the term 'brother', comes from family relationships. The communication of new ideas and fashions and persuasion to drop old ideas can be undertaken very effectively within the family — particularly through the relationship between grandchildren and grandparents. The sense of duty, exemplary service and continuity of service, which the family tends to foster, could be harnessed by the State in the interests of business and the economy as a whole. The welfare functions of the family, including the domestic care of children, the disabled, the sick and the aged, are of major importance, have been overlooked, historically, are difficult to reallocate, and might be encouraged and buttressed by the State in order to achieve greater social equality. Against these arguments, of course, might be set arguments about the containment of individual vitality and the cruel effects of personal vendettas within the family structure, as well as the more traditional arguments about the opposition of the family to the State. These examples are intended only to call attention to the fact that any social organization can have an influence which we value or deplore, but which we have to study comprehensively and in detail if we are to understand. Undoubtedly the Soviet Union found, as Hungary is finding now, that uncompromising emphasis on sexual freedom had repercussions on social order, the birth rate, the psychological health of young children and the popularity of the Government that the regime had not bargained for.

I have attempted to apply Marx's theory of social change to change in the Soviet family. In the causation of change he gives primacy to the influence of economic factors and to the mode of production as the prime mover. We have thrown doubt on this economic determinism, at least as a single factor theory. There are certain logical flaws, particularly in the analysis of the proletarian family, and we are still awaiting a really comprehensive analysis of the relation between family and society. Makarenko's shrewd conception of the family as a cell or collective, which endeared him to Stalin and helped to meet a political problem, bears pondering. The modern sociologist might wonder whether the family does not need treating as an organization, with subtle ramifications throughout the social structure.

Notes and References

1 Geiger, Kent H., *The Family in Soviet Russia,* Cambridge: Massachusetts, Harvard University Press, 1968.

2 New York, International Publishers, 1942.

3 ibid., p. 63.

4 Engels, F., *Principles of Communism,* p. 18.

5 Lane, D., *Politics and Society in the U.S.S.R.,* Weidenfeld & Nicolson, 1970, pp. 356-7.

20 The family of three or four generations in Britain, Denmark and the United States*

In recent years evidence has been accumulating of the close relationships between many older people and their families in Western industrial societies (1). Much of this has threatened assumptions traditionally incorporated in sociological theory which affect our understanding of the processes of ageing and our methods of meeting the problems of the aged. But it has nonetheless tantalized those who have been anxious to establish a preliminary body of knowledge as a basis for the development of the new discipline of social gerontology. For much of this evidence has been unsystematic and confined to certain localities, ethnic groups and social classes. Comparisons between different kinds of evidence are often difficult to make and cannot be pursued at sufficient depth to give strength and solidity to primary hypotheses.

This was one of the reasons given by a group of research workers in Denmark, the United States and Britain for embarking on a cross-national survey of old people. The survey has a long history and its motives and objects have been discussed elsewhere (2). This paper describes its first results. It will be restricted to a provisional analysis of the family relationships of persons aged sixty-five and over in Denmark, the United States and Britain (3).

In each of the three countries roughly 2,500 persons aged sixty-five and over were interviewed at home between April and July 1962. National probability samples of those living in private households were drawn and interviewers used a questionnaire consisting mainly of common questions in a common order, covering five principal areas of interest: health and capacity, occupational status, family relationships, housing and income resources. The research teams held a series of meetings to agree on definitions and techniques during 1960-62 and further meetings to discuss methods of analysis in 1963. Matters of specifically national interest were added to the original design. For example, certain national questions were added to the questionnaire being used in each country. Each country was felt to have individual

* Address given to the Duke University Council of Gerontology, 5 November 1963, and published in Duke University Council on Gerontology, *Proceedings of Seminars, 1961-5*.

customs and institutions which could not be ignored even in an international social survey. When discussing health with an old person in Britain, say, it is natural to introduce questions about the community health and welfare services, such as the home help, district nursing and meals services. These do not exist in the same form in the other countries. In Denmark the survey was also extended to those aged 62-4 (though the data for persons of this age were being analysed separately). In Britain a second national survey of persons aged sixty-five and over was carried out in November–December 1962 (4) and a special additional survey of persons of this age who lived in hospitals and other institutions was carried out in the spring and summer of 1963.

General Features of Contacts with Family

What conclusions may be drawn from the cross-national survey about family relationships? First, *in at least three industrial societies the majority of old people are in close touch with one or more of their children.* In all three countries there was strong evidence that from two thirds to three quarters were in daily or nearly daily contact with at least one of their children; most of these were also in close contact with grandchildren. Indeed the chief surprise was the similarities and not the differences in some of the broad statistical findings. Table 1 gives an example. The proportion of those who had seen at least one of their children on the same day as, or the day previous to, interview, varied

Table 1 Percentage of old people according to most recent occasion of seeing a child (a)

At least one child seen	Old people with children		
	Britain	United States	Denmark
Today or yesterday	69.3 ⎱ 86.6	65.0 ⎱ 83.7	62.3 ⎱ 84.1
Within previous seven days	17.3 ⎰	18.7 ⎰	21.8 ⎰
Within previous month	7.4	6.8	9.8
Within previous year	4.2	7.0	4.8
More than a year ago	1.8	2.5	1.3
Total	100	100	100
Number	1,906	1,996	2,001

(a) The total numbers may not correspond exactly with those in other tables because the information on some questions could not be obtained from everyone interviewed. For clarity the number of persons for whom information could not be classified has been excluded from this table. They numbered 5, 16 and 12 for Britain, the United States and Denmark respectively.

only from 62 per cent to 69 per cent (5). The proportion of those who had *not* seen one of their children on the same day or within the previous week varied only from 13 per cent to 16 per cent (6). There was other evidence that even those who had not seen any child lately had nonetheless experienced some close contacts within the previous year. In Britain, for example, 13 per cent had not seen any of their children within the previous week yet, of these, 43 per cent had stayed with at least one of their children during the previous 12 months, and 35 per cent had had at least one of their children to stay with them — the great majority for at least a week and a few for longer than ten weeks.

Secondly, *even when those without children are drawn into the picture, it still remains true that the majority of the elderly population is in regular and frequent contact with members of the family.* A larger proportion of the British than of the United States and Danish samples of old people lacked surviving children — 23.5 per cent compared with 17.6 per cent and 17.7 per cent respectively. The family and social relationships of this minority of the elderly population deserve special consideration but are only touched upon here. Table 2 includes them in an overall summary of the latest family contacts of everyone in the three samples. Those who had seen at least one of their relatives within the previous seven days numbered 80.0 per cent, 79.5 per cent and 84.1 per cent respectively in Britain, the United States and Denmark. If it is remembered that the majority of those listed as having seen a sibling or another relative but not a child within the previous seven days in fact saw one that day or the previous day (7), it can be said that 60-65 per cent of the elderly population is in daily or nearly daily contact with a relative other than a husband or wife. A number of local surveys in various countries suggest that for these the contact would generally be with a group of from 3 or 4 to 15 persons, including children, grandchildren, sisters and nieces.

But thirdly, *there seems to be an isolated minority of from 10 per cent to 15 per cent of the elderly population (including some married persons) which either has no relatives or sees little of them.* For example, as Table 2 shows, 12 per cent in Denmark, 14 per cent in the United States and 16 per cent in Britain had not seen any relative within the past week. This isolated minority may be smaller than some people would expect. It *may* have increased in the last twenty or thirty years or since the nineteenth century, but unfortunately there is no evidence one way or the other (8). It is nonetheless an important minority, representing between 2 and 2½ million persons in the United States and one million in Britain. Table 2 suggests no more than some of the categories into which this minority falls. It should be noted that some of those listed as not seeing a child or another relative within the last seven days had a husband or wife.

Table 2 Percentage of old people according to most recent contact with a relative

Whether has children/last contact with child/other relative	Britain	United States	Denmark
Has children			
seen at least one yesterday or today	52.9	53.3	51.3
none seen yesterday but at least one seen within last week	13.1	15.3	18.0
none seen within 7 days, but other sib/relative seen within 7 days	4.0	6.3	4.1
none seen within 7 days, and other sib/relative not seen within 7 days	4.5	7.3	} 9.1
none seen within 7 days, and has no other sib/relative	2.0	0.2	
Has no children			
seen at least one other relative within last 7 days	14.0	10.9	14.8
seen no other relative within last 7 days though has one or more	6.3	6.2	} 2.7
has no siblings and/or other relatives	3.2	0.5	
Total	100	100	100
Number in sample	2,500	2,442	2,435
Not seeing relative in previous week	16.0	14.2	11.8

The Role of Widowhood and Incapacity in the Pattern of Family Contacts

Is there any evidence of a strengthening or weakening of contacts with increasing age? Given the broad outline above, do people in extreme old age see less of their relatives than people in their sixties? Is the pattern of contact markedly different for the married than for the widowed, for men than for women, or for the active than for the infirm? These are some of the preliminary questions we must ask in understanding family relationships in old age.

In all three countries proportionately more women than men were in close touch with at least one of their children (though in Denmark the difference was not significant). Moreover, this difference holds generally for each age-group (and also tends to widen among those of higher age), as Table 3 shows. For women in all three countries there is a marked increase, with age, in the numbers who saw one or more of their children within the previous day. This trend holds also for men in Denmark, but not for men in the United States and Britain. When those of one age-group are compared with those of the next, the numbers of men in these two countries who saw one or more of their children on the same or the previous day are found to fluctuate marginally around two thirds.

Table 3 Percentage of men and women in their sixties, seventies and eighties or over who last saw one or more of their children within a day (a)

| | Old persons seeing a child today or yesterday | | | | | |
| | Britain | | United States | | Denmark | |
Age	Men	Women	Men	Women	Men	Women
65-9	67.8	69.5	64.9	64.2	58.9	59.1
70-79	66.1	71.5	59.0	67.4	59.6	64.4
80 and over	62.7	76.3	61.6	79.3	70.8	73.4
All ages 65 and over	66.3	71.7	61.6	67.7	61.4	63.5
Total number in sample	805	1,101	896	1,100	958	1,043

(a) Unclassifiable (for each column reading across): 2, 3, 5, 11, 7 and 5.

These two differences between the sexes and between those of different age are partly attributable, however, to the proportions who were widowed. More of the women than of the men and more of the older than of the younger persons in the samples were widowed. Differences in behaviour and attitude between the sexes are partly explained by such structural differences in the component populations being compared. In the British sample, 70 per cent of the men aged sixty-five and over were married, but only 34 per cent of the women. Table 4 suggests how quickly certain apparent differences between the sexes may disappear when account is taken of structural weightings of this kind. Significantly more widowed than married persons had seen a child within a day, but the differences between widows and widowers, as well as those between married men and married women, were inconsequential.

Table 4 Percentage of widowed and married old persons who last saw one or more of their children within a day (Britain only)

| | Old persons seeing a child today or yesterday | |
Marital status	Men	Women
married and widowed	66.3	71.7
married	62.6	62.9
widowed	75.9	76.9

The two differences are also partly attributable to the greater number of women than of men and of older than of younger persons who were incapacitated. A special scale of incapacity, based on a series of questions about mobility and ability to undertake personal toilet, was applied to the persons in each of the samples. Significantly more of those who were incapacitated than of those who were not had daily contact with their children. A range of other evidence also suggested that married and single children responded to the growing infirmity of their parents, as well as to the loss by one of them of the husband or wife, by intensifying contacts with their parents. They offered a room in their homes or gave considerable aid in the household. The trend with infirmity was not however marked for men. It would seem that once a man was widowed the children tended to feel he was helpless, even if he was still physically active. In Britain and the United States (though not in Denmark) more widowers than widows lived with relatives, and especially with married children. By contrast a woman's need to have independent charge of her household seemed to be recognized for longer. Women often went on living on their own after the death of their husbands and only moved to a married daughter's household, say, when they became really infirm.

The Importance of Family Structure

While bereavement and incapacity are two chief factors explaining variations in the pattern of family contacts in old age there are of course many others. Differences in the structure of the old person's family affect the pattern of contacts. Thus, the frequency as well as the quality of contacts between parent and child will vary according to the sex and marital status of both, the difference in age between them, the number, sex and marital status of any other children, whether there are grandchildren and, if so, their age and sex (9). Table 5 supplies a noteworthy example, however. Quite apart from the differences between the countries in population density, family structure plainly affects how far old people live from their children. Those who have more than one child and also have at least one daughter are much more likely than others to be living with or near one of their children. The data indicate that this holds for both men and women and also for both the widowed and the married. Those who have sons and not daughters are more likely than others to be living at more than an hour's or even a day's journey from their children.

Other data suggest that families with one child only and those with more than one child but either no daughter or no son 'compensate' the elderly parents in various ways. For example, the British survey shows that (i) more sons in families with no daughter than in families with at least one daughter have been seen within the last day by both elderly

Table 5 Percentage of women with different types of family, according to proximity of nearest child (a)

	Women aged 65 and over											
Proximity of nearest child	One son only			One daughter only			More than one child					
							No daughter			At least one daughter		
	Britain	U.S.	Denmark	Britain	U.S.	Denmark	Britain	U.S.	Denmark	Britain	U.S.	Denmark
Same household	22	24	17	38	36	11	31	27	14	52	33	20
10 min. journey or less	25	21	22	21	15	26	31	29	31	23	38	44
11-30 mins. journey	22	16	20	13	14	21	16	17	29	14	14	21
31 mins.–1 hour	10	13	14	9	3	20	8	12	14	6	4	9
Over 1 hr. but less than 1 day	15	13	21	16	17	20	13	10	11	4	8	6
1 day's journey or more	6	12	7	3	14	2	1	4	1	1	2	0
Total	100	100	100	100	100	100	100	100	100	100	100	100
Number in sample	126	91	130	148	131	126	111	116	103	719	773	788

(a) The time of journey was defined as the amount of time usually taken by the child to get to the old person's home from his own home.

men and women; and (ii) more sons in families containing an only child than in families containing two or more sons but no daughter have been seen within the last day by both elderly men and women. In other ways the behaviour and attitudes of old people are affected by whether or not they have the average quota of children of both sexes.

The Importance of Generation Change

Variations in the pattern of family contacts in old age can also be explained, in part, by changes between one generation and the next. More of the older than of the younger persons aged sixty-five and over in the three surveys gave birth to, and still have, large families consisting of four, five and more children. The generations which were able to restrict their children more commonly to two or three in number are only now beginning to reach their sixties and seventies. Moreover, because the younger generations have had their children at a more youthful age, the average distance in years between parents and their children is narrowing. When the present generations of persons in their twenties and thirties reach old age the average distance in years may be as little as 20 to 23, because not only are more marrying but they are marrying earlier and having children earlier. Finally, because expectations of life are lengthening (if only marginally for men aged sixty-five and over in some Western societies) more people are reaching their seventies and eighties. It should be remembered that in various ways the changing characteristics of succeeding generations make it difficult to draw conclusions about the processes of ageing as such.

One of the results of these trends is the rapidly increasing number of great-grandparents. In Denmark 23 per cent, in Britain 22 per cent and in the United States 43 per cent of those with children had great-grandchildren. Already for a substantial minority of the elderly population of Western societies, then, the four-generation family is a reality. In the future the characteristic problems of the family may be those of middle-aged or elderly sons and daughters (whose children are all adults) looking after parents in their eighties, instead of younger sons and daughters, divided between the care of their young children and the care of elderly parents.

The elderly population is also changing from one which had commonly experienced widowhood in middle age to one which experiences it in late middle or early old age. Fewer of the children will have experienced the death of a parent before they attain the normal marrying age (which tends now to be earlier) and fewer of them will have therefore contemplated postponement of marriage so as to provide the survivor with economic and other support. In short, the rising generation of elderly people have fewer children who are still single than their predecessors. Among other things, this will influence the household patterns and preferences of the aged.

Patterns of Household Composition

Family structure and generation change affect our understanding of household composition. People in their sixties tend more often than those in their eighties to have single children living at home but the difference is not striking, for reasons given above. Many other old people live with married children, because when losing a husband or wife they have moved to join one of their married children or have invited the child back to share the parental home. In the Danish survey 20 per cent of those in their sixties but 28 per cent of those aged eighty and over shared the household with a single or married child.

Table 6 shows how common such household arrangements were for the widowed and single. The pattern is remarkably similar for Britain and the United States, with just a slightly larger fraction of the elderly population of the latter living alone and a slightly smaller fraction living with married children. In both countries it was much more common for an old person to be found living with a married daughter than with a married son. By comparing Table 7 with Table 6 it can also be seen that in both countries more widowed than married persons lived with children. In Britain more than half of the 43 per cent widowed and unmarried persons living alone were in daily contact with one or more of their children. A much smaller proportion of old people in Denmark than in the other two countries lived with married children and there was virtually no sign of a preference for living with a married daughter rather than with a married son. A much higher proportion lived alone.

Table 6 Percentage of widowed and single people living in different types of household

Household composition	Britain	United States	Denmark
Living alone	43.0	47.5	61.2
Living with married daughter (and other(s))	13.6	11.0	3.3
Living with married son (and other(s))	5.1	3.1	3.1
Living with unmarried child(ren) alone or with other(s)	18.5	18.3	13.8
Living with sibling(s) alone or with other(s)	11.1	8.7	4.8
Living with grandchild(ren) alone or with other(s)	0.5	1.9	1.1
Living with other relatives	2.6	3.3	1.9
Living with non-relatives only	5.6	6.1	10.7
Total	100	100	100
Number in sample	1,289	1,107	1,107

In Britain relatively more widowed and single women than men were living alone (45 per cent compared with 36 per cent), while in the United States the reverse was true (46 per cent compared with 52 per cent). Otherwise the differences between the sexes tended to follow a similar pattern. In each country rather more widowed women than men lived with single children. The differences between the sexes in the numbers living with married daughters or sons or siblings were marginal. In the United States slightly fewer men than women lived in households of these types, while in Britain slightly *more* men than women lived with married daughters or married sons and about the same number with siblings. Men tended more often to live with people who were not relatives.

While the patterns of household composition for the single and widowed in Britain and the United States were broadly similar, those for the married diverged. In fact the pattern in the United States closely resembled that in Denmark. More married couples in the United States than in Britain lived with no one else (79 per cent compared with 68 per cent). Fewer lived with single children (12 per cent compared with 22 per cent); fewer too with married daughters (1 per cent compared with 4 per cent). These differences might be attributed to (i) the greater mortality at earlier ages of men in Britain (which means that a higher proportion of the U.S. couples are *older* couples whose children are more likely to have married and left home); (ii) there may be a greater shortage of housing for young married couples in Britain than in the

Table 7 Percentage of married people living in different types of household

Household composition	Britain	United States	Denmark
Living with spouse only	67.7	79.1	81.8
Living with spouse and married daughter (and other(s))	3.9	0.8	0.4
Living with spouse and married son (and other(s))	0.7	0.9	1.0
Living with unmarried child(ren) alone or with other(s)	21.9	12.5	13.1
Living with sibling(s) alone or with other(s)	2.0	1.7	0.3
Living with grandchild(ren) alone or with other(s)	1.3	2.0	0.6
Living with other relatives	1.0	1.6	0.4
Living with non-relatives only	1.5	1.4	2.4
Total	100	100	100
Number in sample	1,211	1,335	1,339

United States and Denmark with the result that at any one time more children (particularly daughters) will be found living with elderly parents. Or perhaps the fact that there *has been* a severe housing shortage in Britain in recent decades (particularly in the war and early post-war years) has tended to perpetuate a tradition of 'living upstairs to Mum' in the early years of marriage — at least for some sections of the population. However, their numbers are relatively small and should not be exaggerated.

The Geographical Basis of Family Relationships

From incomplete information about the declining proportion of old people living with their children in industrial societies some theorists have falsely assumed that few old people now live with their children and also that as a result most are isolated from their families. In fact, even though the proportion seems to be diminishing in Britain, Denmark and the United States, a substantial minority still live with their unmarried or married children. But, judging from Table 8, once the proportions of old people sharing a household diminish there may be a corresponding increase in the proportions living within a few minutes' journey. It should also be noted, by comparing Table 8 with Table 1, that although considerably fewer old people in the United States and Denmark than in Britain share a household with children, almost as many are in daily contact with them. This does not, of course, rule out the possibility of a marked qualitative change in the relationships between the generations. However, other data in the three surveys showed that even when not sharing a household, different

Table 8 Percentage of old people according to proximity of their nearest child (a)

Proximity of nearest child	Old people with children		
	Britain	United States	Denmark
Same household	41.9	27.6	20.1
Ten mins.' journey or less	23.5	33.1	32.0
11-30 mins.' journey	15.9	15.7	23.0
31 mins. — 1 hour	7.6	7.2	12.4
Over 1 hour but less than 1 day	9.1	11.2	11.2
1 day's journey or more	1.9	5.0	1.3
Total	100	100	100
Number in sample	1,911	2,012	2,009

(a) Unclassifiable: 0, 0 and 4 respectively.

generations of a family can share many of the activities of daily life. Over a third of those not in fact living with grandchildren said they helped them, by looking after them in the day, giving them gifts and so on. The great majority of old people who were unable to shop, prepare meals or do their housework, were helped by members of their families, whether living at home or elsewhere. In illness four fifths relied on their families for household help rather than upon friends or neighbours, paid help or social services.

In all three countries more elderly women than men shared the household with a child. For the United States sample, the difference was particularly large (31 per cent compared with 23 per cent). Moreover, in all three countries proportionately more of those living at a considerable distance from their children were men. Both these statements, again, can be explained largely by the fact that fewer of the men were widowed.

When unmarried children are ruled out of account, the great majority of old people are still found to be within easy journey of their married children. In Denmark 69 per cent, in the United States 72 per cent, and in Britain 75 per cent of those with married children were within 30 minutes' journey of one of them, most of whom were living with them or within 10 minutes' journey. In Britain 58 per cent of those with married or widowed children had seen one or more of them within the previous day. Studies of the family in Western societies have found that the pattern of contacts with married children corresponds with that with grandchildren.

Table 9 Percentage of old people according to proximity of their nearest married child (a)

Proximity of nearest married or widowed child	Old people with married or widowed children		
	Britain	United States	Denmark
Same household	20.5	15.0	5.2
10 mins.' journey or less	34.0	38.8	34.3
11-30 mins.' journey	20.8	18.4	29.7
31 mins. — 1 hour	9.9	8.3	16.1
Over 1 hour but less than 1 day	11.9	13.3	13.3
1 day's journey or more	2.9	6.2	1.4
Total	100	100	100
Number in sample	1,814	1,942	1,892

(a) United States, 1 unclassifiable.

The Influence of Social Class

While a satisfactory method of defining the social class of elderly persons has not yet been developed, some attempt was made in the cross-national survey to record the main and the last occupation (and industry) of men and of spinsters and also of the husbands of married and widowed women who were interviewed. The occupational classification used by the Registrar-General in Britain differs from that used by the U.S. Census Bureau. The latter was adopted for comparative purposes and occupations were also grouped into broad social classes: white-collar, blue-collar, service workers, farmers, or farm labourers (10).

Table 10 reinforces the conclusions of a number of recent studies in Britain and the United States of the family relationships of professional, managerial and clerical classes. While certain classes may have exceptional characteristics it would seem that in general the inter-generational family contacts of the non-manual classes are only slightly less frequent than of the manual classes. Indeed, as Table 10 shows, the differences between the two broad classes of old people in Denmark were very small indeed, in the United States only a little more marked and even in Britain not striking (11).

When the results of the cross-national survey can be fully elaborated they may lead to some revision of theories which assume that in a

Table 10 Percentage of people of different social class seeing at least one child within a day (a)

| | Percentage seen today or yesterday | | | |
| | White-collar or professional and clerical | | Blue-collar or manual | |
Country	Male	Female	Male	Female
United States	56.1	64.6	61.5	68.5
Britain	57.5	66.4	69.2	73.3
Denmark	59.3	65.3	61.2	63.3
Total no. with children:				
United States	253	308	379	362
Britain	214	283	543	753
Denmark	312	352	332	309

(a) Unclassified   Men   Women
     U.S.   7   86
     Britain   16   32
     Denmark   10   33

fast-changing industrial society the generations within the wider family necessarily become separated and individuals therefore necessarily become more isolated as they get older. It would seem that the social consequences of industrialization and urbanization have been misinterpreted.

The development of social relations in old age will perhaps become clearer as different patterns of family contacts are first systematically described and then tentatively explained. Various data from this survey showed that widowhood and incapacity were more important in explaining differences in the pattern of family contacts in old age than age or sex or even social class. They largely accounted for more of the oldest than of the youngest people aged sixty-five and over being in close contact with their children. It seemed possible that other differences between the oldest and youngest persons of this age in their patterns of family contacts could be explained better by the process of 'generation change' than by the processes of ageing as such.

The research data from the three countries also lend support to the hypothesis that the quality and frequency of interpersonal relationships within the family vary according to family structure. Thus, the quality and frequency of contacts between parent and child vary according to the sex and marital status of both, the difference in their ages, the number, sex and marital status of any other children, whether there are grandchildren and, if so, their age and sex.

Notes and References

1 See, for example, Burgess, E. W., 'Family Structure and Relationships' in Burgess, E. W. (ed.), *Ageing in Western Societies: A Comparative Survey*, Chicago, University of Chicago Press, 1960, and Townsend, P., a new concluding chapter in *The Family Life of Old People*, Penguin Books edition, 1963.

2 For example, Friis, H., 'Cross-National Research on Old Age', *International Social Science Journal*, June 1963; Shanas, E., 'Some Observations on Cross-National Surveys of Ageing', *The Gerontologist*, March 1963. Mr Friis is director of the Danish National Institute of Social Research, which is responsible for the survey in Denmark. Miss Shanas is research associate (associate professor) in the Department of Sociology and Committee on Human Development of the University of Chicago and is directing the survey in the United States. An account of some of the earlier developments will be found in *Cross-National Surveys on Old Age* published by the Division of Gerontology, University of Michigan, 1958, and also in Townsend, P. and Rees, B., *The Personal, Family and Social Circumstances of Old People: Report of an Investigation carried out in England to Pilot a Future Cross-National Survey of Old Age*, published by the London School of Economics, 1959. [See the major report on the cross-national research: Shanas, E., *et al., Old People in Three Industrial Societies*, New York and London, Atherton and Routledge, 1968.]

3 The research in each country was made possible by generous grants from the National Institute of Mental Health and later the Community Health Services

Division, Bureau of State Services of the United States Public Health Service. I should also like to acknowledge the help of the British Treasury in making it possible for the Government Social Survey to offer its valuable research services.

4 The two surveys in Britain, of old persons living in private households represent a collaborative enterprise on the part of research staff of the Government Social Survey, the Cambridge University Department of Applied Economics and the London School of Economics and Political Science. The research was formally launched in December 1961. (See, for example, Townsend, P., and Wedderburn, D., *The Aged in the Welfare State*, Bell, 1965.)

5 The figures include those old people who shared a household with one of their children.

6 In the British survey informants were also asked how often they *usually* saw each of their children. This approach seems to produce a rather similar distribution.

Usually seen	per cent	Last seen	per cent
every day	57.2	today	57.5
at least once a week	25.5	yesterday	11.8
		within 7 days	17.3
	82.7		86.6

7 In Britain over half those saying they had seen a brother or sister within the previous seven days said they had seen him or her today or yesterday.

8 Friedmann, E., 'The Impact of Ageing on the Social Structure', in Tibbitts, C., *Handbook of Social Gerontology*, Chicago, University of Chicago Press, 1960.

9 [See the full analysis in Chapters 6 and 7 of Shanas, E., *et al.*, op cit.]

10 White-collar workers include professional workers and technicians, proprietors, managers and officials; and workers in clerical and sales jobs. Blue-collar workers include craftsmen; operatives and labourers other than farm labourers.

11 It should be noted that farmers and farm workers formed important minorities within the elderly populations of the United States and Denmark and are not included in the table. In Denmark for example 34 per cent of the farmers and 28 per cent of the farm workers lived in the same households as one of their children and another 41 per cent and 42 per cent respectively had seen a child on the same or the previous day.

21 The four-generation family*

The purpose of this paper is to call attention to a little-known fact about old people in industrial societies, and to dwell upon its implications for our understanding of ageing and the aged. In 1962 a cross-national study of people aged sixty-five and over was carried out in Denmark, Britain and the United States (1). Probability samples of around 2,500 persons in each country were interviewed during the same period of the year. Questionnaires and methods of sampling, interviewing and analysis had been standardized.

One result surprised the investigators. A substantial proportion of the elderly populations were found to have great-grandchildren – as many as 40 per cent in the United States, 23 per cent in Denmark and 22 per cent in Britain. The existence on a substantial scale of families of four generations is a new phenomenon in the history of human societies. The emergence of a different structure brings new patterns of relationships but also different experiences of ageing. How has it happened?

This development is not attributable just to improvements in longevity. Average ages at first marriage have diminished and for women in the United States, for example, have been relatively low throughout this century. The age of parenthood has also been diminishing. In the United States the median age of women at the birth of their first children was 23 for those born between 1880 and 1890 but is down to between 20 and 21 for the latest generations to marry. Because of the decreasing number of large families the median age at the birth of the last child has fallen more sharply. Earlier marriage, earlier childbirth and fewer large families inevitably contribute towards a narrowing of the average span in years between successive generations. The larger number of great-grandparents in the United States than in the European countries is attributable in the early decades of this century to the higher rates of marriage, the younger age at marriage and the birth to a larger proportion of women in the early years of marriage of several children.

It would, of course, be profitable to study the family life-cycle in more detail. Among the British sample, for example, it seems that the

* First published in *New Society*, 7 July 1966.

women had become grandmothers on average at 54 years of age and great-grandmothers at about 72. The men had become grandfathers at 57 and great-grandfathers at 75. One immediate thought of relevance to our understanding of human personality is the scope that exists for structural variation in family-building habits. Some women become grandmothers in their late thirties, others not until their seventies.

These structural variations have been given little attention by sociologists and psychologists. If there are shifts of emphasis in family-building practices then there are likely to be big changes in the patterns of family relations and in the types of relationship and of problems experienced by the elderly. With increasing age old people tend to find themselves nearer one of two extremes -- experiencing the seclusion of the spinster or widow who lacks children *and* other near relatives, or pushed towards the pinnacle of the pyramidal family structure of four generations which may include several children and their spouses and twenty or thirty grandchildren and great-grandchildren.

Previous theories about the changes that have taken place in family relations and in the care of the aged during the process of industrialization need to be qualified heavily. When we compare what the family does now with what it did a hundred years ago we are not comparing like with like. Instead of 1 or 2 per cent of the population being aged sixty-five and over there are 10 or 15 per cent. There is the same contrast between developing and advanced industrial societies. In the 'older' type of society old age may have a kind of pedestal prestige. Like the population age pyramids that the demographers produce for us of pre-industrial societies and of societies like Britain in the early stages of industrialization the extended family may have only one surviving grandparent at the apex of a structure consisting of a large number of children and other relatives. Figure 1 suggests how family structure is related to the age structure of the population. Nowadays there may be two, three or all four grandparents alive and often a great-grandparent too. The structure of the kinship network has changed and this has had important effects on the ways in which this network is broken into geographically proximate groupings of households and types of households.

The structure of the extended family — understood as a group drawn from the network of kin whose members meet every day or nearly every day and exchange a variety of services — has changed because of the pressures induced by changing mortality, birth and marriage rates. The relations between ascendant and descendant kin and affinal kin have been strengthened as compared with those with collateral kin: parents and children count more, cousins, aunts and uncles less. There is greater stability at the centre. More people marry. More marry young.

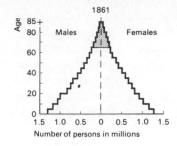
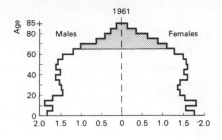

Actual population pyramids in England and Wales in 1861 and 1961

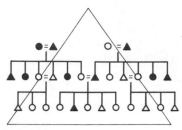

Characteristic example of kinship structure around 1900

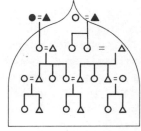

Characteristic example of kinship structure in the second half of the twentieth century

More survive in married couples until an advanced age. Consequently the number of middle-aged and elderly spinsters acting as universal aunts has diminished; there are fewer 'denuded' immediate families (i.e. families of parents and unmarried sibling groups where at least one member is missing) and fewer extended families of certain types — such as widowed women linking in households with their brothers or sisters for the purposes of rearing children and overcoming hardship. The broken marriage and the broken 'home' are no longer dominant constituents of the extended family in a group of proximate households. A model type of extended family is beginning to replace a wide variety of types of families and households, ranging from lone individuals at one extreme to 'kinship' tribes at the other. This family does not necessarily consist of *all* children and grandchildren of an old person, say, but only some of them.

What are the implications for old people in their relations with their families? They are dividing into two broad categories. Those belonging to the third generation more often have a surviving husband or wife than did persons of their age at the turn of the century. Fewer have single children remaining at home and grandchildren who are in their infancy. Since they represent the 'younger' section of the elderly fewer of their children will have to look after them in infirmity, or illness, and they will have more energy to spare for their grandchildren. In various ways it is likely that the rapid relative increase in importance of the third generation, with its younger age-span, will result in much greater emphasis being placed in the future than formerly on reciprocal relations between the second and third generations. This will alter, and complicate, the whole pattern of kinship activity. Moreover, a fourth generation of relatively frail people is also being established — for the first time.

The nature of the problems of old age is therefore changing. A common instance in the past has been the middle-aged woman faced with the problem of caring for an infirm mother as well as her young children. A common instance of the future will be the woman of sixty faced with the problem of caring for an infirm mother in her eighties. Her children will be adult but it is her grandchildren who will compete with the mother for her attentions. The four generations of surviving relatives may tend to separate into semi-independent groupings each of two generations. Similarly there may be a shift of emphasis from the problem of which of the children looks after a widowed parent to the problem of how a middle-aged man and wife can reconcile dependent relationships with *both* sets of parents.

Changes in population structure have far wider and deeper effects than I have been able to indicate here. Insufficient attention has been paid to them in discussing relationships between parents and their children, between husbands and wives, between generations and generally among households and families. The data about the emergence of the four-generation family suggest that the structure of the kinship network has been changing more rapidly than has been supposed. It is therefore likely that changes in family organization and relationships may have been affected less by changes in industrial and economic organization, occupational recruitment and educational selection and organization and more by changes in population structure. This may constitute an argument for reviewing and revising not only theories of change in the process of ageing but also theories of urbanization and the social effects of industrialization.

Reference

1 Shanas, E., *et al.*, *Old People in Three Industrial Societies*, New York and London, Atherton and Routledge, 1968.

Index and index of names

Index

(Names in references and notes appear only at the end of each chapter)

316 Index

Subsistence—*cont.*
  Beveridge assumptions, 42, 54
  class perceptions, 28-9
  concept, 33
  levels in Britain, 101
  levels and the U.N., 47
  and nutrition, 38
  periods of need, 31
  standard, 7, 26-31, 34-5
Supplementary benefits, *see* National Assistance
Supplementary Benefits Commission, 104, 108, 123, 211
Sweden, pensions, 234

Tavistock Institute, 267
Tax relief, 18-19
Taxation avoidance, 46
Terminal illness, 184
Textiles in Lancashire, 64-8
Titmuss, R., 45
  see also Poverty
Trade unions, 13, 17
  and retirement policy, 233
'Two Nations', 58, 60

Unemployment
  defect in statistics, 68-71, 84
  effect on family budget, 72-6
    see also Lancashire
  effect on standard of living, 72
    see also Lancashire
  Insurance Benefit, 81-9
    see also Lancashire
  level, 33

Unemployment—*cont.*
  numbers in poverty, 36
  workshy, 5
United Nations studies, 47
United States
  negroes in poverty, 97
  one-parent families, 55
  poverty, 53, 97
  Social Security Administration survey, 53, 55
  Surveys of the aged, 276
    of the family, 276

Values
  and social services, 155
  Victorian, 6, 17
Voluntary services, 80-81, 182, 227-8

Wealth, problem of failure to tax, 45-6
Webb, Sidney and Beatrice, 17, 136
Welfare Foods, 2
'Welfare State', 4, 6
West Germany
  family allowances, 54, 102
  pensions, 234
West Indians, 98-9
  see also Immigrants
Widowhood and loneliness, 262 ff.
Widows, 261, 262, 263, 293-5
Women
  increasing role of, 233
  isolation of elderly, 246 ff.
  emancipation in Russia, 287
Workhouse, 136
  v. family group, 141, 144
'Workshy', 5, 80

Index of names